Rents, Taxes, and Peasant Resistance

The Lower Yangzi Region, 1840–1950

KATHRYN BERNHARDT

Rents, Taxes, and Peasant Resistance

The Lower Yangzi Region,
1840-1950

Stanford University Press
Stanford, California
1992

Stanford University Press
Stanford, California
© 1992 by the Board of Trustees
of the Leland Stanford Junior University
Printed in the United States of America

CIP data are at the end of the book

Publication of this book was supported by a grant
from the National Endowment for the Humanities,
an independent federal agency

Portions of Chapter 3 previously appeared in
MODERN CHINA (v. 13, 4), pp. 379–410,
copyright © 1987 by Sage Publications, Inc.
Reprinted by permission of Sage Publications, Inc.

To my parents

ACKNOWLEDGMENTS

It is with great pleasure and even greater relief that I can now thank all those people who have offered so much encouragement and assistance over the years. Lyman Van Slyke and Harold Kahn, my teachers at Stanford University, provided a uniquely stimulating and nurturing environment for graduate work and offered invaluable guidance on this book, particularly during its crucial early stages. My cohort at Stanford—Emily Honig, Gail Hershatter, Helen Chauncey, and Randy Stross—greatly enriched and enlivened my time at graduate school. I would also like here to express my gratitude to my undergraduate teachers at Wittenberg University—particularly, Stanley Mickel, Eugene Swanger, Cynthia Behrman, and Peter Celms—who first got me started in the fields of Chinese studies and history.

For financial support for this project, I am indebted to the Social Science Research Council, the Committee for Scholarly Communication with the People's Republic of China, the American Council of Learned Societies, and the Center for Chinese Studies, UCLA. The staffs of the following institutions were most helpful during the course of my research: the Lou Henry Hoover Library at Stanford University, the East Asian Library at the University of Washington, the Tōyō Bunka Kenkyūjo (Tokyo University), the Tōyō Bunko, the National Palace Museum and the Academia Sinica in Taiwan, the history department library of Nanjing University, the Nanjing Municipal Library, the Suzhou Museum, and the First Historical Archives in Beijing.

A number of people made my research abroad a rewarding and memorable experience. I am particularly grateful to Linda Grove for introducing me to the scholarly world in Tokyo and to Tanaka Masatoshi, Saeki Yūichi, Usui Sachiko, and Kishimoto (Nakayama) Mio for accepting me so warmly. Cai Shaoqing of Nanjing University greatly eased my way into various libraries in China and in other ways made my stay there less trying than it otherwise might have been, and Dong Caishi of Suzhou Normal University (now Suzhou University) generously shared his time and vast knowledge of the Taiping occupation of the lower Yangzi valley. I am also beholden to innumerable other scholars in Japan and China for taking the time to discuss mutual research concerns.

Jack Dull, Joseph Esherick, Kent Guy, Elizabeth Perry, and R. Bin Wong read all or parts of the manuscript at various stages of revision and offered much constructive criticism. Joseph Esherick, in particular, gamely read several versions, commenting astutely and at great length on each one. An anonymous press reader's suggestions for final revisions did much to help me tighten up my argument. I am also grateful to Muriel Bell, John Ziemer, and others at Stanford University Press for their professional handling of the manuscript and to Barbara Mnookin for her meticulous copyediting. Finally, my profoundest thanks go to Philip Huang, my best intellectual companion and critic, for all his encouragement and support, and for all our stimulating discussions of the larger historical issues raised in this book.

K.B.

CONTENTS

APPENDIXES

TABLES

TEXT

APPENDIXES

MAPS AND FIGURE

MAPS

FIGURE

Rents, Taxes, and Peasant Resistance

The Lower Yangzi Region, 1840–1950

INTRODUCTION

Throughout China's long imperial history, the political-economic system was supported mainly by the rents and taxes collected from the peasantry. The survival of the system depended on orderly relations between landlords and tenants and between the state and landowners. In the mid-twentieth-century revolution, rents were eradicated, and the political-economic structure came to be based on entirely different principles. How did this transformation come about? Was it, as orthodox Chinese Marxists contend, the result of revolutionary action by an outraged peasantry under the leadership of a committed Communist Party? Or was it, as their detractors would say, the handiwork of a small group of conspirators operating without much peasant support?

This book, taking as its focus the commercially advanced lower Yangzi region, argues that the elimination of land rents was the result not so much of revolutionary action, either by peasant masses or by Communist conspirators, as of a long-term process of change that left the landlord elite tottering on the verge of structural collapse even before the Chinese Communist Party's ascendance to power.

EXISTING APPROACHES

This study both draws on and departs from three major schools of thought on the origins of the Communist revolution in China: the orthodox Chinese Marxist approach, the moral economy approach, and what may be called the market economy approach. The orthodox Chinese Marxist approach locates the roots of the revolution in a worsening of peasant living standards under the impact of commercialization and imperialism. Simply put, this view holds that the expansion of the commercial economy from the late Ming period on, along with the advent of imperialism in the nineteenth century, led to a pronounced differentiation of the farming population into a small number of landlords and rich peasants and a mass of poor peasants and landless hired laborers. With differentiation necessarily came the increased impoverishment of the great majority of peasants, who were subjected on the one hand to impersonal market forces beyond their control and on the other to rising landlord exactions. The result was a deterioration of relations between landlords and tenants and an escalation of open class conflict. The peasantry thus proved very receptive to the appeals of the Chinese Communist Party (CCP), which channeled its discontent into the making of a radically new society. In this interpretation, then, the Communist revolution was the inevitable culmination of the intensification of rural class conflict.[1]

Like the orthodox Chinese Marxist approach, the moral economy perspective highlights the increasing precariousness of peasant life under the impact of an expanding market economy. But it adds to that dynamic an emphasis on the role of the state, especially a state modernizing under the aegis of imperialism. In this view the incorporation of an agrarian society into the capitalist world economy and the extension of the state's reach seriously threatened the peasants' ability to maintain themselves at a subsistence level. The first process brought them into contact with highly unstable market forces, and the second brought them increased taxes. At the same time these two developments also resulted in the dissolution of village redistributive mechanisms that in the past had blunted the impact of subsistence crises on the poorest members of the community. Purely market considerations replaced traditional moral obligations, and peasants, now shorn of the protection that their community had once provided, felt the full force of fluctuating market trends and rising state exactions. In this context peasant collective actions were essentially defensive efforts, and what peasants saw in a revolutionary program like the CCP's was not so much a chance to fashion a new society as an opportunity to restore the moral community and to secure their livelihood.[2]

Unlike the Marxists and the moral economists, the market economists contend that commercialization and incorporation into the world economy proved beneficial to peasant livelihood, and that rural living standards improved as a consequence. As they see it, the revolution came about not because of any deep structural malaise that only a radical social revolution could cure, but because of the influence of one or more immediate political factors—with varying weight given to the inability of Chiang Kai-shek's Nationalist Party to establish a viable rule, the superior organizational ability of the Chinese Communist Party, and the Japanese invasion and occupation of 1937–45.[3]

Each of these perspectives has contributed to the interpretation presented here. From the Marxist approach comes the book's attention to class relations and land rents, from the moral economy approach its emphasis on state-society relations and land taxation, and from the market economy approach its attention to market relations, particularly the use of price data to evaluate the real burden of rents and taxes.

But none of these approaches alone can explain developments in Jiangnan in the nineteenth and twentieth centuries.* By rights the lower Yangzi region should have been at the forefront of the revolutionary process from the very outset. After all, it had all the requisite ingredients for revolution as described by the orthodox Chinese Marxists and the moral economists. The agrarian economy was highly commercialized, landownership highly concentrated, and rural social differentiation highly advanced. Moreover, because of its economic and political centrality, imperialism and state-making had a much greater impact there than in other areas of the country. Yet despite these presumably favorable revolutionary conditions, Communist organizers of the 1920's made little headway in Jiangnan, eventually giving it up for lost and concentrating instead on the hinterland. When the revolution finally came to the region in 1949, it came not as a seizure of power by the masses from below, but as a military conquest by the People's Liberation Army from above.

In other ways as well, the history of Jiangnan defies the central tenets of the orthodox Chinese Marxist and moral economy perspectives. For instance, the Republican period (1912–49) did see an intensification in conflict between landlords and tenants, as the orthodox Chinese Marxist approach would predict, but this was not the result of a rising burden of rent or of a progressive deterioration of peasant living standards. On the contrary, rents held steady or declined in those years, and the escalation in tenant collective action was due more to changing political conditions than to changing economic ones. Likewise, the state did intrude more heavily in rural society in the late nineteenth and early twentieth centuries, as the moral economy approach would predict, but this did not necessarily result in increased exactions and popular agitation against land taxes. On the contrary, for much of the Republican period the Jiangnan peasantry bore a lighter tax burden than it did during the latter part of the Qing period (1644–1912), and the frequency of popular protest against land taxation declined sharply. But paradoxically, as we shall see,

*During the Qing the term "Jiangnan" ("south of the river") referred to the three prefectures of Changzhou, Suzhou, and Songjiang and the department of Taicang in southern Jiangsu and the three prefectures of Jiaxing, Huzhou, and Hangzhou in northern Zhejiang.

increased state intervention in local society *did* bring about an escalation in popular resistance to landlord rents.

The market economy approach is no more successful than the others in capturing the patterns of change in Jiangnan. Overall this perspective has been too much influenced by the simplistic Manichean view of its ideological opponent, orthodox Chinese Marxism. Where the Marxists see progressive peasant pauperization, the market economists insist on growing peasant prosperity. In fact both are right in some sense: advancing commercialization and incorporation into the world economy brought the lower Yangzi region periods of relative rural prosperity, it is true, but also periods of severe economic dislocation. The market economists tend to dismiss those times of economic turmoil as aberrations that had no lasting impact on rural society. The pages that follow will demonstrate that they had a very real impact—indeed, that they redefined the relationship among the state, the elite, and the peasantry in critical ways. The market economy perspective assumes, moreover, that economic growth over the long run generated enough surplus to satisfy the needs of all three parties. In fact the three-way competition over rural output became more intense in the late-Qing and Republican periods.

METHODOLOGY

This work departs from previous scholarship also in its methodology. Rents and taxes are often studied as fixed quantities, a procedure that tells us nothing at all about the changing relationships among the different parties concerned. Rent, for example, involves the two-way relationship between landlords and tenants, in which change in either party can redefine the relationship, even though the rent rate stays the same. A landlord's movement of his residence from village to town would fundamentally alter the nature of the relationship, as would a tenant's increasing participation in the commercial economy; yet again, neither change necessarily implies a change in the amount of rent. It is not enough to look at rents and taxes as simple quantities; they must be studied in the context of evolving social relationships.

In addition, rather than looking exclusively at tax or exclusively at rent, this book analyzes the two together. Tax and rent formed the twin axes around which the relationship among the state, the peasantry, and the elite revolved. They were two closely interdependent matters; a change in one directly affected the other. An increase in state land taxes, for instance, would pressure landlords to raise rents, while a decline in rent receipts might cause them to evade state taxes. To understand rent and tax, each must be viewed in its relationship to the other and not in isolation.

At the same time, the three parties involved in tax and rent are treated as separate and autonomous, each with its own distinctive set of interests. Orthodox Chinese Marxists tend to collapse these parties into two, the landlords and the state on the one hand and tenants on the other. Similarly, the moral economists tend to conflate large elite landholders and small peasant proprietors into the single category of taxpayer and then pit that group against the state. In so doing both schools simplify a complex dynamic. In rent relations the interests of the state and landlords, though overlapping, were not identical. Officials in no sense merely did the landlords' bidding. They had their own agenda of concerns, concerns that compelled close cooperation with the local elite on some occasions and direct confrontation on others. Similarly, in tax relations the interests of large elite landholders and small peasant proprietors were not identical. Each bore a different tax burden (at least in imperial China), and each related to the state in a different way. To ignore these distinctions is to miss some major forces of change, for it was precisely a growing divergence between the concerns of landlords and the state and a growing convergence between those of large landholders and small proprietors that transformed the tripartite relationship in the late-nineteenth and twentieth centuries.

Finally, this book examines the effects that various external influences had on rent and tax relations in the Qing and Republican periods. Among the more important were commercialization and urbanization, China's incorporation into the world economy, the Taiping Rebellion (1851–64), and modern state-making. The impact of these events and processes was cumulative in the sense that the adjustments made in response to one redefined the boundaries of what was permissible in rent and tax, and it was then from within the framework of those new boundaries that the three parties responded to the next challenge, and so on. In this fashion, external influences interacted with rent and tax relations to bring about a gradual realignment in the balance of power among the state, the elite, and the peasantry.

POPULAR RESISTANCE TO RENTS AND TAXES

Tax and rent relations were essentially a competition over rural output. Since each harvest was a fixed quantity, the three-way contest was in effect a zero-sum game: a gain for one party meant a loss for the others. The potential for conflict was all the greater because of the slender margins above subsistence that characterized peasant production. Even a slight decline in yield could easily provoke a fierce struggle over the harvest.[4]

The tension inherent in the trilateral relationship manifested itself most concretely in landowner and tenant resistance to taxes and rents. This resistance took two forms, individual and collective. Individual resistance encompassed a variety of petty, usually covert strategems to frustrate landlord and state extraction—foot dragging on payments, simple evasion, adulteration of the rent or tax rice, and so on. A single instance of noncompliance in itself posed little threat to power and property relations, but in the mass their cumulative weight could have great impact.[5] Just how individual resistance to rents and taxes helped to shape the policies and practices of landlords and state officials in Jiangnan will be a major theme running throughout the book.

Individual noncompliance was by far the more prevalent form of peasant resistance in the period under study, but cultivators on occasion banded together in a collective effort to oppose landlord or state claims. Villagers might launch a rent or tax strike, refusing to pay anything unless the amounts were lowered; they might unite to drive collectors from their community; or they might stage a march on a landlord's residence or a magistrate's office to demand a reduction. In Jiangnan this sort of action generally occurred in large numbers only when rent and tax relations were under particularly severe economic or political strain.

Peasant collective action is significant to the analysis here in several respects. First of all, it serves as a convenient gauge of rent and tax relations. It was during those times of intense overt conflict that the differing interests of the contending parties were the most sharply opposed, and the points of tension in the trilateral relationship the most clearly revealed. Second, changes in the frequency and patterns of collective resistance were often indicative of shifts in the balance of power among the state, the elite, and the peasantry and thus can reveal much about the transformation in their relationship. Finally, collective resistance, like the more prosaic everyday forms of peasant defiance, was an agent of change in its own right. At certain critical junctures in the history of the lower Yangzi region, widespread collective action played an important role in the reshaping of rent and tax relations.

COMMERCIALIZATION, URBANIZATION, AND THE WORLD ECONOMY

We begin with a discussion of landlords, tenants, and the state in the early and mid-Qing periods, when vigorous commercialization and urbanization significantly altered the relationship between landlords and tenants. As the commercial opportunities and the amenities of urban life drew large landowners into market towns and cities, their relations with their tenants became more distant and impersonal; and tenants, for their part, gained greater independence from their landlords as the once-personalistic ties were replaced by strictly contractual ones. This attenuation of the landlord-tenant relationship set the stage for an intensification of conflict between the two over the land and its product. It also prompted an expanded state involvement in rural affairs in general and in rent relations in particular.

With advancing commercialization came also an increasing commutation of rent and tax payments, which, as we shall see, proved to be a major destabilizing force in Jiangnan rural society. The need to acquire cash to pay rents and taxes drew an ever-larger number of peasants, even those involved in grain cultivation and not cash-cropping, into the market economy. This process, what Philip Huang has called extraction-driven commercialization,[6] weakened the link between land productivity and the levels of rent and tax. Once fixed quantities based on average yield, rents and taxes now fluctuated annually with movements in prices and the value of silver and copper in China's bimetallic currency system. Previously, the major economic threat to the delicate balance among the state, landlords, and the peasantry had been declines in yield due to natural or human-made calamities. The commutation of rents and taxes made that balance extremely vulnerable to changing market forces as well.

With China's incorporation into the world economy in the late-Qing and Republican periods, the connection between land productivity and rents and taxes became even more tenuous. Prices and currency values no longer responded just to domestic supply and demand, but also to international market forces. The vulnerability of tax and rent relations to the world market was vividly displayed in the 1840's and 1850's, in the last fifteen years of the Qing, and then again during the depression of the 1930's, when changes in prices and currency values triggered widespread popular protest against the state and the landlords.

The market economy perspective has highlighted the benefits that world trade brought to the Chinese rural economy by raising the demand for agricultural commodities, but it has paid little attention to the ways in which China's links to the international market directly affected the peasantry's tax and rent burden, and even less to the ways in which it aggravated tensions among the state, landlords, and peasants.[7] The omission is a serious one, as I have already suggested. Any assessment of the impact of the world market on the Chinese agrarian economy must take into account the effect that international price and currency movements had on rent and tax relations.

THE TAIPING REBELLION

It is one of the central propositions of this book that the Taiping Rebellion marked a watershed in the changing relations among the state, the elite, and the peasantry in the lower Yangzi region. The rebel occupation of Jiangnan from 1860 to 1864 so disrupted rural society that the reimposition of Qing control after the rebellion necessarily involved a major recasting of rent and tax relations.

The impact of the Taiping Rebellion on rural society has been the subject of considerable debate. In Western scholarship the most provocative thesis has been advanced by Philip Kuhn and Frederic Wakeman, both of whom have relied heavily on the experience of Jiangnan to formulate their conclusions about the relationship between the rebellion and structural changes in local society in the late-Qing and Republican periods.[8] Simply put, they argue that the battle against the rebels irrevocably upset the dynamic equilibrium between the state and the elite, providing the gentry with an opportunity to appropriate the military and administrative functions of weakened county governments and expand their influence in local society. In areas that came directly under rebel control, the power of the gentry was such that the Taipings were forced to abandon their radical land redistribution and social-leveling program in the interests of securing the revenue needed to wage war against the Qing. Unable to eradicate the existing power and property relations, the Taipings chose instead to leave them in place and exploit them for their own purposes. The major beneficiary of rebel rule in the occupied territories, in this view, was the elite, to whom the Taipings granted virtually uncontested dominion over local society in exchange for a steady supply of revenue.

After the suppression of the rebellion in 1864, the argument continues, a weakened state was unable to recapture the authority and control it had lost, and military and administrative power at the local level remained, by default, in the hands of the elite. Subsequently the elite cemented its hold over rural society through the modernization and self-government reforms of the late-Qing and Republican periods. The result was an increasing abuse of power as the local gentry, now unrestrained by the state, overstepped the boundaries governing elite-peasant interaction and evolved into the "local bullies and evil gentry" (*tuhao lieshen*) of the Republican years. Their depredations ultimately became a major grievance fueling peasant support for the twentieth-century Communist revolution.

This book too seeks to explore the connection between the Taiping Rebellion and the Communist revolution. But its findings lead to a different view about the nature of that connection. While rebel rule in Jiangnan did not result in the total restructuring of rural society as prescribed in

Taiping ideology, neither did it, as Kuhn and Wakeman suggest, leave the existing configurations of power and control, wealth and influence, essentially undisturbed. The changes that the Taipings effected in local governance and in rent and tax relations, though far from revolutionary, nevertheless served the interests of the peasantry more than those of the elite. The elite's control of the countryside, I argue, may have been strong enough to compel the insurgents to compromise their ideology, but it was not strong enough to prevent them from enforcing measures detrimental to elite concerns.

The Jiangnan elite did not emerge from the rebellion years with their power intact, much less strengthened. To be sure, a striking expansion of elite influence did occur in Jiangnan in the post-rebellion era. But this development was not a building onto a domination achieved during the rebel occupation, as Kuhn and Wakeman would have it, but rather the result of an effort to restore what had been lost during the disruption of the Taiping years. Moreover, this expansion of elite influence did not, as Kuhn and Wakeman contend, entail a contraction of state power. On the contrary, the functions and influence of both the elite and the state expanded as each sought to redefine its relationship to the other and to the peasantry in the wake of the Taiping Rebellion.

RENT AND TAX RELATIONS IN THE LATE-QING AND REPUBLICAN PERIODS

The crisis produced by the Taiping Rebellion led to extensive modifications in the relationship among the state, the landlords, and the tenantry. First in Suzhou Prefecture in the late Qing and then in much of the rest of the lower Yangzi region in the Republican period, officials intervened in rent relations in ways and to an extent unprecedented in earlier times. This intervention entailed a more comprehensive and organized participation in rent collection and, at the same time, greater attempts to regulate landlords' demands on tenants. Second, landlords, particularly large absentee landholders, mobilized their resources to establish private collection agencies and landowner associations and to negotiate annually with county magistrates on the question of rent ceilings. Together, greater state involvement and landlord mobilization gave rise to new patterns of cooperation and contention between local officials and large landholders.

These two processes help to explain the paradoxical phenomenon noted earlier of stationary or declining rents alongside a rising incidence of tenant protest in Republican Jiangnan. Even as the new patterns of interaction among officials and landlords served to restrain potential increases in rent, I will show, they created conditions conducive to an escalation in tenant collective action. They, moreover, altered the nature of that action. As the state's role in rent relations expanded, local government officials supplanted landlords as the principal targets of tenant protest. To note the rise of an antiofficialism, however, is not to suggest that the relationship between tenants and the state became entirely antagonistic. For the state's involvement in rent relations had two distinct aspects. Officials may have sought to enforce payment, but they also sought to limit the burden on tenants. Reflecting this duality, the Jiangnan peasants saw the state as an aggressor in the collection of rents but as a potential defender of their interests in the setting of rents.

When Communist organizers attempted to mobilize the Jiangnan peasantry in the 1920's, they thus confronted a situation decidedly more complex than that depicted in the orthodox Chinese Marxist argument. The state, far from being a mere agent of the landlord ruling class, had successfully held rents in check. The peasants, far from being receptive to Communist appeals, proved quite resistant to radical action against a state power to which they had repeatedly and successfully turned for help against landlord exactions.

Tax relations, no less than rent relations, were significantly restructured in the period under study. The first move in this direction was the celebrated tax reduction of 1863, a major concession to Jiangnan landowners that greatly eased their burden until the turn of the century. Then, currency fluctuations and escalating exactions by the modernizing Chinese state negated much of the salutary effect of the reforms. The result was a heavier burden in many Jiangnan counties and an intensification of popular collective resistance against land taxation in the final decade of the Qing.

In the Republican period, however, the incidence of peasant actions against taxes declined dramatically—a surprising exception to the trend in other regions in China, where true to the predictions of the moral economy approach, the drive to extract ever more revenue to support state-building efforts triggered an escalation in rural tax protests. In Republican Jiangnan, it will be demonstrated, the level of real taxes (taxes relative to prices of agricultural commodities) went through two distinct phases, initially declining under militarist rule from 1912 to 1927 and then rising precipitously when the KMT (the Nationalist Party, or Guomindang) assumed control of the region in 1927 and launched its ambitious program of state-strengthening. But even under the KMT land taxes were still lower than they had been in the late Qing, and popular protest declined as a consequence.

An equally important reason for the decline, I argue, was a new elite activism in tax matters, itself a reaction to the state's aggressive attempts to consolidate its revenue base. Unlike the imperial state, Republican governments in Jiangnan required large landholders to pay the same rates as small peasant proprietors. This equalization of tax assessments came at the same time as the downward pressure on rents. Faced with increased taxes and depressed rents, large landholders had an immediate economic incentive to lobby the government for remissions and assumed from peasants the initiative for agitating for tax reductions.

On balance, landlords were the losers in the changes of the late-Qing and Republican periods. State intervention undermined the authority of landlords to conduct their dealings with tenants as they saw fit, while tenants, in no small part because of state intercession on their behalf, were able to press their claims against landlords more effectively than in the past. After 1927 especially, landlords were caught in the vise of rising taxes and lowered rents. Their predicament only worsened during the eight years of the Japanese occupation (1937–45) and then the four final years of KMT rule (1945–49). When the Communist Party gained control of the region in 1949, it confronted not a strong landed elite, but one that had already been seriously weakened by greater state intrusion and growing tenant political power.

CHAPTER 1

Landlords, Tenants, and the State in the Early and Mid-Qing

Commercialization was nothing new to the Chinese economy. Dramatic as the changes that took place in the late Ming and early Qing periods were, they were part of an economic transformation that had begun much earlier in the Song (960–1279). What was new was that commercialization now reached down into the villages, drawing both lord and peasant more fully into the market economy. Commercial development was especially advanced in the lower Yangzi valley, which, blessed with fertile soil and abundant water transport, had been at the forefront of the economic transformation since the Song.

The commercialization of the Jiangnan rural economy set in motion a host of other changes that eventually altered the interaction among landlords, tenants, and the state. The relationship between landlord and tenant became increasingly impersonal as landlord ownership became more absentee and fragmented, and increasingly contentious as each party sought new ways to assert his rights to the slowly expanding rural output. In this context tenant resistance to landlord demands escalated greatly, both reflecting and exacerbating the growing depersonalization in rent relations.

The attenuation of the landlord–tenant relationship held a number of important implications for the state. For one, the intensification of tenant rent resistance posed a direct threat to its fiscal viability, since the ability and willingness of landlords to pay land taxes depended on the rent they received from tenants. To safeguard their collection of taxes, Qing officials thus began to lend more coercive support to the collection of rents, becoming in the process more directly involved in rent relations than their predecessors of previous dynasties. For another, with the removal of the elite from the countryside, important tasks such as water conservancy and rural famine relief, which larger landholders had once seen to as community leaders, went unattended, and the state, stepping in to take up the slack, devised policies and programs that established a more direct relationship between the government and the peasantry without the intermediation of landlords.

The state, however, lacked the resources to fill completely the vacuum in the countryside left by the breakdown of landlord-tenant ties, and there emerged in the early Qing a new sort of elite activism—gentry managerialism—that was to characterize Jiangnan local society well into the twentieth century. Gentry managers (*shendong*) performed, in close cooperation with local officials, the tasks and functions that had once been the province of individual landlords. There thus occurred in the early Qing a decided shift from elite power based specifically on the private control of land and peasants to elite power based more broadly on semi-bureaucratic public activity, and from direct relations between landlords and tenants to indirect relations through gentry management.

LANDOWNERSHIP PATTERNS

Landownership and land usage in Jiangnan were every bit as complex in the pre-Taiping period as in the twentieth century. Fragmentary evidence points to the existence of every conceivable kind of owner and cultivator. We find not just the expected landlords, cultivator-owners, tenants, and agricultural laborers, but all the possible combinations of these: part-tenant part-cultivator-owners, part-tenant part-laborers, part-cultivator-owner part-laborers, part-cultivator-owner part-landlords, and even part-tenant part-landlords. The relationship of the owner or cultivator to the land and the relationship between landlord and tenant also assumed myriad forms.

Complexity is the only feature of the pre-Taiping land-tenure system that can be noted with assurance. Though much is known now about Qing property relations, thanks to the herculean efforts of Chinese scholars at the First Historical Archives in Beijing, it is still impossible to determine for any specific locale in the lower Yangzi valley the configuration of landownership and land usage and the predominant form of rental arrangement.[1] The following discussion will perforce be a general account of land tenure in Jiangnan in the early and mid-Qing era.

The limitation of the sources is nowhere more apparent than in the matter of land concentration. That the region was a bulwark of landlordism compared with North China is beyond dispute, but the difference in degree from area to area is hard to pin down. Contemporary statistics are few, and contemporary qualitative statements vague. In the seven-

Map 1. *Jiangnan in the Qing. In the Qing a single city often doubled as the seat of a prefecture and the seat of one or more counties. Thus, Suzhou city was the seat of Suzhou Prefecture and the seat of the three counties of Changzhou, Wu, and Yuanhe; Jiaxing city the seat of Jiaxing Prefecture as well as of Xiushui and Jiaxing counties, and so on. The names of prefectures are in uppercase, and those of counties in lowercase.*

teenth century the scholar Gu Yanwu estimated that nine of every ten peasants in Suzhou cultivated the land of others.[2] His words then became scripture, repeated in most subsequent treatises on Suzhou landownership until the fall of the Qing. The only other data available for Jiangsu show a lower tenancy rate, 50 to 60 percent of the peasant population, for Jiangyin County (Changzhou Prefecture) in 1840.[3] Presumably these figures include part-tenant part-cultivator-owners as well as pure tenants.

As sparse as the information for Jiangsu is, the data for northern Zhejiang are even sparser. Local gazetteers simply mention tenants as a matter of course, without making any attempt to estimate their number. We do, however, have a clue to land concentration in northern Zhejiang from Yan Chen, a native of Tongxiang County (Jiaxing). Referring to a long-standing difference between southern Jiangsu and northern Zhejiang, he wrote in the middle of the nineteenth century:

> In Jiangsu none of the large gentry or wealthy households is without fields and fields of land. Therefore, small households [xiaohu] possess no more than one-tenth of all the land. In Zhejiang, on the other hand, large gentry and wealthy households do not buy land. Consequently, the land there is the property of small households.[4]

Landownership in northern Zhejiang was thus relatively dispersed. Allowing for Yan's use of hyperbole to make a point and taking into account that his small households undoubtedly included some landlords, the tenancy rate in northern Zhejiang, though not as high as in Suzhou, was probably at least as high as the rate of 50 to 60 percent reported for Changzhou Prefecture. A passage in the 1821 gazetteer for Shimen County (Jiaxing Prefecture) bears out this estimate; the majority of the fields farmed by peasants, it notes, was rented land.[5]

To be considered a large landlord by contemporaries, it appears, at least several hundred *mu* of property was required.* The largest land proprietor in Wujiang in the Daoguang period (1821–50) owned more than 10,000 mu. Among the first families of Suzhou, the Pans and the Chengs each possessed at least 2,000 mu. Other large landlords had less bureaucratic influence than the Pans and the Chengs but similar amounts of land; Xu Peiyuan of Changzhou County and Liu Zhaoxun of Wujiang each had several thousand mu on the eve of the Taiping Rebellion.[6] Landowning was commonly just one source of income for such families. Proceeds from usury, commerce, housing rentals, and officeholding supplied the capital to buy land, and income from that property in turn supported these other activities.

More elusive though more numerous were the smaller-scale landlords, described in the sources simply as "well-to-do" (*yinshi*) families or "families with much land" (*tianduo*). The holdings of these people were usually below a couple of hundred mu. Depending on the supply of labor within a household, a person with as little as twenty to thirty mu could be a landlord.

---

*One mu is approximately one-sixth of an acre.

At least by the mid-Qing most of the larger landlords in Jiangnan no longer lived in the countryside near their fields. One eighteenth-century scholar estimated that 40–50 percent of the landowners in Jiangnan lived in county seats, 30–40 percent in market towns, and only 10–20 percent in country villages.[7] An 1846 fishscale register for a polder of 1,420 mu in Yuanhe County shows a similarly high degree of land concentration in the hands of absentee holders, with 17 percent owned by cultivator-owners and landlords of nearby villages, 18 percent by landlords living in Weiting, the nearest market town, and 65 percent by landlords residing in Suzhou city, some thirty *li* away.*

Large-scale landownership had become not only increasingly absentee, but also increasingly fragmented. Absentee landlords seldom possessed contiguous tracts of property, owning instead tiny parcels dispersed over a broad area, frequently over several counties. In the mid-eighteenth century, for instance, a family surnamed Qu of Pinghu County (Jiaxing Prefecture) owned land scattered over 60 percent of the county.[8] And between 1772 and 1886, a landlord family of Yuanhe purchased 490 small separate plots (totaling 990 mu) located in forty different polders.[9]

COMMERCIALIZATION AND THE LANDED ELITE

In the lower Yangzi delta, as Philip Huang has shown in his latest work, commercial development took three major forms: most importantly, the introduction of cotton cultivation and household production of cotton textiles, along with an expansion in sericulture and household production of raw silk and the increased marketing of grain.

As elsewhere in China, the cultivation of cotton in Jiangnan occurred on a large scale only after the techniques for spinning and cloth making began to be widely disseminated in the late thirteenth century. Then, being higher yielding and more easily processed, not to mention warmer, cotton rapidly replaced hemp as the major fiber for the clothing of commoners. In Jiangnan cotton, usually double-cropped with beans or wheat, displaced rice as the major agricultural product in the outer rim running from Zhaowen County east through Taicang Department and then south through the eastern parts of Songjiang Prefecture. Along this stretch, the terrain was too high for the easy irrigation of rice, and, in the coastal areas, the soil too saline for most other crops.

The expansion in cotton cultivation in turn made possible an expansion in peasant family textile production. The spinning and weaving of

---

*"Yuanhe yulin qingce." One li is about a third of a mile. A fishscale register, so called because of its appearance, was a government land register that contained maps of all parcels of land in each precinct (*tu*) and information on the identity and residence of the owners.

cotton in peasant households, mostly done by previously underemployed women and children, spread not only in those counties where cotton was grown, but also in counties where it was not, in which case the family bought the raw fiber at a local market. Since a household typically consumed only a small portion of the cloth it produced (in Songjiang in the mid-nineteenth century only 8.4 of a yearly output of 66.3 bolts), most of its product went to merchants, who then either resold the cloth locally or exported it to other parts of the realm. By the 1830's Jiangnan was exporting about 40,000,000 bolts annually.[10]

A less dramatic but no less significant development was the expansion in sericulture in response to a growing demand for silk clothing by wealthy urbanites. Before the Taiping Rebellion the silk industry in the lower Yangzi region was concentrated east and south of Lake Tai, where mulberry trees were grown on the embankments surrounding the low-lying rice paddies. Peasant families cultivated the trees, raised silkworms, and reeled the raw silk, which they then sold at the market. Because silk looms were expensive and weaving difficult, they rarely wove the raw fiber into cloth themselves. This job was usually performed in the cities and towns by official Imperial Silk Works and by specialized workshops hiring wage labor.[11]

The conversion from rice to cotton along the edges of the region and, to a lesser extent, the increased cultivation of mulberry trees at the center transformed Jiangnan from a grain-surplus to a grain-deficient area. Once considered the breadbasket of China, the region had come by the eighteenth century to depend on imports of 15,000,000 *shi* of rice annually from provinces upriver.*

As the pace of commerce in cotton goods, silk textiles, grain, and other commodities quickened, the marketing network in Jiangnan grew denser with the formation of new towns. According to statistics compiled by Liu Shiji, the number of market towns rose from forty-five to 100 in Suzhou Prefecture and from forty-four to 113 in Songjiang Prefecture between the Zhengde reign of the Ming (1506–21) and the Jiaqing reign (1796–1820) of the Qing.[12] G. William Skinner has estimated that by 1843 about 9.5 percent of the inhabitants of the lower Yangzi macroregion (of which Jiangnan forms the core) lived in towns with populations of more than 2,000.[13] If we look exclusively at Jiangnan, the densely populated and commercially advanced heartland of the lower Yangzi macroregion, the proportion would have been considerably higher. Liu Shiji, for in-

---

*P. Huang, *Peasant Family*, pp. 47–48. A shi is a capacity measure equal to roughly 103.6 liters. A *dou* is one-tenth of a shi, and a *sheng* is one-tenth of a dou, or one-hundredth of a shi. In terms of weight, a shi of unhusked rice equaled about 120 catties (*jin*), or 60 kilograms; and a shi of milled rice equaled about 160–77 catties (80–88.5 kg).

stance, has estimated that as early as the 1740's town dwellers constituted as much as 35 percent of the population of Wujiang County.[14]

For most peasant households, the expanding commercial economy was a lure to produce more than they needed to maintain themselves. The growing demand for grain to feed the urban population as well as those peasants engaged in cotton cultivation provided rice farmers with an incentive to plow more capital and labor into the land to boost its productivity. Since the range of rice yields reported for the late-Ming and Republican periods is virtually identical, an absolute breakthrough in land productivity did not occur in Qing Jiangnan. But as Dwight Perkins has argued, an increase in overall grain output probably did take place as land of low productivity was coaxed by labor and capital into bearing higher yields.[15] More obviously, the growing participation of peasant households in cotton and silk textile handicrafts, most often with previously underutilized family labor, raised their annual income.[16]

Ironically, the same process of commercialization that led peasants to increase their production also put landlords in a more difficult position to capture a share of the expanding surplus. Physically isolated from their land and its cultivators, absentee landlords did not participate in agriculture either as the supervisors of cultivation or as the suppliers of seeds, tools, and draft animals. Nor were they as likely as their predecessors to assist their tenants through hard times with reductions in rent and low-interest loans. The relationship between landlord and tenant not only became increasingly depersonalized, but also increasingly contentious as each sought to assert his claim on the expanding output.[17]

Neither the depersonalization nor the conflict was softened by kinship ties. For the urbanization of the elite also made itself felt in the family networks that shaped much of life in the lower Yangzi valley. In general Jiangnan had a two-tiered kinship system that mirrored the social and physical distance separating the elite and the peasantry—highly articulated and organized lineages among the elite in the cities and towns and more loosely organized descent groups among the peasantry in the villages.* Rarely do we find in the lower Yangzi region the highly stratified rural community so common in South China, particularly Fujian and Guangdong, where lineage ties bound elite and peasant, landlord and tenant, closely together, where elite lineage heads were the village leaders, and where peasant members rented lineage corporate land.[18]

---

*Here I am using the terminology suggested by Patricia Ebrey and James Watson to distinguish among different types of kinship groups. Descent groups are "groups of agnates, defined by *descent* from a common ancestor, who are not all members of a single *chia* or a single line" (their emphasis) and whose "corporate behavior may be limited to activities such as ancestral rites or compilation of genealogies." Lineages are "descent groups that have

The difference between South China and Jiangnan lineages can be seen most clearly in the domain of corporate property. In the lower Yangzi valley lineage landownership generally took the form of charitable estates (*yizhuang*) comprising anywhere from several hundred to several thousand mu of land. The charitable estate of the Fan family of Wu County (Suzhou Prefecture), founded in 1049, was the first of its kind and served as the model for other Jiangnan elite lineages. As the name suggests, the income from estate property was earmarked for various charitable purposes, including relief for widows and orphans, subsidies to promising male students, and the operation of lineage schools, as well as for certain ritual activities such as maintaining ancestral halls and compiling genealogies. Jerry Dennerline has demonstrated that the intent behind this philanthropy, especially the support for widows and orphans, was not so much to bind peasant members more closely to the group as to impress others in the elite marriage market with the lineage's ability to care for the wife and children should the husband die.[19]

Nor did the lineage property itself serve as a bridge between elite and peasant. A high degree of absenteeism and fragmentation characterized corporate landownership no less than it did private landownership. For example, of the eighty-seven charitable estates established in Changshu and Zhaowen from roughly 1550 to 1904, thirty-two were set up by lineages residing in the county seat, thirty by lineages in market towns, and only nineteen by lineages in villages.[20] And in the suburban counties of Suzhou city (Wu, Changzhou, and Yuanhe), forty-one of the sixty-four estates founded between 1049 and 1909 belonged to lineages resident in the city itself, and eight to families in market towns.[21] Moreover, this corporate property consisted of numerous small plots widely scattered across the countryside.

The charitable estates also differed little from large private landholders in their relationship with the peasants who worked the land, being neither demonstrably more lenient nor more exacting in their terms of tenure. In one respect, however, the estates differed greatly from ordinary landlords: they seldom if ever rented corporate property to their own lineage members. In this matter as in others, the Fans of Wu County had set the pattern by specifying in their family rules of 1083 that relatives were not permitted to farm charitable land.[22] As the Chen lineage of Jiashan County explained in the late Ming: "The purpose of charitable land is

strong corporate bases in shared assets, usually, but not exclusively, land." The distinction is important, they feel, because when a group like the lineage provides material benefits for members, "this fact will affect not only how individuals look on membership but also the internal dynamics of the group and the power the group can exert in society." (*Kinship Organization*, p. 5.)

to support relatives of the branch, but relatives are not permitted to rent this land to cultivate for fear that they would someday arbitrarily claim it as their own property."[23] In South China, by contrast, lineage members typically received preference in leasing corporate land.[24]

In short, Jiangnan lineages were predominantly urban families whose influence rested not so much on the control of land and peasants as on success in the civil service exam system and in officialdom. Consequently, though landed property or, more precisely, the income generated by that property, was important to them, territory was not. Corporate land-ownership merely provided a source of income that could be tapped to perpetuate the lineage through education and acts of charity. It made no great difference where the land was located or who the cultivators were so long as they were not lineage members. Kinship organizations in the lower Yangzi region did not form a strong personal link between land-lord and tenant and therefore did not serve to mitigate tensions between the two to any great extent.

TERMS OF TENURE

The attenuation of the landlord–tenant relationship within the context of commercialization brought about significant changes in the terms of tenure. The physical separation of landlord and tenant was accompanied, first of all, by a shift from sharecropping to fixed rents. For landlords resident in cities and market towns, fixed rent was a more convenient method of collection since it did not require their presence in the fields at harvest. They paid a price for the convenience, however, by sacrificing in years of exceptional yields the share that would have been theirs under sharecropping. For tenants the trade-off was a heavier burden in years of dearth in exchange for a higher return in years of plenty.

In Jiangnan fixed rents in kind predominated, but fixed rents in money were not uncommon, especially for land on which cotton and other cash crops were grown. Rents for the autumn rice harvest ranged from 0.8 to 1.8 shi of husked rice per mu, or 40 to 60 percent of an average to superlative yield (2–3 shi per mu).[25] Rents for the spring wheat crop ran from 0.3 to 0.6 shi per mu, or 25 to 60 percent of the average yield of 0.7 to 1.2 shi. Not all landlords required a spring wheat rent, and those who did typically compensated their tenants with an autumn rice rent several tenths of a shi (dou) lower than the local norm.[26]

In much of the region, particularly in the rice-growing areas, the amount of fixed rent changed little through successive generations of landlords and tenants. As an official noted in the early part of the Qian-long reign (1736–95):

[The current rents in Jiangnan] are the amounts of old that have been passed down through generations. Even when land changes owners, the tenant generally enters into a contract [with the new proprietor] to pay the old rent, an amount known by everyone. Therefore, rent cannot be increased when the price of land rises or reduced when the price of land falls.[27]

Customary practice in fact made it difficult for Jiangnan landlords, especially those in rice-growing counties, to raise fixed rents. Peasants who leased paddy land generally entered into contracts that specified the amount of rent due but no termination date. As long as the cultivator dutifully paid his rent in full, he could not, by the terms of the agreement, be asked to quit the tenancy. Nor could the landlord raise the rent during the course of his tenure. In the event of default, the tenant could be replaced, but the incoming party generally contracted to pay the same amount in rent.[28]

Some landlords tried to circumvent this strong social dictate against raising fixed rents by resorting to other, equally questionable practices. Although strictly prohibited by official statute, not a few used rent measures (*zuhu*) 6 to 16 percent larger than the government grain tax measure, the standard of comparison.[29] Others manipulated a form of payment called *zhezu*, in which rent was fixed in kind but rendered by the tenant in copper *cash*. Each year at harvest, the landlord was to set the commutation rate for the fixed rent (the *zhejia*, expressed in so many *cash* per shi of rent) at a level equal to the prevailing market price. But few landlords could resist the temptation of setting the rates at a higher level, for by doing so, they could change the amount of rent owed by the tenant without tampering with the fixed amount in kind.

Despite what seemed an obvious advantage for the landlord, fixed rent paid in kind remained the dominant form of collection in Jiangnan during the early and mid-Qing years.[30] In fact, the zhezu method would bring a landlord more income than payment in kind only if pressing circumstances forced him to sell the in-kind rent at its low post-harvest price. If, for example, a landlord accepted rice as payment in the fall and held it until the following spring when the price attained its annual high, he could get more money for each shi of rent than he could get with zhezu collection. During the eighteenth century in particular, a long-term increase in grain prices, as well as seasonal fluctuations, favored landlord speculation in rice, thus making fixed rent paid in kind the preferred method of payment.

The fixed rent stipulated in a written tenancy contract, labeled "original rent" (*yuanzu*) or "regular rent" (*zhengzu*), was not necessarily what the cultivator had to deliver each year. Often a distinction was drawn between nominal rent (*xuzu*, literally, "empty rent"), the figure in the contract, and actual rent (*shizu*), a lower amount required of the tenant. The discrepancy between the two could be quite large; by the middle of the nineteenth century, for example, tenants of land near Suzhou city paid actual rents 20 percent lower than the nominal ones.[31] Since this distinction will figure prominently in later discussions of rent reductions in the late-Qing and Republican periods, let us pause here for a brief look at how it arose.

The earliest mention of actual rent comes from a 1760 gazetteer for Wuzhen and Qingdunzhen, two towns straddling the border of Huzhou and Jiaxing in Zhejiang. In that locale, the gazetteer reports, tenancy contracts stipulated a nominal fixed rent, but peasants verbally pledged to deliver a lower fixed amount (the shizu) each year, regardless of the quality of the harvest. The final rent due was then determined on the basis of the yield; a larger amount was added to the minimum shizu when the harvest was good, a lower amount when it was poor.[32] This arrangement combined the risk-sharing of sharecropping with the inflexibility of fixed rents and may well have come into being during the transition from the one form to the other. Yet it differed from conventional fixed commodity rent in that the tenant forfeited his claim to a reduction during years of below-average yields in return for a smaller annual fixed charge. And conversely, the landlord relinquished the possibility of gaining the full amount of the stipulated nominal rent during years of average to superlative harvest in exchange for a lower but guaranteed yearly return. This method of calculating rent persisted under various names in certain Jiangnan counties until land reform in the early 1950's.[33]

More commonly, actual rents were simply rents fixed at a lower rate than the nominal rent without any provision for the tenant to pay more in exceptional years. Furthermore, tenants generally retained the right to negotiate for a reduction in bad years. This type of arrangement was customarily granted to peasants who had either paid a deposit on assuming a tenancy or bought the topsoil rights to the property as a way to compensate them for the considerable outlay of money involved.[34]

In addition to rent tenants had to pay surcharges, the amounts and varieties of which varied throughout the region. The Qu family of Pinghu collected four kinds of extra-rental fees in the 1740's and 1750's: *jiaomi*, *hushou*, *yangmi*, and *saodimi*. The first, jiaomi ("foot rice"), covered the expenses and salaries of the landlord's rent dunners (*cuijia*). The other three, subsumed in the Qu rental contracts under the heading "Expenses for Handling Grain" (*ban liang zhi fei*), duplicated exactly the customary fees that Pinghu landowners paid when they delivered their tribute rice to government granaries. Hushou refers to the man who measured the grain and, by extension, the consideration paid to him; yangmi ("sample rice") was the handful of rice the tax collector grabbed from the landowner's basket, ostensibly to evaluate its quality (*yangpin*); and saodimi ("sweep ground rice") was the gratuity paid to the granary worker who swept up the grain that fell out of the tax measure onto the floor. The Qus thus had either shifted the burden of these fees onto their tenants or, more likely, adopted the same nomenclature for similar commissions to their own granary personnel. They calculated the jiaomi at rates of 4.0 to 4.5 percent of each shi of rent rice, and the other charges at a combined rate of 0.7 percent. For every shi of rent, then, a Qu tenant paid an additional .047 to .052 shi in surcharges.[35]

The Qus' range of surcharges is atypical, since the tendency during this period, particularly among larger landlords, was a streamlining of extra-rental fees. Landlords of Suzhou, for example, levied a single surcharge, *limi* ("strength rice," calculated at roughly 3 percent of the rent), to cover the expenses and salaries of dunners and granary personnel.[36] But the Qu levies were otherwise in keeping with the general trend toward the deper-sonalization of surcharges. Wealthy landlords of the Qing, unlike their Ming predecessors, did not require those charges—labor service, gifts, and the like—that symbolized and reinforced the personal subordination of their cultivators. The standardized fees they set were clearly closer to the surcharges added to land taxes than the gifts and services rendered by a peasant to his lord.

Rent and surcharges composed a tenant's yearly financial obligation to the landlord, but even before assuming cultivation, a peasant in early and mid-Qing Jiangnan often had to pay a hefty deposit, usually called *dingshouyin*, as protection against default.[37] When a peasant relinquished a tenancy either voluntarily or at the request of the landlord, he was sup-posed to get a refund of the deposit minus the amount of any unpaid rent. Among the land documents of the Qu family are several promis-sory notes of tenants who still owed a certain portion of the deposit. The largest amount was 1.6 taels of silver per mu, which, at the current rice price of 2–3 taels per shi, equaled 0.53 to 0.80 shi of rice. Assuming that the party to the note may have already paid some of the deposit, the balance represents the minimum dingshouyin required by the Qus. The total amount was probably the equivalent of a year's rent (1.0 to 1.2 shi on Qu paddy land), the generally accepted standard for tenant deposits.[38]

On a per-mu basis, the amount of the rent deposit might not appear excessive. But tenants did not live off a single mu of land. In the case of Qu property, they typically contracted for three to fifteen mu at a time. A tenant who rented the higher amount of land thus had to pay as a deposit anywhere from thirty to fifty-four taels, a sum of money that in the mid-eighteenth century could purchase one and a half to five mu of paddy.[39]

As mentioned, tenants were often compensated for their outlay of funds with a lower annual rent than the nominal rent. It is not clear whether the Qus had adopted this practice, but even if they had, it would have taken a tenant several years to recoup his initial outlay, and only then if he had not gone into debt to raise the money to pay the deposit. The landlord, by contrast, would fare well under this arrangement, since the interest he could earn by lending the deposit at the legal interest rate of 3 percent a month exceeded the income lost with the lower annual rent.*

The term dingshouyin had a second meaning in Jiangnan. As well as designating a security deposit, it denoted the purchase price for cultivation rights in the system of dual ownership. Dual ownership of land was a practice in which the ownership rights, the subsoil rights (*tiandi*), and the cultivation rights, the topsoil rights (*tianmian*), were clearly separated. The holder of the subsoil, recognized as the legal owner of the property, was responsible for taxes and received rent from the holder of the topsoil. Both parties were free to mortgage or sell their respective rights, and a change in the status of one did not affect the other.

The possession of the topsoil gave the rights owner a number of advantages. First, rent on it was commonly several dou lower than the rent for land with no topsoil-subsoil division.[40] Second, this rent was remarkably stable. The fixed amount in kind during the initial division of a plot into topsoil and subsoil generally remained the maximum rent for that land. A landlord–subsoil owner could lower the rent, but he could not easily raise it, even when the topsoil changed hands.[41] Two-tiered ownership, as we shall see in subsequent chapters, acted as a powerful check on potential increases in fixed rents in kind in Jiangnan during the nineteenth and twentieth centuries. Third, topsoil owners acquired a security lacking in other tenure arrangements. Only in the case of rent default could a landlord evict the guilty party, and then only when the accumulated amount in arrears added up to the original purchase price of the topsoil rights (in which case the landlord could confiscate the topsoil as payment of the rent debt).[42] And finally, in owning the topsoil, the tenant had a piece of property to dispose of as he saw fit—sublet, mortgage, or sell.

Co-ownership of land in Jiangnan appears to have begun to take hold in the Ming.[43] The scattered evidence points to the existence of the system in most prefectures of Jiangnan by the mid-Qing but does not allow us to estimate how much land was involved. The most that can be asserted

---

*For example, if the Qus required the equivalent of one year's rent as security deposit—say 2–3 taels (1.0 shi) and compensated the tenant very generously with a lowered rent of 0.8 shi, they would lose 0.2 shi or 0.4–0.6 tael annually (assuming constant rice prices). But if they loaned out the deposit of two to three taels at the rate of 3 percent a month, they would gain 0.72–1.08 taels in interest the first year. By the end of five years they would have lost a total of two to three taels in rent but gained 3.60–5.40 taels in interest at the flat rate of 3 percent a month, and 7.30–10.97 taels at an annually compounded rate.

is that dual ownership was sufficiently widespread to have been identified in several mid-Qing sources as the root of many of the ills of Jiangnan land tenure.[44]

The Qing material also suggests that co-ownership was much more common in the rice-growing than in the cotton-growing areas of the lower Yangzi region, a pattern that is revealed more clearly in twentieth-century rural surveys.[45] One origin of the system, implied in the term for topsoil rights in Changzhou Prefecture, "ashes and fertilizer" (*hui-fei*), helps to explain this geographical distinction. In an attempt to re-cover from the severe depopulation and devastation following the wars of the Ming-Qing transition, landlords granted surface rights to cultiva-tors as an incentive or as compensation for capital or labor investments in land reclamation and improvement. Since the creation and mainte-nance of paddies required both more labor and more money than cotton land, co-ownership became more widespread in places where rice was the principal crop.

In other cases dual ownership rights came into being when cultivator-owners, in need of cash or hard pressed by taxes, transferred the subsoil rights to their property to another party, but continued to work the land as tenants with topsoil rights. The transfer could take the form of an outright sale or of a mortgage with the subsoil as security.

The use of the same term to designate a rent deposit and the price of cultivation rights suggests that the topsoil-subsoil distinction also traced back to the practice of requiring deposits. A tenant, when quitting the land for which he had paid a dingshouyin, would prefer to forfeit that deposit and sell the cultivation rights illegally at a higher dingshou price to another peasant. Or a landlord, to avoid refunding a deposit to an out-going tenant, would require the new cultivator to pay the dingshouyin to the old one. A trade in tenancies thus developed among cultivators, and the term dingshouyin also came to represent the price of a tenancy. After a tenancy had been in circulation for a while, it acquired the right of alienation and became known as the topsoil to the land. Eventually cultivators were able to buy the topsoil directly from landlords.[46]

Once topsoil rights had been created for a plot of land by whatever means, the subsoil owner–landlord could no longer demand a security deposit from the tenant–topsoil owner. Customarily, the parties to the transfer of topsoil rights were required to inform the landlord–subsoil owner of the transaction, but the incoming tenant, precisely because of his ownership of the topsoil, owed no security deposit. As dual ownership spread throughout the rice regions of Jiangnan, then, it eased out security deposits—hence the twentieth-century pattern in which topsoil-subsoil rights were more common in the rice-growing counties, and security deposits more common in the cotton-growing ones.[47]

Fueling the expansion in co-ownership in Jiangnan was an ever-increasing population pressure on the land. In 1393, when the Ming government carried out its most thorough and reliable population census and land survey, cultivated acreage per capita stood at 7.96 mu for Jiangsu and 4.93 for Zhejiang. By 1820 population growth had reduced those figures to 2.5 and 1.7, respectively. In Jiangnan, the most fertile and densely populated part of these two provinces, the amount of cultivated land per person was even less—1.58 mu.[48]

The land scarcity of the early and mid-Qing, as one might expect, meant escalating land prices, whether for land with no divided rights, for subsoil rights, or for topsoil rights. But of the three, the cost of topsoil rights increased the fastest. In the middle of the eighteenth century, the price of topsoil rights in Suzhou Prefecture hovered around two to three taels of silver a mu, some 9 to 26 percent of the price of land with no divided rights; by the end of the century, peasant land hunger had pushed the range to 57–86 percent.[49] Because of this inflation, co-ownership proved to be a mixed blessing for the tenantry. It gave a cultivator secure tenure, a lower, more stable rent, and the authority to sell, mortgage, or sublet the tenancy, but he had to pay dearly for all this.

In sum, the changing terms of tenure in Jiangnan during the late Ming and early Qing represented a significant recasting of power and property relations in response to the commercialization of the rural economy and the urbanization of the elite. In the new, purely contractual relationship between landlord and tenant, the two continually jockeyed for rights to the slowly expanding rural output. Through fixed rents and co-ownership of land, tenants acquired the right to any improvement in land productivity, a gain that under the old sharecropping system they would have had to share with their landlords, as well as protection against arbitrary eviction. Landlords, as one might expect, were not content to let their tenants retain all of this surplus and sought to cash in on it with security deposits, surcharges, nonstandard rent measures, and, through zhezu, higher rents. Their efforts were often stymied by tenant rent resistance.

TENANT RENT RESISTANCE

As used in the primary sources, the term rent resistance (*kangzu*) covers a wide range of tenant actions—from simple default, to the adulteration of rent rice, to violent attacks on a landlord's person or possessions. None of this was unique to the Qing, to be sure. Tenants had resorted to these tactics down through the ages.[50] But the rent resistance of the Qing was of an altogether unprecedented scale.

The particular terms of land tenure in Jiangnan during the Qing favored this tendency. In sharecropping the tenant's almost total dependence on his landlord for his means of livelihood made defiance a risky proposition at best. In the eighteenth century sharecropping was still practiced widely in North China, and a governor-general of Liangjiang wrote of its role in shaping the tenant-landlord relationship there:*

> Tenants in the north live in village housing owned by landlords. They also depend on their landlords for oxen, plows, and seeds. Thus, once they quit a tenancy, not only do they no longer have land to cultivate, they also are without houses in which to live. Tenants therefore fear their landlords, and landlords work their tenants as if they were slaves.[51]

In sharecropping, moreover, the landlord was a very immediate presence. Sometimes either he or his agent oversaw the process of cultivation from beginning to end. At the very least one or the other went to the land at harvest to assess the quality of the crop and determine its division, often then taking the landlord's share directly from the field. Under such close supervision, the sharecropper had little scope for rent default or other forms of resistance.

The tenants of Jiangnan were under no such constraints. As the Liangjiang governor-general went on to point out:

> Tenants in the south live in their own houses and supply their own draft animals and seeds. They merely rent land to cultivate from landlords. Except for rent payments, the tenants and landlords have little to do with each other. Should the tenant relinquish the tenancy, he still is able to provide for himself. Therefore, tenants regard landlords as being of little account. And landlords are unable to tyrannize tenants to any great extent.

By all accounts, Jiangnan tenants made the most of their opportunities to vent their grievances. A work on the customs of Taicang, for instance, listed rent resistance as one of the evil practices of the area, along with gambling and excessive litigation.[52] Memorials to the emperors frequently cited chronic rent default as the reason for shortfalls in the landowners' tax quotas. So pervasive was the problem that a special idiom developed to describe different types of tenants. Those who dutifully fulfilled their obligations were "conscientious tenants" (*liangdian*), as opposed to the "obstinate tenants" (*wandian*), "cunning tenants" (*diaodian*), or "deceitful tenants" (*jiandian*) who dodged them. Even more perfidious were the tenant "sticks" or toughs (*diangun*), who combined in their persons the rent default of the obstinate tenants with the bullying behavior of "local sticks" (*digun*).[53]

---

*The jurisdiction of the Liangjiang governor-general covered Anhui Province, Jiangsu Province, and the northern section of Zhejiang Province.

Official discussions of rent resistance attached these pejorative labels uniformly to all tenants guilty of misdeeds in their dealings with landlords. The government view of tenant disobedience rarely distinguished between a disinclination to pay and an inability to pay. All delinquency was "resistance" (*kang*) and portrayed as deliberate and unjustified. Official sources thus convey the impression that all tenant resistance was offensive in nature, aimed not so much at defending one's subsistence as at improving one's lot in life.

In fact tenant motives in the early and mid-Qing were mixed. Resistance in years of poor harvest was primarily a defensive, restorative measure, an attempt to coerce landlords into honoring the traditional obligation of reducing rents during times of disaster. Yet as officials and gentry frequently noted in dismay, a reluctance to pay rents in full was evident in bountiful years as well. "The crafty among the tenants pay only eighty or ninety percent of the rent even in years of exceptional harvest," wrote an official, indicating the Jiangnan tenantry as a whole. Another official wrote of Suzhou peasants that "there are many tenants who do not pay their rents in full even in years of bumper crops," and the Jiading County gazetteer of the Kangxi period (1662–1722) took the same sour view, noting that "whether the harvest is good or bad, [tenants] always default on their rents."[54]

Curiously, official dismay at the persistence of rent delinquency during times of plenty was not matched by an open acknowledgment that it could be prompted by financial hardship in lean years. Seldom did the emperors or their officials publicly attribute rent default to peasant poverty. It was not that they were unaware of the burden of rent or unsympathetic toward cultivators who had fallen on hard times. In fact, as we will see, they frequently exhorted landlords to lower rents during years of widespread crop failure. But even as they urged such reductions, they were at pains to paint tenant resistance as the activity of evil people who, in the official stock phrase, "seized the pretext of poor harvest to resist rents."

If the emperors and officials recognized the link between rent resistance and subsistence crises, why were they so reluctant to make the connection explicit in their public pronouncements? Simply put, they also recognized the threat that rent resistance posed to the perpetuation of the landlord-tenant relationship and the ideological norms supporting that relationship. Rent reduction in times of adversity was all well and good, but it was something to be given by landlords and not something to be taken or assumed as their due by tenants. As the Jiangsu governor Yin Jishan put it in a 1730 memorial about a rent strike in Chongming County: "Cultivating the land and paying rents is the duty of the people. How then can we tolerate the stubborn resistance of deceitful tenants?"

If the harvest was not up to par, "[tenants] should ask their landlords for concessions in rents. Why must they gather together and break the law?"[55]

In appeals to tenants to renounce their evil ways, officials generally employed the language of obligation and reciprocity. This one, the work of the Jiangyin County government in 1742, is typical:

> All over the realm it is the rule that tax payments are made from rent payments [*liang cong zu ban*]. Landlords spend much money to purchase land, but being unable to cultivate all of their property themselves, they recruit tenants to undertake the work in their stead. They hope the rents that tenants pay, in addition to covering tax payments, will support their families. Tenants, for their part, rely upon farming for their livelihood. They suffer from being propertyless themselves and therefore undertake the cultivation of landlord land, depending upon what's left after paying rent to support themselves. In this way landlords and tenants, as connected to each other as arms and fingers, partake of the same joys and the same sorrows.[56]

This passage is full of the stock phrases that routinely appeared in such pronouncements—namely, that landlords put forth the capital and tenants the labor, that landlords and tenants were both financially dependent on the quality of harvest and shared the same risks and benefits, and, finally, that landlords relied on rent payments to meet their land tax obligations.

The last notion captures both the essence of the relationship between land rents and land taxes and the real source of the official reluctance to acknowledge publicly the relationship between poverty and tenant default. In a region characterized by high rates of tenancy, the state's fiscal viability ultimately depended on the landlords' ability to extract rent. Official sympathy toward the plight of the tenantry thus tended to flag when default threatened to disrupt the flow of revenue from the countryside to the state treasuries.

Individual Rent Resistance

Peasants were a wily lot, or so literati and officials complained. They were wont to employ a variety of ruses to cheat landlords out of their rightful due. Instead of delivering the clean, dry rice called for in tenancy agreements, they would mix it with chaff or moisten it with water. In years of drought, flood, or insect infestation, they would claim more crop damage than had actually occurred and refuse to pay the stipulated rent. Worse, some obstinate tenants delivered nothing at all, electing instead to use the rice to repay debts in order to keep their lines of credit open or, if they had planted the early-ripening variety, to sell the entire crop immediately after harvest in order to get the highest possible return before more grain came onto the market and drove the price down to its annual low.[57]

Most exasperating of all were the topsoil owners who, it was said, treated the land as if it were their exclusive property and, as a consequence, were even more remiss in their obligations than the ordinary tenant. Often emotionally and always financially attached to their land, topsoil owners, "crouching over it like a tiger," guarded their claims from landlords and other tenants alike.[58]

Landlords in fact had little protection against the determined tenant–topsoil owner. The threat of eviction, their main defense against default and other unacceptable practices, carried little weight with these "crouching tigers." Although topsoil owners did not have absolute security from eviction, they could not be ousted so long as the amount in arrears was less than the original cost of the topsoil. A landlord would thus be forced to put up with an unruly tenant for a considerable length of time. Unless the tenant agreed to sell the topsoil to the landlord or to another peasant, there was no way to cut the period short. Until the matter of the ding-shouyin was settled, the recalcitrant party typically refused to vacate the land, often forcibly preventing the new tenant from working it (*bachan*).[59]

The landlords' physical remove made individual resistance all the more difficult to handle. Into this breach stepped the state, which, under the principle that "taxes come from rents," began to throw its weight more heavily behind rent collection. Landlords were permitted to report cases of default to local officials, who then instructed yamen runners and rural functionaries—*dibao*, *dizong*, *jingzao*, and the like—to dun the delinquent tenants. If they could not or would not pay up, they could be arrested, brought to trial, punished with eighty lashes of the heavy bamboo, and then detained in prison until they did so or at least until the start of the agricultural busy season, in the fourth month.[60]

Government assistance was a great boon to hard-pressed landlords, enabling many to collect more rent than they could ever have collected on their own. But reliance on official help did not always proceed smoothly or produce the desired results, for tenants found ways to manipulate the process of government dunning to serve their own rent-resisting ends. Tenant toughs were known to incorporate a stint in prison into their annual cycle of cultivation, secure in the knowledge that they would be set free in the fourth month even if they had not cleared their debt. In a more widespread practice, peasants paid the locally based dibao, dizong, and jingzao semiannual gratuities in return for protection against the consequences of default. Government runners sent to the countryside to press for rents could also be lured away from their appointed task with bribes; the amount, of course, had to exceed the fees that landlords had paid to secure their services. If the detention of a tenant was ordered, the runners and judicial clerks would delay first the arrest and then the trial, squeezing money from the landlord the entire time. When a tenant died in prison from disease or maltreatment, his family, with the connivance of government personnel, would attempt to extort compensation from the landlord by threatening him with a lawsuit.[61]

The fees demanded of landlords for official intervention made reliance on that form of rent collection an expensive proposition. For the less wealthy and influential, the cost could prove prohibitive. "Powerful families and large lineages with much land," one Suzhou gentryman commented in 1834, "are able to petition the government to dun for rent. Their tenants still fear the dunners." Smaller landlords, unable to bear the costs of official help, could "only let their tenants defiantly default on rents. . . . Even in years that are not ones of poor harvest, their rental income is not sufficient to pay taxes. Hence, among these landlords, there is not one who does not wish to get rid of his property and relieve his descendants of the burden. His only fear is that he cannot do it quickly enough."[62]

Another gentryman expressed the same sentiment more poetically.[63]

> The autumn crop is piled on the threshing floor.
> Most peasants have harvested ten shi or more.
> "Taxes come from rents," the officials decreed,
> "So you must pay rents with all due speed."
>
> The powerful gentry, they set strict deadlines.
> And their tenants come, all trembling with fright,
> Promptly delivering all their best rice
> And letting them measure out what they might.
>
> With the poor and powerless, the tenants make bold,
> Openly defaulting on rents, both new and old.
> When the landlord comes to visit and humbly begs,
> The tenant gives him broken rice all mixed with dregs.
>
> The landlord winnows the broken grain and sifts out the chaff,
> But what remains is not enough to cover the tax.
> Then he is arrested and beaten for default.
> His request that the tenant be dunned brings no result.
>
> He tries to sell his land, but no one wants to buy.
> So then he must place it in a powerful gentry's keep.
> Everyone says the new crop will be ready for harvest soon.
> Aiya! All the poor landlords just stand and silently weep.

Smaller landlords, in fact, were not as resigned to tenant default as this poem would suggest. Unable to secure government assistance, they undertook dunning personally, often with fatal results. Most of the violence that grew out of individual rent resistance occurred between tenants and these small, locally resident landlords.[64] Larger, absentee landlords were insulated from the violence by distance and their corps of private and public dunners.

Collective Rent Resistance

Individual rent resistance was by far the more pervasive form of tenant defiance in the early and mid-Qing periods. However, when cultivators were balked in their efforts to settle things on their own, they occasionally banded together to oppose landlord claims. Nearly all the recorded incidents of collective tenant action in Jiangnan during the Qing had as their aim a temporary reduction in rent. In this respect the region differed from other areas in China, where the abolition of surcharges and the institution of cultivation rights and fixed rents remained issues of contention between landlords and tenants throughout the late-seventeenth and eighteenth centuries.[65] In the lower Yangzi valley, as extra-rental exactions were being pared down and as fixed rents and topsoil rights were becoming firmly established, tenant dissatisfaction came to be focused almost exclusively on the issue of rent.

Each instance of collective action against rent in Jiangnan, while varying in its particulars, conformed to one of two general patterns of protest. In the first, the activities of the tenants could potentially progress through three stages, becoming more violent and hence more likely to incur government suppression at each stage. Resistance of this type began with a strike in which tenants declined to pay their rents in full. The strike was sometimes accompanied by efforts to negotiate a reduction with landlords. If the landlords acceded to the strikers' demands or took no action against them, thus in effect acquiescing to the reduction, the resistance was a peaceful one.

If, on the other hand, landlords refused to accept the reduction and tried to collect rents personally or with the aid of private and public dunners, the protesters, entering into the second stage of resistance, used force to defend their default. Zealous collectors would be beaten, sometimes to the point of death, and their rent rice boats would be destroyed. At this juncture the county magistrate, apprised of the situation by yamen runners and landlords, was faced with a dilemma. The law demanded that he arrest the peasants who had attacked the collectors and their boats, yet an attempt to do so might incite them to even more determined resistance and even greater violence. In some instances local officials chose to remain aloof from the conflict in the hope that the contending parties could work out their differences without further involving the government. If the magistrate decided to intervene in the dispute, he proceeded with caution, first ordering dibao and runners to apprehend the chief troublemakers, and bringing in a small force of soldiers only as a last resort.

Should these efforts fail, what the magistrate feared the most might come to pass: a true uprising in which the homes and granaries of the landlords were attacked and looted. The escalation in violence at this third and final stage and the threat it posed to public order invariably stiffened the magistrate's resolve to terminate the conflict, and he would now dispatch a larger contingent of government troops to disperse the protesters and capture their leaders. Frequently, a mere show of official force was sufficient to persuade the tenants to disband without a fight. At times, however, they stood their ground and engaged the soldiers in furious but necessarily short-lived battles, their primitive weaponry—hoes, cudgels, spears, and knives—being no match for the firearms of their foes.

In the second and less complex pattern of resistance, tenants backed up their protest with a show of force at the outset. Proclaiming their intention to default on rents, they would immediately gather and proceed en masse to attack their landlords' residences and granaries. Here tenant violence was not a response to landlord dunning or official attempts at suppression, but a measure calculated to convince landlords of the futility and danger of rent collection.

The kinship ties and communal activities that structured village life gave Jiangnan communities a cohesion that could be of tremendous use in mobilization for such collective action. The Jiangnan landscape was dotted with single-surname villages (Yao Family Harbor, Gao Family Village, Western Jin Village, and the like), indicating that they were founded by families of the same descent group. Seldom were villages able to maintain this original familial purity over time, but even after the devastating wars of the Taiping Rebellion, many Jiangnan villages were still dominated by one descent group. For example, two-thirds of the population (514 people) in Qianxiang Village (Wuxi County) in the early 1930's belonged to the Tang group, and 80–90 percent of the population (532) of neighboring Houxiang Village bore the surname Lü.[66]

Villagers also drew collective strength from their shared religious life. Usually when organizing a rent protest, peasants met at their village temple to devise their strategy and to pray to the gods for assistance. In some places local temples played a direct role in tenant resistance. In the countryside of Shuanglinzhen in Guian County (Huzhou), peasant life centered around temple associations. Each year an association collected dues from village residents to finance the annual fair and other activities. It invested any surplus funds, dividing the interest among the contributing households. Whenever the crops suffered even slight damage from insects or inclement weather, it was reported, the association became a vehicle for rent resistance. The members would congregate at the temple, pray to their gods, and decide on an acceptable level of rent. They would then drive away any landlord who came to the village and attempted to collect more than this amount.[67]

This sense of solidarity among peasants extended beyond the boundaries of their own villages to encompass the members of neighboring communities. The pattern of land tenure and the nature of agriculture in Jiangnan, especially in the rice-growing areas, made for a fair amount of contact among peasants of different villages. The peasants who in 1846 farmed the 1,420 mu of the Pin polder in Yuanhe County, for instance, resided in eleven different villages surrounding the property. While there was some tendency for peasants to rent the fields nearest their own village, on the whole there was much intermingling within the paddy, with cultivators from different villages farming adjacent plots.[68]

Neighboring villages were in any event tied together by their common interest in maintaining the irrigation and drainage system and regulating the water level of their polders. Intervillage cooperation was especially critical, as the following passage suggests, when a polder needed to be drained during the summer rainy season.

> After planting, if excessive rainfall causes flooding, the people must assemble paddle wheels to drain the water. These are called water carts [*da pengche*]. Each time there must be hundreds of them. People are distributed according to the amount of land, carts according to the number of people, and the amount of water drained depends on the number of carts. A marker is placed in the water and the level is checked constantly. The people take turns paddling the wheels, day and night without rest. There is a schedule by which the people assemble and disperse, and rules by which everything is regulated.[69]

The teamwork and discipline needed for polder management could form a strong enough bond among tenants of different villages to draw them into taking collective action.

Still, these familial, religious, and economic ties were no guarantee of solidarity, for a community could be just as ridden with conflict over access to land as the landlord and peasant were over the issue of rent. With land so scarce and tenancies so expensive, cultivators were forced to compete with one another for fields to farm. This struggle weakened the potential for collective action in two ways. In the first place it fostered a feeling of ill-will among tenants that could be as strong as or even stronger than any shared enmity toward landlords. Anger over the loss of a tenancy was sometimes expressed against the landlord but more commonly against the more vulnerable target, the new tenant, who was accused of "usurping cultivation" (*duozhong*). The landlord may have been responsible for depriving one of land, but it was another peasant who made his action possible by being willing to take over. A Jiashan peasant, evicted for default in 1771, captured the essence of this dynamic when he upbraided his successor with the words, "You have no shame, making it so that I have no land to farm."[70] Other dismissed tenants resorted to more than scathing remarks, refusing to leave the land and attacking the new cultivator when he began working in the field. Such disputes, which frequently resulted in the death of one of the contending parties, created hostilities and divisions in the village that undermined the unity necessary for effective protest.[71]

Second, before entering into any collective rent resistance, tenants had to weigh the chances and benefits of success against the possibility and consequences of failure, and the scarcity of land heightened the risks of a failed protest. A participant would face not only possible legal punishment for rent default and for any crimes of violence, but possibly worse, the loss of a valuable tenancy. The prospect of jeopardizing their access to land made tenants hesitant to take part in collective action.

Well aware of this reluctance and the reasons for it, tenant leaders employed a variety of techniques to overcome it, ranging from subtle persuasion to outright intimidation. They arranged for the staging of plays, whose sole purpose, as one account noted, was "to unite the hearts" of the tenants. Recruits were asked to enter into blood pacts and swear oaths of resolve in front of the images of their local gods. The compliance of those who remained hesitant was secured through threats to their property and public demonstrations of disfavor outside their homes. Tenant organizers were not above a little chicanery in their effort to rally people to their cause. In Jiangyin County in the 1750's, for instance, some organizers posed as rent dunners and in that guise propagated their resistance scheme.[72]

In their use of these tactics, tenant leaders showed a firm grasp of the principle of safety in numbers. The larger the number of protesters, the greater the likelihood that most would escape the economic and legal consequences of their actions. Landlords, overwhelmed by the number of participants, would not be inclined to evict so many tenants, since it would be difficult to find others to farm the land. Officials also tended to treat the participants leniently, in part because they lacked the resources to capture, try, and punish all those involved in a large-scale resistance and in part because they feared that harsh reprisals would drive the people into a rebellion against the state. When faced with a rent uprising, therefore, the government applied the same distinction between leaders and followers that it used in dealing with other forms of popular protest. Leaders were pursued vigorously and punished as fully as possible under the appropriate legal statutes; followers were considered to be unwilling or unwitting participants, people who had been either coerced or duped into joining the protest, and ought not to be chased down. Any who happened to fall into government hands were usually merely reprimanded and ordered to return home and resume work on their fields.

Tenant organizers had one thing going for them in their mobilization efforts: large-scale protests, even those that encountered government suppression and resulted in the arrest and prosecution of the leaders, were seldom entirely fruitless. Indeed the nature of collective resistance against rents was such that it is difficult to describe the results in the familiar terms of success and failure. True, one can speak of an unqualified success if the landlords agreed to tenant demands for a rent reduction. But the reverse did not always hold true; a refusal to accede to tenant demands did not necessarily mean that the resistance was an utter failure.

This seeming paradox can be explained by the dynamics of collective action against rents. Unlike food riots, workers' strikes for higher wages, or tenant struggles aimed at the abolition of surcharges or the establishment of cultivation rights, rent resistance (and tax resistance as well) was undertaken not to gain something but to keep from having to give something. The method of resistance—the withholding of rents—thus automatically achieved the resisters' goal, a reduction in rents. Subsequent tenant actions, such as negotiations with landlords and attacks on collectors and government troops, were largely defensive, designed to protect a fait accompli. These specific measures might end in defeat; the landlords might prove unwilling to negotiate or the government might intervene to quell the violence and arrest the leaders. But these failures for the resisters did not always translate into victory for the landlords. Although some of the protesters might be persuaded to abandon the fight and pay what they owed, others held out. The longer they did so, the more they drew on their autumn or spring crop to sustain their households, and the less likely the landlords were to receive any part of the harvest. So in the end, no matter what the government or the landlords did, the tenants achieved their original objective of not paying rents in full for that collection period.

The Link Between Rent Reduction and Tax Remission

In their actions of the early and mid-Qing, peasants did not deny the landlords' right to rents, but only disputed the amounts they were required to pay, especially in years of lowered yields. For the increasing numbers of Jiangnan tenants who paid fixed rents in cash or kind, this issue was especially critical, since that arrangement generally did not carry any specific provisions for a poor harvest. At most, rental contracts merely stated that "the general customs of the area will be followed in the event of damage from flooding, drought, or insects."[73] This clause seemed to promise a rent reduction in such circumstances, but the vagueness of the wording left much room for conflict.

Peasant claims to a rent reduction were strongest when landlords had received a remission in tax. Since taxes came from rents, the tenants reasoned, landlords who did not have to pay the full tax need not receive the full rent. In the early part of the Qing, this argument had the support of the Kangxi Emperor who, following the precedents set in the Yuan and the Ming, issued a series of edicts ordering landlords to pass along some of the benefits of tax remission to their tenants. The penalty for not doing so was 100 blows with the heavy bamboo and the refund of the overcharge to the tenant. The Kangxi Emperor further decreed in 1710 that, in the future, 70 percent of any tax reduction should accrue to the landlord and 30 percent to the tenant. (Thus, in the event of a tax remission of, say, one dou per mu, the landlord was to reduce rents by 0.3 dou per mu.)

During the Yongzheng reign (1723–35) and the early years of the Qianlong reign (1736–95), the government backed away from this stance, making rent reduction in years of tax remission a purely voluntary matter.[74] This new policy became enshrined in the Qing legal code, which expressly forbade local officials from forcing landlords to share a tax remission with tenants. If a landlord decided to do so, the statutes stated, an appropriate division would be the 70–30 ratio.[75]

The reason for the shift in Qing policy is not hard to find. The early Qing's propensity to follow Ming precedent aside, two primary considerations lay behind the Kangxi Emperor's policy of compulsion: the need to assert Manchu authority over the Chinese elite and the need to ease the burden on tenants so as to promote the resettlement and reclamation of the vast tracts of land left devastated by the wars of the Ming-Qing transition. By the early eighteenth century these tasks had been largely accomplished, and other concerns came to the fore. With the merging of the labor service tax (*ding*, levied on male adults) into the land tax (*di*) in the second quarter of the eighteenth century, property became the sole unit for taxation. The fiscal health of the state thus came to depend even more heavily than before on the ability and willingness of landlords to deliver their land taxes, which in turn depended on the ability and willingness of tenants to deliver their rents.

This fiscal chain was clearly threatened by the escalation in tenant resistance in the more highly commercialized regions of the realm, an escalation that the Yongzheng and Qianlong emperors and their high officials attributed in part to the policy of compulsory rent reduction. Tenants, they complained, withheld their rents in years of inferior harvests in the hope that landlords would receive a tax remission, but when a tax break was enacted, they demanded a larger rent reduction than the law required; and if there was no tax break, they would still refuse to deliver their rent in full. In short the policy of compulsory rent reduction came to be perceived as a liability that at once alienated landlords and encouraged tenants to hold back rents. To the Qing government, then, it made sense to relinquish some of its authority over landlords in the interests of securing its tax base.[76]

But the severing of the connection between tax remission and rent reduction did not result, as the Yongzheng and Qianlong emperors hoped, in a decrease in tenant resistance. Although no longer backed by imperial sanction, peasants in Jiangnan and elsewhere continued to claim that a landlord's tax remission entitled them to a rent reduction. The rent resistance, both individual and collective, this attitude inspired became such a grave problem that local officials were ordered to be sure that peasants did not learn of imperial edicts urging landlords to make voluntary reductions. As the Qianlong Emperor put it in 1777, such edicts "should not be announced publicly lest crafty tenants use them as a pretext to resist rent. . . . Tenants are all ignorant rustics, and if the edicts are made public, they will invariably interpret them as imperial orders to reduce rents, and the wicked practice [of rent resistance] will gradually spread."[77] Such injunctions had little effect, for it was the very fact of the tax remission, not knowledge of an imperial edict, that encouraged tenant resistance.

THE ROLE OF THE STATE

The turn away from compulsory rent reduction notwithstanding, the Qing period was in general a time of increasing state intervention in rural affairs, particularly in two domains: water conservancy and famine relief.

In the early Ming, water management, except for the largest projects, had been a purely local concern, coordinated and supervised by local community leaders under the *lijia* and *tiantouzhi* ("head of the field") systems.* But the smooth functioning of these systems depended on the oversight of the local landlords, and once they left to take up residence in the towns and cities, the systems broke down.[78]

---

*The lijia system, instituted in 1381, divided local communities into two units—the li and the jia—for the purpose of tax collection and corvée duty. The li comprised 110 households and was administered by the *lizhang*, a post that rotated among the 10 largest households (based on their holdings and the number of male adults). The other 100 households were divided into 10 units (jia), each under the command of a *jiashou*. The responsibility for mobilizing and supervising peasant labor to dredge rivers, maintain dikes, and the like fell to the lizhang, aided by the *tangzhang* (dike administrator) and the *liangzhang* (grain tax administrator), both labor-service positions. In the "head of the field" arrangement, adjoining property owners alone were responsible for the upkeep of polder ditches and embankments, since in principle they benefited most from the irrigation and drainage these provided.

In the sixteenth and seventeenth centuries, as water facilities fell into a worsening state of disrepair, county governments in Jiangnan cast about for new methods of management. Eventually, they decided on a combination of measures. First, rural residents were to provide the labor for conservancy projects strictly on the basis of landownership (*zhaotian paiyi*) rather than, as in the lijia, on the basis of both landownership and adult male labor (ding). Second, in the case of leased land, the landlords were to supply the funds and provisions, and the tenants the labor (*yeshi dianli*). This measure was particularly significant, since tenants had formerly been classified as supernumerary households (*jiling*, literally "odds and ends"), which meant that, though they had frequently performed the polder repairs under the landlord-dominated "head of the field" system, they had not been called on to work on the larger-scale projects administered through the lijia.[79] In fact, according to Hamashima Atsutoshi, they were not even mentioned in the major Ming compendia on water control.[80] With the adoption of the *yeshi dianli* policy, tenants were now viewed by the state as objects of water-control policy.

In the new system the supervision of polder repairs became the responsibility of the polder head (*yujia* or *tianjia*), a post that circulated among the wealthier resident landowners. The actual work was done by the cultivators, peasant proprietors and tenants alike, based on the amount of land they farmed. Tenants received compensation for their labor from their landlords, usually in the form of rent discounts. Under this arrangement, unlike the "head of the field" system, the burden for polder work was spread evenly among all cultivators, for the polders were now small enough, after a widespread partitioning in the late Ming and early Qing, that most plots of land adjoined the embankment.[81]

For undertakings too large to be handled by such local arrangements, various labor procurement and management techniques emerged. For some projects, the *zhaotian paiyi* and *yeshi dianli* procedures of labor recruitment were followed; others relied on workers hired with official funds, private contributions, or land levies. These larger-scale endeavors were supervised variously by provincial and county officials, subcounty functionaries, deputized expectant officials, and members of the local gentry.[82]

As for rural relief programs, Mori Masao has argued that these too became increasingly state-conceived and state-run after the seventeenth century. In the early Ming the government, though attentive to the needs of cultivator-owners stricken with poor harvests, largely left the fate of tenants in the hands of landlords. By the end of the Ming, however, this policy of nonintervention was becoming difficult to sustain as absentee landlordism grew and as conflict between tenants and landlords intensified. The government, changing tack, began to establish relief regulations and programs that explicitly included the tenantry as a category eligible for state aid. The involvement of the state in the landlord–tenant relationship through relief programs drew praise from some landlords and criticism from others, who exhorted their fellows to fulfill their traditional responsibilities by extending low-interest loans and rent reductions to tenants in times of need. By the eighteenth century, Mori contends, the voices of dissent had been silenced, and inclusion of the tenantry in government relief programs had become accepted as a matter of course.[83]

Ironically, the state's increasing involvement in the landlord–tenant relationship was accompanied by a decreasing official concern about the growth of landlordism itself. During the early part of the Ming, the labor service system was at least as crucial to the maintenance of the state as the taxes exacted from landowners. Through the corvée, the populace supplied manpower for the military, water conservancy, the lijia system of tax collection, and sundry other tasks that in later times were performed by hired labor and yamen clerks and runners. Since tenants were exempt from lijia service as "odds and ends," it was in the state's interest to promote an independent peasantry and to discourage the amassing of land by landlords. To this end (as well as to avenge himself against the Jiangnan elite, which had supported his opponent's claim to the throne), the founding emperor of the Ming had confiscated much of the land of Jiangnan landlords and converted it into state property farmed by government tenants. His successors, however, did not continue his aggressive measures, and the land slowly crept back into circulation among private proprietors. By the end of the Ming, landlordism had regained its hold in the lower Yangzi valley.

Faced with this resurgence, the state in the late Ming and early Qing periods, rather than seeking to change the nature of landholding to conform to the tax and labor service systems, elected instead to accommodate to the changes in landholding. It recognized the de facto conversion of labor duty into monetary payments and instituted a series of reforms that linked the commuted service tax more closely to the ownership of land. The amalgamation of the labor service tax (ding) and the land tax (di) in the second quarter of the eighteenth century completed the process. Landownership became the sole basis for the taxation of the rural populace, and the state no longer concerned itself as much with limiting landlordism. Its attention turned instead to ensuring that landlords had the means to pay their taxes.[84]

But it also had to contend with a new element. Increasingly throughout the Qing, gentry managers (*shendong*) moved in to fill the leadership vacuum left by the departing landlords. For this group the management of large-scale water conservancy programs and rural relief activities, in particular, became an important source of income. Since there was considerable overlap between the categories of gentry and landlord, many of these managers were landlords as well. But they did not act in that capacity as their predecessors had; their endeavors were public projects undertaken in conjunction with government officials and gentry peers. Put another way, the specific functions of the landlords became generalized to the gentry as a whole.[85]

This recasting of elite involvement in local affairs both reflected and aggravated the growing distance between landlord and tenant. Large landholders, now ensconced in the cities and towns, no longer functioned as village leaders and no longer performed the community tasks that had once been their responsibility as landlords. Instead, they involved themselves in civic affairs and what rural tasks they might take on frequently had little to do with their own land and their own tenants. Their influence came to be based more on connections with the government than on patron-client ties with the peasantry.

Confronted with a default of landlord responsibility, the state expanded its power in the domains of water conservancy and rural relief, instituting programs that established a direct official connection with the tenantry without the intermediation of landlords. But the state also retrenched, to the extent that it released landlords from the obligation of passing along to tenants the benefits of a tax remission. It was a position that the Qing would find difficult to maintain after the onset of a new crisis in landlord-tenant relations in the mid-nineteenth century.

CHAPTER 2

Popular Resistance in the 1840's and 1850's

From roughly the start of the Qing until the nineteenth century, rent relations in the lower Yangzi valley, for all the numerous changes, remained quite peaceful. To be sure, local natural disasters frequently aggravated the competition between lord and peasant, pushing them into violent confrontation over the harvest, but on the whole and in the eighteenth century especially, landlords and tenants shared an unprecedented prosperity that kept the number of violent clashes down.

Then, mounting population pressure on both physical and government resources, a worsening state fiscal crisis, foreign intrusion, and growing local disorder began to strain the social fabric throughout China, but especially in the more advanced coastal areas such as Jiangnan. By the 1840's the region was confronting a crisis that seriously threatened both the elite's and the state's grip on rural society. A severe inflation in the value of silver relative to copper all but wrecked the economy, resulting in a sharp decline in the prices of agricultural commodities, a precipitous rise in land taxes, and increasing landlord pressure on tenants to pay, if not higher rents, at least the current amounts in full. Political difficulties compounded these economic woes as first the British in the early 1840's and then the Taiping rebels in 1853 brought war to the region. One result of this political and economic turmoil was a marked escalation in popular resistance to rents and taxes.

LAND TAXATION IN JIANGNAN

The phrase "the land taxes in Jiangnan are the highest in the empire" is a familiar refrain in Qing treatises on taxation, and for good

reason. Although the area contained only 5 percent of the country's registered taxable acreage, it was saddled with 10 percent of the national
diding quota and a whopping 40 percent of the national tribute quota.[1]
As Table 2.1 shows, in 1753 the average statutory quota in Jiangnan (the
diding and tribute tax combined; the equivalent of .1355 shi of husked
rice) was about three and a half times the national average (.0384 shi).
Within the region itself, the quotas ranged widely across prefectures,
with Jiaxing Prefecture carrying the heaviest average burden (.2043 shi)
and Taicang Department the lowest (.0808 shi). In a number of places, of
course, the burden was heavier than the average. In Wu County (Suzhou
Prefecture) in the 1750's, for instance, 65 percent of the cultivated acreage
had a stipulated quota of .1722 shi of husked rice per mu for the tribute
tax and .1245 tael of silver per mu for the diding, which at the current
rice price of 1.7 taels per shi made for an overall quota of either .2454 shi
or .4172 tael.[2]

Had Jiangnan landowners been able to pay just the quotas, their tax
burden would not have been especially onerous. The 1753 average equaled
about 4.5–6.8 percent of an average to excellent rice harvest (2–3 shi per
mu). Even in Wu County, which bore the heaviest tax, the quota required only about 8–12 percent of a rice harvest. The problem was that
these statutory amounts became the basis for further taxation, particularly from the second half of the eighteenth century onward. By 1750, as
Wang Yeh-chien and others have pointed out, these national quotas were
of fixed amount, but the local governments' share, never abundant, had
become woefully inadequate. To raise the funds needed for growing public expenditures, local officials, forbidden to tamper with the basic quotas,
effectively raised the level of taxation by levying surcharges (*fushou*) and
by setting conversion rates above prevailing market prices (*lezhe*).[3]

The most important of these surcharges were the wastage fees (the
haoxian on the diding, the *haomi* on tribute grain), originally levied to
make up for any losses in the melting down of tax silver into ingots and
the transporting of tribute rice to the capital. These supplementary fees
were the only surcharges the central government recognized as legal. All
others were considered illegal exactions. In 1753 surcharges, both the
legal and the illegal, amounted to 21 percent of the basic tax, boosting
the Jiangnan average to .1637 shi, or 5.5–8.2 percent of a rice yield of 2–3
shi (Table 2.1). For Wu County, this meant a final bill of .2969 shi, or
roughly 10–15 percent of a harvest.

The diding had long been assessed and collected in taels of silver, but
by the end of the eighteenth century, local landowners normally paid it in
copper *cash*, which had become an important medium of exchange with
the expansion of copper mining in Yunnan. Those who did so were at
the mercy of the conversion rates (*zhejia*) determined by county magistrates, who could—and typically did—set them higher than the prevail-

TABLE 2.1
Land Taxes in China, 1753
(average diding plus tribute per mu)

Area	Quota		Surcharges		Total tax	
	Shi	Tael	Shi	Tael	Shi	Tael
China	.0384	.0576	.0091	.0137	.0475	.0713
Zhili	.0260	.0390	.0063	.0094	.0323	.0484
Shandong	.0279	.0419	.0077	.0115	.0356	.0534
Henan	.0329	.0493	.0085	.0128	.0414	.0621
Shanxi	.0401	.0602	.0104	.0156	.0505	.0758
Fengtian	.0452	.0452	.0107	.0107	.0559	.0559
Shaanxi	.0639	.0639	.0186	.0186	.0825	.0825
Gansu	.0373	.0373	.0101	.0101	.0474	.0474
Jiangsu	.0599	.1018	.0118	.0201	.0717	.1219
Zhejiang	.0606	.1030	.0112	.0190	.0718	.1220
Fujian	.0670	.1139	.0161	.0275	.0831	.1414
Guangdong	.0354	.0601	.0108	.0184	.0462	.0785
Anhui	.0586	.0820	.0130	.0182	.0716	.1002
Jiangxi	.0464	.0649	.0102	.0143	.0566	.0792
Hubei	.0206	.0289	.0047	.0066	.0253	.0355
Hunan	.0344	.0481	.0072	.0101	.0416	.0582
Guangxi	.0509	.0611	.0110	.0131	.0619	.0742
Sichuan	.0123	.0148	.0037	.0044 ˙	.0160	.0192
Yunnan	.0460	.0552	.0218	.0261	.0678	.0813
Guizhou	.0927	.1113	.0244	.0292	.1171	.1405
Jiangnan	.1355	.2304	.0282	.0479	.1637	.2783
Suzhou	.1944	.3304	.0427	.0727	.2371	.4031
Songjiang	.1707	.2902	.0355	.0604	.2062	.3506
Taicang	.0808	.1374	.0157	.0267	.0965	.1641
Changzhou	.1240	.2108	.0243	.0415	.1483	.2523
Hangzhou	.0946	.1608	.0178	.0303	.1124	.1911
Jiaxing	.2043	.3473	.0427	.0725	.2470	.4198
Huzhou	.0839	.1426	.0180	.0306	.1019	.1732

SOURCES: Wang Yeh-chien, *Land Taxation*, p. 70; Wang Yeh-chien, *Estimate of Land-Tax Collection*, table 26; Liang Fangzhong, pp. 401–13.

NOTE: I have used Liang Fangzhong's 1820 data for the Jiangnan prefectures. Since there is very little difference between Liang's provincial figures and Wang's, the prefectural acreages (and the quotas) presumably did not change much between 1753 and 1820. The national and Jiangnan regional averages were derived by dividing the total national or regional quota (surcharges and total tax) by the total national or regional acreage. Hence, the national and Jiangnan averages do not equal the averages of the different columns. Since the tribute tax was calculated in shi of grain and the diding in taels of silver, the figures in the columns under "shi" represent the grain quota and surcharges (originally expressed in shi of rice) plus the diding quota and surcharges converted into shi equivalents at the going market price. Similarly, the figures in the columns under "tael" represent the diding quota and surcharges (originally expressed in taels of silver) plus the estimated market value of the grain quota and surcharges in taels of silver.

ing silver-copper exchange rate, thus to turn a tidy profit when they converted the taxes back into silver for remittance to upper levels of the bureaucracy.

County magistrates also manipulated the tribute conversion rate to their advantage. In theory at least, landowners had the right to decide whether they would deliver their tribute in kind or in currency. For the latter form of payment, the copper *cash* conversion rate was to be derived by first commuting the statutory quota in shi into its equivalent in taels of silver based on the prevailing rice price and then converting that into *cash* based on the market ratio between the two currencies. In their computations, however, county magistrates used inflated figures for the rice–silver and silver–copper ratios, again profiting by collecting more in copper *cash* than they would subsequently have to spend to purchase the grain to be sent north to Beijing.

On top of all this, landowners had to pay various fees to the yamen clerks and runners who assisted in the process of tax collection. Imperial statutes, in recognition of these functionaries' low salaries and their need to supplement this inadequate income with customary fees, allowed some charges—for example, fifty copper *cash* for each shi of tribute tax to help cover the yamen runner's expenses when he went to the villages to hand out tax notices. But clerks and runners often demanded more than what was legally permissible or demanded additional fees that were not provided for in the imperial statutes (a fee for entering the government granary, a fee for the grain measure, a fee for the tax receipt, and a fee for the granary watchman, to name just a few). In addition, clerks and runners practiced other extortionate tricks of the trade—using tax measures larger than the statutory standard, manipulating the scales when weighing the tax monies, paying the tax on behalf of unsuspecting landowners and then requiring restitution at exorbitant interest rates, or simply demanding that the landowner pay more than the required amount and then pocketing the difference. In Jiangnan in the first half of the nineteenth century, such exactions, both the legal and the illegal, could increase a landowner's tax bill by as much as 10 to 20 percent.[4]

THE ECONOMIC CRISIS OF THE 1840'S AND 1850'S

Until roughly the 1820's a general inflation in prices made these Jiangnan tax rates bearable, but then China began to be hit by a series of economic jolts, and by the 1840's and 1850's severe economic dislocations had rendered the region's heavy tax burden virtually intolerable. At the heart of the difficulties lay a rise in the value of silver relative to copper, from about 1,000 *cash* to a tael at the turn of the century, to at least 2,000 *cash* per tael by the 1840's—a phenomenon noted not only for the commercially advanced lower Yangzi region but for less developed areas as well.[5]

Scholars have attributed this doubling in the copper price of silver to a number of different factors. Some link it to a debasement of copper currency brought about by declining copper production and the widespread counterfeiting of substandard coins. Others, mirroring the dominant opinion of the Qing court, argue that the monetary imbalance resulted from the outflow of silver to pay for illegal opium imports. Finally, in a more recent work, Lin Man-houng emphasizes China's growing integration into the international economy and the effects that a worldwide scarcity of silver in the first half of the nineteenth century had on China's internal currency situation.[6]

Whatever its cause, the change in the relative value of silver and copper reversed the inflationary trend in the copper prices of agricultural commodities. Between the early 1820's and the early 1840's, the price of rice in Jiangnan fell a full 50 percent, and from the 1830's to the 1840's, the price of wheat dropped about 30 percent. Cotton prices continued to grow into the early 1840's; then a noticeable decline set in there, too, due in part to exceptionally good harvests in 1844 and 1846 and in part to a decrease in demand for domestic cotton textiles with the influx of less expensive foreign products after the Opium War.[7]

The rise in the value of silver and the fall in prices adversely affected nearly all social groups to one degree or another. During the 1840's low prices and a crisis in credit drove merchants and shopkeepers into bankruptcy, producing a general contraction in commercial activities. For peasants this meant shrinking income from household handicrafts and off-season employment just as their returns from agriculture were decreasing and their land taxes increasing.

For the government, the silver inflation and price deflation meant a rise in expenses and at least the threat of a decline in revenue. Since government business was transacted in silver, its expenses rose along with the value of that currency. And since the tribute tax was ideally to be pegged to market trends, the government's income from land taxation stood to fall along with the price of rice. The Qing land tax system, however, cushioned the government from the worst effects of the economic turmoil. The potential loss of revenue could be made up to some extent by adding on surcharges and/or raising conversion rates. In fact, as the value of silver rose and the price of rice fell, the government's effective rate of taxation steadily climbed. At minimum, the doubling of the value of silver from 1,000 *cash* to 2,000 *cash* meant the taxpayer paid twice as much as before in the diding tax alone. In Jiangnan in the 1840's and 1850's, silver inflation, plus the addition of surcharges and the standard practice of setting above-market conversion rates, produced diding rates ranging from 2,900 to 5,000 copper *cash* per tael of tax.[8] The tribute rate shot up even more dramatically, despite the fall in the price of rice. In the 1840's

TABLE 2.2

The Land Tax Burden for Cotton in Changshu County, 1798–1856

(rates per mu of the most common grade of land)

Date	Qianliang (1)		Tribute (2)		Total tax (1) + (2)	
	Dan	Cash	Dan	Cash	Dan	Cash
1798–99	—	367	—	825	—	1,192
1821–22	.102	327	.191	615	.293	942
1828	.070	311	.204	907	.274	1,218
1836	.036	304	.153	1,286	.189	1,590
1845	.089	417	.365	1,725	.454	2,142
1846	.079	297	.230	879	.309	1,176
1853[a]	.112	362	.424	1,371	.536	1,733
	.112	362	.205	664	.317	1,026
1856	.094	362	.313	1,221	.407	1,583

SOURCE: Usui, "Shindai fuzei kankei sūchi no ichi kentō," pp. 108–13.

NOTE: One dan = approximately 110 pounds.

[a] In 1853 the tribute tax in Changshu County was reduced as a result of reforms introduced by the Jiangsu governor. The higher figures are the pre-reform taxes, and the lower ones the post-reform rates.

and 1850's, rates as high as 8,000 to 10,000 *cash* per tax shi (4–6 times the current price of rice) became commonplace.[9]

Numerous contemporary accounts speak of the increasing burden of land taxes in Jiangnan as well as in other parts of the realm during the Daoguang and Xianfeng reigns. Precisely how onerous this burden became in the lower Yangzi valley can be seen in a set of statistics compiled by Usui Sachiko. Taking into consideration the silver-copper ratio, the conversion rates, surcharges, and the price of agricultural goods, Usui has drawn up a tax schedule for Changshu County (Suzhou Prefecture), for which information on prices and taxes is particularly abundant.[10] The most common grade of land in Changshu carried a quota of 0.165 shi in tribute grain and from 0.105 to 0.148 tael of silver in the *qianliang* tax.* Usui's data, reproduced in Tables 2.2 and 2.3, give the amount of rice or cotton that a proprietor of this grade of land had to sell to pay the entire tax in copper *cash* and the amount of rice he had to deliver to the government if he paid the tribute portion in kind.

In 1845, when the conversion rates were exceptionally high, the payment of both the qianliang and the tribute tax in *cash* consumed 45 percent of an autumn harvest of cotton (average yield 1 dan, or about 110 pounds per mu) and from 38 percent to 58 percent of a harvest of rice (average to

*In Changshu, as well as in other Jiangnan counties, the land tax was divided into a qianliang tax and a *caomi* tax. The qianliang consisted of the diding plus that portion of the tribute grain tax, principally transport surcharges, that had been commuted permanently into silver. The remaining portion of the tribute, the caomi, was assessed in rice.

superlative yield 2–3 shi). For landowners able to pay the tribute levy in kind, the per-mu burden in 1845 was somewhat lower, 0.687 shi or 23–34 percent of a yield of rice. In 1846 and again in 1853, the magistrates of Changshu lowered the conversion rates for the tribute rice by about one-half, but landowners were still required to pay a tax substantially higher than the quota of 0.165 shi.

Rising taxes weighed more heavily on some Jiangnan landowners than others. Special exemptions were granted to families designated in the registers as "large households" (*dahu*), a term referring primarily to gentry families. These often substantial tax breaks were the work of county magistrates and their underlings, not a matter of Qing policy. Since the late Ming, in fact, the gentry had been systematically deprived of most of its legal tax privileges. By the late eighteenth century the only exemption to which landowners with academic ranks were entitled under the law was part of the ding, or labor portion of the amalgamated diding tax. Nevertheless, it was common practice throughout Jiangnan for county magistrates to collect tribute tax from large households at a "short rate" (*duanjia*) significantly lower than the "long rate" (*changjia*) demanded of the "small" or commoner households (*xiaohu*). In Changshu and Zhaowen counties, for example, the short rate in 1842 (5,200 *cash* per shi of tribute quota) was less than half the long rate (10,920 *cash*).[11] For the tribute tax collected in kind, large households received similar considerations. In the early 1850's large households of Suzhou city paid only 1.2 to 1.3 shi of rice for each shi of the stipulated quota, compared with 3 to 4 paid by the others.[12]

TABLE 2.3
The Land Tax Burden for Rice in Changshu County, 1798–1856
(rates per mu of the most common grade of land)

Date	Qianliang (1)		Tribute in money (2)		Total tax (1) + (2)		Tribute in kind (shi) (3)	Total tax in shi (1) + (3)
	Shi	*Cash*	Shi	*Cash*	Shi	*Cash*		
1798–99	.189	367	.424	825	.613	1,192	.173	.362
1821–22	.101	327	.188	615	.289	942	.306	.407
1828	.156	311	.454	907	.610	1,218	—	—
1836	.136	304	.562	1,286	.698	1,590	.388	.524
1845	.225	417	.925	1,725	1.150	2,142	.462	.687
1846	.156	297	.459	879	.615	1,176	.462	.618
1853[a]	.158	362	.600	1,371	.758	1,733	.413	.571
	.158	362	.285	664	.443	1,026	.413	.571
1856	.061	362	.204	1,221	.265	1,583	.413	.474

SOURCE: Same as Table 2.2.
[a] Pre- and post-reform rates.

Some Jiangnan counties had three different tribute rates: one for upper gentry (*jinshi* and *juren*), one for lower gentry (*shengyuan*), and one for commoners.* In Taicang Department the rates were 4,000, 7,000–8,000, and 10,000 *cash* per shi of tribute, respectively.[13] And in Haiyan County (Jiaxing Prefecture) in 1848–49, small households were charged three to four times the stipulated quota, lower gentry the quota, and upper gentry less than the quota.[14]

Large households secured further decreases by taking advantage of the yamen practice of "selling disaster" (*maihuang*), in which clerks and runners literally sold tax remissions to the highest bidders. A problem already in the eighteenth century,[15] "selling disaster" became even more prevalent after the 1820's, when the governors of Jiangsu and Zhejiang began routinely reporting natural disasters year in and year out, in good times and bad. But the reductions the imperial court obligingly granted were not distributed equally among landowners, for yamen clerks and runners sold them to large households. It is not clear whether large households earned the right to buy the tax cuts because of their standing or whether they were classified as large households precisely because they were able to purchase the reductions. But the upshot was that landowners of small household status rarely received their share of the remissions, even when a poor harvest gave them a legitimate claim. Thanks to the practice of short rates and the sale of remissions, large households were able to escape the worst of the tax hikes of the mid-nineteenth century.[16]

Landowners who lacked the protection of gentry status, cultivator-owners and landlords alike, had two recourses when they found it impossible to continue as small household taxpayers. They could entrust the payment of their taxes to gentry brokers in the illegal practice of proxy remittance (*baolan*), or they could rid themselves of the burdensome property. In proxy remittance a gentryman paid a small household's taxes at his own reduced rate. In the short run the arrangement benefited both parties, the gentryman through the fees he charged for his services and the small household through lowered taxes. Unfortunately, no information has come to light detailing the actual amount of grain or money that a commoner landowner had to hand over to a gentry broker. But given the staggering difference between large and small household tax rates in many locales, a proxy remitter could surely demand a fee that left the client ahead, but was crippling nonetheless.

Perhaps for this reason tax brokerage was unable to prevent hard-

---

*A candidate acquired the shengyuan degree after passing the prefectural exam, the juren degree after passing the provincial exam, and the jinshi degree after passing the metropolitan exam. Because only jinshi and to a lesser extent juren could be assured of receiving an official post in the Qing, a large political and social gap separated them from the shengyuan, hence the conventional distinction between upper and lower gentry.

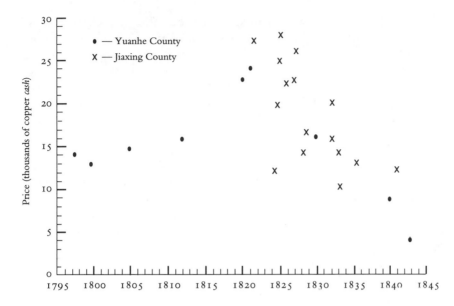

Prices of paddy land sold in Yuanhe and Jiaxing, 1797–1843. Prices are rounded to the nearest 500. Sources: "Shilu yiji"; and the Huai papers.

pressed commoners from resorting to the other alternative, selling their property. The extent of the increase in land concentration prior to the Taiping Rebellion is difficult to determine, especially for Jiangnan, where ownership was already highly unequal. Officials of the time did lament that "the rich are getting richer, and the poor poorer," and that the number of small households was decreasing at an alarming rate.[17] It was a trend that had predictable snowballing effects. As the tax base contracted, local officials reacted by raising the rates for small households, who then had even greater incentive to seek the shelter of a gentry broker or to sell their property to a large landowner. This shrank the tax base even further, prompting local officials to attempt to collect even more from the remaining commoner landowners.

All landowners, large and small households alike, were affected by one of the results of rising taxes and declining grain and cotton prices—a fall in the value of land. After rising steadily throughout the eighteenth century and into the nineteenth, land prices peaked in the 1820's and then dropped steeply. Paddy land in Huating County that had sold for 40,000 to 50,000 copper *cash* a mu in the first decade of the nineteenth century, the local gazetteer notes with perhaps a touch of hyperbole, commanded only 10,000 *cash* in the 1830's.[18] Price data culled from land sale contracts from Jiaxing County and a land purchase register from Yuanhe County show a similar, if less drastic, drop. (See the figure above.)

Land declined not only in resale value, but also in profitability. In Wujiang County in the 1790's, when a shi of rice sold for as much as 3,400 *cash*, a mu of top-grade paddy purchased at the average price of 17,000 copper *cash* and rented out for 1.2 shi earned a pre-tax profit of 24 percent annually; in the 1840's, with rice prices hovering around 2,000 *cash*, the same plot brought a pre-tax return of only 14 percent.[19] Land purchased at the depressed prices of the mid-century, of course, gave a better rate of return.

Confronted with a decline in the profitability of his property on the one hand and higher taxes on the other, a landlord of the mid-nineteenth century would have been tempted to recoup his losses by raising rents. There are some examples of landlords doing precisely that, but overall the historical evidence does not lend itself to any generalization about a widespread increase in rents to match the increase in taxes. Raising rents would have been the logical course only if landlords were already collecting what was owed in full. In fact, they were not. Consequently, it was to this end that they bent their efforts.

Those efforts did not meet with much success, for tenants were also hard hit by the economic slump of the mid-nineteenth century. For peasants who paid fixed rents in money, declining prices meant that rent absorbed a larger portion of their income from the harvest. Tenants of the lineage land of the Dong family in Guijiashi (Zhaowen County), for instance, paid in 1838 a rent of 1,400 *cash* per mu of cotton land. At the high cotton prices common in the 1830's (8,000 to 9,000 *cash* per dan), that amounted to only 16 to 18 percent of the income from one mu (average yield one dan). The lower cotton prices of the 1840's and 1850's drove the percentage up considerably—to 39 percent in 1846 and 44 percent in 1853.[20] For tenants who owed fixed rents in kind, primarily for rice and wheat crops, the proportion of rent to total income from a harvest did not change with the fall in prices, but the overall decline in household income from farming, handicrafts, and off-season employment made that rent all the more burdensome.

The deflation of the 1840's and 1850's thus bore heavily on tenants and landowners alike. The response was widespread individual resistance to rents and taxes, a simple refusal to pay what was owed. That failing, they often took the next step, banding together for collective action. Collective protest against rents and taxes escalated greatly in Jiangnan during the 1840's and 1850's. In this, the lower Yangzi region was hardly unique. The currency problems and the recession of mid-century were national in scope and provoked the same sort of popular resistance in other regions.[21] But in Jiangnan the highly commercialized rural economy, as well as the widespread commutation of rents and taxes, made landowners and tenants particularly vulnerable to price and currency fluctuations. The result was a greater number of collective actions against rents and taxes (fifty-seven) during this time than in any other part of the realm.

SOCIAL DISORDER

The rent and tax uprisings of the 1840's and 1850's took place amid growing disorder in Jiangnan local society. Memorials to the emperor speak repeatedly of increased banditry on land and piracy at sea and of an expanding underworld of gambling, salt smuggling, and opium trafficking.[22] The Lake Tai area was particularly bedeviled by the appearance of a new criminal element called "gunboat" (*qiangchuan*) gangs, a name derived from the fast, three- to five-man boats, fully equipped with fowling pieces, the gangs used to roam the surrounding waterways. Their economic mainstay was the proceeds from the gambling dens they operated, but they also dabbled in salt and opium smuggling.[23]

Contributing in no small measure to the disorder was the chaos wrought when Jiangnan became a battlefield of the Opium War (1839–42). In spring 1839 the Daoguang Emperor, determined to save the Chinese people and the Chinese economy from the deleterious opium trade, dispatched the eminent statesman Lin Zexu to Canton to eradicate opium smoking and smuggling there. Lin's vigorous campaign provoked in the fall of 1839 the outbreak of a full-scale war with Britain, which was equally determined to protect the profitable opium trade, as well as to force China to open up more ports of trade. Initially fought in the Canton area, the war reached close to Jiangnan in the fall of 1841, when the British captured several counties in Ningbo Prefecture and Ningbo city itself. They then made this important port their headquarters throughout the winter while waiting for reinforcements from India. They began a new offensive in May 1842, taking Zhapu in Jiaxing Prefecture, then Shanghai, and finally the strategic city of Zhenjiang. With the Grand Canal, the country's main north-south artery, blocked, and the British poised for an attack on Nanjing, the Chinese forces soon surrendered. Under the peace agreement, the Treaty of Nanjing, the British gained, among other concessions, the opening of five ports, including Shanghai and Ningbo, for foreign trade and residence.

The Opium War in Canton, as Frederic Wakeman and Philip Kuhn have demonstrated, led to a militarization of that city's hinterland.[24] To supplement inadequate government troops, local officials hired mercenaries (*yong*); and to protect their towns and villages, the gentry as well as some commoners formed militia (*tuanlian*), composed of either mercenaries or peasant minutemen. Whether or not a similar process occurred in Jiangnan as well, we do not know. The two major compendia of sources on the Opium War do contain materials that note in passing that Jiangnan officials recruited mercenaries and the gentry organized militia in the areas under attack by the English.[25] But these references are too scattered and cryptic to say how full the mobilization was.

Two things are clear, however: first, what local militia there were in Jiangnan were, in conception as well as in action, defenses against, as one official put it, both "internal" and "external" bandits; and second, whatever level of militarization was achieved during the war, it was not sustained thereafter.[26] The turmoil of the Opium War years provided local bandits (*tufei*) in the lower Yangzi valley with abundant opportunities to loot and plunder at will. Bandits, for example, destroyed the Shanghai yamen even before the arrival of the British troops.[27] There were also numerous rice riots; in Pinghu County (Jiaxing Prefecture) crowds attacked and robbed the granaries of some 600 wealthy households.[28] Once the war was over and the activities of the local bandits and rice rioters had subsided, the mercenary bands and gentry militia disbanded, in contrast to the Canton region where, Wakeman demonstrates, they persisted in defiance of government orders to demobilize. Militarization thus did not take hold as firmly in Jiangnan as in Guangdong.

If the Opium War in the lower Yangzi valley did not leave in its wake a militarized local society, it nevertheless did introduce a new element of instability to the area. Until the war Jiangnan had been relatively free of Ming restorationist secret societies. Afterward, with the opening of Shanghai and Ningbo as ports of foreign trade, Guangdong and Fujian merchants, compradors, porters, sailors, and opium smugglers poured into the region, bringing with them the illegal Triad organization, a branch of which, the Small Sword Society (Xiaodaohui), seized the city of Shanghai in 1853 and held it until early 1855.

Even as the officials and elite of Jiangnan had to contend with the Small Sword Society to the east, they faced an even greater military and ideological threat to the west, with the capture of Nanjing and Zhenjiang by the Taipings in 1853. The most culturally iconoclastic and physically devastating of the series of rebellions that swept China in the mid-nineteenth century, the Taiping Rebellion had begun in 1851 in Guangxi Province among a predominantly Hakka group called the Society of God-Worshippers.* The society's god was the Christian god, and its leader Hong Xiuquan claimed to be the second son of God, who had received from the Heavenly Father the mandate to restore China to a state of Christian grace. In practical terms, this mission translated into eradicat-

---

*The Hakka were latter-day northern Chinese immigrants to Guangdong and Guangxi. A subethnic group with their own dialect and distinctive customs, they were constantly in conflict with the much larger population of original settlers. The tensions between the two groups frequently broke out into murderous feuds.

ing Confucianism, Taoism, and Buddhism and seizing political power from the demonic Manchu rulers. Hong Xiuquan and his group envisioned an egalitarian, classless society based on the communal ownership of property and the communal worship of God.

In January 1851 the rebels, numbering about 20,000, began their long march north. Government forces were unable to halt the advance of the "long-hairs" (*changmao*), so called because they cut off their queues and let their forehead hair grow to show their defiance of the Manchus.* On March 19, 1853, the Taipings, now close to half a million strong, captured Nanjing and proclaimed it the capital of their new order, the Heavenly Kingdom of Great Peace (Taiping Tianguo). Zhenjiang fell shortly after. Jiangnan itself was not to fall to the Taipings until 1860, but the very proximity of the rebels directly influenced events in the region in the 1850's.

COLLECTIVE ACTION AGAINST RENTS AND TAXES

This, then, was the larger context in which the rent and tax uprisings of the 1840's and 1850's took place. They rolled across Jiangnan in two waves, one in the period 1840–46 and a much larger one in 1853, the year the Taipings arrived in Nanjing and the Small Sword Rebellion erupted in Songjiang and Taicang. Several of these collective actions have been richly documented; they are the subject of this section and of the analysis that follows.

Zhaowen County Uprisings, 1842 and 1846

> A black cloud completely covers the sky.
> The tribute rate's 14,000 *cash* high.
> The officials must once have been bandits.
> We sell our children, but our taxes we can't satisfy.[29]

Few parts of Jiangnan escaped the rash of rent and tax struggles that broke out in the 1840's and 1850's. From Songjiang in the east to Huzhou in the west, landowners and tenants gathered, often several thousand strong, to resist the claims on their harvests. Provincial officials considered a number of these conflicts serious enough to be drawn to the attention of the Daoguang and Xianfeng emperors, but surpassing them all in

---

*When the Manchus conquered China, they forced Chinese men to adopt their own headdress—a high shaven forehead and a queue—as a symbol of submission to the new dynasty. The penalty for not doing so was death. For a fascinating analysis of the political and symbolic meaning of hair in the Qing period, see Philip Kuhn's latest work, *Soulstealers*.

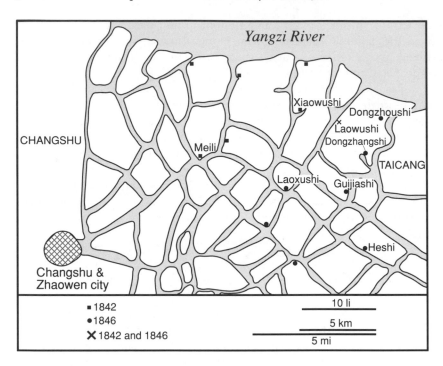

Map 2. Market towns attacked in the Zhaowen tenant uprisings of 1842 and 1846. Only the towns named in the text are shown. Lushi was near Xiaowushi. Its exact location cannot be determined. Source: Chongxiu Chang-Zhao hezhi gao (1904).

tenacity and destructiveness was a series of protests in Zhaowen County in northern Suzhou Prefecture. Fortunately for us, a Zhaowen landlord, Zheng Guangzu, chose to chronicle these events, giving us an all-too-rare picture of things from an insider's point of view.[30] Zheng lived in Dongzhangshi, a market town of several hundred households in the cotton and wheat belt of northeastern Zhaowen. A landowner of substantial means and holder of a minor academic rank, he played an active role in local affairs, devoting much time to famine relief, water conservancy, and, as we shall see, the maintenance of law and order.[31]

Zheng Guangzu relates that the trouble in Zhaowen began in 1842 with a protest among tenants of Suzhou garrison land near Xiaowushi and Lushi. Rents from garrison land (*tuntian*) constituted the principal means of support for the *qiding*, the hereditary group of boatmen who manned the tribute rice vessels. Although this income was exempt from government taxation and thus not affected by the increasing tax rates, the qiding had been steadily raising the rents for the autumn cotton crop. By the early 1840's they were demanding as much as 1,700 *cash* per mu, some 500 to 1,000 *cash* higher than the rent for nearby Taicang garrison land. The tenants of the Suzhou garrison felt the injustice of this disparity all the more keenly because the price of cotton had begun to decline after the exceedingly high prices of the 1830's. Until 1842 they had coped by defaulting openly and enduring stints in the cangue at the subcounty magistrate's yamen in Laowushi.

This passive resistance was transformed into violent protest when the qiding and their dunners arrived in the countryside to collect both rents for the fall harvest and back rents from previous years. Their callous disregard of the peasants' welfare, Zheng reports, particularly incensed two brothers surnamed Wang, who had spent several months of 1841 locked in cangues for default. The Wangs mobilized their fellow garrison tenants to drive the qiding from the area.

What began as a struggle against the qiding quickly escalated into a widespread uprising against other landlords. In this enlarged protest discontent focused not on increased rents but on the landlords' unwillingness to grant reductions in the regular amounts. Tenants in eastern Zhaowen, hearing that landowners had received a tax remission, had hoped that their landlords would see fit to decrease rents accordingly. In the end their hopes were dashed, and they threw in their lot with the original band of garrison protesters, vowing to avenge themselves against wealthy families who charged extortionate rents (*xiongzu*).

The tenants selected as their leader one Min Yuanyuan, whom Zheng describes as an experienced middleman and guarantor (*zhongbao*). It was a wise choice. As the go-between for peasants in their contractual dealings with landlords, Min possessed a higher degree of literacy and a larger knowledge of the world outside the village than the average cultivator, attributes that he put to good use in the resistance.[32] Under his guidance the tenant force, initially numbering around sixty people but growing as the protest continued, attacked over the course of five days the subcounty yamen in Laowushi and the residences of at least fifteen landlords and several rent dunners. All escaped personal injury, but the tenants plundered most of their homes for grain, money, and other valuables and set some on fire. The violence of the peasants' actions caused Zheng Guangzu to speculate that they were wildly out of control, "unable to stop even when they realized the danger of continuing." It was "as if a spirit was stirring them up." Indeed, so great was their frenzy, he writes, that it generated a tornado that pulled them along in its wake.

Actually, the tenants displayed more method than madness in their demonstration against rents. Consulting among themselves, they determined in advance which landlords and dunners to strike. From the fact that the people singled out resided in ten different market towns and villages, some at least twenty li from Lushi and Xiaowushi, it is quite clear that the protesters did not indiscriminately attack whoever was closest to hand, but went out of their way to get at those who had most earned their resentment. Even at the height of their jacquerie, the tenants exercised restraint in the punishment they meted out to their foes. They spared the house of one dunner, for instance, because another person held the mortgage on it. This sort of consideration for the consequences of their actions suggests that the protesters were moved by a calculated rather than an unbridled rage.

Several days into the uprising the Zhaowen magistrate arrived in the countryside with a small force of soldiers and runners to suppress the protesters. Zheng Guangzu and two other landlords (who, unlike Zheng, had suffered tenant attack) raised bands of "country braves" (*xiangyong*) to assist the magistrate in his campaign. Since capture seemed imminent, Min Yuanyuan drowned himself in a river. Secondary leaders were arrested and then executed, and those followers who were apprehended received lesser sentences for crimes against property.

The 1842 tenant uprising was a prelude to a larger-scale rent struggle in eastern Zhaowen in 1846. The two incidents overlapped somewhat in geographical area and objects of attack, but by and large the resisters of 1846 went after different landlords residing in different market towns and villages. This fact does not rule out the possibility that the tenants of the earlier conflict joined in the later one, but such a connection cannot be documented. Perhaps more important than any continuity in targets and participants was the inspiration that the 1842 collective action gave to the protesters of 1846.

Yet a more timely source of inspiration was a tax resistance movement that had begun four months before the second rent conflict. And the background of that dispute lay in the tribute rice baolan scams for which Zhaowen and neighboring Changshu were justly notorious. By the mid-1840's, one official estimated, a hundred or so large households in Changshu were paying taxes at the "short rate" on behalf of 90 percent of the small households. No comparable figures exist for Zhaowen, but baolan was judged to be no less a problem there.[33] Such rampant proxy remittance yielded the expected results. To make up the deficit in revenue, the county magistrates raised the conversion rates for the remaining small household taxpayers, thus forcing even more of them to seek gentry protection, which in turn compelled additional increases in tax. By 1845 this dynamic had pushed the "long rate" for the tribute tax to six times the price of rice.[34] For the average small household in Changshu and Zhaowen, tribute payments alone required about 37 percent of a harvest of cotton (0.365 dan of an average yield of a dan) or 31 to 46 percent of a harvest of rice (0.925 shi of an average to superlative yield of 2 to 3 shi; Tables 2.2 and 2.3).

In the fall of 1845 this situation came to the notice of the Jiangsu governor Li Xingyuan and the Suzhou prefect Gui Danmeng, who moved to put an end to proxy remittance and the excessively high rates on which it fed. They broke up a large ring run by three juren, two shengyuan, and one retired and one active tribute tax clerk, and prohibited the distinction between large and small households and the practice of proxy remittance. Henceforth all Changshu and Zhaowen landowners, gentry and commoner alike, were to deliver their tribute tax directly to the government collection chests at the uniform rate of 4,970 *cash* per shi, half the previous small household "long rate." [35]

The Changshu magistrate put the new regulations into effect immediately, and landowners were reported to have "eagerly delivered" their tax at the new reduced rate. The Zhaowen magistrate Yu Cheng, however, delayed implementation and continued to collect the tribute levy at the former extortionate level.[36] His tardiness brought some forty wrathful landowners from Meilizhen to the gates of his office in the first month of 1846. After destroying the furnishings in the main yamen court, the crowd wrecked the house of Xue Zheng'an, the retired tribute clerk who had been implicated in the baolan scandal.

The instigators of this incident were a landowner by the name of Ji Cuicui and a ruffian (*tugun*, literally "local stick") called Jin Deshun. Ji Cuicui, in addition to his indignation about the Zhaowen magistrate's failure to carry out the tax reforms, held a grudge against Xue for an earlier disagreement over the amount of tribute grain he owed. Jin Deshun had led a checkered life as first a monk, then a pirate, and then the holder of a minor military rank awarded for his service in capturing his former pirate comrades. At the time of the tax revolt, he was living off his skills as a doctor. Jin did not own any land, but he too harbored a grudge against the former clerk for refusing to cut him in on the proxy remittance ring.[37]

After the disturbance at the county seat, Jin and Ji and their followers fled back to Meili, where they set about mobilizing several thousand people in preparation for the anticipated official reprisals.[38] This secular aid was supplemented by sacred assistance. Gods, speaking through child mediums, informed the protesters that 3,000 heavenly soldiers had been dispatched to keep government forces at bay, and divinations cast at local temples further assured them that they would come to no harm.

Magistrate Yu Cheng did little to cast doubt on these oracles. Soon after the attack on the yamen, he sent some runners to Meili to arrest the ringleaders, but Jin and Ji, with the help of some of their supporters, killed two of their number and drove the rest away. Apart from this aborted effort, Yu took no action, apparently neglecting even to report the matter to his superiors, probably for fear that his own role in provoking the tax revolt would be exposed.

No serious military challenge was put to the resisters for half a year. Then, in the summer of 1846, with the outbreak of the second rent conflict in Zhaowen and of a tax uprising in nearby Taicang, in which the participants were reputed to have been consciously emulating the example of Jin and Ji, Magistrate Yu's bungling of his county's tax dispute came to light. Governor Li removed him from his post and ordered the Suzhou prefect, Gui Danmeng, and the newly appointed Zhaowen magistrate to lead provincial soldiers to Meili to suppress the resistance movement. This force soon captured Jin Deshun, Ji Cuicui, and twenty of their followers. Jin and Ji were beheaded; five of the supporters were strangled for their role in killing the runners, and the other fifteen were permanently exiled to a distance of 3,000 li.[39] For good measure Prefect Gui ordered the "arrest" of the local gods for their part in inciting the tax resistance. He instructed that their images be tied up and transported to Zhaowen city for display at the city god's temple as a warning to other troublemakers who might similarly be inspired by favorable celestial responses. A year later the gods, their sentences served, were carried back to Meili in a formal procession complete with the appropriate musical accompaniment.

This movement was still three months' away from suppression when the 1846 tenant uprising erupted in the countryside surrounding Dongzhangshi, Zheng Guangzu's place of residence. Once again, as in the original protest against the qiding in 1842, the immediate cause of peasant discontent was rising cash rents at a time of declining prices. Landlords, the tenants charged, were increasing the conversion rate for spring wheat rents in total disregard of the fall in grain prices. Added to this concern was the rumor, how well-founded it is impossible to say, that landlords also intended to raise the autumn cotton rents by 20 percent, the penalty fee for late payment from 30 *cash* to 100 for each 1,000 *cash* of rent, and security deposits by as much as 500 percent.

However strong their grievances, though, the tenants, mindful of the disastrous fate that had befallen the earlier rent protesters, were at first reluctant to press their case against their landlords. Even the auspicious results of divinations did not dispel their fears. What apparently tipped the balance was the assumption of leadership positions by Jin Shangui, a "local stick" who, according to Zheng, "left no evil deed undone," and Wang Simazi and Zhang Rongrong, also identified only as "local sticks." To pluck up the courage of the hesitant peasants, these leaders emphasized the Meili tax protesters' success thus far in eluding capture.

On a date prearranged by Jin Shangui, a group of tenants met at a nearby temple and then drew up and posted placards warning landlords that their homes would be destroyed if they did not lower the conversion rate for the wheat rent. Receiving no sign of acquiescence, the "local sticks" and their tenant supporters then set off to carry out their threat.

Under the slogan of "smash rack-rents" (*da xiongzu*), the crowd, eventually growing to a perhaps exaggerated size of 7,000 to 8,000 people,[40] plundered and wrecked the residences, granaries, and/or commercial establishments of at least 35 people in Dongzhangshi, Dongzhoushi, Laowushi, Laoxushi, Lushi, Guijiashi, Heshi, and neighboring villages. The landlords who suffered attack were either of lower gentry or commoner status. At one point in their weeklong uprising, the tenants surged past Zheng's residence in Dongzhangshi on their way to destroy the charitable estate offices of another landlord family. Zheng congratulated himself on his exemption from attack, attributing it to the goodwill he had amassed among peasants for his work in water conservancy and famine relief.

Day after day the people who had suffered at the tenants' hands filed to the Zhaowen yamen to report the crimes and appeal for an immediate suppression of the protest. After much urging on their part, Magistrate Yu decided to do battle with the culprits himself and to that end raised a band of country braves by signing on at random, Zheng notes contemptuously, "the weak, the old, and the destitute." The composition of his crew must have alarmed the magistrate as well, for instead of pitting this motley force against the tenants, he went to Suzhou city to request that provincial soldiers be dispatched to restore order. In response Governor Li sent the Suzhou prefect, Gui Danmeng, and a contingent of government soldiers to eastern Zhaowen, where they quickly dispersed the protesters and captured Jin Shangui and Wang Simazi (but not their fellow leader Zhang Rongrong, who had fled) and more than thirty followers. After this campaign Magistrate Yu was deprived of his post for his incompetence in dealing with the rent resisters and for his failure to arrest Jin Deshun and the tax protesters. Prefect Gui returned to Zhaowen two months later to put an end to the Meili tax resistance.

Despite the eventual suppression of the 1846 rent and tax revolts in Zhaowen, they did score some successes. Governor Li and Prefect Gui, conceding the legitimacy of the protesters' grievances even while deploring their methods, ordered Zhaowen landlords to levy rents at commutation rates no higher than market prices and instructed the new magistrate to implement the governor's 1845 tribute tax reforms.[41] The extent to which landlords abided by the new rent regulations is not readily apparent. The county experienced no further violent demonstrations against rents until 1853, when the arrival of the Taipings in Nanjing and Zhenjiang and the eruption of the Small Sword Rebellion in Taicang and Songjiang ignited tenant uprisings throughout Jiangnan. The intensity of the 1853 protests in eastern Zhaowen suggests that the six-year interlude in collective action against rent was more the product of tenant caution than of landlord compliance with the governor's instructions.[42]

The fate of the tribute tax reforms is more evident. The conversion

rate steadily crept up from the reform level of 4,970 *cash*, to reach 6,600
to 6,800 *cash* in 1853. Though burdensome, this amount was still about 40
percent lower than the pre-reform rate. The distinction between large and
small households proved less amenable to change. By 1848 large households were again paying their taxes at short rates, engaging in proxy
remittance, and cornering the market in disaster points.[43] Nevertheless,
as with rent revolts, no more violent protests against taxes were reported
for Zhaowen for the remainder of the 1840's.

In general the rest of Jiangnan also experienced a hiatus in violent collective action against rents and taxes between 1846 and 1852–53, the only
recorded incident being a prolonged tax resistance struggle in Shimen
County (Jiaxing) from 1847 to 1849.[44] Individual resistance to the claims
of landlords and the state continued, but county magistrates, having
learned well the lessons of their predecessors, were loathe to move against
the defaulters and risk provoking a reaction that, if mishandled, could
result in their dismissal from office. Thus until 1849, when a disastrous
flood produced a wave of rice riots, a semblance of law and order prevailed throughout the valley.

The Rice Riots of 1849

> The village behind beats the drum, the village in front the gong.
> Men and women, like wolves and tigers, fierce and strong,
> Gather together in a tumultuous throng
> And to the gates of rich families move along.
> Here, hoards of rice are swept completely clean,
> And there, stores of grain are suddenly gone.[45]

During the late spring and summer of 1849, rain fell in the lower
Yangzi region for nearly fifty consecutive days. The water control network, which had not been adequately maintained for several decades,
was severely overtaxed, and fields, villages, and cities were inundated.
The calamity struck just when farmers were harvesting their winter crops
and planting the summer ones, one of the most vulnerable times in the
agricultural cycle. As a result ungathered wheat rotted in the fields, new
crops of rice and cotton either could not be sown or else drowned as
seedlings, and the price of grain soared. Thousands of rural residents,
their food stores from the previous autumn harvest long depleted, converged on yamens to agitate for disaster relief. Others raided the shops
of grain merchants and the granaries of rich landowners, determined to
"seize rice" (*qiangmi*) or to "eat large households" (*chi dahu*).[46]

In response to the violence inspired by the specter of famine, the government attempted to arrange a more orderly transfer of grain from the
haves to the have-nots. Officials enjoined merchants and wealthy families

to sell their hoards of grain locally at low prices and to contribute funds to relief bureaus for redistribution to the needy. These efforts had mixed results. In some counties "the gentry and the rich" (*shenfu*) rallied and donated large amounts of cash and grain for relief. In others the handsome profits to be made from speculation overcame any sense of civic duty or fear of the unruly poor, and donations from the wealthy were very disappointing. The magistrate of Huating (Songjiang) was so dismayed by his county's failure to raise funds that he issued an announcement warning rich households that his only recourse now was to "let the people themselves call on each of you in person to seek food. . . . Some of you will be dragged outside your homes, and others will be cursed and reviled. But all you should do is obediently submit [to this treatment]."[47]

The relief measures that the officials and gentry were able to piece together were clearly inadequate, and rice rioting continued unabated throughout the summer and fall. It became so acute in some places that rich households hired mercenaries or otherwise formed defense groups to provide for their own protection. In eastern Zhaowen, for example, Zheng Guangzu pulled together his family members, hired hands, and "familiar tenants" (*shudian*) into a fighting force, and set out to do battle with the rioters. His campaign earned the approval of the magistrate, who gave him the authority to shoot on sight. Zheng's militia eventually captured twenty-four culprits and was instrumental in quelling the worst of the Zhaowen rioting.[48]

The Lilizhen Rent Resistance Movement, 1852–55

> We'll stab Cai Lingxiang and revile his wife.
> The marshes everywhere brim with strife.[49]

Jiangnan was slow to recover from the devastation of the flooding. The wheat crop in many areas could not be planted in the fall of 1849, and grain prices remained high throughout 1850. During the first several years of the new decade, though the area as a whole was spared catastrophes of the magnitude of the 1849 flood, harvests in certain locales were not up to par.

One such area was Wujiang County, which was hit by a drought in 1852. The poor rice harvest in the fall prompted tenants of the Beitangzi polder near Lili market town to launch a rent protest that was to continue intermittently for the next two and a half years.[50] The Lili resistance differed from the Zhaowen protests in several respects. Unlike the Zhaowen protesters, the Wujiang tenants did not immediately resort to violence against landlords, one reason for the movement's longevity. Further, in their choice of targets, the Wujiang tenants proved to be more selective

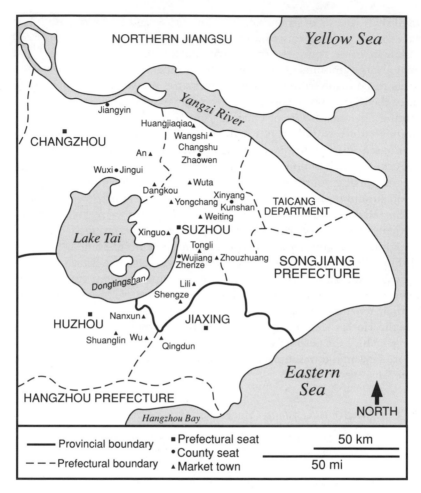

Map 3. The Lake Tai Region, ca. 1850

than the Zhaowen peasants, concentrating their forces primarily against three prominent gentry households—those of Yin Zhaoyong, a vice-president of the Board of Rites; Shen Shitang, whose son, Gaozhong, served on the Board of War; and the juren Cai Lingxiang. A contemporary wrote of these landlords that "they presume upon their political influence to oppress the people of the countryside. They are extremely cruel and are looked upon with fear and loathing." [51]

The organizers of the Lili resistance were members of the Lu family, most notably Lu Xiaozhong and his cousin Lu Xiaoheng, men who, as the governor-general and governor explained in a joint memorial, were not bandits (*fei*) but just ordinary peasants. In the fall of 1852 the Lus called together more than 200 of their fellow tenants for a meeting at a local temple. There, the group entered into a pact, agreeing that no one would pay more than 50 percent of the usual amount of rent.[52] The resisters passed out leaflets in neighboring villages announcing their intent, threatening noncompliant tenants with the destruction of their homes, and requiring everyone to donate thirty to forty *cash* for expenses. They then studded the mouth of the local harbor with wooden posts to block the entry of the boats of landlords, rent dunners, and yamen runners. Despite these careful preparations, the resistance of 1852 crumbled quickly when the participants heard that the county magistrate had sent soldiers to arrest them. The Lu cousins and the other main conspirators hid, and their supporters, admitting defeat, delivered rents as usual.

This setback might have spelled the end of collective action against rents in Lili had not the Taiping army captured Nanjing and Zhenjiang the following spring. Emboldened by the proximity of the rebels and capitalizing on the fact that the attention of officials was directed more toward that threat than toward unrest at home, the Lus and their followers resumed their protest in the fall of 1853. This time they demanded that landlords permit them to deliver only 0.53 shi per mu in rent, which amounted to even less than they had been willing to deliver the previous year. When their demand was not met, they adulterated the rent rice with substandard kernels and chaff.[53]

The government took no action against the Lili tenants until the fall of 1854, when Yin Zhaoyong sent a memorial to the court complaining that the Wujiang magistrate was allowing "local bandits" to run rampant and requesting an immediate investigation into the matter.[54] The Wujiang magistrate was thereupon stripped of his office, and a former incumbent, Zhou Murun, was assigned the task of leading official troops and country braves against the protesters. This time news of an impending government attack did not cause the Lili tenants to disperse without a fight. In fact, it pushed them into violence. Surmising the authorship of the memorial responsible for the decision to suppress the resistance, they raided the Yin family compound in Changtian Village and kidnaped a tutor and several relatives. They also attacked the residence of Cai Lingxiang in Lili town and seized several of the family servants. The tenants transported their prisoners back to Beitangzi polder and locked them up, presumably intending to use them as hostages should the need arise. When the expected government reprisals did not take place immediately, the Lus released the captives unharmed.

For reasons that are not clear, Zhou Murun did not attend to the rent protesters until the spring of the following year (1855). On his arrival in the tenants' territory, he quickly captured Lu Xiaoheng. In retaliation his cousin, Xiaozhong, staged attacks on the residences of Yin Zhaoyong, Shen Shitang, and Cai Lingxiang, and seized four new hostages, including two granary managers (*zhangfang xiansheng*) from Shen's establishment. The tenants announced that they would release their prisoners only after Lu Xiaoheng had been set free. Zhou Murun refused to bargain and engaged the resisters in a pitched battle on a nearby waterway. The tenant force of 400 to 500 boats outnumbered the 60 to 70 vessels under Zhou's command, but what the government side lacked in numbers was more than compensated for by a superiority in firearms. Zhou ordered his troops to fire cannons and muskets directly into the mass of poorly armed tenants, who soon broke rank and fled. Then, proclaiming that "jade and stone [both good and evil people] will burn together," he gave his soldiers free rein to kill and loot throughout the area. Within a week Lu Xiaozhong and ten of his followers joined Lu Xiaoheng in captivity. The Lus were executed in Suzhou city, and their heads were sent back to Lili for display. Every day thereafter, it was reported, the tenants gathered at the temple to burn candles and incense and to beseech the gods to eliminate the landlords, officials, and soldiers. Their piety so badly frightened the governor and the prefect that they had the temple destroyed.[55]

The Small Sword Uprising in Songjiang and Taicang, 1853

> You magistrate perched so high on your pillow,
> Of the people's suffering what do you know?
> Our wives will beg and to the loan association we'll go.
> But we won't sell our children to pay the taxes we owe.[56]

Just as the arrival of the Taipings in Nanjing and Zhenjiang in 1853 gave new life to the rent resistance movement in Lili market town, so it ushered in a dramatic escalation in popular protest throughout the rest of Jiangnan. In that year alone there were thirty-two collective actions against rents and taxes, a sixfold increase over the number of conflicts reported for 1852 (Table A.1). Disorder of this magnitude, which would have been a cause for considerable concern among officials and the elite even in "ordinary" times, took on alarming dimensions in the face of the anticipated Taiping invasion. Local discontent, it was feared, could all too easily coalesce into a rebellion against the government just when a unanimity of purpose was needed to deal with the Taiping threat. More frightening yet was the possibility that local rebels and the Taiping insurgents would find common cause and join forces to wrest the region from Qing control.[57]

These fears were partially confirmed in early September 1853, when the Small Sword Society of Shanghai triggered an uprising in Song-

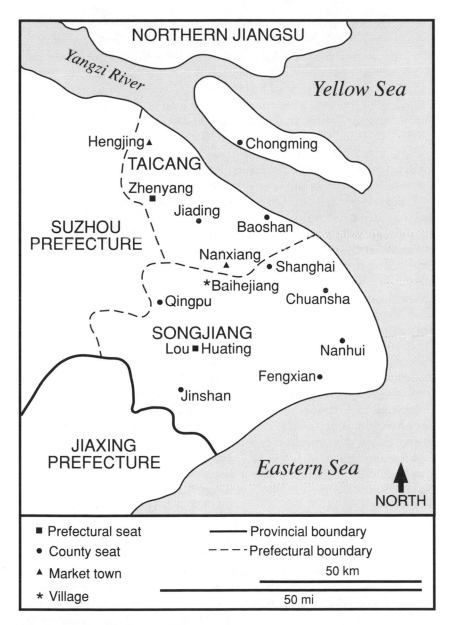

NORTHERN JIANGSU

Yangzi River

Yellow Sea

Hengjing▲

TAICANG

Zhenyang■

Jiading●

SUZHOU
PREFECTURE

Baoshan●

Nanxiang▲

●Shanghai

*Baihejiang

●Qingpu

Chuansha●

SONGJIANG

Lou■Huating

Nanhui●

Fengxian●

●Jinshan

Chongming●

JIAXING
PREFECTURE

Eastern Sea

↑
NORTH

■ Prefectural seat   —— Provincial boundary

● County seat   - - - - Prefectural boundary

▲ Market town   50 km

* Village   50 mi

Map 4. Songjiang Prefecture and Taicang Department, ca. 1850

jiang Prefecture and Taicang Department.[58] A Triad offshoot organized shortly after the (unrelated) Small Sword Rebellion in Amoy in May 1853, the society was a confederation of seven existing associations: the Small Sword Society, the Double Sword Society (Shuangdaohui), and one other unspecified gang, all composed of Guangdong immigrants; the Bird League (Niaodang) and the Green Turban Society (Qingjinhui) of Fujian natives; the Ningbo League (Ningbodang) of Ningbonese; and the indigenous Hundred Dragons League (Bailongdang). The amalgamated group presumably called itself the Small Swords, a common appellation for Triad branches, because its leader, Liu Lichuan, had headed the smaller Guangdong society of the same name.[59]

The thirty-three-year-old Liu, originally of Guangdong peasant stock, had migrated to Shanghai in 1849, bringing with him a command of pidgin English picked up during a sojourn in Hong Kong and credentials as a member of the Triads. In his new city he set about organizing other Guangdong natives into the Small Sword group, meanwhile supporting himself first as an interpreter for a Western enterprise and then as a market broker in the sugar trade. When these jobs ended, he turned to medicine to scratch out a living. In the time-honored tradition of leaders of heterodox groups in China, Liu used his medical skills to lure people to his cause. Every patient was a possible recruit, and Liu made the most of these possibilities by treating the indigent free of charge, a generosity that added to his own reputation and that of the society he represented, attracting many urban poor to the Small Sword banner.[60]

Beneath Liu Lichuan in the Small Sword hierarchy was an echelon of secondary chiefs of diverse occupations: a foreigner's groom; a tea merchant; several government mercenaries; Li Xianyun, the director of two Fujian shipping guilds; and Li Shaoqing, the head of a Guangdong shipping guild.[61] Of particular interest here was the involvement of the two Lis, attesting (along with other evidence) to a strong structural link between merchant guilds in Shanghai and the seven associations that made up the Small Sword Society. Behind their façade of respectability as guild managers, Li Xianyun and Li Shaoqing had been prominent figures in the Shanghai underworld even before their participation in the Small Swords. As patrons to the criminally inclined among their fellow provincials, they enjoyed close connections with Fujian and Guangdong secret societies. At the end of August 1853, when rumors of an imminent Small Sword uprising reached official ears, Wu Jianzhang, the military intendant of the Suzhou-Songjiang circuit, summoned Li Xianyun, Li Shaoqing, and four other guild directors (two headed Guangdong groups; the others, Ningbo and Shanghai groups). At the meeting Intendant Wu proposed to the assembled directors that *they* disband the Small Sword Society. Wu's appeal, the congruence between the number of the Small Swords' component groups (counting the two Fujian guilds Li Xianyun headed), and the Lis' criminal connections all suggest that the Small Swords were in fact the underworld arm of the seven guilds represented at the meeting.[62]

In the end the directors refused to comply with Intendant Wu's wishes. Instead, they submitted a politely worded petition in which they lamented the increase in local disorder and the toll it was taking on commerce and generously offered to convert the Small Sword Society into a militia to protect the streets of Shanghai. The wherewithal for this, they suggested, should come from gentry and merchant contributions solicited by the circuit intendant's office itself. Wu Jianzhang did not miss the threat implicit in the directors' proposal and agreed to raise the money in the misguided hope of buying peace. With the funds he provided, Liu Lichuan and the guild directors cum Small Sword leaders expanded their rebel force, labeled it a militia, and in early September 1853 deployed it in revolt against the Qing dynasty.[63]

Crucial to the success of the Small Sword assault on Shanghai and other cities in Songjiang and Taicang was the participation of the rural populace. At its inception the society had been strictly a Shanghai urban group, composed predominantly of unemployed Fujian and Guangdong boatmen; it had few links with cities other than Shanghai, let alone with the peasantry. This was a situation, the Small Sword leaders understood, that had to be remedied before there could be any thought of mounting an attack. Liu Lichuan and the other chieftains had therefore assiduously cultivated some contacts with indigenous bandit gangs and local men of influence who could provide the society with the manpower needed to launch a widespread revolt.

The most fruitful of these connections was Zhou Lichun, a forty-year-old peasant and tax resistance leader of Baihejiang Village in northern Qingpu County. In the early 1850's Zhou was serving as his precinct's *baozheng*, a post that included among its duties the collection of land taxes. From the description of a Jiangsu financial commissioner in 1866, it was a much-abused position:

> Formerly, the *baozheng* of Qingpu suffered from being tied down [*kun*] to a rotation. In their years of responsibility to make up for the tax default of others, many went bankrupt. In the fourth year of the Jiaqing reign [1799], a stele was set up, forbidding this practice. Thereafter, a *baozheng* was to be nominated by the landowners of the *tu*, and his duties were to be restricted to notification and dunning. Should abuses such as *baolan* or embezzlement arise, the *baozheng* was to be held solely responsible and those who selected him were not to be troubled. Recently, however, tax notices have been issued by the tax runners of each *tu* and collection undertaken by the *baozheng*. When the latter embezzles the funds, the runner accuses the landowners of an injudicious selection and forces them to make restitution for

the misappropriated monies. Actually, the *baozheng* of today are chosen by
the runners, but are claimed to have been selected by the landowners. Innocent people are being punished for the misdeeds of the *baozheng*. Thus, the
evils of *kunbao* ["tied to the post of *baozheng*," e.g. forced to act in rotation
as that functionary] have been abolished in name, but not in practice.[64]

If the typical *baozheng* was as predatory as this suggests, Zhou Lichun
was the exceptional functionary, for he used his position to protect the
interests of the landowners of his precinct. As a result, he had reportedly
earned the trust and respect of his fellow taxpayers.[65]

Zhou's involvement in the Songjiang-Taicang uprising began mod-
estly as the leader of a tax resistance movement in Qingpu. In early
summer 1852, the magistrate, apparently without any authorization from
his superiors, tried to collect some 1850 taxes from which landowners
had been exempted by imperial decree. This effort meeting with little
success, he had some tax runners beaten to impress on them the urgency
of their task. One of these hapless men was the runner for Zhou's precinct, who appealed to the baozheng to lead a group of landowners to
the yamen to report poor harvests in the hope that the magistrate would
permit the remission to remain in force and thus spare him further punishment. Zhou Lichun and several hundred taxpayers, no doubt acting
more in their own interests than for the sake of the runner, marched into
Qingpu city, destroyed the house of the tribute grain clerk who had had
a hand in rescinding the exemption, and then forced their way into the
yamen to present their case to the magistrate. When he refused to listen
to their appeal, the crowd of landowners beat him severely.[66]

Zhou Lichun and his followers immediately fled back to Baihejiang
Village. Zhou carried on in hiding for the next year, and his prestige and
power grew. Drawing on his connections with other baozheng, he made
pacts with the landowners in villages of more than twenty precincts not
to deliver taxes to the government. The protesters extorted money from
wealthy households for expenses and recruited martial arts experts for
protection. Zhou Lichun, as one account put it cryptically, "became entrenched" in the northern Qingpu countryside; and government troops,
dispatched on three separate occasions, were unable to penetrate the ring
of defense his supporters had drawn around him.[67]

The Qingpu resistance, while far-reaching in its consequences, was
initially but one of a number of popular protests against taxes in the eastern part of Jiangnan in 1853. Early in that year more than 2,000 taxpayers
in Nanhui County attacked government offices twice with the intention
of slaying the magistrate; he managed to escape unharmed both times.
Three granary clerks in neighboring Fengxian were not so fortunate; a
group of landowners, enraged by a 10 percent increase in the tribute

conversion rate, boiled them to death in a vat of vegetable oil. In early summer rural residents of Huating County set fire to the boats of mercenaries who had accompanied the magistrate to the countryside to dun for the payment of taxes. Shortly thereafter a runner mobilized a crowd to storm the Shanghai yamen in protest of tax collection.[68]

Jiading County to the north of Qingpu was also having its share of difficulties. Zhu Chengcong, a resident who participated in the suppression of the Small Sword rebels, provides a succinct account of the succession of events that formed the background to the uprising there. The Jiading revolt, he begins, "was brewing during the magistracy of Chen Rong and reached fruition during the term of Feng Han. . . . In 1849 Chen Rong undertook a spot-check of property deed tax slips [*shuiqi*].[69] Whenever the name of the family member on the deed slip did not match the name of the landowner in the tax register, the officials and clerks conspired to accuse the parties involved of tax evasion, thus causing great turmoil in the countryside." In late spring of the same year, "rain fell heavily for ten days. Rural residents created a disturbance at the yamen, ostensibly to report flooding but actually to vent their anger over the deed slip affair. The magistrate fled and hid in the house of a Daoist priest of the Sanxiao Hall. Thereafter the people regarded the officials with contempt." When midsummer did see extensive flooding, "an even larger crowd entered the city and looted large households and plundered rice shops. The magistrate merely ordered that the rioters be given money and rice so that they would disperse. He never investigated and dealt with the instigators of the incident." In 1850 Chen Rong attempted to collect land taxes that had been remitted by the emperor. "The people complained unceasingly. Cases of banditry occurred daily. In 1852 Feng Han succeeded to the magistracy. Reports of banditry multiplied, but he just ignored them." The uprising in Jiading, Zhu concludes, was "just retribution from Heaven."[70]

The times were ripe for revolt, and various people urged Zhou Lichun to take up the banner and overthrow the local Qing government. Zhou, however, did not become convinced of the possibility of a successful revolt until the summer of 1853, when he forged ties with the Small Sword Society in Shanghai and several local bandit gangs from Jiading. In July 1853 some Small Sword members were robbed of their cargo by a Qingpu strongman of Zhou's acquaintance while on an opium run between Shanghai and Suzhou. Aware of Zhou Lichun's influence in the area, the smugglers sought him out to request his help in securing the return of their goods. Zhou complied and retrieved the opium. When word of this deed reached Shanghai, the Small Sword chieftain Li Shaoqing, seeing in the tax resistance leader a potential ally, went to Baihejiang and escorted Zhou to Shanghai for a meeting with Liu Lichuan. It is not clear whether Zhou formally joined the Triads, but an alliance of some sort was formed, and Liu Lichuan selected him to be one of the leaders in the Taicang-Songjiang insurrection.[71]

One month after his conference with the Small Swords in Shanghai, Zhou Lichun added two local bandit gangs to his ranks, the Arhat League (Luohandang) and the Three Sword Society (Sandaohui). The Arhat League, based in nearby Nanxiang market town in southern Jiading County, had been formed the previous summer by the monk Sheng Chuan and the brigand Xu Yao in a formal ceremony that bound several hundred bandits, vagrants, and craftsmen together in sworn brotherhood. The group's primary activity in the ensuing months had been banditry, for which Xu Yao and some others were arrested and imprisoned in cages in front of the Jiading yamen in the spring of 1853. In mid-August the other league members mobilized hundreds of rural residents, invaded the city, and freed the prisoners in an attack on the yamen. Magistrate Feng Han fled, and in the absence of any government authority, the league patrolled the streets of the city for the next several days, extorting money from the rich, and then departed. Xu Yao subsequently led his followers to northern Qingpu and merged forces with Zhou Lichun.[72]

One of the prisoners released by the Arhats was a bandit named Chen Mujin, who, with the assistance of several "local sticks," promptly organized some 1,000 men into the Three Sword Society. Their initial intention was to loot rich households in Taicang and then journey to Nanjing to join the Taipings, but instead they followed the path of the Arhat League and threw in their lot with Zhou Lichun.[73]

With his ranks thus fortified and Jiading city shown to be vulnerable to attack, Zhou Lichun finally consented to raise the banner of revolt, and the Small Sword Rebellion began. The insurgents took Jiading city on September 5, 1853, and then within the next two weeks seized Shanghai, Baoshan, Nanhui, Chuansha, and Qingpu. The capture and occupation of these cities took place amid a display of the standard trappings and slogans of the Triads. Rebel banners carried the phrases "Overthrow the Qing, restore the Ming," "Follow the will of Heaven, put the Way into practice," and "Exterminate greedy and corrupt officials"; and proclamations declared that the corruption of officials and the unwillingness of the rich to succor the poor had driven the people to revolt. Among other things the rebel leaders promised a moratorium on land taxes for three years.[74]

The rapidity and success of the Small Swords' offensive attest more to a lack of preparation on the government side (despite ample warning of plots afoot) than to any absolute superiority of rebel organization and numbers. At most the cities they took were protected by small forces of mercenaries thrown together at the last minute by county magistrates.[75] Conspicuously absent in the attempt to repulse the rebel onslaught were any gentry-organized militia. Although officials in Taicang and Song-jiang and some members of the elite had been lobbying for the formation of local defense groups ever since the Taiping conquest of Nanjing and Zhenjiang in the spring, their efforts were to no avail. The gentry as a whole, apparently not sharing the same sense of urgency, evinced a marked reluctance to contribute any funds or managerial expertise to militia affairs.[76]

This reluctance gave way to enthusiasm only after the cities had fallen to the insurgents. Then the gentry response, though belated, was swift, and the militia formed under its auspices played a critical role in recovering some of the cities from rebel control. In Jiading, for example, the juren Wu Lin, who had been urging his peers to participate in self-defense preparations since the Arhat League's occupation of the city in August, finally received the assistance and funds he needed to raise a militia. He recruited some youths skilled in fighting, but the bulk of his force consisted of peasants put off from the rebel cause by their inability to enter the sealed-off city to sell their cotton crops. On September 22 this militia, in conjunction with government troops transferred from the imperial siege of Nanjing, recaptured Jiading. Zhou Lichun was apprehended (according to some reports, by the disgruntled peasants themselves) and sent to Suzhou for interrogation and execution.[77] On the same day government troops ousted the Small Swords from Qingpu and Baoshan. Within the next five days local militia led by several lower gentrymen recovered Nanhui, and the rebels in Chuansha fled to Shanghai.[78] Thus, with the exception of Shanghai, which the Small Swords held until February 1855, the cities of Songjiang and Taicang were restored to Qing rule in less than a month.

The recapture of the county cities, however, did not spell the end of popular protest in Songjiang and Taicang. Throughout the fall of 1853 and well into the spring of 1854, tenants and landowners in those areas continued to engage in violent collective action against rents and taxes. Collective resistance then abated, and no further organized protests occurred until the Taiping invasion in 1860. The rest of Jiangnan also experienced a decline in the frequency of collective actions against rents and taxes after 1853. From a high of thirty-two in 1853, their number dropped to one to three a year for the remainder of the decade.

ANALYSIS OF POPULAR RESISTANCE
TO RENTS AND TAXES

To describe these events is of course not to truly understand them. For that we need to pay more attention to such matters as leadership, goals, and targets of attack. Though as we saw in the Zhaowen County example collective actions against taxes and rents were not always unrelated, for the purpose of analysis, they are better treated separately.[79]

Collective Rent Resistance

As in the Zhaowen resistance against the qiding in 1842 and the Lilizhen rent struggle of 1852–55, leadership for collective rent resistance came primarily from the tenants' own ranks. The sources variously identify the leaders by their residence (*xiangmin* "country person"), their occupation (*diannong* "tenant farmer"), or their occupation and their moral character (*diangun* "tenant stick"). There are instances, however, in which the occupation or status of the leaders is not clear. In Zhaowen in 1846, for example, "evil sticks" (*egun*) assumed command of the tenant resisters; in 1853 a local bandit (*tufei*) launched a struggle against landlords in Wuxi; and in neighboring Jingui in the same year, the protest was led by several local bandits and a *dizong*, a rural functionary similar to a dibao or a baozheng.[80]

The local bandits and "evil sticks" in these incidents may or may not have been tenants themselves. The dizong could have been one, too, supposing that a local magistrate held to the general rule that rural functionaries should be propertyless in order to prevent a conflict of interest. But even if this particular dizong was not a tenant himself, his assumption of the position did not necessarily mean that he then became a lackey of the officials and the elite. As noted in Chapter 1, rural functionaries frequently found it in their own best interests to collude with tenants in defrauding landlords. The leadership of the dizong in the Jingui collective action may have sprung from this sort of previous association with tenants.

The terms local bandits and evil sticks are definitions more of activities than of occupations. Therefore, tenants who resisted rent and attacked landlords became, by their very actions, deserving of these pejoratives. Indeed, in several accounts of the collective actions of the 1840's and 1850's participants begin as "tenants" and end up as "local bandits" and "evil sticks."[81] Leaders may well have undergone the same transformation.

On the other hand, the tendency for collective rent resistance to escalate into a widespread looting of prosperous households, as demonstrated in the Zhaowen incidents, suggests that such leaders could have been outlaw elements of long standing and not tenants after all. Officials of the time wrote quite cynically of this alliance between bandit leaders and their tenant followers, maintaining that bandits, to gain manpower for their nefarious schemes, deliberately inflamed tenants and, "under the pretext of rent resistance," led them in the looting of rich families. A more accurate view would be that both parties shared a common target—wealthy landlord households.

Of the disputes in which the tenants' grievances are recorded, only the protest against the qiding in Zhaowen in 1842 and the large-scale uprising against landlords there in 1846 involved increased rents. Significantly, these disputes concerned not rents fixed and paid in kind, but wheat rents fixed in kind and paid in cash (zhezu) and/or cotton rents fixed and paid in cash. The Zhaowen landlords came under tenant fire because they were increasing the conversion rate for wheat rents and the cash amounts for cotton rents in total disregard of the decline in prices. Landlords in other areas of the cotton-wheat belt where rents of this sort were common may also have resorted to raising rents to cope with high tax bills, though the volatile climate of the 1840's and 1850's made this less than an attractive option. When tenants were routinely defaulting on the current amounts and were also quick to air their displeasure, there was little to be gained and much to be lost by attempting to raise rents. In the rice-growing counties, where fixed charges paid in kind predominated, rent hikes were even less of a possibility because of the strong customary law forbidding them, especially when the tenant possessed the topsoil.

The battle between landlords and tenants in the lower Yangzi valley in the mid-nineteenth century was thus joined not so much over increasing rents as over the regular amounts. Occasionally, as in the first year of the Lili resistance (1852), tenants justified their refusal to deliver their rents in full on the grounds of poor harvest. In other instances they based their demands for a reduction on the fact that their landlords had received tax remissions. These two rationales for resisting rents—poor harvests and tax exemptions—were not as closely intertwined in the mid-nineteenth century as in the past, when tax remissions had been accorded almost exclusively because of substandard yields. In the 1840's and 1850's, as noted previously, the provincial governments of Jiangsu and Zhejiang secured reductions for landowners as relief from implausibly high tax rates, regardless of the quality of the harvest. There thus occurred the parallel phenomenon of tenants demanding rent reductions even in years of excellent harvests.

Whatever the motivation behind their collective resistance, tenants attacked landlords of every complexion—upper gentry landlords, lower gentry landlords, and commoner landlords. Status counted for little; it was those of substantial means, the landowners with at least several hundred mu, who tended to be targeted. Frequently, the objects of attack are specifically identified as large or wealthy households in the sources. In other cases the extent of their holdings can be inferred from one or more factors: their methods of rent collection (i.e., the use of dunners and gra-

nary boats), their residence in a market town or county seat, their need
to maintain a granary for all the rent rice they took in, and their close
association with the local government, which enabled them to petition
for official assistance in dunning. That the tenants should go after these
landlords is hardly surprising. Although the relationship between a small
landlord and his tenants could be just as fraught with tension, any violent conflict between them was more a spur-of-the-moment, small-scale
brawl than a full-fledged collective action, because of the relatively few
numbers of people involved. Moreover, insofar as tenant protest included
the looting of granaries and houses, the larger, wealthier landlords were
the more tempting targets.

Tenants, however, did not lash out blindly at all wealthy landlords.
Lists of potential victims were drawn up in several incidents, and some
large landholders were reportedly attacked by mistake because of erro-
neous information about the true target's place of residence. In their selection of victims, the tenant protesters employed a rough notion of justice,
the content of which is most clearly revealed by those practices they considered to be instances of "collecting rack-rents" (*shou xiongzu*): exacting
a fixed charge larger than the local norm, setting the conversion rate for
commuted rent higher than the market price for the product, refusing to
grant reductions in years of substandard yields, or declining to share the
benefits of a tax remission.

Just as important as the amount of rent in assessing a landlord's fair-
ness was the manner of its collection. A high rent could be less onerous
if the landlord routinely turned a blind eye to default. Conversely, a low
rent could be unduly burdensome if the landlord relentlessly dunned for
its payment regardless of the cultivator's economic circumstances. While
all landlords who were excessively zealous in the pursuit of rents were
open to the charge of rack-renting, the larger, wealthier ones were especially vulnerable since, as the tenants reasoned, they were more able, and
ought to have been more willing, to absorb a certain amount of default.
The most despised of all were those who, to use the stock phrase, "relied on their influence to dun for rents"—that is, who prevailed on their
connections with local officialdom to have tenants arrested and beaten
for default. Peasants so resented this sort of treatment that on several
occasions in the 1840's and 1850's the incarceration of some of their fellows sparked retaliatory attacks on landlord residences and rescue raids
on government jails.[82]

In his account of the Zhaowen uprisings, Zheng Guangzu raises the
possibility that tenants judged landlords not only on the matter of rent,
but also on their participation in activities beneficial to peasant livelihood.
In explaining why the protesters of 1846 bypassed him, Zheng does not
link his escape from attack to any charitable treatment of tenants on his

part (the most logical and straightforward connection for him to make had there been any grounds for it). Instead, he attributes his good fortune to the peasants' gratitude for his contribution to water conservancy and famine relief programs.

No doubt all other things being equal, giving freely of his time and money to activities that promoted the general welfare of the peasants could count in a landlord's favor and protect him from attack. But this was not so sure a thing as Zheng suggests. In fact several people who were attacked in the 1842 and 1846 Zhaowen conflicts boasted records of public service at least as noteworthy as his.[83] Any benefits accruing to tenants from their landlords' participation in public projects were too uncertain and remote to offset the more immediate concern of unreasonable claims on their harvest. A landlord's hefty donation to the county relief chest could not compensate for his failure to reduce rents in years of crop failure. Nor could his service at a river-dredging bureau make up for his refusal to grant discounts in rent to reimburse tenants for the labor and cash they had expended in polder repairs.[84]

In the end Zheng's civic activities did not save him either. In the fall of 1853 several hundred peasants, reportedly enraged by his exploitation of official connections to dun for rents, destroyed the furnishings and burned the interior of his house. During the fray one tenant was arrested. Several days later a larger group, this time some 1,000 strong, assembled outside his gate and threatened to wreck his residence completely if the apprehended tenant was not set free. After the Zhaowen magistrate bowed to this demand and released the prisoner, the crowd dispersed without inflicting further damage on the beleaguered landlord's compound.[85]

Zheng Guangzu's initial exemption from attack and his subsequent fall from grace were probably bound up with the enthusiasm he displayed for the use of military force during the 1842 rent protest and the 1849 rice riots. Fear of his considerable martial resources deterred the tenants in 1846, and a desire for revenge for his deployment of his forces against peasants fueled their attack on his residence in 1853. Zheng and the other private landowners who raised forces to combat the tenants in 1842 are not the only examples of gentry or landlord suppression of rent struggles in the 1840's and 1850's. Government troops were responsible for putting down the majority of the tenant uprisings during these two decades, but when official forces fell short in providing the protection landlords desired, gentry- or landlord-organized groups of mercenaries (some of which, like the Zhaowen militia in 1842, were formed specifically for the purpose of quelling fractious peasants) stepped into the breach. During a rent struggle in Wuxi in 1853, for instance, the landlords under attack hired thugs skilled in martial arts to defend them, while some of the leaders of a simultaneous tenant protest in neighboring Jingui were captured by Zhao Zhenzuo, the gentry manager of the Changzhou prefectural militia bureau, and his band of 600 mercenaries. And the juren Wu Lin of Jiading, after ousting the Small Sword rebels from his city, turned his men against a large-scale rent strike in the western part of the county.[86]

The use of militia to put down peasant protest in 1853 was part of an intensification of conflict between landlords and tenants in the lower Yangzi valley. The arrival of the Taipings to the west, coupled with the outbreak of the Small Sword Rebellion at home, had touched off a dramatic escalation in resistance to rents. One landlord complained that "although this year is one of unusually good harvest, tenants everywhere are unwilling to pay rent."[87] Data from the registers of a Suzhou bursary confirm this observation. In 1850, 1851, and 1852, only 5 percent, 8 percent, and 12 percent of the tenants of 900 mu of bursary-managed land in Changzhou County defaulted on all or part of the rent; in 1853, despite excellent yields, the figure skyrocketed to close to 50 percent.[88] Even more alarming than the extent of individual resistance was a sharp rise in the number of tenant collective actions: from six incidents over the thirteen years 1840–52 to twenty-two in 1853 alone (Table A.1).

Moreover, these struggles took on a different tone. In the pre-1853 episodes tenants tended first to attempt to negotiate a reduction, withholding rents primarily to pressure landlords into acceding to their requests. In 1853 they were more likely to refuse to pay anything at all. By "swallowing rents" (*tunzu*), as this activity was called, tenants were not only taking advantage of the general turmoil of the times to avenge past wrongs, but also anticipating the imminent arrival of the Taipings and a possible end to rent collection forever.

Collective Tax Resistance

The descriptions of the tax protests of the 1840's and 1850's, like those of the rent uprisings, are usually quite sparing of details. Less than half the accounts, for example, record the names of the leaders of the tax protests, and only about a third note their occupation or status. What information we have, however, shows an assorted group: a monk who had defaulted on his tax, cultivator-owners, "local bullies" (*tuhao*), commanders of gunboat gangs, and, in several cases, such as the Qingpu movement, rural functionaries who transformed the apparatus of tax collection into an instrument of resistance.[89]

Interestingly, the one group we would expect to be represented is absent from the list: men of gentry status. None of the organizers is identified as a degree-holder or turns up on gazetteer lists of successful examination candidates. It is of course possible that the unnamed leaders in the more cryptic descriptions were actually gentrymen or that the named leaders were of certain lowly ranks, especially purchased ones, not worthy of note in local gazetteers. But, then, how are we to explain the fact that gentry are occasionally mentioned as tax resistance leaders in other parts of China in the nineteenth century—in accounts of the same nature as those for the lower Yangzi valley and hence no more or less complete?[90]

Explaining why something did not happen is clearly a tougher task than explaining why something did happen. Indeed, gentry leadership, particularly that of shengyuan, would be an easier case to argue. In some Jiangnan counties landowners of this rank, though not charged the outrageously high taxes required of commoners, still had to pay more than the higher-ranking juren and jinshi. Moreover, as practitioners of proxy remittance, many lower gentryman were already engaging in a form of resistance to the state's demands. Elsewhere in China these baolan networks sometimes furnished the leadership, organization, and manpower for collective action against land taxation.[91] Finally, there was no lack of gentry in the lower Yangzi valley who commiserated with the peasantry's plight and spoke out eloquently on its behalf. Yet none of these things—self-interest, a ready-made organizational base, or righteous indignation—propelled the Jiangnan gentry toward assuming the command of a collective tax protest.

To my mind, the absence of gentry leadership can be attributed to a disjunction between motivation and opportunity. Gentrymen who had the means to organize a following for resistance lacked the desire to do so, and, conversely, those who may have had the desire lacked the means. Proxy remitters were the most suitable candidates for gentry leadership of Jiangnan tax protests because of their roots in the countryside and their connections with commoners. But they were also the least likely candidates because of their interest in maintaining a status quo that was highly profitable for them. After all, why risk the exposure of the baolan ring by attacking the yamen and the government collectors? Why agitate for a reduction in taxes that would only lower one's margin of profit by narrowing the gap between the small household rate and one's own large household rate? It is interesting to note in this regard that when gentry proxy remitters in other parts of China mobilized their clients for protest, it was generally in reaction to official attempts to break up the baolan network.[92] The government in Jiangnan tended to be less than diligent in its efforts to curb proxy remittance, its suppression of the ring in Zhaowen and Changshu in 1845 and its repeated injunctions against the practice notwithstanding. As long as the government continued to be lax, gentry tax farmers had little reason to jeopardize their lucrative businesses by organizing their clients for collective action against high taxes. Other gentry landowners, especially those residing in market towns and county seats, had more tenuous ties to commoners in the countryside and would have found it difficult to gather a following for a protest even had they desired to do so. It was thus the high degree of absentee landownership and the urbanization of the elite, plus the widespread existence of proxy remittance, that together inhibited gentry participation in collective protests against land taxes in Jiangnan.

The lower Yangzi valley also differed from other regions in that militia did not serve as vehicles of resistance. A number of scholars have noted the connection between the militarization of local society and the escalation of violent protest against land taxes in various parts of China. Elizabeth Perry, for example, finds the one clearly linked to the other in the Huaibei region of North China:

> In the mid-nineteenth century, the proliferation of militia was associated with a dramatic rise in the frequency and scale of tax resistance in Huai-pei. The relationship was two-fold. In the first place, the surcharges levied to support the organization of militia were a cause of considerable resentment. In the second place, these same militia in turn offered an organizational base for opposition to government policy. . . . Under the pretext of local defense, peasants were encouraged to stockpile weapons and participate in military training. The result was a powerful force that could be mobilized to promote local interests when these conflicted with government demands. . . . Hundreds of cases have been recorded of militia leading assaults on county offices, burning tax registers, and killing magistrates and other officials.[93]

The same phenomenon occurred in parts of South and Central China.[94]

In Jiangnan, however, militia formation was too intermittent, too urban-oriented, and too closely linked with the local government to furnish an organizational basis for tax uprisings. As we saw, the limited mobilization of defense groups during the British invasion of the lower Yangzi valley in the early 1840's did not lead to a wholesale and enduring militarization of local society. In the decade after the Opium War, the few militia units that were mustered to deal with specific instances of indigenous disorder were disbanded once they had accomplished their purpose. Not until 1853 did members of the elite undertake a more widespread organization of militia, and even then they did so only when, as in the Songjiang-Taicang Small Sword Rebellion, social unrest had come uncomfortably close. Moreover, the militia sponsored by gentrymen in 1853 were generally urban-based mercenary bands of unemployed tribute grain sailors, dispossessed peasants, bandits, and the like rather than village defense corps of taxpaying landowners. They also operated in close conjunction with the local government and its troops and were at times deployed to suppress local riots.

The Jiangnan tax uprisings also lacked the close connections with secret societies found in some areas. In the Small Sword Rebellion of 1853, the society members mobilized landowners not for tax resistance as such, although the remission of taxes was a plank in their political platform, but for typical secret society causes. The specific grievances that landowners had against the government were thus subsumed under the society's goals of overthrowing the Qing and equalizing wealth, goals that by definition were not part of the remedialist demands of tax resistance.

In Jiangnan the closest approximation to secret society leadership of tax revolts was the guidance provided on occasion by the gunboat gangs that roamed the waterways around Lake Tai. Essentially river pirates, these men were more interested in the profits to be made from opium smuggling, gambling, and pillaging than in any anti-Manchu ideology. Like the bands of roving brigands (*gu*) that proliferated in Guangdong and Guangxi in the mid-nineteenth century, the Jiangnan gunboat gangs moved easily between the roles of predator on and protector of the established order. Their mobility and martial prowess made them a formidable threat to the lives and property of the settled population, but these same qualities also made them a popular source for mercenary recruitment. During the turbulent 1850's wealthy merchants employed the gangs to guard their cargo en route to distant markets; landlords hired them to accompany their rent collectors to a hostile countryside; and members of the local elite, especially in 1853, recruited them to man their defense bureaus. The government also availed itself of their services, engaging them to supplement inadequate official forces. In their capacity as government mercenaries, gunboat sailors often carried out the tasks of escorting yamen runners to the villages to dun for taxes and ferrying apprehended tax resisters to the county jails.[95]

But also like the gu bandits of South China, the gunboat gangs were not without a streak of social banditry, and some commanders deployed their forces to resist rather than to assist tax collection. Qian Rongzhuang, the leader of a fleet of several hundred boats in Guian County (Huzhou) is a case in point. A descendant of generations of yamen runners, Qian was incensed by the chronic abuses in the tribute grain collection in his home county. Sometime in the mid-1850's (the exact date is not clear) he assembled the landowners of several tens of polders near his native village and arranged for them to sail to the Guian yamen together to negotiate a reduction in the tribute tax. With white banners calling for justice fluttering above their boats, Qian and the landowners streamed into Huzhou city. The Guian magistrate, fearful of a riot, promptly acceded to their demand that they thereafter be required to pay only 70 percent of the tribute tax. This agreement continued for several years, the taxpayers dutifully delivered the reduced levy, and the commander's fame grew.

Soon after his foray into Huzhou, Qian Rongzhuang set up a gambling den in the market town of Nanxun. Then, in 1859, in response to a government campaign against both gunboat gangs and gambling, Qian disbanded his followers and surrendered to the Guian yamen. He died as a result of the flogging he received for his part in the tax resistance. Qian's original protest against official corruption and high taxes and his final act of contrition set him apart from other gunboat leaders in the eyes of his contemporaries, one of whom called him a most righteous person.[96] There were other cases of the sort, but not many. Most of the identified protest leaders were taxpayers themselves, whether landlords or cultivator-owners.

As with rents, collective action against land taxes increased and changed character between the 1840's and the 1850's. During the earlier decade five of the six recorded incidents were provoked either by a magistrate's refusal to permit landowners to report poor harvests (*baohuang*) entitling them to tax reductions or by his dilatoriness or unfairness in implementing a remission once an appeal had been accepted. By the 1840's, as we have seen, the practice of securing tax remissions from Beijing by falsifying harvest conditions had become routine, yet landowners did not share automatically or equally in the benefits, since clerks and runners monopolized their apportionment. The only recourse open to peasants too lowly or poor to "buy disaster" was to report poor harvests to the magistrate in the hope that he would override his underlings and grant them a reduction. In the 1850's resistance through baohuang gave way to an outright refusal to pay taxes, and the incidence of collective protest against state exactions rose dramatically. All together, twenty-three collective actions against land taxes were reported for the 1850's (as opposed to six for the 1840's), ten of which took place in 1853 alone (Table A.1).

The escalation in both tax and rent resistance in 1853 thoroughly alarmed the officials and the elite of Jiangnan. The Suzhou gentryman Feng Guifen captured the fears of the times when he wrote that "the peasants, glaring like tigers stalking their prey, are waiting in secret for the chance to strike against us."[97] They would get that chance, many believed, with a Taiping invasion of Jiangnan. Confronted in 1853 with the twin perils of an intensification of social unrest at home and the likelihood of a rebel offensive from the west, some gentry and officials retreated into a fatalistic passivity or engaged in a last-ditch effort to feather their nests. Others responded to the crisis by organizing militia to suppress local disorder and to prepare for the anticipated war with the Taiping rebels.

The crisis of 1853 brought forth a more creative response—an attempt at land tax reform in southeastern Jiangsu Province. The author of the program was the self-same man who felt the peasants' glare so keenly—Feng Guifen. A scholar well known for his views on statecraft and his arguments for more gentry participation in local administration and one of Suzhou's largest absentee landholders, Feng had earned his jinshi degree in 1840, and after serving in Beijing as a compiler in the Hanlin Academy and as an examiner in the civil service system, had retired from formal official life in 1845. He returned to his home and devoted himself to his writings and local affairs and to advising Jiangnan officials about a range of intractable problems. One such problem was the administration of the grain tribute tax, a subject to which Feng had given much thought. He was the principal architect not only of the tax reform of 1853, but also, as we shall see, of a more comprehensive and lasting reform ten years later.

In 1853 Governor Xu Naizhao, acting on Feng's proposal, instructed all county magistrates in the Suzhou-Songjiang-Taicang tax circuit to eradicate the small household–large household distinction and to reduce tribute grain conversion rates to a uniform 4,000 copper *cash* per shi. Like earlier attempts at reforms of this nature, the 1853 measures had little chance of success. Only small households who paid at exorbitant rates stood to benefit. The reforms demanded financial sacrifices from large households, magistrates, and yamen clerks and runners that few were willing to make. Protest from these quarters came fast and furious, eventually leading to the abandonment of the program in mid-1854.[98]

In his 1853 formulations on tribute tax reduction and equalization, Feng did not address the question of rent decreases, even while noting the numerous tenant attacks on landlords. Nowhere in his writings of this time did he urge landlords to pass on some of the benefits of his proposed tax reduction to their tenants, let alone suggest that a lowering of rents be made compulsory. His omission no doubt stemmed in part from a pragmatic desire to make his fiscal proposals as palatable as possible to landlords of large household status; any advocacy of rent reduction would only have strengthened their opposition to tax equalization.

More generally, Feng's omission was in keeping with the precedent established in edicts of the Yongzheng and Qianlong emperors that left the question of rent reduction in times of tax reduction to the discretion of individual landlords. This reluctance to intervene in the landlord-tenant relationship against the interests of landlords pervaded the official response to rent resistance as well. Although there are instances in the 1840's and 1850's of an official ordering a decrease in rents in the wake of a tenant protest, they are few and far between.[99] Not until the Taiping Rebellion had exacted its toll from landlordism in Jiangnan did Feng Guifen and the government break with tradition and see mandatory rent reduction as a necessary corollary of tax reduction.

CHAPTER 3

The Taiping Occupation of Jiangnan, 1860 – 1864

In the end the pincer-like threat to Jiangnan was removed in 1855, when Qing forces ousted the Small Swords from Shanghai and the Taipings launched expeditions north, west, and south, but not east. Moreover, news from the front, initially discouraging, became more heartening as the end of the decade approached. By 1856 the Taipings had secured strategic cities along the Yangzi River, from Wuchang in Hubei to Zhenjiang in Jiangsu, and had routed the Qing imperial encampment outside Nanjing. But then bloody dissension among the rebel leaders in Nanjing later that year claimed the lives of the Eastern King, Yang Xiuqing, and the Northern King, Wei Changhui, as well as thousands of their supporters, and impelled Shi Dakai, the Assistant King, to quit the city with his troops in 1857 and strike out on his own, first in South and then in West China. With this loss of important military leadership and the consequent demoralization of the movement's adherents, Taiping forces were unable to hold their own against Qing troops and the Xiang Army, a formidable regional force organized by a Hunanese official, Zeng Guofan. The Qing commanders retook Zhenjiang at the end of 1857, and by 1860 the insurgents were on the defensive everywhere and once again besieged at Nanjing by regrouped imperial forces.

Equally encouraging to the region's officials and elite was the relatively peaceful climate at home. The tax and rent uprisings of 1853 had been suppressed. Collective actions against taxes continued throughout the remainder of the 1850's, particularly in northern Zhejiang, but with diminished frequency and intensity. Tenants, though still widely defaulting on rents, did not engage in collective violence against landlords. Even in 1856, when a severe drought and hordes of locusts reduced yields in some areas by as much as 70 percent, no organized rent protests occurred.[1] The reason, one observer commented, was that landlords and tenants now "shrink from one another in fear."[2] As events would prove, conflict had merely been suspended, not resolved, but the suspension was a welcome respite nonetheless.

The easing of the threat from the Taiping "long-hairs" and the comparative peace at home brought about a relaxation in local vigilance. With no immediate threat, defense efforts were difficult to sustain. Some militia bureaus foundered on complacency and corruption and were closed down. Others remained in existence primarily as supply agencies for government armies and continued to collect contributions and sell examination ranks, but they did not actively recruit and train mercenaries or peasant militiamen.[3]

The officials and elite of the lower Yangzi valley would not have been so complacent about the region's security had they given credence to the prophecies making the rounds of villages and towns. Freak births warned of impending disaster. Comets streaking through the night sky foretold war. And most ominously, the ground throughout Jiangnan began to sprout long, black hair.[4]

What the prophecies predicted came to pass in 1860. The Taipings, fortified by the revival of central authority in the person of Hong Ren'gan, the ailing Hong Xiuquan's cousin, and the rise of three brilliant military leaders, Chen Yucheng, Li Xiucheng, and Li Shixian, set out to regain the offensive. They began with a thrust into Jiangnan as a diversionary maneuver to lure imperial forces from the encirclement of Nanjing. In March 1860 Li Xiucheng and Li Shixian led their troops through Anhui Province and Hangzhou Prefecture to attack Hangzhou and Huzhou cities. Their ruse succeeded. Government troops hurried from Nanjing to defend the Zhejiang cities. The two Lis then withdrew from Zhejiang and rushed back to Nanjing to do battle with the depleted forces at the imperial camp. In May the Taipings again destroyed the Great Camp of Jiangnan.

The siege of Nanjing now broken, the rebel leaders convened to discuss their next move. After much debate they decided on an all-out attack on rich Jiangnan. With the lower Yangzi as an economic base, efforts then would be made to retake the middle Yangzi area. Accordingly, Li Xiucheng and Li Shixian set off toward Suzhou city. Along the way they routed Qing forces at Jurong and Danyang in western Jiangsu; then, in late May, they took Changzhou and Wuxi cities. On June 2 the Taiping army marched virtually unimpeded into Suzhou city.* The two com-

---

*The ease with which the Taiping army took Suzhou city was due in part to the surrender of two expectant officials in charge of guarding several of the city gates. One was Li Wenbing, who was none other than Li Shaoqing, formerly of the Small Sword Society. During the battle over Shanghai from 1853 to 1855, Li had switched to the Qing, an action for which

manders then struck off in different directions. Li Shixian led his army south to capture Wujiang and Zhenze counties in Suzhou Prefecture and Jiaxing Prefecture in northern Zhejiang. Meanwhile Li Xiucheng headed east, capturing the rest of Suzhou Prefecture and several counties in Taicang Department and Songjiang Prefecture. Misled by some foreigners' assurances of neutrality, he committed a mere 3,000 soldiers to an assault on Shanghai in mid-August. French and British troops handily repulsed the attack, and Li, declining to press the issue, went to Zhejiang to defend Taiping-occupied Jiaxing city from a Qing counterattack.

Except for the capture of Jiaxing Prefecture, the Taiping offensive of 1860 was not as successful in northern Zhejiang as in southern Jiangsu. Attacks on Hangzhou and Huzhou cities encountered stiff resistance. The rebels finally took Hangzhou in December 1861, after Li Shixian's occupation of eastern and southern Zhejiang had isolated the city. The conquest of Huzhou proved to be even more difficult. Defended by a vigorous militia, the city managed to hold on until May 1862.

In general the Taiping occupation of Jiangnan was short, geographically uneven, and constantly threatened by enemy attacks from without and treachery from within. The longest the rebels held any place continuously was four years (Changzhou Prefecture from May 1860 to May 1864). Some areas, notably Shanghai city and several counties in Songjiang, escaped rebel rule altogether. Other areas, particularly counties in Huzhou and Hangzhou prefectures, were successively captured by the Taipings, retaken by Qing forces, and then recaptured by the rebels. And throughout their four-year occupation of the region, the Taipings were embroiled in major battles and minor skirmishes with enemy troops and resident defense leagues.

Yet no matter how short-lived and tenuous their occupation of any place in Jiangnan turned out to be, the rebels, on taking an area, sought to impress on it their own brand of rule. Taiping governance of the lower Yangzi valley did not result in a complete restructuring of power and property relations as prescribed in the rebels' ideological tract "The Land System of the Heavenly Dynasty." But neither did it leave rural society untouched, as some writings on the subject imply. An examination of the system of local government and the land policies instituted by the Taipings reveals that, while the world was not turned upside down in Jiangnan, it certainly was knocked askew.

---

he was rewarded with the position of expectant circuit intendant. For his assistance in capturing Suzhou, Li received a high position in the Taiping army and became the occupying commander of Kunshan County, Suzhou Prefecture. (Wang Tao, "Wengyou yutan," pp. 1024–25.)

POPULAR RESISTANCE AND ASSISTANCE
TO THE TAIPINGS

The Taiping drive through the lower Yangzi valley in 1860 galvanized residents to mobilize for self-defense. In the cities and the larger market towns, the officials and elite resurrected the procedures used in 1853—the formation of militia or self-defense bureaus, the recruitment of mercenaries, and the organization of *baojia* as a patrol system and conscription pool. The mobilization appears to have been much fuller than in 1853, giving the defense efforts of 1860 a depth that the earlier ones lacked. Whereas the pertinent sources for 1853 are virtually mute on the subject of militarization in places other than cities and the larger market towns, the materials for 1860 speak repeatedly of the formation of militia (*tuanlian*), people's militia (*mintuan*), and even polder militia (*yutuan*) in the countryside.[5] These rural defense groups, most commonly called "white heads" (*baitou*) for the white cloth they wrapped around their heads to distinguish themselves from the red-turbaned Taiping rebels, are usually identified by the name of the small market town or village that served as their headquarters, suggesting that natural, as opposed to administrative, units formed the basis of organization.[6]

The most formidable militia complex in southern Jiangsu was organized in the spring of 1860 in a triangle overlapping the borders of Changzhou and Changshu counties in Suzhou Prefecture and Jingui County in Changzhou Prefecture. Market town militia bureaus lay at each point of the triangle: the Dangkouzhen bureau in Jingui, headed by the juren Hua Yilun; the Wutazhen bureau in Changshu, headed by the gongsheng Cao Heqing; and the Dongyongchang bureau in Changzhou, headed by the jiansheng Xu Peiyuan.* Among them, the bureaus were able to mobilize over a hundred militia groups within a forty- to fifty-li radius of Dongyongchang.[7]

Of these three militia leaders, the most notorious and the most richly documented is Xu Peiyuan of the Dongyongchang bureau.[8] As the following passage from a fellow countyman suggests, Xu and his three brothers, all holders of purchased academic degrees, were archetypical rural strongmen (*tuhao*), notable more for their wealth, martial prowess, and bullying ways than for any scholastic excellence:

> Outside of the Qi gate of Suzhou city [20 *li* north], there is a market town called Yongchang. The several brothers of the rich Xu household are so

---

*The gongsheng and jiansheng degrees could be acquired by hereditary privilege, examination, special recommendation, or purchase. Xu Peiyuan bought his rank; how Cao Heqing acquired his is unknown.

cunning, fierce, and skilled in the martial arts that all the countryside fears them. They own several thousand *mu* of land. When paying taxes, they pay at the low large household "short rate" and feign poor harvests. Yet when collecting rents, they do not permit the slightest default. In the tenth year of the Xianfeng reign [1860], when the Taiping bandits were pressing close to Suzhou city, the Xus feared that the peasants would take advantage of the general chaos to vent their resentment against them. They therefore put forth the funds to hire several thousand unemployed men and to manufacture weapons, all in the name of self-defense. They also recruited their tenants by seducing them with sweet words, telling them that those who exerted an effort and assisted them in defense would have their rents canceled for two years. The number of people under the Xus' command thus grew. They extorted donations from all households. No one dared disobey them.[9]

So powerful were Xu Peiyuan and his brothers that the militia bureaus in other market towns in northern Changzhou, even those in towns larger than Dongyongchang, yielded to their command.[10]

Next to the Xus and their defense network, gunboat gangs provided the most effective resistance to the Taiping advance, especially in southern Suzhou Prefecture (Wujiang and Zhenze counties) and in Jiaxing and Huzhou prefectures. Shen Paishi of Xiushui County (Jiaxing) commanded one such gang. Shen had forged ties with Qing officialdom before the arrival of the Taipings. In the mid-1850's he had sailed to Guian County in Huzhou to assist the magistrate, his blood brother, in collecting land taxes, and in 1858 he had, for a time, merged his band with the army of a Zhejiang official. When the rebels launched their Jiangnan campaign in the spring of 1860, Shen welded the gunboat groups in his territory into a strong militia and fought the Taipings throughout Jiaxing Prefecture.*

Unlike the freewheeling Shen, other gunboat commanders were tied to a particular area and operated in close conjunction with the local elite. The most illustrious commander of this type was Fei Yucheng, the sixty-year-old leader of defense efforts in Zhouzhuangzhen on the Yuanhe-Wujiang border in Suzhou Prefecture. Fei, described as a heroic knight-errant by a scholar who otherwise looked askance at the brigand's gambling dens and opium dealings, had committed his force of several hundred boats to

---

*Shen Zi, "Bikou riji," pp. 328–29. Not all gang leaders immediately took up arms against the invaders. A few, such as Bu Xiaoer of Wujiang and Jin Yushan of Wuxi, initially joined forces with the rebels and were appointed to positions in the local Taiping administration. But the realization that such activities as opium smuggling and gambling would not be tolerated came quickly, and they transferred their allegiance to the Qing. For short biographies of Bu Xiaoer and Jin Yushan, see Harigaya, "Taihei Tengoku senryō chi-iki no sōsen shūdan," p. 21.

local defense preparations.[11] In 1853, at the behest of the elite of Zhou-zhuang, he set up a self-defense bureau there. Then, in 1856, the Suzhou prefect ordered him to capture bandits and other gunboat leaders. His failure to arrest Sha Ge, the "godfather" of the Wujiang-Zhenze gangs and Fei's nominal superior in the gunboat hierarchy, resulted in his own imprisonment.

Fei was not destined to languish in detention for long, however. The Jiangsu governor recognized his contribution to the maintenance of law and order and soon had him released. On the recommendation of Han Chong, a commissioner of the Suzhou Supply Bureau (the joint gentry-official agency in charge of raising defense funds), Fei then received the rank of jiansheng (conditioned on a donation of 740 taels to the agency). When Suzhou fell to the Taipings in June 1860, Fei, who had been patrolling the gates of the city, fled to Zhouzhuang, with Commissioner Han and several other eminent Suzhou gentrymen close on his heels. Back in Zhouzhuang, Fei, at the urging of Han and others on the spot and of Jiangsu officials from the sanctuary of Shanghai, expanded his gunboat force, coordinated the people's militia along the Yuanhe-Wujiang border, and used his considerable military resources to protect the region from the Taipings and the elite from local bandits and unruly peasants.[12]

For Fei and other Jiangnan militia leaders, the escalating local disorder that accompanied the rebel invasion was a major preoccupation. Crowds of residents, variously identified as local bandits, peasants, and tenants, looted pawnshops and rich households. Again, the targets were often, though by no means always, selected on more specific grounds than wealth. In some outbreaks, punishment was reserved for "all those rich households who, relying upon their influence to collect rents, [had] incurred the long-standing resentment of the peasants" and "those who [were] harsh in rent and debt collection."[13] Some of the fiercest and most extensive conflicts took place in Changshu and Zhaowen, where, one gentryman claimed, peasants and local bandits wreaked more destruction on life and property than the Taipings.[14] Among the casualties there was the newly refurbished house of the embattled Zheng Guangzu.[15]

The local discontent fueling these assaults on landlords, usurers, and the rich did not coalesce into large-scale organizational and military support for the Taipings. In this respect Jiangnan differed markedly from eastern and southern Zhejiang, where the Lotus Cupule Gang (Lianpeng-dang), the Gold Coin Society (Jinqianhui), and the Eighteen Bureaus (Shibaju) tenant organization fought alongside rebel troops in battles against Qing armies and loyalist militia.[16] Popular protest in Jiangnan remained localized and discontinuous. The peasants there were in essence continuing their ongoing war with their private enemies. Yet the changed context endowed their age-old actions with a new significance. Peasants and local bandits, one landlord noted, were awaiting the arrival of the Taipings "with the intention of welcoming them with food and drink."[17] More concretely, peasant violence took a toll on the defenses and the spirit of the region's protectors, thereby expediting the Taiping advance.

On several occasions that violence was in direct aid of the rebels. In Jiangsu, immediately before the Taiping attack on Changzhou prefectural city, peasants killed Zhao Zhenzuo, the gentry militia leader who had led his mercenaries against tenant protesters in 1853.[18] The rebels' way into Changshu from Jiangyin County was cleared by the people of Zhouzhuangzhen (Jiangyin), who led the army across a nearby river and then joined in the fight against local militia forces.[19] And in Zhejiang the guidance of a peasant was instrumental in the conquest of Haiyan County.[20]

With only these and a few other isolated instances of peasant assistance to the Taipings to go by, we are in no position to assess the extent and depth of popular support for the rebels in 1860. True, contemporary accounts, written by literati hostile to the Taipings, speak occasionally of people entering the ranks of the insurgents voluntarily. A native of Wu County, for instance, wrote in dismay that "few men and women have committed suicide. Some even happily follow the bandits. They do not know shame."[21] But statements of this nature are rare. More commonly, the accounts refer to people who somehow ended up with the enemy as "captives" (*beiluzhe*), sometimes adding that they then became Taiping followers. No doubt the catch-all category of "captives" included people who joined the Taipings willingly in the first place, whether out of conviction or for the employment opportunities in the rebel camps.[22]

What support the local populace might have been tempted to render to the Taipings in 1860 was qualified by one overriding concern. The Taiping advance meant war, and war meant the destruction of crops, the disruption of trade routes, pillage, rape, and death. As reiterated in account after account, Qing troops were responsible for much of the wrack and ruin in Jiangnan, to the point that, as one gentryman lamented, "the people fear the Qing soldiers, but not the Taiping bandits."[23] Yet the behavior of the Taiping troops, though more praiseworthy than that of the Qing soldiers, was still far from perfect. Li Xiucheng acknowledged in his confession that in Jiangnan the absorption into the Taiping army of defeated Qing soldiers and other elements whose main interest was the spoils of war seriously undermined the exemplary discipline that had once distinguished the rebel movement.[24] These new recruits received little, if any, ideological indoctrination; and punitive measures against rape and indiscriminate killing and looting proved only partially effective.

There was thus a tension in the peasants' response to the Taiping invasion—a tension that made possible both peasant uprisings against the local elite in anticipation of the rebels' arrival and a banding together with the local elite in defense against both rebel and Qing soldiers. As the Taipings emerged victorious in county after county, local residents, elite and commoner alike, were quick to render tribute as a token of surrender and to purchase the door placards (*menpai*) that would bring them immunity from attack and Taiping protection against the depredations of Qing troops. At this juncture peasants were at most hopeful that Taiping rule would be more just than Qing rule and at least willing to be persuaded that the Taipings indeed had succeeded to the Mandate of Heaven.

THE TAIPING SYSTEM OF LOCAL GOVERNMENT

Throughout the four-year Taiping occupation of the lower Yangzi valley, the structure of rebel rule reflected the military strategy that had secured the region in the first place. Not surprisingly, the Taipings made prefectural and county cities and large market towns their targets of attack, and these same cities and towns then became the loci of their power. Except for some tinkering with the border between Suzhou and Jiaxing prefectures, the rebel rulers retained the administrative boundaries of the Qing prefectures and counties. Jiaxing, Huzhou, and Hangzhou prefectures remained part of a province that the Taipings continued to call "Zhejiang," while the prefectures and department of southeastern Jiangsu— Changzhou, Suzhou, Songjiang, and Taicang—were divided off from Jiangsu to form a separate province named "Sufu."

The neatness of the Taiping administrative structure masks a bewildering array of local rebel officials who possessed an equally confusing number of military ranks, civil posts, and titles of nobility. As a rule the army leader who led the successful campaign against a city or town became its occupying commander (*shoujiang*). In theory the commander of a market town was subordinate to the county commander, the county commander to the prefectural commander, and the prefectural commander to the provincial commander. But in practice a proliferation of ranks and titles as the rebellion matured had produced a confusion in the chain of command, from the supreme rank of king (*wang*) on down. Li Xiucheng's superior position as the ruler of Sufu and Zhejiang, for instance, was based more on his experience, reputation, and the backing of Hong Xiuquan than on his title of king, since several commanders in Jiangnan had been elevated to this rank and were thus Li's equal in the rebel hierarchy. This confusion continued down the line of administrative units, with prefectural commanders holding the same ranks as their nominal subordinates in the county cities, and county commanders possessing the same ranks as market town commanders.[25] One important consequence of the disarray in the command structure was a lack of uniformity in Taiping policy. Commanders routinely ignored orders emanating from the Heavenly King in Nanjing and Li Xiucheng in Suzhou, and instituted programs of their own making. The rebel administration of Jiangnan thus showed wide variation from area to area.

Once ensconced in the cities and large market towns, the Taiping commanders engaged in what was largely a peaceful pacification of the countryside. They posted announcements, such as the one below issued in Changshu and Zhaowen, urging people to lay down their arms, return to their homes, and deliver tribute:

> You people of the countryside and towns of Changshu and Zhaowen basically have commendably kind and generous natures. You thus could not but be deluded by that mercenary scoundrel Wang Yuanchang.* Over the summer and fall [of 1860], you have suffered greatly at his hands. Now Wang most likely will be unable to deceive you any longer for he has fled the area and will not dare to show himself again. His Majesty the Loyal King of Sufu understands the circumstances thoroughly and has specifically ordered us to enter the city with our weapons sheathed. This we have done, without committing the slightest offense against the people. Hereafter, if you wish to return home and work in peace, all that needs to be done is for the residents of each precinct to prepare pigs, sheep, oil, salt, and other goods, select one or two reliable people to lead the way with banners on which the words "tribute payment" are written in large characters, and then, with gongs and drums sounding slowly at the rear of the procession, carry the goods into the city and present them to us.

After the presentation of tribute, the people were to return home, compile population registers, and deliver them to the Taipings. In return they would be issued door placards listing the names and ages of the members of each household. "When our Taiping brothers see the placards, they will not dare to disturb you. You can live peacefully as before. The old and the young, men and women, can sleep soundly without worry." Noncompliance would bring a large force of soldiers that would "trample the area flat, sparing not even the chickens and the dogs."[26]

Little further inducement was needed to persuade residents to give up the fight and offer tribute as payment for peace. Groups of people went in droves to the cities and towns to render tribute to the rebels.[27] The leadership of these tribute missions, the geographical areas they represented, and the amount of the payment varied from case to case. The organizers included militia leaders, merchants, rich landlords, village elders, dibao, and jingzao; and the organizational units for tribute presentation were market towns, villages, or precincts (tu).[28]

---

*Wang Yuanchang's militia, stationed in the northeastern corner of neighboring Jiangyin County, had been the major force blocking the Taipings' entry into Changshu.

In several instances market town leaders acted on behalf of both the town itself and the surrounding villages. In Wangshi, for example, a town of some 400 to 500 households in northern Changshu, a group of market brokers learned that Wang Shengming, an Anjing mat peddler of their acquaintance, had thrown in his lot with the rebels. Under Wang's guidance, the brokers made arrangements for tribute presentation. They ordered each household to post the character for "submission" (*shun*) on its front door, and each person to wrap his or her head in red cloth, and sent porters to nearby villages to summon jingzao and village elders for a consultation. When a column of 300 or so Taiping soldiers approached, Wang led a delegation of townspeople and village elders out the gate to escort them into town. A discussion then followed, during which it was decided that the town should offer 1,000 taels of Chinese silver and 1,000 yuan of foreign silver in tribute. The soldiers then departed, and the market brokers and village elders hastened to collect the funds. Everyone contributed, the women their jewelry and the peasants their livestock and poultry. After amassing the necessary tribute, Wang and the brokers delivered the money to the Changshu commander at the county seat. In return they received an official Taiping banner to display in a prominent place as evidence of the town's surrender. They also received orders to collect one yuan from each household for door placards. Other towns and villages in Changshu followed Wangshi's example, and the county was soon pacified.[29]

The amount of tribute demanded of the people of Wangshi was unusually large. The town of Huangjiaqiao in Changshu delivered only one pig, twenty yuan, and ten taels of silver; in Wu County the town of Xingguo offered ten pigs, twenty ducks and chickens, and forty shi of rice; and each precinct of Dongtingshan, the hilly islands in Lake Tai, paid twenty yuan.[30] These low amounts suggest that tribute collection was not merely a way for the Taiping leaders to garner necessary supplies and funds, but also, and perhaps more importantly, a way for them to meet the people of influence in the countryside. The rebel commanders subsequently appointed many of the leaders of tribute missions to posts within local Taiping officialdom.

Not all areas in Jiangnan were as quick as Wangshi to submit to Taiping rule. The militia network of Xu Peiyuan, Cao Heqing, and Hua Yilun in the Changshu-Jingui-Changzhou border region and that of Fei Yucheng in Yuanhe continued to fight the rebels after other places had been pacified. As the long summer of 1860 wore on, however, and as neighboring towns and villages capitulated one after the other, these militia leaders came to see the wisdom of at least a nominal submission to Taiping control. Cao Heqing of Wutazhen (Changshu) surrendered to the Taiping army immediately after the conquest of the county seat in mid-September and soon became a trusted adviser of the Changshu commander Qian Guiren. During the next several months Fei, Xu, and Hua each concluded a mutual nonaggression pact with the Suzhou commander Xiong Wanquan. In exchange for ceasing hostilities and delivering a certain quota of taxes and supplies, the militia leaders received almost absolute control over their home bases. Only these men and members of their bureaus, the agreements stipulated, had the authority to collect land and commercial taxes and to appoint local officials in their areas of influence. No Taiping soldier was permitted to enter these regions or to interfere with their governance.[31]

Elsewhere in Jiangnan the Taipings retained the right to appoint natives as *xiangguan*, or "rural officials," and through them to supervise closely the management of local affairs. In its ideal form the xiangguan structure of administration was part of a political, military, and religious hierarchy modeled after the classical system of local control described in the *Rites of Zhou (Zhouli)*, a work ascribed to the Duke of Zhou (11th century B.C.). As outlined in the Taiping document "The Land System of the Heavenly Dynasty," residents of an area were to be divided into groups of five families, each headed by a *wuzhang* (corporal). With these five-family groups as the basic building blocks, larger units were to be formed in the following manner:

Number of families	Unit head
25 (5 wuzhang groups)	*liangsima* (sergeant)
100 (4 liangsima groups)	*zuzhang* (lieutenant)
500 (5 zuzhang groups)	*lüshuai* (captain)
2,500 (5 lüshuai groups)	*shishuai* (colonel)
12,500 (5 shishuai groups)	*junshuai* (general)

The responsibilities of the unit heads went beyond the military function their names suggest, for they also were to act as the administrative and religious leaders of their groups.[32]

But the Taiping leadership was more successful in implementing this system of control in its armies than among the inhabitants of conquered territory. By the time the rebels took the lower Yangzi valley, the military and religious duties of the xiangguan had fallen by the wayside, and their sole remaining responsibility was administration. And even in this respect the system as instituted in Jiangnan fell far short of the ideal. Imposing organization based solely on population and in defiance of natural boundaries and settlement patterns had never been an easy task in China, as the history of the baojia and lijia systems attests. The xiangguan apparatus tended to be based on geographical areas, whether the prefecture-county-xiang-du-tu units of the Qing administrative hierarchy or the city–market town–village units of the economic hierarchy, rather than on groups of people. The system that took shape in Jiangnan was thus not the neat pyramidal structure outlined in the Taiping land program. In general, xiangguan were appointed in a rather random fashion without much attempt to conform to the ideal or to make the system uniform from county to county.

Another major departure from the ideal was the appointment of local men as the *zongzhi* of prefectures and the *jianjun* of counties, positions not part of the original conception of political organization. Equivalent to Qing prefects and county magistrates, the zongzhi and jianjun were accountable to their prefectural or county commanders.

Immediately subordinate to the jianjun in the xiangguan hierarchy were the junshuai, whose numbers and jurisdiction differed from county to county. The countryside of Changshu and Zhaowen, for instance, was divided into eight camps, with a junshuai in charge of each. In Yixing County (Changzhou Prefecture) the old Qing administrative unit of the township (*xiang*) became the territory of two or three junshuai. In other areas junshuai were appointed to the larger market towns.[33] The number of lower-level xiangguan—the shishuai, lüshuai, zuzhang, liangsima, and wuzhang—within each junshuai's jurisdiction, as well as their units of control, is difficult to determine from the scattered references in the sources. One observer estimated that Changshu and Zhaowen counties had more than 2,000 xiangguan of these ranks. In Wuxi a shishuai was appointed for every five precincts, and a lüshuai for every two.[34] The position of lüshuai (in charge of 500-family groups) appears to have been the lowest level of xiangguan appointed regularly by the Taipings in the Jiangnan countryside. The relevant materials, at any rate, make only occasional mention of the appointment of zuzhang, liangsima, and wuzhang.

The xiangguan undertook numerous tasks for their Taiping overlords, foremost among which was the gathering of revenue and supplies for the war effort. They compiled population and land registers, collected household levies and property and commercial taxes, sold the mandatory boat permits, shop licenses, and road passes, and filled rebel requisitions for wood, bricks, boats, and sometimes manpower. In addition they helped to administer the Taiping civil service examinations, managed water conservancy, handled civil litigation, maintained local law and order, and implemented relief measures, such as the distribution of gruel to the poor and the resettlement of refugees.[35]

Finding willing recruits for all these posts was only part of the rebels' task. They also had to recruit residents to perform the myriad chores that the administration of a large region entailed. The Taiping kings in their palaces, lesser rebel commanders in their halls, and xiangguan in their bureaus all needed clerks, messengers, doctors, porters, accountants, guards, and the like. One commander in Jiaxing Prefecture launched a public campaign to entice members of the community with a broad range of skills into the rebel camp. In an announcement issued in 1861, he urged the following types of people to come forward and offer their services: people well versed in astronomy, astrology, and mathematics; people with a knowledge of geography, topography, and the strategic possibilities of the area; people well read in the work of Sunzi and with a knowledge of military strategy and the deployment of troops; people familiar with local conditions and customs; people learned in history and political affairs; people with clerical skills; people with exceptional ability in the martial arts, horsemanship, and marksmanship; "heroes of the greenwood" (brigands) who were willing to forsake their evil ways; itinerant entertainers and opera performers who were fleet of foot; and physicians and surgeons.[36]

The men appointed xiangguan in Jiangnan came from backgrounds and stations in life as diverse as the categories in this recruitment notice: upper gentry, lower gentry, and indigent scholars; former Qing magistrates, yamen clerks, and runners; large landlords, small landlords, and peasants; rich households, well-to-do households, and beggars; dibao, polder heads (yujia), and village elders; merchants, peddlers, and shopkeepers; militia leaders, gunboat commanders, and local strongmen; Daoist priests, Buddhist monks, and martial arts instructors; carpenters, butchers, and doctors; and "local sticks" (digun), local bandits (tufei), and vagrants (wulai).

The heterogeneous composition of the xiangguan reflects the Taipings' haphazard recruitment and appointment procedures. In theory local residents were to participate in the selection of the full complement of xiangguan through the public nomination (*gongju*) of suitable candidates. But in fact the higher-level xiangguan were appointed outright by the rebel commanders, and the lower-level ones by either the commanders or their xiangguan superiors.[37] The main criterion governing the selection of xiangguan was expediency. As newcomers, the Taipings at best had only a sketchy knowledge of the society now under their control. Yet they had to set up a local bureaucracy as quickly as possible to gather the region's riches for the Taiping coffers. The commanders did not have the luxury of time to make a judicious selection of xiangguan (if that indeed had been their intention). Men who in some manner or another—whether as organizers of tribute missions, former militia leaders, or volunteers for service—had become visible to the commanders were immediately appointed. Some of those singled out, much to the horror of their contemporaries, took to their posts with alacrity, others only with great reluctance. Still others who were called on to serve refused outright, often at the cost of economic reprisals against their families.[38]

A fair number of the people who became xiangguan, particularly those from the lower classes, were undoubtedly rebel sympathizers, but examples are hard to come by, since contemporary writers rarely acknowledged conviction as a possible motivation for serving the Taipings. According to them, people who volunteered for or willingly took up posts did so out of the greedy desire to accumulate wealth, and those who accepted positions reluctantly did so out of the noble desire to protect their families and neighbors from the abuses of the Taiping rebels and the other xiangguan.[39] Once in the rebel camp, however, this distinction sometimes became blurred as the outsiders became insiders and built up a stake in the Taiping status quo. "In the beginning," one gentryman wrote, "they felt it was difficult to serve as *xiangguan* and [only did so] because they feared humiliation at the hands of the long-hairs." But as time passed "they gradually came to see eye to eye with the bandits. They acquired the manner of the bandits and lost their own original nature."[40]

Aiding this transition from reluctant to willing collaborator were the seemingly limitless opportunities for unscrupulous xiangguan to get rich quick. Few received emoluments from the Taipings. Instead they deducted their "salaries" and bureau expenses from the taxes and levies they gathered for their overlords. As the conduits for the flow of the area's wealth, xiangguan found it a relatively easy matter to collect more from the people and deliver less to the Taipings, keeping the balance for themselves. All other administrative duties, from refugee relief to civil litigation to water control, presented further occasions for graft, squeeze, and influence peddling. Periodic Taiping crackdowns on xiangguan corruption proved no more effective than Qing prohibitions had against malfeasance within its officialdom.

Though perhaps not as common, but just as worthy of note, were those xiangguan who earned the commendation of their contemporaries for their honesty in office, their solicitous care of destitute refugees and needy scholars, and their attempts to curb the excesses of their bureaucratic peers.[41]

TAIPING GOVERNANCE:
FEUDAL POWER OR PEASANT POWER?

The mixed composition of the xiangguan has long fueled a lively debate among Chinese historians about the class character of Taiping rule. Some scholars contend that the Taiping movement remained true to its peasant origins throughout the rebellion; peasants dominated the xiangguan ranks, and rebel rule worked for their interests. Other scholars maintain that the exigencies of war and subversion from within ultimately transformed the Taiping government into a "feudal, monarchical rule" in which political power remained in the hands of the landlord class. Among those of the second school there is some disagreement over the timing of the transformation. Some historians date it from the establishment of the Heavenly Capital at Nanjing in 1853, and others assert that the "feudal" aspects of the rebellion gained the upper hand only after the leadership was shaken by the internecine conflict in 1856.[42]

Because of the varied class membership of the men who became xiang-guan, both schools of thought are able to muster evidence for their argument. For every example that the feudal-power proponents can raise of a landlord serving as a xiangguan, the peasant-power advocates can find a counterexample. Both sides, in their determination to divide all xiang-guan and all local society into the two opposing camps of landlords and peasants, do considerable injustice to a complex historical record. The peasant-power theorists, in particular, err in their facile identification of all nonlandlord, nonmerchant, and nongentry xiangguan as members of the peasantry when, in fact, only a very small number are explicitly referred to as peasants in the sources. In this respect the feudal-power theory, with its more numerous cases of landlord xiangguan, holds an evidential edge over the peasant-power theory.

This difference of opinion reflects not only the ambiguity of the source material, but, more important, divergent approaches to the question of the nature of Taiping rule. The feudal-power theorists take the ideals of the Taiping movement as their analytical starting point and view the realities of rebel rule in light of those ideals. Insofar as the goals of the rebellion included divesting the local elite of its property and power and reorganizing society along *Zhouli* lines, the Taiping record was abysmal. The feudal-power theory thus concentrates on the failures of the rebel movement and, in doing so, emphasizes the continuities between local society under the Qing and local society under the Taipings. The peasant-power theorists, on the other hand, tend to take as their point of departure not the ideals of the rebellion, but local society as it existed before the arrival of the Taiping army. They therefore dwell on the points of discontinuity between the two rules, giving a more reformist slant to the rebel administration of occupied territories.

In general, Western scholarship on the Taiping Rebellion is in tune with the perspective and substance of the feudal-power theory, although its analytical focus is the gentry rather than the landlord class. Philip Kuhn and Frederic Wakeman, for instance, contend that apart from the city of Nanjing, the Taipings did not effect changes in the power structure in the territory under their control; they merely coopted the existing local leaders to serve as xiangguan. Unlike the feudal-power theorists, however, who do not go so far as to argue that the landlord class reaped financial and political benefits from Taiping rule, Kuhn and Wakeman further maintain that the gentry, freed from the constraints placed on them by the Qing government, came to enjoy a virtually uncontested dominion over local society.[43]

If mere numbers are used to evaluate the composition of the xiangguan, the argument for a strict continuity in power relationships between Qing and Taiping society has much validity. People who had had some power, wealth, or status in local society before the arrival of the Taipings—former Qing officials or military men, landlords, gentry, merchants, members of rich or well-to-do families, militia leaders, yamen employees, subcounty functionaries, and polder heads—accounted for almost 70 percent of the 127 local officeholders on whom we have specific information (see Table 3.1). The impression of continuity is reinforced by the examples of Xu Peiyuan and Fei Yucheng who, though they did not hold xiangguan positions, were granted almost total control of their pre-Taiping spheres of influence, and by the many instances of gentry and yamen clerks and runners who staffed the xiangguan bureaus and occupied themselves with the daily administration of local affairs.

But this continuity in personnel is misleading. There was in fact a considerable change in the configuration of power, a point frequently overlooked in assessments of the xiangguan. Table 3.1 shows that, though the higher posts tended to be dominated by members of the elite, they were by no means off-limits to men of lower status. Those appointed to the highest positions of zongzhi and jianjun (equivalent to Qing prefects and county magistrates) included a subcounty functionary, a domestic servant, a mat peddler, and a yamen runner. And more than half of the junshuai, who typically were in charge of market towns or townships, and shishuai, who held jurisdiction over several precincts, were of nonelite status.

Men of prominent status, then, did not monopolize the highest xiangguan offices, nor were people of humble backgrounds consigned to the lowest ranks. As a result, many people now rose to positions of power that had been beyond their reach in Qing society. Conversely, men whose wealth or influence had commanded them fairly high positions in the elite under the Qing now found themselves as xiangguan of the lowest ranks, serving more as hostages to tax collection than as officials with any real authority. This scrambling in the pattern of power, plus the appointment of many men of nonelite status, tells a quite different story from what the numbers alone suggest; the imposition of Taiping rule brought significant changes in local power relations, changes that undermined the elite's hold over rural society.

The question of the class character of the xiangguan is bound up with the issue of the land policies instituted by the Taipings. Both the feudal-power theory and the peasant-power theory recognize that the rebels nowhere implemented their revolutionary land redistribution program, and both attribute this failure, though with different emphasis, to the exigen-

TABLE 3.1

Status of 127 Xiangguan in Jiangnan

(percent)

Category	Zongzhi/ Jianjun (15)	Junshuai/ Shishuai (70)	Lüshuai/ Zuzhang (18)	Unspecified (24)	Total (127)
Elite (70)					
Former officials (3)	20.0%				2.4%
Qing military (3)	6.7	2.9%			2.4
Militia leaders (5)	6.7	2.9	5.6%	4.2%	3.9
Gentrymen (20)[a]	26.7	8.6	16.7	29.2	15.7
Merchants (15)	13.3	10.0	5.6	20.8	11.8
Landlords (3)		4.3			2.4
Landlord-merchants (3)		4.3			2.4
Rich family (16)		14.3	22.2	8.3	12.6
Well-to-do family (2)			5.6	4.2	1.6
SUBTOTAL	73.4%	47.3%	55.7%	66.7%	55.2%
Nonelite (57)					
Yamen employees (8)	6.7%	8.6%	5.6%		6.3%
Subcounty functionaries (5)[b]	6.7	4.3	5.6		3.9
Polder heads (2)		2.9			1.6
Professionals (8)[c]		10.0	5.6		6.3
Employees (8)[d]	6.7	5.7	16.7		6.3
Peasants (6)		5.7		8.3	4.7
Poor family (1)			5.6		0.8
Artisans/peddlers (7)	6.7	7.1		4.2	5.5
Disreputable out- law types (12)[e]		8.6	5.6	20.8	9.4
SUBTOTAL	26.8%	52.9%	44.7%	33.3%	44.8%

SOURCES: Bernhardt, pp. 237–42; Dong Caishi, "Taiping Tianguo de xiangguan," pp. 717, 720–21; Heqiao Jushi, pp. 190–200; Wang Tianjiang, "Guanyu Taiping Tianguo de xiangguan," pp. 130–37; Yuan Zhen et al., pp. 17, 23; "Lihu yuefu," p. 168.

NOTE: Columns do not total 100 because of rounding.

[a] Holders of civil and military academic degrees.

[b] Dibao and precinct and township managers (tudong and xiangdong).

[c] Priests, doctors, geomancers, and martial arts teachers.

[d] People in the private employ of others, such as domestic servants, rent dunners, clerks in stores, and waiters.

[e] Vagrants, "local sticks" (tugun), bandits, gamblers, mercenaries, and gunboat commanders.

cies of war and the opposition of the landlord class. Where the two differ is on the question of what shape property relations *did* assume during the occupation. The feudal-power theory, in keeping with its argument that political power remained with the landlord class, dwells on the Taipings' affirmation of landlord ownership of land and the right to collect rents. The peasant-power theory highlights the rebels' reforms.

Here again, proponents of both theories can find extensive corroboration for their perspectives. Either school, however, would be hard put to document for any county a direct connection between the composition of the xiangguan and the land, rent, and tax policies instituted there. Counties where men of nonelite status were prominent in the rebel bureaucracy did not necessarily have reformist land policies, and, conversely, counties where men of the elite clearly dominated did not necessarily have conservative ones. Instead, the conservative and reformist elements co-existed as integral components of a fiscal plan that owed its origins more to expediency than to ideology.

THE LAND SYSTEM UNDER THE TAIPINGS

First issued in early 1854, the document "The Land System of the Heavenly Dynasty" contained a blueprint for the total reorganization of the agricultural and fiscal systems of Chinese society. Private ownership of land was to be abolished and the land thus freed distributed to all individuals, young and old, male and female. Each adult (sixteen years or older) was to receive one mu of top-grade land or its productive equivalent in inferior land, and each child half a mu. At harvest a household was to keep sufficient grain to feed itself and seed the next year's crop. Any surplus grain was to be deposited in public granaries set up for each twenty-five family (or liangsima) unit and given out to families as the need arose for wedding, birth, or funeral expenses. Any grain in excess of the needs of a particular liangsima group would be channeled to grain-deficient units.[44]

This rigidly egalitarian program was destined to remain merely an ideal. Soon after its formulation, a severe food shortage in Nanjing forced the Taiping leaders to abandon any plans they may have had for its implementation. In the summer of 1854 Yang Xiuqing, Wei Changhui, and Shi Dakai memorialized Hong Xiuquan for permission to order residents in rebel territory in Anhui and Jiangxi to "deliver land taxes as usual." The Heavenly King gave his consent and thus set the government on the course it was to maintain until its defeat in 1864. To ensure a steady flow of income, existing property relations were to be left intact and exploited in the fashion of the Qing state. Tenants were to deliver rents to their landlords, and landowners were to deliver taxes to the Taipings.[45] The reprint of the land document sometime after 1860 (the exact date is not clear) indicates that the rebels continued to accord land redistribution a place in their ideology, but the pressures of war and the demand for revenue prevented them from carrying out such a vast undertaking.

A restructuring of property relations was thus not on the insurgents' agenda for Jiangnan. Nothing speaks so forcefully of their failure even to attempt to implement their program there as the utter silence in the sources not only about land redistribution as a Taiping practice, but also about land redistribution as a Taiping ideal. None of the available contemporary materials mentions the land law even while recording, often in minute detail, nearly all other aspects of life under rebel rule. Since many of the authors were landlords who otherwise discussed matters pertaining to their property, it is safe to assume that the Taiping land program was not widely known.[46]

This suggests that at least by 1860 the Taipings were no longer even exploiting their land program as a way to garner peasant support. The rebels came to the lower Yangzi valley not so much as a liberating force but as an occupying army whose primary aim was to extract as much revenue as possible to fuel the fight against the Qing. This concern dominated all others, producing a welter of continually changing and seemingly contradictory policies. The Taipings affirmed, both in word and in deed, the current land system. They honored existing claims of ownership in land registration drives, issued announcements calling on the populace to pay rents and taxes as usual, and made rent and tax default a crime, punishable in some places by decapitation.[47] Yet maintaining the system was not a goal in itself, merely a means to another end. Taiping support of existing property relations was contingent. Where the current arrangements did not produce the expected revenue, rebel commanders were quick to adopt measures that, if they did not work sweeping changes in the pattern of landownership, did seriously undermine landlord control over the land and its cultivators.

The need for revenue was not the only ingredient in the making of the Taipings' land policies. With the conquest of Jiangnan the rebels inherited not a tabula rasa on which they could inscribe their designs at will, but a region with a recent history of widespread and violent conflict over rents and taxes. Landowners and tenants, after several decades of fierce resistance to what they perceived as unreasonable claims on their surplus, proved less than amenable to Taiping demands on their income and through their opposition helped to determine the direction of rebel policy.

The land system that took shape in Jiangnan during the occupation was thus not the result of a systematic and consistent application of some comprehensive Taiping program. Rather, it was formed in each area by different combinations of expediency, landlord acquiescence or opposition, and peasant resistance.

Landlord-Tenant Relations

The Taipings arrived in Jiangnan with the intention of tapping into the existing mechanisms of revenue extraction and, to that end, ordered landowners to deliver taxes, and tenants to deliver rents. But what was desirable in principle, they quickly discovered, was often not workable in practice. In the majority of counties Qing land and tax records had perished in the burning and looting of yamens. Many landowners had fled their homes, and those who stayed were reluctant to report their holdings. Moreover, landlord attempts to collect rents met with fierce tenant resistance.[48]

Under these circumstances, collecting taxes on the basis of landownership was all but impossible. The Taiping commanders in a number of counties therefore elected to dispense with the customary procedure and levy taxes on the basis of cultivation instead. When ownership and cultivation coincided, the new method of collection did not differ from the old. For landlord land, however, the Taiping government by-passed the owners altogether and began gathering taxes directly from tenants.

The practice of tenant payment of taxes (*zhuodian qizheng*) became fairly widespread in the autumn of 1860, with evidence pointing to its adoption in Suzhou, Changzhou, and Jiaxing prefectures and Taicang Department. In some places, like the suburban counties of Suzhou city (Wu, Yuanhe, and Changzhou), only those tenants whose landlords had fled were required to pay taxes. If the landlords returned, the tenants were to pay them the back rents minus the amount they had paid in tax. Landlords still in residence were to continue to collect rents and pay taxes as usual.[49] In other places, such as Wuxi, Jingui, Changshu, and Zhaowen counties as well as Taicang Department, the Taipings applied the new policy to all rented land. After the tenants had paid taxes, landlords were permitted to collect what rents they could. No provision was made for the collection of back rents on the return of a refugee landlord.[50]

Some Chinese scholars have interpreted this development as a kind of a "land to the tiller" program (*gengzhe you qitian*). Unable to carry out a full-fledged redistribution of land amid the turmoils of war, they argue, the rebels chose instead to pass ownership from landlords to tenants through the *zhuodian qizheng* arrangement.[51] But their evidence for this claim is not persuasive. Though some sources suggest that the tax obligation canceled the cultivator's rent obligation, especially when the landlord was no longer in residence, there is no indication that the Taiping government intended *zhuodian qizheng* to be anything other than a convenient method of tax collection.

Still, the policy did throw into question whether tenants who paid tax were also obligated to pay rent. Most tenants chose to believe that the shift in tax liability entailed a transfer of ownership as well, or, at the very least, released them from their rent obligations.[52] Tenants in Wuxi and Jingui, it was said, "now regard leased land as their own property and therefore do not deliver any rent."[53] In Changshu and Zhaowen peasants warmly welcomed an arrangement that required less of them than the landlords had expected. "Since they avoid paying rents," one observer noted, "they are delivering taxes eagerly."[54] When landlords tried to assert their claim on the harvest, tenants took the position, defending it with force if necessary, that they did not have to deliver rents because they had already paid taxes.[55]

Tenants may well have been genuinely confused about their duties under the new policy, but in light of the history of Jiangnan tenant protest, one suspects their position was more willful than innocent. As discussed in previous chapters, Qing officials, in their appeals to tenants, typically had explained the need for rent collection in terms of landowners' tax liability—tenants had to deliver rents so that their landlords would have the wherewithal to pay taxes. The broad effect of these appeals ran counter to their intention, inspiring resistance rather than compliance. Tenants subverted the official logic to their own ends and refused to pay rents in full whenever their landlords received remissions in taxes: since landlords did not have to pay the entire amount of tax, they did not need to receive the entire amount of rent. Under the *zhuodian qizheng* practice, peasants pushed this reasoning to its inevitable conclusion: since landlords no longer had to pay any tax, there was no reason for them to receive any rent.*

By all accounts the rent resistance of the fall and winter of 1860–61 weakened the landlords' already tenuous hold over their tenants. Changshu and Zhaowen landowners complained of receiving virtually no rents for the autumn harvest.[56] In Wuxi and Jingui absentee landlords living in the county seat suffered the same fate, although proprietors residing in the countryside were able to coax a few dou out of their tenants.[57] Elsewhere in Jiangnan, especially in those locales where customary taxation procedures remained in force, landlords fared somewhat better, but even they were able to collect only a fraction of the regular amounts of rent.[58]

---

*An interesting outgrowth of this perception of the relationship between taxes and rent occurred in Changshu and Zhaowen in the spring of 1864, one year after the Taipings had been driven from those two counties. Regular Qing land taxation did not resume in Jiangnan until the fall of 1865. Until then landowners were charged special land levies, which were generally collected only in the autumn, there being no provision for the spring portion of the diding tax. According to Ke Wuchi, *Louwang yongyu ji*, p. 100, landlords in Changshu and Zhaowen, fearful that tenants would refuse to deliver the customary spring wheat rents on the grounds that no taxes were being collected, actually imposed a local land levy on themselves (80 *cash* per mu for philanthropic purposes) as an inducement to their tenants to pay rent.

Like landlords, the Taipings were dissatisfied with the financial arrangements of 1860. Throughout the summer and fall of that year, the rebel commanders conducted a vigorous campaign to register land and compile fiscal records to replace those lost during the fighting. They repeatedly issued orders to landowners and tenants to report their holdings and dispatched lower-level xiangguan, former yamen clerks and runners, and subcounty functionaries to carry out field surveys.[59] These efforts were not entirely successful. The concealment of land was rife, and the surveys were too time-consuming to yield quick results. By the end of 1860, therefore, much land had not yet entered the rebel tax rolls, representing a substantial reserve of untapped revenue.[60]

By 1861 the commanders of a number of counties, appreciating the need for a change, moved to repair matters by partially discontinuing tenant payment of taxes, implementing rent reduction, directly involving xiangguan bureaus in the collection of rents, and making landlord registration of land a condition for receiving rents. With this cluster of policies, they hoped to placate both landlords and tenants, and at the same time increase their revenues by ensuring the registration of land. As with any plan that attempts to honor competing claims on fixed resources, no one was completely satisfied with the new arrangements, least of all landlords.

Of the measures adopted in 1861, the one most calculated to appeal to landlord interests was the curtailing of tenant payment of taxes. In those areas where the practice had been applied to all landlord land (Taicang, Changshu, Zhaowen, Wuxi, and Jingui), the Taiping commanders stipulated that resident landlords should resume collecting rents and delivering taxes; tenants would retain the tax liability only for the property of refugee proprietors.[61] This partial restoration of the customary pattern of rent and tax payment deprived tenants in these locations of their much-used excuse for nonpayment of rents, thus enabling those landlords who had suffered under the *zhuodian qizheng* policy to regain some control over their land.

Yet any economic benefit landlords might have derived from this change in policy was all but negated in some counties by mandatory reductions in rent. Varying from place to place, the Taiping-stipulated rents ranged from 0.4 to 0.8 shi of rice per mu, or roughly 30 to 80 percent of the pre-Taiping average (1.0 to 1.2 shi). The cost of these reductions was borne entirely by landlords who, despite their decreased rental income, were still expected to shoulder the full burden of land taxes and miscellaneous expenses and levies. As a result they generally earned in the end no more than 0.1 to 0.3 shi per mu, and that paltry sum only if their tenants paid the lowered amounts of rent in full.[62]

Without being privy to the discussion among the Taipings that resulted in the decision to decrease rents, it is difficult to determine exactly what motivated the move. In the case of their relationship with landlords, sheer necessity forced the rebels to act in ways contrary to the goals of their movement. But in this instance ideology and expediency dovetailed so neatly that they cannot be easily disentangled. The reductions in rent may well have been, as the advocates of the peasant-power theory contend, simply an embodiment of the commitment to alleviate the suffering of the peasantry. But in that case, why had the Taipings not ordered the reductions in the fall of 1860 immediately after their conquest of Jiangnan? The fact is, aside from several Wujiang market towns, where rents were indeed lowered immediately, most reductions occurred in 1861 only *after* tenants had demonstrated quite forcefully that they would not tolerate the high amounts. The Taiping administration, bowing to their wishes, lightened their burden, it seems, primarily in the hope that they would then feel obliged to deliver at least the decreased rents, which in any case were more than many peasants had been willing to pay when left to their own devices.

If this was the intention, the Taipings must have been sorely disappointed, for opposition to rents did not abate after the reductions. It was especially prevalent in those counties where tenants in 1860 had interpreted their payment of taxes under the *zhuodian qizheng* policy to mean either that the land had passed into their ownership or that they were no longer required to render rents. When the cancellation of the policy proved them wrong, they were not disposed to resume paying rents, even at the lowered rates.[63]

The third of the new policies, making xiangguan tax bureaus responsible for collecting rents from tenants, had precedents in Wujiang County, where such agencies were in operation in several market towns as early as the fall of 1860.[64] The bureau personnel collected the rents from tenants, deducted land taxes, miscellaneous levies, and their own expenses, and then handed the remaining cash or grain to landlords. Now, in 1861, similar bureaus were set up in many other parts of Jiangnan—Yuanhe, Wu, Changzhou, and southern Changshu (Suzhou Prefecture), Wuxi and Jingui (Changzhou Prefecture), and several places in Jiaxing Prefecture.[65]

The proponents of the feudal-power theory view this network of rent bureaus as an unequivocal example of Taiping support for the landlord class in Jiangnan. The rebel government did more than just allow the continuation of the landlord-tenant relationship, they argue; it created an infrastructure to facilitate the landlords' collection of rent. But that argument ignores the thrust of the policy. Assisting and thereby placating landlords was of concern, to be sure, but the bureaus were slated to serve the Taiping government first and landlords only incidentally, an ordering of priorities most evident in the fact that landlords were prohibited from gathering rents privately.* If they hoped to receive any income from their land, landlords had to register their property with the bureaus. Channeling rent payments through its own bureaucracy was thus a way for the rebel administration to extend its control over the revenue generated in the countryside. Simply by virtue of having tenant rents pass through its hands first, the government increased the likelihood that landlords would register their property, and that land taxes, miscellaneous levies, and expenses would be paid.

The arrangement further guaranteed that the Taipings and their xiangguan would not be the ones forced to bear the cost of a shortfall in rental income. The bureaus, rather than promising the landlords a certain percentage of whatever was taken from tenants, assigned them a fixed share of the stipulated reduced rent—for instance, as in the southern part of Changshu County, 0.24 shi out of a reduced rent of 0.7 shi per mu.[66] The remainder was divided among land taxes, miscellaneous levies, and bureau expenses, all of which had precedence over the landlord's claim. Given the tenant propensity for default and the xiangguan talent for embezzlement, it is hardly surprising that landlords frequently did not receive even this small portion of the harvest.[67] Bureau rent collection, far from being a boon to hard-pressed landlords, effectively placed them on a very capricious Taiping dole.

The uncertainty of receiving one's share of the rent, along with a fear of the consequences of making one's presence and wealth known to the rebels, accounts for the adamant opposition that landlords in some places displayed toward bureau rent collection. In the summer of 1861, for example, the Changshu commander Qian Guiren ordered landholders in the northern part of the county to report their property to the tax bureaus. Those who registered more than 200 mu of land were to be classified as "large households" (*dahu*), to what end Qian did not specify. After the autumn harvest the bureau staff was to collect 0.8 shi of rice from each mu of rental land, 0.2 to 0.3 shi of which would then be handed over to the landowner. Any attempt at the concealment of holdings, Qian further decreed, would result in the confiscation of the property in question. De-

---

*Similarly, the Taipings prohibited rent collection agencies that were not under their bureaucratic control. A group of landlords of Tonglizhen (Wujiang County), for example, set up a rent bureau in late 1860. When the Wujiang jianjun heard of this effort to collect rents privately, he ordered the bureau to inform the local rebel authorities of the location, amount, and ownership of the land under its management. The Tongli landlords decided to close their agency rather than comply with the jianjun's orders and thereby subject themselves and their clients to Taiping land taxation. (Juanpu Yelao, "Genggui jilüe," p. 101; Zhi Fei, "Wujiang gengxin jishi," p. 44.) The Taiping government sometimes dealt harshly with landlords who violated the injunction against private rent collection. In 1861 the head of a private rent bureau in northern Changshu was executed, and his associates severely beaten (Gong Youcun, "Ziyi riji," p. 389).

spite this threat few northern Changshu landlords followed Commander Qian's orders for fear of incurring extra xiangguan and Taiping exactions if they registered with the bureaus.[68] Qian's plans for bureau rent collection thus fell through.

Undaunted, Qian then ordered landlords to purchase land certificates (*tianping*), the Taiping document of landownership, as a prerequisite for collecting rents privately. Once again, he threatened the noncompliant with confiscation, and once again, few landlords complied. "They are clearly aware," a gentryman explained, "that [because of tenant resistance] they would not necessarily receive any rents [even with the certificate] and, moreover, are deeply concerned that they would suffer endless hardships should the bandits find out who they are."[69] This time Qian made good his threat and expropriated the property of the defiant landlords, who consequently received no rental income for the remainder of the occupation.[70]

Commander Qian's policy of making the receipt of rents contingent on the registration of land was part of a general trend evident in 1861 and 1862 in some of the other areas where rent collection was not routed directly through xiangguan bureaus. Without official documents certifying that they had duly reported their holdings, landlords were not entitled to collect rents privately. Occasionally, as in several market towns in Wujiang County, landlords received a special rent permit for each mu of reported property.[71] More commonly, as in northern Changshu, the Taiping land certificates, which the government began to require of all proprietors in 1861–62, provided the necessary proof of registration.[72]

The Taipings and their xiangguan generally issued land certificates to landowners who had clear title to the property. But in Tonglizhen (Wujiang County) tenants were permitted in 1862 to buy the certificates for the land they cultivated for 360 copper *cash* per mu (about one-tenth of the current price of land). "[Since] the rented land becomes their own property," one contemporary commentator wrote, "the peasants are secretly delighted and are coming forward one after the other to purchase the land certificates."[73] Presumably the certificate acted as the title deed to the property, and the tenant did indeed become the legal owner under Taiping law. The purchase of land certificates by Tongli tenants is the most unambiguous instance of any rebel "land to the tiller" measure. It remains, however, an isolated case.

By the end of the rebel occupation, then, a variety of rent and tax arrangements had emerged in Jiangnan: landlords collecting rents and paying taxes as of old, landlords receiving rents through bureaus, landlords collecting no rents, tenants paying rents to bureaus, tenants paying taxes in their landlords' stead, and, in Tonglizhen, tenants paying taxes as cultivator-owners after having purchased land certificates. Along the rather tortuous path that culminated in this mix of procedures, the Tai-pings were guided more by expediency than by ideology. Initially their need for revenue produced an intention to conserve and exploit the exist-ing mechanisms of revenue extraction. Then when it became apparent that relying on conventional methods of rent and tax payment was not the most effective way to reap the riches of the region, they introduced a series of modifications in the fiscal system. On the whole these alter-ations were far from congenial to landlord interests. In some areas land-lords were denied the right to any rent because of their failure to register their land. In others they were forced to entrust the collection of rent to bureaus, which frequently appropriated their share. And where landlords were permitted to collect rents privately, they were often compelled to do so at reduced amounts set by the rebel government.

Despite the generous reductions accorded to tenants in some coun-ties, rent resistance continued to be a major source of financial instability for both the landlords and the Taiping administration.* And during the occupation period, as in the past, peasant opposition to rents often took on a violent cast. Because of the particular collection arrangements that came into being under rebel rule, xiangguan and their bureaus became objects of tenant attack as frequently as individual landlords. In some locales peasant protest against bureau rent collection was so fierce that the managers elected to shut down rather than risk repeated assault.[74]

It was in their reaction to rent resistance that the Taipings most fully demonstrated the ambivalence of their position vis-à-vis the Jiangnan peasantry. Unable to reconcile their conflicting roles as an army of lib-eration and an army of occupation, the rebels were at times conciliatory and at other times brutal in their treatment of tenant protesters. In the fall of 1861 several xiangguan bureaus in northern Changshu announced their intention to collect both rents and taxes from tenants. In response the peasants attacked the bureaus, demanding that they be required to pay only tax and no rent. When called on to arrest the wrongdoers, the Changshu commander Qian Guiren declined to do so and, moreover, agreed to the protesters' demands. Tenants across the border in a village near An market town (Wuxi) were not as fortunate. Their rent strike at the end of 1861 (after the county had reverted to tenant payment of rent and landlord payment of tax) brought a force of Taiping soldiers, who, in the pitched battle that followed, burned their village to the ground.[75]

---

*In northern Changzhou County (Suzhou), for example, where rents had been uniformly reduced by half on the order of the hegemon and Taiping collaborator Xu Peiyuan, nearly 80 percent of the tenants on 900 mu of land managed by the bursary of a Shen family failed to deliver any rent to the collection bureaus in 1861, and 94 percent defaulted entirely on their reduced rents in the following year (Natsui, "Jūkyū seiki chūyō Soshū no ichi sosan," pp. 18–20).

Land Taxes

Land taxes during the Taiping period were of concern to landlords, cultivator-owners, and tenants who were obligated under the *zhuodian qizheng* policy to pay the imposts on behalf of their landlords. The rebel administration adopted the form of Qing land taxation and levied both the diding and the tribute tax, but it invested this form with a new content by changing the rate of collection. Whether the overall movement was up or down is problematical. In 1860 the Heavenly King Hong Xiuquan ordered a general reduction of 10 percent in land taxes in Jiangnan; that his orders did not go unheeded is indicated by several tax receipts from Suzhou Prefecture.[76] Similarly, Li Xiucheng stated in his confession that under his rule landowners in Suzhou were not required to pay their taxes in full; and indeed, so grateful were they that they honored him by erecting a memorial arch that bore the legend "The People Will Never Forget."[77] Other Jiangnan residents, however, did not share these sentiments and complained that the land tax burden under the Taipings was even heavier than it had been under the Qing.[78]

Which set of opinions accurately reflected the realities of land taxation during the rebel occupation is not easily determined. To compare the tax burdens of the two governments, several variables must be taken into consideration: the stipulated quotas, surcharges, the form of payment (money or grain), the conversion rates for silver and rice into copper *cash*, customary fees, miscellaneous levies, market prices for agricultural goods, and, finally, the relative value of silver and copper currency. Unfortunately, information on this full range of variables is not available for any single county under both regimes. Moreover, since taxation under both the Qing and the Taiping was characterized by wide variations in amount, only the most drastic increases or decreases would be visible. More subtle changes cannot be detected. In the circumstances, what follows must necessarily be a tentative comparison.

To reiterate briefly, the amount of tax a landowner was required to pay was determined by the statutory quota and the rate of collection. Under the Qing the quotas remained fixed at low levels, and increases were brought about primarily by raising the conversion rate of silver into copper *cash* for the diding and of rice into copper *cash* for the tribute tax. Accordingly, the quotas were low, and conversion rates high.

This pattern was reversed under Taiping rule. The stipulated amount of tax tended to be fixed at high levels, and the conversion rates at low ones. The Taiping land tax quota included such miscellaneous levies as a gunpowder levy, a dike construction levy, a firewood levy, bureau expenses, and fees for tax collectors. With these additional items, the stipulated land tax quota in some places came to 0.6 to 0.7 shi per mu, three

TABLE 3.2

The Land Tax Burden in Southern Changshu County, 1860–1862

(rates per mu for rice paddy)

Category	1860		1861		1862[a]	
	Shi	*Cash*	Shi	*Cash*	Shi	*Cash*
Conversion rate per shi		3,000		2,400		2,700
						2,900
						3,200
Tribute tax	.40	(1,200)	.37	(888)	.54	(1,458)
					.57	(1,653)
					.60	(1,920)
Diding tax		160				1,020[b]
Bureau expenses		200	.05	(120)		
Collection fees			.03	(72)		140
Land certificate			.10	(240)		50
Salt levy					.02	(54)
					.02	(58)
					.02	(64)
Total tax		1,560		1,320		2,722
						2,921
						3,194
Equivalent in rice[c]	.26–.31		.22–.26		.45–.54	
					.49–.58	
					.53–.64	

SOURCE: Gong Youcun, pp. 393, 416, 418, 420, 439, 468.

NOTE: The cash equivalents of tax items originally quoted in shi are shown in parentheses. They have been calculated on the basis of the conversion rates in the first row.

[a] The multiple numbers represent the three consecutive tax payment periods and deadlines. The penalty for missing a deadline was both a higher conversion rate and a higher tax quota.

[b] Includes dike levy.

[c] These figures represent the amount of rice a landowner would have to sell to acquire the copper *cash* to pay tax. They have been calculated at rice prices of 5,000 and 6,000 *cash* per shi.

or more times the Qing quota. But this increase in the quota was off-set by conversion rates that were on a par with or lower than prevailing currency values and grain prices.

The interplay of high quotas and low conversion rates is illustrated in the land tax collection of the xiangguan bureaus in the Wutazhen vicinity of southern Changshu. The items in the tax schedule, their amounts, and their conversion into copper *cash* are given in Table 3.2. A comparison of these figures with those for Changshu in the years preceding the rebellion (Tables 2.2 and 2.3) shows that the total tax in copper *cash* required of tax-payers by the Taipings in the early 1860's was equal to or higher than the amounts demanded by the Qing during the 1840's and 1850's. From this kind of analysis, some Chinese scholars have concluded that Changshu's tax burden was heavier under the Taipings than under the Qing.[79]

That conclusion is not fully warranted. Unlike the Taiping schedule, the Qing figures do not include any miscellaneous imposts on land or the customary fees paid to yamen personnel. For lack of information on those items, the best we can say is that the gap between the two sets of figures was smaller than the tables suggest. More important, the amount a landowner rendered in *cash* to either the Qing or the Taiping is not, by itself, an adequate gauge for assessing the tax burden, for it fails to indicate what proportion of the harvest a cultivator had to sell to obtain the necessary currency. To determine this, the price of rice and the conversion rates must be taken into account. From 1861 onward, when the effect of the disruption of rice imports from Central China began to make itself felt in grain-deficient Jiangnan, the price of rice in Changshu shot up to 5,000–6,000 *cash* per shi.[80] Since the Wutazhen bureaus set their conversion rates at half the price of rice, the landowner had to sell much less grain than he had formerly sold to raise the money for taxes. The per-mu burden in southern Changshu during the Taiping years thus tended to be the same as or lower than the per-mu burden in the 1840's and 1850's.*

The high tax quota of southern Changshu was by no means unique. In some counties in Jiaxing Prefecture, for instance, the quota climbed to 0.7 shi of rice and 800 *cash* per mu (Pinghu County) and 0.48 shi and 4,300 *cash* (Jiaxing County) by 1862 (Table B.1). We do not have conversion rates for these counties for that year, but judging by other years, they were commensurate with the price of rice in Zhejiang, which ranged from 6,000 to 10,000 *cash* per shi.[81] Pinghu landowners would therefore end up owing the equivalent of 0.78 to 0.83 shi of rice, and Jiaxing landowners, 0.91 to 1.2 shi. (This extraordinarily heavy tax burden probably owes to a serious underreporting of property in this case. During the fierce fighting in Jiaxing Prefecture in 1860, nearly all the local yamens' land and tax registers had been destroyed. By the fall of 1862 only some 20–30 percent of the land in the prefecture had been reported to the rebel authorities, who then taxed it heavily enough to compensate, at least in part, for the unreported, hence untaxable land.[82])

Other counties in Jiaxing Prefecture and some in Suzhou Prefecture managed to keep the land tax quota fairly low. Tribute grain notices issued to taxpayers in Haiyan and Shimen counties in Jiaxing show quotas of less than 0.2 shi a mu, roughly the equivalent of the tribute quota for these counties under the Qing. Taxpayers in Tongxiang in 1861 were charged 0.2 shi in rice and 700–800 *cash* (or 0.07–0.13 shi based on rice prices of 6,000 to 10,000 *cash* per shi), for a total burden of 0.27–0.33 shi. The

---

*Unfortunately, the pre-Taiping data for the rest of Jiangnan do not permit similar comparisons, at most indicating that the actual tax was two to three times the stipulated quota. For data on the Taiping period alone, see Table B.1.

amount required of taxpayers in Wujiang, Wu, and Changzhou counties in Suzhou was equally low (Table B.1).

The main reason that the Taipings, despite their pressing need for revenue, were able to keep taxes at low levels in these and other counties was that they exploited one group of landowners much more fully than the Qing. In assessing taxes, the rebel government made no distinction between large and small households. Large households that had been able to evade much of the land tax through a combination of legal exemptions and well-placed bribes were now required to pay all imposts on their property in full. Nor was this the end of it, for the wealth and status that had earned these families privileges under the Qing now made them prime targets for rebel and xiangguan exactions. The wealthy among the landlords became the objects of periodic search-and-seizure campaigns, called "striking the vanguard" (*da xianfeng*), in which squads of Taiping soldiers would cart away their stores of grain, cash, and other valuables. Sometimes the expropriation of wealth took the form of forced loans and special rich-household levies.[83] The fear of the larger landlords of northern Changshu that they would be subject to extra exactions if they registered their land was not unfounded.

Land taxes during the occupation period thus varied depending on the area, the year, and even the status or wealth of the taxpayer. The burden in each county tended to grow heavier year by year as the Taiping military situation and need for revenue became more desperate. Although land taxes seldom reached the relatively dizzying heights of the 1840's and 1850's, landowners in some counties had to pay three to four times as much as the Qing-stipulated quotas, amounts that they found just as intolerable under the rebels as they had under the Qing. And they expressed their dissatisfaction in the same manner as they had under the Qing—in tax uprisings.

As tax farmers for the Taiping government, the xiangguan bore the brunt of this popular indignation. Though assaults on xiangguan and their bureaus by irate landowners took place in nearly every county during the rebel occupation of Jiangnan, the majority of the recorded incidents occurred in Changshu and Zhaowen, where land taxes were particularly onerous. No collection season there went by without a number of attacks on xiangguan, often resulting in their deaths and the destruction of their homes and bureaus.[84]

The xiangguan tax collectors were beset from above as well as from below, for they were held personally responsible for any shortfall in their jurisdictions. Failure to fulfill quotas frequently led to beatings or confiscation of the hapless collaborator's personal wealth. Some xiangguan fled or committed suicide to escape these penalties.[85]

THE END OF TAIPING RULE

The position of the xiangguan became even more precarious as preparations for a determined campaign against the Taipings began, spearheaded by Li Hongzhang. In the 1850's Li, a jinshi from Hefei, Anhui Province, and a protégé of Zeng Guofan (now the Liangjiang governorgeneral), had raised a regional army in his home province, the Huai Army, so named after the major river running through Anhui. In the spring of 1862, he received, upon the recommendation of his mentor, the governorship of Jiangsu and moved with his army to Shanghai. There he fortified his troops with battalions drawn from Zeng's Xiang Army. Also under Li Hongzhang's at least nominal command was the Ever-Victorious Army, a force of some 3,000 to 4,500 mercenaries trained and led by first the American adventurer Frederick T. Ward and then the English officer Charles George Gordon.

News of the preparations afoot in Shanghai for major battles with the Taipings sparked retaliatory attacks on the rebel collaborators throughout the lower Yangzi valley. Again, a large number of the recorded incidents occurred in Changshu and Zhaowen. In the spring of 1862 "tens of thousands" of people, responding to the false rumor that the Huai Army had already begun operations against the rebels, went from town to town, burning bureaus and killing xiangguan. They were suppressed by Taiping troops led by the Changshu commander Qian Guiren and the Taicang commander Qian Shouren.[86]

Ironically enough, the same two commanders who jumped to defend the rebel bureaucracy against the attacks of the populace were at this point deeply involved in a conspiracy that would undo Taiping rule from within just as it was being threatened from without. The conspiracy, forged soon after the Taipings had gained control of the lower Yangzi valley, involved three local strongmen, Xu Peiyuan, Fei Yucheng, and Cao Heqing; two other Taiping field commanders besides the Qians, Li Wenbing of Kunshan and Xiong Wanquan of Suzhou; and three Qing officials in Shanghai, Xue Huan (Li Hongzhang's predecessor as governor of Jiangsu), the circuit intendant Wu Xu, and the Suzhou prefect Wu Yun. When the opportune moment arrived, the conspirators in rebel territory and their Qing contacts in Shanghai were to launch simultaneous attacks on the Taiping army.

The conspirators' first attempt at insurrection, the taking of Suzhou city in February 1862, failed when Li Xiucheng returned unexpectedly from the battlefront in Hangzhou. Though aware of the plot, the Loyal King did not take sufficient measures to ensure that a second attempt at mutiny would not be made. He ordered the execution of Li Wenbing and transferred Xiong Wanquan to Jiaxing but left the other conspirators in their positions of power.

The second attempt came a year later, in January 1863. The plans called for the Changshu commander Qian Guiren to go to Suzhou and invite Li Xiucheng to come to his county to review troops. Once Li arrived in Changshu, he was to be killed. The plan misfired. After Qian had set off for Suzhou, one of his fellow conspirators launched the mutiny precipitously in Changshu. The Taicang rebel commander, Qian Shouren, followed suit a few days later. In Suzhou the Loyal King dispatched his trustworthy subordinate Tan Shaoguang to Changshu to do battle with the mutinous Taiping troops, ordered the execution of the strongman Xu Peiyuan and the decimation of his militia, and sent Qian Guiren to Hangzhou with instructions to atone for his part in the plot by working for the Taiping cause.[87]

Soon after the mutiny the Huai Army and the Ever-Victorious Army set out from Shanghai to wrest Jiangnan from the rebels. They were aided along the way by the mutinous Taiping battalions, local militia, gunboat gangs, and bands of rural residents who, as in 1862, attacked xiangguan. In early December 1863 erstwhile Taiping defenders of Suzhou city killed Tan Shaoguang and surrendered to Li Hongzhang. Meanwhile, in Zhejiang Governor Zuo Zongtang, a Hunanese jinshi and another of Zeng Guofan's protégés, waged war against the rebels, occupying the key cities of Jiaxing and Hangzhou in late March 1864. As Li Hongzhang and Zuo Zongtang scored victory after victory in Jiangnan, Zeng Guofan's Xiang Army, now under the direct command of his brother Zeng Guoquan, drew ever closer to the Heavenly Capital at Nanjing from the west. The Heavenly King, Hong Xiuquan, died of illness on June 1, and the Xiang Army broke through the walls of Nanjing on July 19, 1864, set fire to the city, and slaughtered its inhabitants. The Taiping leaders who had escaped this final conflagration—among them Li Xiucheng—were apprehended and executed. With the recapture of Huzhou city in Zhejiang in late August, the entire lower Yangzi valley was once more under Qing control.

The Taiping occupation of Jiangnan, though relatively short-lived, left its mark on the imaginations of the survivors and their descendants. The memory of the rebels was kept alive through stories and songs, annual commemoration ceremonies, and occasional sightings of "ghost soldiers" engaged in an ongoing, ethereal battle.[88] For Jiangnan literati the Taiping occupation became a universal point of reference, a great watershed between life when it was sweet and life now turned sour. The pre-rebellion era was perceived in retrospect as a golden age, a time when peasants were diligent, officials honest, and the gentry public-minded. Now, all bore the tarnish of the Taiping calamity.

However exaggerated, these literati pronouncements about the lingering effects of the Taiping occupation give some indication of the depths to which the Jiangnan elite was shaken by the rebellion. The physical destruction alone was appalling. By the end of the rebellion, cities and towns that had once been centers of a thriving commercial network lay gutted by fire, with only scorched walls standing as testimony to their former importance. In much of the countryside piles of rubble marked the sites of former villages, and vast tracts of land were no longer under cultivation. Millions of people had died or had fled their homes for safety elsewhere.

But the impact went beyond physical devastation, bad as it was. The Taiping occupation also took a toll on power relationships in rural society. Contrary to the impression given in standard Western scholarship, Taiping rule did not rest lightly on Jiangnan. True, the rebels' overriding concern, the need for revenue for their war effort, led to practices supportive of the status quo—the appointment of members of the local elite to xiangguan posts, the affirmation of landlord landownership and the right to collect rents, and assistance in the suppression of tenant protest. Yet this same concern also resulted in policies disruptive of existing power and property relations. Because of the Taiping commanders' unfamiliarity with the region and their need to set a local officialdom in place quickly, they recruited xiangguan from all social stations. Thus, many men of nonelite status acquired an authority that they were not reluctant to use against their erstwhile social betters.

The local elite lost economic ground as well. Unlike the Qing government, the rebel administration granted no privileges to wealthy and influential households, requiring them to pay land taxes in full and, moreover, demanding of them special levies and contributions. The landlord class as a whole suffered a serious decline in rental income as a result of the Taiping policies of land confiscation, tenant payment of taxes, bureau rent collection, and mandatory rent reduction.

CHAPTER 4

Reconstruction and Post-Taiping Rural Society, 1864 - 1911

With the retaking of the lower Yangzi valley, the Qing government and its loyalist gentry inherited a region that had been physically devastated by the ravages of war and politically and socially challenged by the particularities of Taiping rule. Accordingly, the government and the elite set themselves to two major tasks: recruiting peasants to resettle and reclaim the countryside and reestablishing conventional power and property relations. These endeavors constituted a small part of the large, countrywide undertaking known as the Tongzhi Restoration (so called because it took place during the reign of the Tongzhi Emperor; 1862–74). Despite its name, the aim of the movement was not a mere restoration of China to its pre-rebellion state. What was at stake, in the words of Mary Wright, was "the revival of Confucian values and institutions, but so modified that they might endure."[1] A spirit of innovation thus infused the Restoration; and reconstruction in Jiangnan partook of that spirit, giving rise to new relationships, institutions, and practices that came to characterize rural society there for the remainder of the Qing.

It was, for example, during the era of reconstruction that we find the significant expansion of gentry influence that several scholars have identified as the most significant consequence of the Taiping Rebellion, notably Philip Kuhn and Frederic Wakeman. However, so far as Jiangnan is concerned, the expansion of elite power was not, as they suggest, the result of the Taiping practice of coopting members of the elite to serve as xiangguan or of a continued militarization of local society. Further, it was not a development that was bound to be inimical to the interests of the state.[2] On the contrary, the expansion of elite influence took place within the context of a general cooperative effort between the gentry and the government to recover the control over rural society that both had lost during the years of the Taiping occupation.

In rent relations that cooperation led to new patterns of interaction among the local government, landlords, and tenants. More and more landlords, either unwilling or unable to deal with their tenants themselves, now entrusted the care of their property to bursaries (private rent collection agencies) and charitable estates. Through these sorts of institutions, they were better able to bring collective force to bear on local officials in their efforts to gain greater state support for rent collection. Their efforts paid off, and the postbellum era saw an intensification of official participation in dunning, principally in the form of government-run tenant-dunning bureaus. But this was not an unmixed blessing, for local officials also became more fully involved in setting rents. In this, initially at any rate, they acted not so much on their own initiative as at the behest of politically prominent members of the elite, who feared that rent relations could never be set to rights if the burden on tenants was not regulated.

Still, this pattern emerged only in areas like the Suzhou suburban counties of Wu, Yuanhe, and Changzhou, which recovered relatively quickly from the physical devastation of the wars. In other areas, where the destruction had been much more severe and recovery was slower, a different dynamic prevailed. There, a continuing shortage of labor and an abundance of land tipped the balance of power decisively in the tenantry's favor. But not for long. As these areas filled up with settlers, tenants lost their edge, the balance began to right itself, and, as we shall see in the next chapter, rent relations in the twentieth century came to be characterized by the same landlord mobilization and state involvement that had come into being earlier in Suzhou.

In tax relations the key to the reimposition of government control over the countryside was the celebrated reform of 1863. Sometimes portrayed in the secondary literature as the culmination of a centuries-long campaign to lighten Jiangnan's disproportionately heavy burden, the Tongzhi tax reduction is better seen as an attempt to regain the allegiance of those small landowners who had so repeatedly and so vehemently demonstrated their opposition to Qing taxation in the more recent past.[3] The reform did achieve much of this desired effect. It significantly reduced the burden on Jiangnan landowners, resulting in an overall decline in the frequency of collective action against tax until the turn of the century. Then, as China's currency situation became more and more unstable and as the state increased its exactions to finance its program of modernization, the level of taxation rose dramatically and so too did the volume of popular resistance.

THE GENTRY AND RECONSTRUCTION:
THE EXPANSION OF ELITE POWER

As one might suppose, the reconstruction effort proceeded at different rates and with different emphases throughout the valley, depending on the amount of physical destruction sustained during the wars. In minimally damaged places the rehabilitation of agriculture and the restoration of power and property relations were largely accomplished within a few years after the Qing victory. In heavily battered areas, where population resettlement and land reclamation posed a greater challenge, recovery was slow, continuing at least for the remainder of the century.

On the whole the three prefectures of northern Zhejiang suffered more heavily than southeastern Jiangsu. Hardest hit were the counties in Hangzhou and Huzhou adjacent to Anhui. As the main point of entry from that province into Zhejiang, these border areas were repeatedly thrust into the thick of major battles and were constantly shuttled back and forth between Taiping and Qing control. Some counties changed hands as many as six times between 1860 and 1863. The continual warfare had predictable results on life and land. Contemporaries estimated that at the end of the rebellion no more than 10 to 20 percent of the original population remained and that, in 1866, up to 80 percent of the arable acreage still lay uncultivated. The eastern sections of Hangzhou and Huzhou and the entire prefecture of Jiaxing fared somewhat better; by 1866, at any rate, 40 to 60 percent of the land was being farmed.[4]

In southeastern Jiangsu only Changzhou Prefecture sustained damage of the magnitude common in northern Zhejiang. In 1864 Li Hongzhang described the war-torn prefecture: "I have surveyed an area of up to one hundred and several tens of *li*. . . . Villages and towns are destroyed and the cultivated land has all become waste. White skeletons lie on the thorns. There are definitely no residents."[5] All told, an estimated 70 percent of the pre-Taiping population of Changzhou had either perished in the fighting or fled to safety elsewhere. And as late as 1874, ten years after the rebellion, as much as 50 percent of the land had not yet been brought back into production.[6] A few other counties, notably Kunshan, Xinyang, Jiading, and Jinshan, were also heavily devastated, but overall the countryside in Suzhou, Songjiang, and Taicang had been spared the worst of the fighting. As a result, by 1868, 80 percent of the land was under cultivation.[7]

But no county in the lower Yangzi valley emerged from the rebellion completely intact, and a formidable array of tasks confronted the Qing. Cities and villages had to be rebuilt, waterways repaired, the population resettled and counted, the land reclaimed and registered. Jiangnan officials quickly recognized that reconstruction lay beyond the meager resources of the government and would have to depend heavily on active elite participation. Just as the state had encouraged gentry activism in the 1840's and 1850's to cope with popular unrest and the Taiping threat, so it would now rely on the elite's assistance to reestablish the Qing order. To that end the government permitted the gentry in the post-rebellion years an even greater hand in the administration of local affairs than it had enjoyed in the decades immediately preceding the Taiping occupation.

Reconstruction in Jiangnan was carried out primarily through a network of reconstruction bureaus (*shanhouju*) and supplementary agencies such as land reclamation bureaus and refugee bureaus, which were jointly directed by officials and upper gentry and staffed by lower gentry, yamen clerks and runners, and subcounty functionaries. In general the gentrymen who served in the various bureaus had not occupied xiangguan posts under the Taipings. Indeed, one of their responsibilities as bureau personnel was to assist the local government in bringing collaborators to justice. Some former xiangguan were arrested and executed.[8] Most, however, were permitted to atone for their crime by paying fines to the reconstruction bureaus. In principle only those men who had served the rebels voluntarily could be fined; those who had been coerced into serving or who had accepted posts in an effort to protect their communities were to be spared.[9]

The principle was seldom upheld in practice. The extortion of fines from former xiangguan was too lucrative to allow for considerations of justice. Rarely did the bureaus even put up a pretense of investigating a person's motives for becoming a xiangguan. They simply dispatched personnel to the countryside to ferret out the guilty, determine their financial worth, and collect a suitable fine.[10] Their victims were in no position to dispute this summary justice; should they refuse to pay, they faced certain arrest and possible execution.

The policy of fining Taiping collaborators generated much controversy. Contemporary writers criticized the dispensers of justice for being too harsh on men who had held low-ranking positions in Taiping officialdom and not harsh enough on higher-ups. Acting as lüshuai, zuzhang, and the like, the critics contended, had brought the incumbents nothing but trouble, since they had been personally liable for the tax quotas of their jurisdictions. Many had been pressed into service in the first place and had subsequently suffered physically and financially for failure to deliver taxes in full. To add to the burden of these people by exacting fines was a grave miscarriage of justice.[11]

Worse still, many critics felt, men who had amassed great wealth by extorting money, grain, housing, and other valuables from the people were being let off far too lightly. Some Wujiang gentrymen, thoroughly incensed by the lenient punishment meted out to the xiangguan who had dominated Shengze market town, even tried to remedy the situation. In a petition to the government they accused the Shengze collaborators (most of whom were the relatives and hangers-on of a rich landlord family) of bringing financial ruin to many and of extending active assistance to the Taiping army in its battles against the Qing. Instead of receiving the death sentences they so richly deserved, the petitioners explained, the Shengze collaborators had escaped prosecution by making generous contributions to the Suzhou gentryman Pan Zongwei. (It is unclear whether Pan pocketed the contributions or accepted them on behalf of the Suzhou reconstruction bureau.) Indeed, thanks to Pan's continuing patronage, some of the Shengze xiangguan had even obtained minor managerial positions in local society; one, for example, had become a manager of the firewood levy in Suzhou city.[12]

The Wujiang gentry's petition does not tell us about the ultimate fate of the other Shengze collaborators. What is clear, however, is that postbellum Shengze was dominated not by this company of former xiangguan, but by its victims, those gentrymen who had endured physical and economic hardship under Taiping rule.[13] For the most part this situation prevailed in other areas of Jiangnan as well. Discredited by their collusion with the Taiping insurgents, most of the erstwhile xiangguan were barred from positions of influence in the post-Taiping order.[14]

One exception to this general scenario may have been the Xu family of Changzhou. Under the arrangements between the militia leader Xu Peiyuan and the Taipings, the Xu brothers had acquired dominion over the northern section of their county. Though never entirely clear of the taint of collaboration, despite Peiyuan's participation and eventual death in the 1863 mutiny, the Xus emerged from the occupation with an influence that had been beyond their reach before the rebellion, and they remained a landlord family of considerable wealth and notoriety well into the Republican period.[15] All the same, the Xus never regained the power they had enjoyed under Taiping rule. With the return of the Suzhou city gentry from exile in 1864, they became just one of a number of elite families, and a relatively minor one at that. Moreover, their newfound and, in the eyes of many, ill-gotten influence did not go uncontested. As we shall see, the Suzhou city gentry made a concerted effort to undercut the Xus' power during the rent reduction campaign of 1866.

But in the end the Xus were a unique case. For the majority of gentrymen who served the Taipings, the end of the occupation spelled the end of the power they had held as rebel collaborators. The expansion of elite influence in the lower Yangzi valley, therefore, cannot be tied to the incorporation of gentrymen into the Taiping structure of rule.

Nor, let me repeat, can it be located in any enduring militarization of local society. Just as Edward McCord has demonstrated for Hunan,[16] a militarized society was not a legacy of the Taiping Rebellion in Jiangnan. The militia that had participated in the final Qing campaigns were disbanded once the rebels were defeated and popular unrest entered its immediate postwar lull, and though gentry periodically organized self-defense groups at the request of the government throughout the remainder of the nineteenth century, these units were routinely dissolved as soon as the threat had passed.[17] An informal military structure was not the source of gentry power in the post-Taiping period.

Instead, elite influence in the late Qing expanded principally along two avenues: the semiofficial, in which gentrymen worked closely with the local government, and the extrabureaucratic, in which gentrymen pursued activities outside regular bureaucratic channels. These two avenues converged to form what Mary Rankin, in her study of the gentry in Zhejiang in the late Qing, has called "the public sphere" of elite activism.[18] Elite public management was not something new to the post-rebellion period, for, as we have seen, gentry managers had been prominent in the administration of community affairs since the early Qing, but in the late Qing both the scale and extent of that management expanded considerably.

The semiofficial route to influence took the concrete form of joint gentry-official bureaus and rural directorships. These institutions, which came into being during the reconstruction era, had a twofold effect on the range of gentry power. First, they provided a more formal structure for what had previously been the informal responsibilities of gentry managers—for example, water conservancy and relief activities. Second, they allowed the elite entry into certain administrative areas, primarily the fiscal realm, where the state had always jealously guarded its own prerogatives. Through the complex of rural directorships and bureau managerial positions, gentrymen in the post-Taiping period were incorporated more fully into the formal system of government and thus were able to exercise their influence in ways that had not been available to them prior to the rebellion.

Two of the semiofficial bureaus through which the gentry extended its influence in the post-Taiping years—the reconstruction and land reclamation bureaus—have already been mentioned. In addition to these agencies, which were temporary bodies established to deal with an exceptional situation, there were more enduring ones that assisted government officials in the routine administration of Jiangnan society. The most important of these were:

1. The maritime transport bureaus (*haiyunju*), which were in charge of the transport of tribute rice up the coast to Beijing.
2. The commercial tax bureaus (*yaliju*), which were in charge of the

collection of commercial taxes, including the likin, the internal transit tax.

3. The salt gabelle (*yanliju*) and salt sales supervisory bureaus (*duxiaoju*), which oversaw the distribution and taxation of salt.

4. The baojia bureaus (*baojiaju*), which implemented and supervised the baojia system of rural control.

5. The sea wall construction bureaus (*tanggongju*), which were responsible for constructing and maintaining sea walls along the coast.

6. The river conservancy bureaus (*hegongju*), which were in charge of the dredging of waterways and the construction and repair of river dikes.

These bureaus, headed by circuit intendants or deputized expectant officials, included among their staffs a number of gentry managers.[19]

Other gentrymen, as *xiangdong* (township managers), *qudong* (ward managers), and *tudong* (precinct managers), undertook a wide variety of duties on the local level. They compiled land, tax, and population registers, supervised water works, collected commercial taxes, and, on occasion, organized baojia and militia groups. The origin of these rural directorships is obscure. Some evidence suggests that they existed in parts of Jiangnan as early as the 1830's. In other localities they first appeared during the militarization of the turbulent 1850's and early 1860's as a kind of administrative adjunct to militia units. In any event they became common only during the era of reconstruction. From the mid-1860's on county magistrates routinely relied on rural directors for assistance in local governance.[20]

Rural directors were appointed by a magistrate on the recommendation of members of the elite. Most were degree-holders, mainly shengyuan but sometimes juren as well, although academic credentials do not seem to have been a prerequisite for office.[21] Once selected, a rural director could remain at his post indefinitely, there being no fixed term of tenure. Some precinct directors in Wuxi, for example, occupied their positions for more than twenty years.[22] To a certain extent, though, continuation in office was contingent on performance, and negligence or corruption could bring dismissal by the county magistrate.[23]

The opportunities for corruption in office were abundant. Like the gentry managers affiliated with the various bureaus, rural directors did not receive salaries from the government but simply paid themselves from funds put at their disposal for certain projects and from customary fees collected during the execution of their duties. Although some directors, noted for their honesty, took only what was considered their rightful due, others engaged extensively in extortion and embezzlement, acquiring a reputation for corruption rivaling that of yamen clerks and runners.

Included in the range of activities that were more clearly gentry-conceived and gentry-run were various philanthropic pursuits, such as the founding of charities for widows, orphans, and other needy people and the establishment of academies (*shuyuan*). These sorts of extrabureau-cratic elite institutions predated the Taiping Rebellion, to be sure, but in nothing like the numbers that came after. In southeastern Jiangsu, for example, there were seventeen academies by 1735 and thirty-one by 1820; during the period 1864–1904 thirty more were established.[24] The founding of charities (*shantang*) also picked up pace in the late Qing. In the suburban counties of Suzhou city (Wu, Changzhou, and Yuanhe) members of the elite established twenty-three new welfare facilities from the 1860's to 1902, this in addition to rebuilding most of the forty-seven that had been established between 1676 and 1857 and destroyed during the Taiping wars.[25]

The elite's expansion in the sphere of public activity, as Rankin has noted, did not necessarily mean that state authority and power declined as a consequence. Rather, to use her words, the enlargement of the public sphere, first through the reconstruction efforts in the immediate post-rebellion period and then through the modernization reforms of the first decade of the twentieth century, created "an intermediate area where the state and society met. In the nineteenth and twentieth centuries, it was a dynamic and expanding sphere, which neither governmental nor societal leaders could fully claim as their own. . . . The public sphere became a place where new power might be sought, new conflicts could arise, and new relationships could develop."[26] She also demonstrates how the relationship between the state and the elite in this new sphere changed in the late Qing from one of close cooperation during the era of reconstruction to one of extreme contention during the first decade of the twentieth century as the dynasty lost legitimacy.

For our purposes, some amendments must be added to Rankin's analysis. First, even though many of these activities impinged on the rural populace, the expansion of gentry influence in the public sphere was over-whelmingly an urban phenomenon that did little to bridge the growing gap between elite and peasant. The semiofficial bureaus and elite charities and academies, with rare exception, were based in market towns and cities. Even many of the rural directors did not reside in country villages. Gentry activism of the late Qing thus reinforced the trend, evident since the early Qing, toward the urbanization of elite interests.

Second, the public sphere should also include those formerly private areas of elite activity that the state now considered proper objects for its regulation and control, and not just, as Rankin tends to see it, those formerly exclusive areas of state activity that the elite now participated in more fully.[27] The late Qing was a time of both an expansion of elite influence and an extension of the state's reach into local society, and it was the intersection of the two that created and defined the public sphere. This perspective is crucial to an understanding of the dynamic between landlords and local officials in the post-rebellion period. For as we shall see later in this chapter, it was this changing interaction that placed rent relations within the scope of the newly emergent public sphere.

THE REORDERING OF THE COUNTRYSIDE

Planning for the restoration of the Qing order began in earnest in the spring and summer of 1863, when Li Hongzhang's Huai Army and the foreign Ever-Victorious Army scored major victories against the Taipings in eastern Jiangsu. Of central importance in these plans was a permanent reduction of the land taxes in the lower Yangzi region, a measure approved by the court in 1863 and scheduled to go into effect in 1865. The architects of the 1863 tax reform intended it to serve several purposes simultaneously. They hoped, first of all, that a decrease in what landowners owed would result in an increase in what they actually paid. In a joint 1863 memorial Zeng Guofan and Li Hongzhang, who, along with Feng Guifen, were the most ardent supporters of the proposal for southeastern Jiangsu, explained that for decades the amount of tax the central government had received from that area had fallen far short of the statutory quotas.[28] That being the case, they suggested, it would be best to accept the fact that the existing quotas were impossible to collect and reduce them, thereby earning the gratitude of landowners, who would then deliver their taxes willingly and in full.[29] The reformers also presented their program as a way to undermine popular support for the Taipings. The censor Ding Shouchang, the major advocate of tax reduction for northern Zhejiang, wrote in an 1863 memorial: "If we are to strike fear in the hearts of the bandits [the Taiping rebels], we must first win the hearts of the people. If we are to win the hearts of the people, we must first reduce the heaviest tax quotas."[30] Finally, there was also concern that high taxes would discourage the immigration so needed to repopulate the countryside.[31]

The land tax reforms of 1863 were more comprehensive than those launched a decade earlier in Jiangsu by Feng Guifen and the provincial governor. Whereas the 1853 reforms had called only for a lowering of the tribute conversion rate and the equalizing of payments between large and small households, the 1863 package included a reduction in the tribute quota, a decrease in surcharges and the conversion rates for both the diding and the tribute tax, and an eradication of differential rates for gentry and commoner families. The amount of reduction in the tribute tax varied. The quota for the Suzhou-Songjiang-Taicang circuit was to be lowered by one-third, that for the three northern Zhejiang prefectures by eight-thirtieths, and that for Changzhou Prefecture by one-tenth. To give the reforms a better chance for success, the power to determine surcharges and conversion rates was transferred from the county to the provincial government. Henceforth, only provincial officials would have the authority to raise or lower taxes.[32]

The responsibility for carrying out the reforms was entrusted to two joint official-gentry commissions, a tax reduction bureau (*jianfuju*) in Jiangsu and a general tax reorganization bureau (*qingfu zongju*) in Zhejiang. In addition to deciding how the tribute reductions were to be distributed among individual landowners, these bureaus had to compile new land registers to replace those lost during the war. Assisting them in this chore was a host of other organizations, including local tax reorganization bureaus, reconstruction bureaus, land reclamation bureaus, and the agencies in charge of collecting provisional land levies.

Provisional Rent and Tax Measures

In the two years before the reforms took effect, 1863 and 1864, the government suspended the paying of tribute and diding taxes. This two-year moratorium, however, did not relieve Jiangnan landowners of all imposts on their property. Funds were still needed to fuel the war machines of Zeng Guofan, now the Liangjiang governor-general, of Li Hongzhang, the Jiangsu governor, and of Zuo Zongtang, the Zhejiang governor, for the final drive against the Taipings. Furthermore, revenue had to be raised for reconstruction and relief projects in places newly recovered by the Qing. Accordingly, in the summer of 1863 Li Hongzhang and Zuo Zongtang authorized local officials and gentry to set up bureaus for the collection of a land levy (*mujuan* or *tianjuan*), part of which would go toward military provisions and part toward reconstruction and relief.

That fall, the machinery for collecting the levy was put into place in areas already restored to Qing control, primarily Songjiang Prefecture, Taicang Department, all counties of Suzhou Prefecture except Wu, and sections of Jiaxing Prefecture. Collection bureaus, headed by deputy officials and prominent gentry managers and staffed by yamen clerks and runners, were established in cities and market towns. In some locales (Changshu, Zhaowen, and several areas in Songjiang) the network of bureaus extended more fully into the countryside, with branch agencies in each precinct under the management of jingzao, dibao, and rural directors. This apparatus inevitably added another item to the landowner's bill, a fee to cover bureau expenses.[33]

In their efforts to collect this revenue, the bureaus confronted the same problems that had plagued the Taiping government when it first sought to exact taxes from Jiangnan landowners—the loss of government fiscal records, the absence of many landlords, and a widespread resistance among tenants to rent payment. And to deal with these problems, the bureaus adopted some of the same methods that the rebels had employed. Chief among them were a government-decreed rent reduction, the collection of the land levy directly from tenants (*zhuodian qizheng*), the establishment of rent collection bureaus, and a requirement that landlords register their land as a prerequisite for receiving rent. The levy and rent measures of 1863–64 bear relating in some detail, for several survived the resumption of regular tax and rent collection in 1865 to become enduring features of post-Taiping rural society.

In his original instructions on the collection of the land levy, Li Hongzhang, adopting the suggestion of several influential Suzhou gentry landlords, ordered local officials to enforce a 50 percent reduction in the pre-Taiping rents.[34] This measure was grounded in the realization that tenants would be unlikely, in any event, to deliver their dues in full. In some areas rents would not be forthcoming because of the substantial damage that harvests had suffered in the recent fighting. In areas where crops were only minimally damaged, peasants would be disinclined to pay high rents after the reduced amounts of the Taiping years. Rather than run the risk of massive tenant protest with a sudden reimposition of regular rents, it was deemed better to accept the lowered amounts for the time being, in the hope that such a demonstration of landlord largess would move peasants to pay at least half the normal amount.

The order for rent reduction placed the regulation of tenant payments directly within the purview of the gentry-official levy bureaus. Besides collecting levies and assisting in the compiling of land registers, bureau personnel were to ensure that no landlord exceeded the 50-percent ceiling on rent. The land registration, levy, and rent procedures used by the bureaus in 1863, with some minor variations, conformed to one of two general patterns. First, in Changshu, Zhaowen, and several counties in Songjiang Prefecture, the agencies instituted the practice of *zhuodian qizheng*, instructing jingzao, dibao, and rural directors to collect the land levy and expenses directly from tenants. Bureau clerks then subtracted this sum from the tenant's reduced rent and entered that amount onto an official notice. To secure this notice and hence the right to collect rent privately, a landlord first had to report his holdings.[35]

Second, in parts of Jiaxing Prefecture and in Yuanhe, Changzhou, Wujiang, and Zhenze counties of Suzhou, either the land levy bureaus or separate rent collection bureaus (*shouzuju*), following the example of the xiangguan bureaus of the Taiping occupation, collected the entire amount of reduced rent from tenants. After the bureau had deducted its share for the levy and expenses, the remainder was handed over to the landlord when he came to register his land.[36]

In 1863, as during the Taiping period, reduced rents, the practice of *zhuodian qizheng*, and bureau rent collection tended to benefit tenants, the bureau staff, and the military coffers of the government more than landlords. Tenants, unmoved by the calculated generosity of reduced rents, defaulted openly on the lowered amounts. In Changshu and Zhaowen, where levies were gathered directly from tenants, leaving landlords to collect the rent as best they could, tenants refused to pay any rent at all, claiming, as they had under the Taipings, that their payment of taxes cancelled their rent obligation.[37]

Landlords did not fare much better in those counties where rent collection was entrusted to bureaus. In 1863 the bureau in Tonglizhen (Wujiang), for instance, collected only 40 percent of the total amount of reduced rents owed for the land within its jurisdiction. What remained as the landlord's share after the deduction of levies and expenses was much less than the originally proposed 0.25 shi per mu. The reluctance of Tongli tenants to pay the reduced rents in full, one landlord explained, was due to the change that the Taiping Rebellion had wrought in "the hearts of the people."[38]

Tenant resistance and the hardships that landlords suffered on this account prompted the provincial authorities to modify the procedures for levy and rent collection. In the fall of 1864 landlords were assessed for military, reconstruction, and bureau expenses on the basis of rental income and not, as in 1863, on the basis of landownership. This new rent levy (*zujuan*), expressed in so many copper *cash* per shi of rent rice, relieved landlords of the burden of having to pay a fixed sum to the government regardless of what they received from tenants. There is also some indication that officials upped rents from 50 to 60 percent of the pre-Taiping amounts.[39] At the same time officials took steps to return the direct control of the land to landlords. In Changshu and Zhaowen the authorities discontinued the *zhuodian qizheng* policy, thus depriving tenants of their much-used justification for not paying their rents.[40] Elsewhere in Suzhou Prefecture, where rent collection had been routed through bureaus, officials now permitted landlords the option of collecting rents personally after they registered their property and received official rent notices.[41] Finally, now that the levy was tied to landlord income, the government had a greater stake in rent collection. To ensure the payment of rent, dunning bureaus (*cuizuju*), manned by yamen runners, were established in some areas.[42]

With the resumption of regular, though now-reduced, land taxes in the autumn of 1865, the apparatus for the collection of rent and levies was dismantled. Rent relations, it was hoped, could be restored to their antebellum footing without the need for direct state involvement. This hope, however, proved illusory. A continuing instability in the landlord-tenant relationship led to the resurrection of some of the policies adopted in 1863 and 1864, most particularly official participation in the setting of rents and the establishment of government dunning bureaus.

Labor Recruitment and Land Reclamation Policies

The provisional tax and rent measures of 1863 and 1864 applied only to land still under cultivation. For fields that had gone to waste, officials had to devise another set of policies to encourage resettlement and land reclamation. Two concerns directed the Qing's efforts in this regard. The decimation of the population and the devastation of farmland in many Jiangnan counties afforded the state a rare opportunity to reshape land-ownership there into a pattern more to its liking. By promoting small peasant ownership, it could establish a direct relationship with a greater number of cultivators and thus free itself of the often troublesome inter-mediation of landlords. Yet officials also had to take care to honor existing property rights so as not to alienate the elite, whose support was so vital to the restoration and viability of the dynasty.

Two basic principles thus informed state resettlement and reclamation policies—"Land Reverts to the Original Owner" (*tian gui yuanzhu*) and "Recruit Cultivators and Return Land to the Tax Rolls" (*zhaoken shengke*). These principles in turn gave rise to two different types of labor recruit-ment and land reclamation—*rentian*, literally "claiming one's ownership of land," and *renken*, "undertaking the reclamation of land."[43] Rentian re-ferred to fields claimed by an owner, who, after proving his rights to the property with title deeds or affidavits from neighbors or subcounty func-tionaries, was to have sole responsibility for bringing the land back into production either by working the field with family labor or recruiting tenants to do so. Renken applied to fields unclaimed by previous owners. For land of this type officials were to recruit cultivators, who would re-ceive legal ownership of the property after they had begun to pay full taxes on it. To ensure that both processes went as smoothly as possible, the government permitted land in process of reclamation a period of tax exemption ranging from three to ten years.[44]

The Qing policy makers, knowing full well that the severe depopula-tion in numerous Jiangnan counties required the recruitment of cultiva-tors from outside the region, instructed local officials and gentry man-agers to see that outsiders were accorded the same considerations and concessions as natives in the reclamation of land. In terms of numbers, the recruitment efforts were quite successful. Immigrants, called "guest people" (*kemin*), poured into Jiangnan in two waves. In the decade immediately following the rebellion, most of the guest people who settled in Hangzhou, Huzhou, and Jiaxing were refugees from Ningpo and Shaoxing prefectures and shack people (*pengmin*) from the hills of Taizhou and Wenzhou prefectures in southeastern Zhejiang. The first immigrants to reach the devastated areas in southern Jiangsu, by contrast, were refugees fleeing the severe famine that struck the northern part of the province in 1866. Included also in this first group of settlers were demobilized soldiers from the disbanded regional armies.

The second wave of immigration began in the 1880's, when famine refugees from Hunan, Hubei, Henan, and northern Jiangsu settled throughout the lower Yangzi valley. During this period as well, guest people from the eastern and southern parts of Zhejiang crossed into Jiangsu to reclaim land in Kunshan and Xinyang counties in Suzhou Prefecture and land throughout Changzhou Prefecture. Soon after the recruitment of settlers began, immigrants came to outnumber natives in the more seriously ravaged counties.[45]

The relationship between guest people and natives was far from amicable. Contemporary sources invariably characterized immigrants as a shifty and arrogant lot, prone to lawlessness and quick to violence. Their strange dialects, clothing, and customs made them targets of derision, and their reputation for making free with the possessions of others made them objects of suspicion. Natives accused the newcomers of a host of crimes against property, including illegally appropriating land, houses, farm tools, and animals, cutting down trees to build makeshift shacks, and, if they were engaged in sericulture, picking leaves from the mulberry trees of others.[46] Tension between the two groups frequently erupted into murderous feuds, adding a new element of disorder to Jiangnan rural society.[47]

The hostility between natives and immigrants complicated the officials' already difficult task of attracting and retaining cultivators. Unlike natives, whose ties to their homes were more than economic, guest people had little to keep them in one place should richer prospects beckon elsewhere. Famine refugees from North China, in particular, did not form a dependable supply of labor. As a local gazetteer put it, "The people [from the north] come in swarms, settle like ants, gather like crows, and scatter like wild beasts."[48] Being neither rice-eaters nor rice-growers, these northerners felt out of place in Jiangnan. Many, moreover, owned land in their native provinces and had migrated south merely to tide over a rough spell. Once conditions improved in the north, they would desert their fields in Jiangnan and return home.[49]

The fear of losing precious farm labor gave rise to a serious contradiction between the two principles of *tian gui yuanzhu* and *zhaoken shengke* and their accompanying practices of rentian and renken. The principle of reversion to the original owner required that that person, if still alive, be given sufficient opportunity to return and reclaim his property (rentian). Yet the principle of *zhaoken shengke* demanded that officials recruit cultivators to farm the land (renken) so that it could be restored to productivity and taxable status as quickly as possible. Faced with this dilemma, a local official had to choose between two less-than-ideal options. He could adhere strictly to the principle of reversion to the original owner and let the field lie fallow on the chance that someone might come forward to assert ownership rights. By following this course, however, he would be violating the principle of *zhaoken shengke* and would have to withstand considerable pressure from his bureaucratic superiors to restore wasteland quickly to production and to the tax rolls. Alternatively, he could abide by the second principle and let the field be reclaimed by a cultivator other than the original owner. Should the owner subsequently return, that person would have to work out some agreement with the reclaimer about compensation for labor and capital costs and about the future disposition of the field.

What made this last solution, on the surface the easier one, problematical was that many peasants, especially immigrants new to an area, were reluctant to reclaim land of such ambiguous legal standing. As Governor-general Ma Xinyi explained in an 1869 memorial:

> Reclamation of wasteland requires an extraordinary amount of labor and capital. Draft animals, seeds, and farm implements all must be purchased, and the reclaimers must build thatched cottages in which to live. When the original owner suddenly returns after a field has been returned to production, he might repay the reclamation expenses, extend the tenure of cultivation [e.g. keep the reclaimer on as a tenant], or sell the land to the cultivator. But the peasant is not at all pleased. Reclaimers are impoverished peasants who wish the land to become their own property. If there might be an original owner, then they clearly know that the field could not become their own. So why should they be willing to exhaust themselves doing the reclamation work for other people?[50]

Moreover, those peasants who did farm fields of unclear legal status in the expectation of acquiring the property did not always relinquish the land when the original owner turned up. Many stood their ground and refused to vacate the reclaimed land, an action that often led to endless litigation and sometimes to violent confrontation.[51]

In an effort to resolve the contradiction between the two policies, Ma Xinyi, in an 1866 memorial concerning Zhejiang and an 1869 one concerning Jiangsu, set some guidelines weighted heavily in favor of reclaiming peasants. In the Zhejiang regulations he urged officials to recruit cultivators for fields as yet unclaimed by original owners. Should the owner subsequently come forward to claim the land, his rights should be honored, but he would have to reimburse the peasant for his labor and capital investments and/or retain him as a tenant. If after several years (precisely how long Ma did not say) the field remained unclaimed by the owner, it was to revert to the reclaimer. Ma's Jiangsu regulations of 1869 went further, establishing a specific deadline for a claim of original ownership. Anyone who had not come forward by the end of 1870 would forfeit all rights to the land, and reclaimers would acquire legal ownership.[52]

The extent to which Ma Xinyi's regulations were actually followed lies at the heart of a debate among Chinese scholars about the pattern of landownership in the postbellum period, a debate made the more lively by the lack of statistics. Did Qing reclamation policies and practices promote a growth in small peasant proprietorship? Or did they promote a restoration of landlordism? Li Wenzhi takes the first line: thanks largely to the implementation of Ma's policy, cultivator ownership expanded significantly throughout the lower Yangzi valley, not only in the most heavily devastated areas of southwestern Jiangsu (here including Changzhou Prefecture) and northern Zhejiang, but, to a lesser degree, in comparatively lightly devastated southeastern Jiangsu as well.[53] Others contend that there was no appreciable change in landownership. According to Mao Jiaqi, for example, local officials did not follow Ma's policy, continuing to honor prior property claims long after the deadline had passed. The result, he concludes, was a revival of landlordism even in the most severely damaged areas of Jiangnan.[54] Taking the middle road, Wang Tianjiang maintains that the differing degrees of devastation resulted in much geographical variation in landownership patterns in the postwar years. Overall, southwestern Jiangsu and northern Zhejiang experienced a pronounced increase in the amount of land owned by peasants, while land in southeastern Jiangsu remained concentrated in landlord hands.[55]

Although, as these divergent views suggest, the transformation in Jiangnan land tenure patterns cannot be charted with any precision, an impressionistic picture can be drawn by considering both the geographical variation in the extent of devastation and the impact of government reclamation policies. In general Suzhou, Songjiang, and Taicang experienced no marked increase in cultivator ownership of land. In the 1880's, 80 to 90 percent of the peasants in Suzhou and 50 to 60 percent of those in parts of Songjiang were reportedly tenants, figures in line with pre-rebellion estimates.[56] Having escaped the worst of the fighting, much of the land in these areas had remained under continuous cultivation during the rebellion, and after the Qing victory the resettlement of the countryside proceeded relatively quickly. By 1868, according to the Jiangsu governor Ding Richang, a full 80 percent of the arable acreage was under production.[57] Moreover, except in the most severely depopulated locales, such as Kunshan and Xinyang and the southernmost section of Suzhou Prefecture bordering Zhejiang, wasteland was reclaimed principally by natives under tenancy contracts.[58] Both the rapid reclamation of land and the comparatively small role of guest people in that process indicate that original owners still in residence or recently returned from exile quickly asserted their rights to their property. With so small an amount of land of ambiguous legal status, the number of peasant proprietors could hardly have increased significantly under Ma's 1869 policy.

Nevertheless, some reworking of the pattern of ownership did occur. In Songjiang Prefecture, for instance, landownership became more dispersed among numerous petty landlords, few of whom possessed enough property to be rated large landholders. According to several newspaper accounts of the 1880's, only a handful of families in Huating and Lou counties owned fields numbering in the thousands of mu, and in Fengxian and Nanhui proprietors with as much as 1,000 mu were very rare. In this respect postbellum Songjiang contrasted sharply with Suzhou, where large landlords were not only relatively common but also more politically influential.[59] This distinction persisted into the Republican period and made for very different sets of relations between landlords and officials in the two areas.

In the Jiangsu prefecture of Changzhou and the three northern Zhejiang prefectures of Hangzhou, Huzhou, and Jiaxing, depopulation was much more severe and wasteland much more extensive than in southeastern Jiangsu. The war had also taken a heavier toll on elite families. Contemporaries wrote that few rich households had survived the turmoils in Wuxi and Jiangyin (Changzhou), and that in northern Zhejiang old illustrious families had either perished or fallen on such hard times that they had to sell their land and other valuables to survive.[60]

These conditions furnished fertile soil for an expansion of peasant proprietorship. Officials abetted the process with measures that favored reclaimers over previous owners. Ma Xinyi's regulations seem to have been enforced to a considerable degree in southwestern Jiangsu and northern Zhejiang, especially as time passed and the chances of original owners appearing to claim their property became increasingly remote. In 1880 the governor-general, Liu Kunyi, credited Ma's policy of 1869 for much of the progress that had been made in the reclaiming of wasteland in southwestern Jiangsu.[61]

In northern Zhejiang as well, local officials adopted a policy that favored the rights of reclaiming peasants, especially immigrants, but not exactly in the fashion envisioned by Governor-general Ma. The difference turned on the government imposts levied on peasants who undertook to reclaim wasteland. Despite the impression conveyed in some works on the subject, the imperially sanctioned period of tax exemption did not always absolve reclaimers of all government charges. In practice the moratorium often applied merely to the regular taxes, the diding and the tribute tax. Throughout Jiangnan (and in Anhui Province as well) unclaimed wasteland was by no means free for the asking, and reclaimers generally had to invest more than just reclamation costs when they took on the land. County officials either designated unclaimed fields as official land (*guantian*) and then sold it to interested parties or charged an annual fee variously called a levy (*juan*) or rent (*zu*). This fee was lower than the regular tax and was to give way to regular taxes once the land was returned to productivity and the reclaimer was vested with property rights.[62]

In northern Zhejiang, however, county officials commonly did not enter this land onto the regular tax rolls even after it had been brought back into full production, because to do so meant losing the fee from the property and reducing the revenue available for local use. There thus arose a distinction between fields reclaimed by original owners, which were subject to regular taxation, and fields reclaimed by others, which were subject to the lower official rent or levy. As might be expected, the property in the former category was in the possession of Zhejiang natives, while the latter, identified as "guest wasteland" (*kehuang*), was monopolized by immigrants. Since it was to a county's financial benefit to keep as much land as possible in the "guest wasteland" category, local officials defended it from both the demands of the upper levels of government and the claims of original owners. When called by their superiors to account for the status of land that had once been waste, they either replied that it had not yet been brought back under cultivation or insisted that assessing immigrants with the regular tax would induce them to look for cheaper fields in some other county. When presented with proof of prior ownership, they invariably, as the current saying went, "protected the immigrant and oppressed the native" (*bike yatu*). The preferential treatment accorded reclaimers in property disputes helped to foster an expansion in cultivator ownership in the three northern Zhejiang prefectures.[63]

RENT RELATIONS

The geographical variations in the destruction of life and property during the rebellion resulted not only in differences in the pattern of landownership but also in differences in the relative strengths of landlords and tenants. And these differences directly affected the type of peasant resistance to rents that took place in each area. In Changzhou Prefecture in Jiangsu and the three northern prefectures of Zhejiang, the abundance of land and shortage of labor decisively shifted the balance of power in the tenantry's favor. Consequently, tenants in those areas, while widely engaging in individual resistance to landlord demands, did not resort to collective action to press their claims.

In the counties of Suzhou Prefecture that had sustained comparatively minimal damage, tenants did not enjoy the same sort of leverage, but their brief taste of nonpayment of rents and reduced rents during the Taiping years made them less compliant in their dealings with landlords once the Qing was restored. To cope with continuing widespread default, members of the elite and government officials in Suzhou established procedures and institutions that significantly altered the relationship among tenants, landlords, and the state. This restructuring of rent relations in turn encouraged an escalation in tenant collective action.

Changzhou Prefecture and Northern Zhejiang

In Changzhou and northern Zhejiang the extreme destruction of life and land during the Taiping wars brought dramatic, if only temporary, changes in the balance of power between landlord and tenant. Because of the critical shortage of labor, landlords had to grant generous terms of tenure merely to attract cultivators. Rents were extremely low or nonexistent during the period of reclamation, but even afterwards they could not be raised quickly for fear of scaring away the precious labor. In the immediate post-rebellion years, tenants in these locales paid rents as low as several hundred *cash* or several dou of grain per mu. But landlords could not count on receiving even these small sums, since tenants frequently defaulted openly, secure in the knowledge that they probably would not be evicted, and that even if they were, finding other fields to farm would be relatively easy.[64]

The initial abundance of land exerted another adverse effect on landlords' rental income in Changzhou and Zhejiang. With land so plentiful and labor so scarce, peasants often abandoned the time-consuming practice of intensive rice farming, electing instead to plant over relatively broad stretches of land. Immigrants from the north were especially apt to adopt this method, since they were not well versed in wet-field riziculture.[65] The yield thus fell short of capacity, and with it the amount of rent the tenant was willing to pay. Unfortunately for the landlord, his land, once reclaimed, was returned to the tax rolls at its old grade of productivity, thus placing him in the bind of lacking sufficient rent to cover the tax. In Jiashan County (Jiaxing) the rent for fields planted extensively was no more than a few hundred *cash* per mu, compared with a tax as high as 700 *cash*. Any attempt to raise the rent, the local gazetteer explained, only drove the cultivators away to seek cheaper land elsewhere.[66]

For landlords who suffered such a disparity between rent and tax, landownership had become a losing proposition. Complaints about the burden of landownership abound in the sources. One wit had it that "field [*tian*] may lie at the bottom of the character for rich [*fu*], but it actually forms the top of the character for burden [*lei*]" (*tian nai fu zi zhi di, shi wei lei zi zhi tou*).[67] Ridding oneself of the burden, however, was easier said than done because of a glut of land on the market. And even if a proprietor was fortunate enough to find a buyer, he could not hope to gain much from the deal because of exceedingly low prices. As late as the 1880's, a mu of paddy in Jiaxing County could be had for less than five taels, a far cry from the sixteen to twenty-four taels in the peak years of the 1820's; in less heavily damaged Yuanhe County (Suzhou), by contrast, land prices had nearly regained their 1820's level by the 1880's.[68]

While Changzhou and Zhejiang landlords were bemoaning the burden of landownership, their tenants no doubt were extolling its virtues. A marked expansion in dual ownership accompanied land reclamation throughout Jiangnan, and in the heavily damaged areas in particular. New topsoil rights came into being in two ways. When an original owner returned to discover that his land had been reclaimed by another, he might keep the cultivator on as a tenant and grant him alienable topsoil rights as reimbursement for reclamation costs. Alternatively, landlords offered topsoil ownership up front as an inducement to recruit cultivators. In any case, the tenant, as was customary, automatically paid less rent than his fellows paid on "undivided" land.[69]

Moreover, in some areas of northern Zhejiang, tenant topsoil owners continued to be held liable for land taxes, a practice that had been dropped in southeastern Jiangsu as early as 1864.[70] Given the lowered productivity of this land and the difficulty of collecting much rent, it was seemingly to the landlord's advantage to have the tenant retain that liability for this property (called *yuhuatian* in Jiaxing and *jinhuatian* in Jiashan). But in the end the arrangement, just like the practice of *zhuodian qizheng*, fostered even greater resistance to rents. Tenants of this land in Jiaxing and Jiashan, for instance, paid at most a rent of only one to two dou per mu, and that only in years of good harvest.[71]

Somewhat paradoxically, the demographic changes that generated much individual resistance among Changzhou and northern Zhejiang tenants also brought about a lengthy hiatus in collective action against rents. Changzhou and northern Zhejiang, the site of eleven of the twenty-eight tenant actions in Jiangnan in the 1840's and 1850's, experienced no further collective protests aimed explicitly against rents until 1907 (see Tables A.1 and A.2). With so much unoccupied land nearby, tenants who found the landlords' demands intolerable now had the option of flight or avoidance, an individual resistance strategy not many could afford to adopt in the prewar years.[72] This was particularly the case for guest tenants, who lacked close ties to their new homes. The very existence of this option for tenants, of course, also helped to limit the landlords' demands and to make them wary of applying too much coercion in rent collection. Thus the very same low population density that made Changzhou and Zhejiang landlords so vulnerable to tenant claims also made tenants less likely to engage in collective action to press those claims.

Suzhou Prefecture

Just as the absence of tenant collective actions in Changzhou and northern Zhejiang in the late nineteenth century can be linked to the weakness of the local landlords, so their increase in Suzhou can be attributed to the relative strength of the landlords there. The elite landlord families of Suzhou city and its environs came out of the Taiping wars in much better shape than their counterparts in the more heavily contested areas of the lower Yangzi valley. Those who had not sought refuge in Shanghai or places north of the river had found some protection in the territories under the control of Xu Peiyuan and Fei Yucheng in Changzhou and Yuanhe. However much these families may have suffered financially and emotionally during the rebellion, they at least survived with their lives and property claims intact.[73] They were therefore able to regain their footing relatively easily and quickly. But it was not all that secure a footing, confronted as they were by continuing widespread tenant default.[74]

The elite and local officials in the suburban Suzhou counties (Wu, Changzhou, and Yuanhe) were clearly aware that a simple restoration of the old rural order would not suffice to quell tenant disobedience or prevent the recurrence of a catastrophe of the magnitude of the Taiping Rebellion. Their efforts to impose a new sort of order on the countryside transformed the relationship among the state, landlords, and tenants in this area of Jiangnan. This transformation involved three distinct but very much interrelated trends. First, the local government began to involve itself much more directly in setting and collecting rents. Second, Suzhou landlords, acting out of a heightened sense of shared interests, mobilized their resources to establish rent collection agencies and to regulate the level of rent. Third, at least in part because of these two developments, the suburban Suzhou counties experienced a dramatic increase in the frequency of tenant collective action.

Increasing government intervention in the landlord–tenant relationship in Suzhou was manifested immediately after the rebellion in what Feng Guifen called "the final task of tax reduction," a permanent decrease in rents.[75] In the fall of 1866 the Jiangsu financial commissioner, responding to the petition of Feng and other upper gentrymen of Suzhou city, ordered landlords in Wu, Yuanhe, and Changzhou to reduce rents permanently. In the Feng proposal rents equal to or less than one shi per mu were to be reduced by 2 percent; for higher rents, the one-shi portion was to be lowered by 2 percent and the rest was to be cut by half. Thus a rent of 1.3 shi would be lowered to 1.13 shi (0.98 + 0.15). No rent could exceed 1.2 shi, which meant that any amount above 1.44 had to be slashed to that level.[76] Soon after the Feng plan was adopted in the suburban counties, authorities ordered similar reductions in Wujiang, Kunshan, and Xinyang, also in Suzhou Prefecture.[77] Once these regulations were promulgated, landlords in the six counties were legally bound to reduce rents and were subject to official punishment if they did not comply.

Whether and to what extent landlords in these locales followed the new rent law is difficult to assess. No evidence on the fate of the reform in Wujiang, Kunshan, and Xinyang has come to light. The historical record for Wu, Changzhou, and Yuanhe is more helpful, but not all that one could desire, either. Large landlords and bursaries there did implement a reduction, but whether it was anything more than a reduction on paper is open to question because of the distinction between nominal and real rents. In his polemic *The Investigation of Rent* (1884), the Yuanhe landlord Tao Xu accused the Suzhou city landlords of applying the government-decreed reduction to nominal rents only, a move that narrowed the gap between nominal and actual rents but did not decrease the amounts tenants had to pay.[78]

Although some landlords no doubt resorted to this subterfuge, others carried out the reduction in spirit and not merely in form. Rental contracts and registers of large landlords and bursaries, for example, sometimes preface the amount of rent with the phrase "reduced actual rent" (*jian shizumi*), indicating that a reduction was undertaken in the real and not just in the nominal rent.[79] Bursary registers in particular are valuable aids in assessing the fate of the reform, since they deal in actual rents, recording the amount collected and the amount still owing for different plots of land. In their studies of the records of two Suzhou bursaries, Natsui Haruki and Frank Lojewski have discovered that rents were lowered on the bursary-managed land by some 2 to 15 percent. Natsui has further calculated that, on average, rent reduction consumed 60 percent of the savings that a landlord earned through the tax reforms.[80] The Tongzhi rent reduction thus broke with the precedent established in the eighteenth century by which the benefits of tax remissions were to be divided thirty-seventy between tenant and landlord.

Considering how much decreased rents offset the gains from the tax measures and how easily the regulations could be circumvented by simply lowering the nominal rate, some may find it surprising that any landlords would effect a genuine reduction. In the circumstances of 1866, however, a permanent rent reduction was not so unthinkable as it would have been half a century earlier. Landlords, after all, had not received the full amounts of actual rents since at least 1860, if not earlier. The resumption of regular tax and rent collection in 1865 had not resulted in any appreciable increase in their income because of a continuing disinclination among tenants to honor their debts, a disinclination no doubt bolstered by the belief that they should share some of the benefits of the tax reduction. In 1865, for instance, the bursary of a Suzhou family surnamed Shen collected only 10 percent of the rent due on seventy-five mu it managed in a polder in Changzhou County.[81] So even with an actual reduction, landlords might receive more income from their land than they had received in the recent past. Moreover, although there had not been as great a loss of life in the three Suzhou counties as in other parts of Jiangnan, labor was still in short supply immediately after the rebellion. To keep cultivators working their land, the landlords may have felt that a reduction in rent was necessary.

Fear of official reprisal appears not to have been a major concern. There is, at any rate, only one recorded case of a landowner being brought to legal account for failure to follow the rent law. Xu Peirui, a younger brother of Xu Peiyuan and the head of the family after Peiyuan's death in 1863, was fined 2,000 strings of copper *cash* (roughly the equivalent in 1866 of 1,300 taels) for allegedly failing to reduce the rent on 1,000 mu of land he managed for his nine-year-old grandnephew. In levying this fine, the government acted not on its own initiative but at the urging of a group of urban Suzhou gentrymen, among them Feng Guifen. As Xu Peirui interpreted the matter, the gentrymen's attack was not so much an effort to enforce the rent reduction as an attempt to undercut his family's influence and to avenge his brother Peiyuan's confiscation of their rents during the Taiping occupation.* Aside from this ambiguous case, there is no evidence to suggest that the Suzhou government enforced the permanent reduction with the same vigor and the same outpouring of resources it brought to bear in the collection of rent.

Still, even a weak effort represented a departure from the government's past attitude toward the landlord-tenant relationship. Before the Taiping rebellion the Qing state, while quick to support landlords in their claims on tenants, was reluctant to infringe on their rights to conduct their dealings as they saw fit. Even as tenant obligations to landlords entered the

---

*The misunderstanding, Xu Peirui claimed, arose from the fact that he had issued payment notices to the tenants of this land before the reduction was announced. When it came time to collect rents, he had actually given the peasants a larger discount than the official regulations called for. His foes among the Suzhou gentry had taken the rent notices as evidence of his failure to comply with the new regulations. For Xu's correspondence on this dispute, see "Shuangli bian," *Jindaishi ziliao,* 34 (1964), 100–105.

realm of public policy, the treatment of tenants remained largely a private matter, one not subject to official legislation. The blow dealt to the rural order by tenants and Taipings in the mid-nineteenth century forced the state to recognize that, for that order to survive, the autonomy of individual landlords would have to be curtailed, by government decree if necessary. This recognition was shared by those large gentry landlords who had proposed the permanent rent reduction in the first place.

Another development that gave the rural order in Suzhou a different character now was the kind of heightened sense of landlord collectivity expressed in the growth of bursaries (*zuzhan*) and lineage charitable estates (*yizhuang*). Unalike as these institutions were in many respects, they served landlords in a similar fashion. With the resources of many proprietors to draw on, they were able to support legions of private rent dunners and to command ready official assistance for rent collection and the suppression of tenant resistance. These institutions were thus particularly important for smaller-scale landlords who did not have the clout to secure government help on their own.

As the dominant collective landlord force in rural society in Wu, Changzhou, and Yuanhe after the rebellion, bursaries were once thought to have been purely products of the postbellum era in Suzhou. But as the work of Natsui Haruki has demonstrated, some existed at least a decade before the Taipings conquered Jiangnan,[82] and others got their start during the occupation as refugee landowners entrusted the management of their property to friends and relatives remaining at home. Located in Suzhou city and the larger market towns of the three suburban counties and owned primarily by degree-holding landlords, the bursaries managed the land of others on commission. The services they rendered encompassed all aspects of landownership and land rental: signing on and dismissing tenants, determining levels of rent, rent collection itself, land purchases and sales, the payment of taxes, and all the bookkeeping these myriad tasks entailed. Since most bursary owners, as degree-holders, were classified as large households (*dahu*), they were able to extend to their clients substantial tax breaks through proxy remittance. And as the caretakers of significant amounts of property, they enjoyed a special relationship with local officials, who made yamen personnel available to them for dunning and who consulted with them regularly about matters pertaining to landownership and rental.

Unlike bursaries, whose sole purpose was the management of landlord land, the charitable estate, as we have seen, consisted of corporate land, the income from which was used to support lineage activities such as relief to needy members, subsidies to promising male students, and the maintenance of the ancestral hall. Ever since the founding of the Fan estate in the eleventh century, charitable estates had been a legitimate and officially sanctioned way for lineages to reinforce their own cohesion and their position in the community. But like bursaries, they flourished in the late Qing, as elite lineages, taking advantage of the greater availability of land, sought to reassert themselves after the devastation of the Taiping years. In Suzhou Prefecture alone at least eighty-eight estates were founded after 1864. Each typically had 500 to 1,000 mu of land, and each, as a charity, received special tax considerations from the government.[83]

But in fact these estates were more than charitable enterprises, performing certain bursary-like functions for lineage members. A branch family, under the guise of donating land to the main line's charitable estate, would in reality merely entrust its management to the estate personnel. The rental income remaining after the payment of taxes reverted not to the estate but to the branch family for private use. This arrangement gave the landlords of a lineage the same rent collection and tax benefits that the bursaries provided their clients.[84]

The bursaries and charitable estates of Suzhou, far from inhibiting rent resistance as they were designed to do, tended to foster it. Certain practices in particular sparked frequent and vehement protest. For one, the rent collectors did not hesitate to use physical intimidation and violence. When official and private dunners, called "Uncle Chicken-catchers" (*zhuoji dashu*) by the local peasantry, went to the countryside to press for the payment of rents in arrears, they readily and illegally resorted to brute force if persuasion failed, sometimes bringing on the death or suicide of a beleaguered tenant.[85] When a landlord requested the detention of a delinquent peasant, he purchased from the prison guards the type of beating the inmate was to endure. The array of choices included "one beating every five days" (*wuri yibi*), "one beating every three days" (*sanri yibi*), and "blood beating" (*xiebi*), in which the peasant was lashed with a bamboo cane until his blood started to flow.[86] The severity of the punishment meted out to tenants in Suzhou so frequently exceeded the one session of eighty strokes permitted by law that the Jiangsu provincial government felt obliged to issue several regulations reiterating the legal limit.[87]

Ironically, the chronic default that landlords cited as justification for this harsh treatment stemmed in part from the particular form of rent payment they demanded of their cultivators. By the 1870's commuted rents (*zhezu*, rent stipulated in kind but paid in currency) had replaced the delivery of grain as the preferred method of collection among the bursaries, charitable estates, and wealthy individual landlords in Suzhou city and its environs.[88] The increasing popularity of commuted rents can be attributed to a number of different factors. In the first place, they were encouraged by the government-decreed rent reduction of 1866. By switching from payment in kind to payment in cash, a landlord could comply outwardly with the official regulations, while ensuring that his income suffered no real decline by setting the conversion rate at a high enough level to compensate for his lowered fixed rent. They were also encouraged by the expansion of co-ownership in Suzhou after the Taiping Rebellion. Given the difficulty of raising the fixed rents of topsoil holders, the only way a landlord–subsoil owner could increase his take from the land was by requiring payment in currency. Declining grain prices in the late 1870's and early 1880's further encouraged the adoption of zhezu collection, since with this method a landlord could keep his commutation rate (in effect, *his* rice price) artificially high and shift the financial loss to his tenants.

Finally, this trend was related to another that we will take up in some detail later in the chapter: the commutation of tribute tax payments. In the post–rebellion period the government increasingly collected the tribute tax in currency. With commuted rents, landlords were spared the trouble of marketing an in-kind payment to raise the money for the tribute tax. Moreover, by collecting rents in cash at conversion rates higher than the prevailing prices, they were able to protect themselves from the post-harvest dip in grain prices.

Suzhou landlords, making the most of the flexibility of commuted rents, typically set the conversion rates at levels at least 10 to 20 percent and sometimes as much as 60 to 70 percent above the current price of rice, thereby effectively raising rents by corresponding amounts.[89] Such large gaps between market prices and rental commutation rates ran directly counter to customary norms, and landlords came under harsh criticism for their insensitivity to the tenantry's economic difficulties.[90] The Suzhou landlords defended their actions by pointing to the even larger gap between market prices and the tribute tax conversion rates.[91] It was not an empty argument. In 1879, for instance, when the Jiangsu tribute conversion rate was 118 to 135 percent higher than the prevailing rice prices in the Suzhou market, the rental commutation rates charged by the Suzhou bursaries were only 39 to 50 percent higher. Later years likewise show a significant disparity: 110 percent vs. 34 percent in 1880, 106 percent vs. 35 percent in 1900, and 124 to 169 percent vs. 47 to 77 percent in 1904.[92] When deciding on the rental conversion rate, therefore, Suzhou landlords considered not only rice prices but also the tribute conversion rate. Commuted rents provided landlords with a way to pass on more of the tax burden to their tenant cultivators.

Tenants felt the baneful effect of zhezu payment most acutely in years of good harvest, when the profits they might have gained from higher yields were offset by unusually low post-harvest prices and the consequent need to sell more rice than usual to acquire the money to pay rent. In the autumn of 1878, for example, an exceptionally bountiful harvest in

TABLE 4.1
Currency Exchange Rates, Rice Prices, and Suzhou Rental
Commutation Rates, 1872–1909
(Index: 1892–96 = 100)

Category	1872–1876	1877–1881	1882–1886	1887–1891	1892–1896	1897–1901	1902–1906	1907–1909
Values								
Exchange rate[a]	1,212	1,141	1,149	1,087	1,065	927	902	936
Rice price[b]								
Yuan	2.91	3.27	3.08	3.17	3.64	4.91	5.72	6.73
Cash	3,530	3,727	3,535	3,449	3,843	4,558	5,168	6,316
Rental zhejia[c]								
Yuan	1.85	2.00	1.96	—	1.96	3.23	3.67	5.59
Cash	2,243	2,280	2,250	—	2,151	3,011	3,318	5,212
Index								
Exchange rate[a]	114	107	108	102	100	87	85	88
Rice price[b]								
Yuan	80	90	85	87	100	135	157	185
Cash	92	97	92	90	100	119	134	164
Rental zhejia[c]								
Yuan	94	102	100	—	100	165	187	285
Cash	104	106	105	—	100	140	154	242

SOURCE: Table B.3.

NOTE: The values in this table and those that follow are period averages.

[a] Cash per yuan.

[b] Price per shi.

[c] Conversion rate per shi of rent.

Suzhou drove the price of rice down to a mere 1.5 to 1.6 yuan of foreign silver per shi; at the current exchange rate, this amounted to only 1,500–1,600 cash. Since the conversion rates set by landlords that year ranged from 2,500 to 2,800 cash per shi, tenants had to market 56 to 87 percent more rice than the fixed amount in kind to raise the cash for their rents. In these circumstances, which peasants called "a good harvest turned poor" (shuhuang), it was to the cultivator's advantage to delay paying rent until the price of rice rose.[93]

Newspaper accounts and Suzhou bursary records demonstrate that the gap between rice prices and commutation rates, always present, widened in the last years of the Qing, producing an increase in real rent. Table 4.1 shows that fluctuations in the conversion rates expressed in copper cash stayed more or less on course with changes in the cash price of rice through 1896. In the next thirteen years the rental rates in cash rose 2.42 times, while the price of rice in cash went up only 1.64 times. Rents in real terms thus climbed 48 percent (2.42 ÷ 1.64).

This rent hike, however, applied only to those increasingly few tenants still able to sell their crop for copper cash. Many peasants were paid in foreign silver, which had emerged as an important medium of exchange in the Jiangnan marketplace after the Taiping Rebellion. Landlords were willing enough to accept the silver currency but persisted in expressing the commutation rate in *cash*. Rents were thus affected not only by the discrepancy between commutation rates and rice prices, but also by fluctuations in the values of the two currencies.[94] Between 1872–76 and 1902–6 the value of foreign silver relative to copper *cash* dropped 25 percent as the worldwide slide in the silver market made itself felt in China (Table 4.1). This meant that tenants had to sell a larger portion of their crop to obtain the silver equivalent of the copper amount specified in the zhezu rates. Between 1892–96 and 1907–9 commuted rents paid in silver went up 2.85 times, yet the price of rice in silver rose only 1.85 times. As a result commuted rents in silver underwent a greater real increase in the last years of the Qing than commuted rents in copper—54 percent as opposed to 48 percent.

As the discrepancy between market prices and conversion rates grew, so did the number of rent defaults, periodically prompting the larger and more politically influential Suzhou landlords and bursary owners to ask provincial and county officials to intervene and impose a ceiling on commuted rents. The official rates, though usually set above the prevailing market prices for rice, were still considerably lower than those charged by some landlords. During years of poor harvest the county magistrates or the Suzhou prefect, again at the behest of the Suzhou gentry, took the additional step of ordering landlords to lower rents even further.[95] As with the 1866 rent reduction campaign, the government did not follow through in its enforcement of these orders, but what is significant here is that local officials had now begun to perceive the regulation of tenant rents as part of their administrative duties.

Their freedom of action, however, was circumscribed by the wishes of the large Suzhou gentry households. In their collective effort to stabilize rural society after the turmoils of the Taiping occupation, wealthy Suzhou landholders were quick to use the influence and resources of the state to back the collection of rents and to restrain their immoderate peers, but less amenable to any official initiative that might undermine their own control of their land and tenants.

The state's limited ability to mandate changes in the landlord-tenant relationship in Suzhou was best demonstrated in a heated dispute between local officials and a number of large landlord families in the winter of 1880–81. The magistrates of Changzhou, Yuanhe, and Wu counties proposed to their superiors that all rents for land owned by landlords residing in the city be collected by the jingzao, the precinct functionary who assisted yamen personnel in land registration and tax and rent prompting. The urban landlords, the magistrates argued, relied so heavily on official assistance in dunning that government personnel might as well assume responsibility for collection as well. So bold a move would also serve to mitigate the harsh treatment that peasants suffered at the hands of the urban landlords who, the officials stated, displayed much less sympathy for cultivators than their rural counterparts.

No sooner had this proposal reached the provincial government than some twenty urban landlords fired off a petition of their own. Mincing few words, they refuted the charges leveled against them, condemned rural landlords for *their* callousness toward tenants, and pointed out in great detail the infeasibility of the magistrates' suggestion. Victory was theirs in the end, for the provincial government did not approve the plan.[96]

Throughout this acrimonious dispute not a single word was written about its true cause. The magistrates of Changzhou, Yuanhe, and Wu may well have been sincere in their desire to improve the lot of the tenantry, but their pronouncements on this score seem forced, and conveniently overlook the fact that their county administrations willingly and profitably participated in the harsh rent collection that they now deeply deplored. The real purpose behind their proposal was to clamp down on the land tax evasion at which the large Suzhou landlords were so adept. Just like the Taipings and their collection bureaus, the magistrates hoped to ensure the payment of taxes through the simple expedient of having rents pass through official hands first. What remained after the government had taken its share would be handed over to the landlords. For Suzhou families that had endured this arrangement during the Taiping Rebellion and that remembered well the inroads it had made on their rental income, such a prospect was a frightening one indeed. They marshaled as many arguments as they could against the proposal, short of baldly admitting their concern about being forced to pay more in taxes.

The dispute of 1880–81 spotlights the fundamental conflict of interest between landlords and state officials in the matter of rent collection. The state assisted landlords in rent dunning primarily out of concern for land taxation; landlords had to be assured of rent so that they could pay tax. When all went well, when officials found the level of payment to be at least satisfactory, then the fundamental conflict of interest rarely manifested itself. But when the government found the landlords' level of payment inadequate, it considered collecting taxes from tenants directly, thereby asserting the primacy of tax over rent and placing itself in more direct competition with landlords over the cultivator's product. Unable to prevent this during the Taiping occupation, the large Suzhou landlords now had the political clout to block such a measure, and the magistrates of the suburban counties again concentrated on helping landlords in rent dunning as a way to improve tax collection.

Beginning in 1886 this state assistance assumed a new form with the establishment of rent-dunning bureaus (*zhuizuju*). Like their precursors of 1864, they also served as tenant debtor prisons. Every autumn after the thirty-day rent payment period had passed, bursary managers and large landlords of Suzhou petitioned the prefect to set up these bureaus at the principal city temple, the Xuanmiaoguan, and in the larger market towns in the suburbs. Upon the receipt of the names of tenants in arrears and the appropriate fee (1,500 *cash* per tenant in 1886), the yamen personnel in charge of the bureaus would dispatch dunners to the countryside to press for payment. Should the rent not be forthcoming, the errant tenant could be arrested, taken to the bureau, flogged, and then put in a cangue. In some years during the last several decades of the Qing, some forty to a hundred peasants a day were reportedly "processed" this way at the main bureau in the Xuanmiaoguan.[97] The tenant remained imprisoned until the rent was paid or until the bureaus were shut down at the beginning of the agricultural busy season in the fourth month of the following year.

Rent-dunning bureaus represented the extreme form of a development that became increasingly evident in the post-Taiping period: the separation of the prosecution of defaulting tenants from the regular judicial system. Before the Taiping Rebellion landlords had been required to proceed through the expensive process of litigation to secure the official incarceration and punishment of tenants. Now, through the services provided by the dunning agencies, landlords were able to circumvent the courts entirely. Tao Xu lamented in his *Investigation of Rent* that of all those accused of crimes, "be it rebellion or moral depravity," only tenants were denied the chance to refute the charges against them in a magistrate's court.[98] To simplify the procedure even further, bursaries, charitable estates, and the larger individual landlords of Suzhou were allowed to keep a supply of official arrest warrants on hand and to submit the filled-in forms directly to the bureau, thus eliminating even the need to file formal complaints at the yamen.[99]

Between them, the state and the landlords' own institutions, the bursaries and charitable estates, produced a rural order in Suzhou that was superficially stronger but fundamentally weaker than the antebellum order. It was superficially stronger because rent collection and dunning had become more systematic and efficient. But in fact this very efficiency and the brute force on which it ultimately depended further loosened the already faltering bonds between landlord and tenant. The growing recourse to sheer physical coercion indicates that the ideological norms underpinning rent relations had lost their persuasiveness; no longer could Suzhou landlords rely on appeals to Confucian ethics to compel tenants to fulfill their obligations. In the short run the brutal efficiency of the rent collection apparatus no doubt discouraged many would-be defaulters, but in the long run it only served to encourage an escalation in open class conflict in Wu, Yuanhe, and Changzhou. Though landlords in these counties had been plagued by a widespread peasant disinclination to pay rent in the 1840's and 1850's, they had not been the targets of tenant uprisings. Indeed, none of the twenty-eight recorded collective actions against rent in these two decades took place there. After the Taiping Rebellion the situation reversed itself, and between 1873 and 1912 more cases of collective action against rents occurred in the three suburban Suzhou counties than in any other single place in the region (see Table A.2).

The lower Yangzi valley as a whole experienced a dramatic upsurge in tenant protest in the last decade of the Qing in response to rising levels of rents, frequent natural disasters, and the general turmoil surrounding the overthrow of the dynasty. From 1902 through the winter of 1911–12, twenty-four collective actions aimed explicitly at rents (along with tax resistance in three cases) took place, compared with three in 1873–81, six in 1882–91, and five in 1892–1901 (Table A.2).* The "high tide of rent resistance," as contemporaries called it, began in 1907 in several counties in Jiaxing Prefecture and reached its peak in the autumn and winter of 1911–12, when massive flooding and the 1911 Revolution plunged the region into chaos. The wave of tenant protest then inundated nearly every corner of Jiangnan. In Kunshan County more than 130 villages united in a collective resistance to rent collection. Thousands of peasants in Shimen and Haiyan counties in Jiaxing violently refused to pay rents on the grounds that their landlords had received tax remissions because of the flooding. And in Tonglizhen (Wujiang) tenants demanded that their landlords hand over the title deeds to the land, insisting that "a change in dynasties" meant a transfer in landownership.[100] To contemporaries the rent struggles of 1911–12 so resembled the tenant protest of the Taiping period in frequency and intensity that they referred to them as the "resurrection of the Heavenly King Hong Xiuquan."[101]

LAND TAXATION

Like tenant collective actions against rents, landowner protest against land taxation intensified greatly in the last decade of the Qing. There were fifty-one actions against taxes (including the three cases of joint tax-rent protest) from 1902 through the winter of 1911–12, against only four in 1873–81, two in 1882–91, and two in 1892–1901 (Table A.2).† The 1863 land tax reform, it seems, was largely successful in its goal of easing

---

*These figures do not include collective appeals to officials for harvest investigation (*baohuang*) in which the goal of the appeal is not specified in the sources. If we assume that a reduction in rents was an aim of these incidents, then the figures would rise to four for the period 1873–81, twelve for 1882–91, five for 1892–1901, and thirty-five for 1902–11.

†If tax reductions were a goal of appeals for an investigation of the harvest, there would have been five tax protests in the years 1873–81, eight in 1882–91, two in 1892–1901, and sixty-two in 1902–11.

the burden on Jiangnan landowners—at least until the turn of the century. Then, as we will shortly see, a combination of factors—a widening gap between conversion rates and rice and currency prices, changes in the relative value of silver and copper, and the imposition of new surcharges and levies—brought about a round of tax hikes and an escalation in landowner collective action.

The Land Tax Burden

Before assessing the effects of the Tongzhi tax reform in more detail, let us briefly review its major components. The reform, first of all, called for a permanent reduction in the tribute tax by one-third in the Suzhou-Songjiang-Taicang circuit, by one-tenth in Changzhou Prefecture, and by eight-thirtieths in the Hangzhou-Jiaxing-Huzhou circuit. It also called for a decrease in surcharges and more equitable tax conversion rates. To ensure compliance with these regulations, as well as uniformity from county to county, the responsibility for determining surcharges and conversion rates was to shift from the local to the provincial government. Finally, the reform called for the abolition of proxy remittance and differential rates of payment for gentry and commoner households.

Differential rates and proxy remittance. It was on this last point that the Tongzhi tax reform first foundered. The regressive distinction between large and small households proved to be as difficult to eliminate in the post-Taiping period as it had been in the past, and gentry landowners continued to receive special consideration. In Changshu and Zhaowen local officials exempted large households from the 1,000-*cash* "public expenses" (*gongfei*) portion of the tribute tax, and in the suburban counties of Suzhou city large households paid their tax at a "short" conversion rate some 30 to 40 percent lower than the commoners' "long" rate.[102] In other counties gentry families were granted the privilege of paying the diding in taels of Chinese silver, a privilege that relieved them of the increases built into the copper *cash*–Chinese tael and copper *cash*–foreign silver conversion rates.[103] And everywhere yamen clerks and runners still conducted a flourishing business of "selling disaster" (*maihuang*) to gentry households.[104]

The survival of the large-small household distinction ensured the survival of proxy remittance. In the post-Taiping period the practice was particularly prevalent in the suburban counties of Suzhou city, where the relationship between proxy remitters and small and medium-scale landlords had become institutionalized in the bursary system.[105] As the following account from a late Qing newspaper makes clear, tax evasion was a major incentive for consigning the management of rental property to a bursary:

TABLE 4.2

Currency Exchange Rates and Diding Conversion Rates in
Southeastern Jiangsu, 1879–1909

Period	Exchange rate		Diding rate	
	Cash per tael	Index	*Cash* per tael	Index
1879–1881	1,601	100	2,200	100
1882–1886	1,608	100	2,200	100
1887–1891	1,521	95	2,200	100
1892–1896	1,491	93	2,160	98
1897–1901	1,298	81	2,000	91
1902–1906	1,262	79	2,240	102
1907–1909	1,311	82	2,400	109

SOURCES: Wang Yeh-chien, *Land Taxation*, pp. 118–19; *Chuanshaxian zhi*, 8: 23a–24b.

TABLE 4.3

Rice Prices and Tribute Grain Conversion Rates in
Southeastern Jiangsu, 1879–1909

Period	Rice price		Tribute rate	
	Cash per shi	Index	*Cash* per shi	Index
1879–1881	3,422	100	3,285	100
1882–1886	3,535	103	3,432	104
1887–1891	3,449	101	3,392	103
1892–1896	3,843	112	3,752	114
1897–1901	4,558	133	4,132	126
1902–1906	5,168	151	4,912	150
1907–1909	6,316	185	6,852	209

SOURCES: Zou Dafan et al., pp. 235–36; *Chuanshaxian zhi*, 8: 22b–24b.

Among the landlord families of Suzhou city, there have always been those called *guanye* and those called *ziye*. Large households are the *guanye*, and small households the *ziye*. The *ziye* pay their taxes in full, not daring to default even a little bit. The *guanye* do not attend to their land personally, but leave everything up to their accountants, who engage in all sorts of financial trickery. For this reason much of the tax owed by the *guanye* falls into arrears. It now has gotten to the point that the *ziye* are enlisting their property under the names of the *guanye*. This is called "entrusting land to a bursary" [*jizhan*].[106]

Tax conversion rates.   The record on other aspects of the tax reform is more mixed. Provincial determination of the diding and tribute conversion rates seems to have resulted in greater uniformity among counties, at least in southeastern Jiangsu. Moreover, as Tables 4.2 and 4.3 demonstrate, until the turn of the century the provincial rates in southeastern Jiangsu closely followed fluctuations in the price of rice and in the copper-silver exchange rate. Then, as the state grew ever more desperate for revenue, the diding conversion rate no longer adhered as much to changing currency values, and at the close of the decade the tribute conversion rate was climbing at a faster pace than the price of rice. The growing gap between the conversion rates on the one hand and the price of rice and the copper-silver exchange rate on the other brought about automatic increases in a landowner's tax bill.

Such divergences had contributed to the sharp rise in the tax burden in Jiangnan in the 1840's and 1850's, but their impact was even greater now because of an increasing commutation of tribute payments. In theory landowners were to decide whether to deliver their tribute in kind or in currency, but in practice that decision was often made by local officials, who preferred payment in currency for its convenience. By the early twentieth century most, if not all, of Jiangnan's tribute was collected in money, which officials then used to buy rice to transport up the coast to Beijing.[107] Compulsory commutation meant that few Jiangnan landowners could escape the hikes built into the tribute conversion rate by paying the tax in kind. Furthermore, the need to market more rice to pay their tax drew them even more fully into the commercial economy, making them that much more vulnerable to price movements and currency fluctuations.

On top of this, landowners were now saddled with yet another official rate, one that came into being in response to the increasing use of foreign silver in the post-Taiping period.[108] Local officials permitted payment of taxes in this currency, but in computing the amount a landowner owed, they did not convert tax taels and tax shi directly into foreign silver. Instead, they took the conversion rates in copper *cash* and changed them into foreign silver at an exchange rate they themselves set. Though their *cash*–foreign silver rates paralleled the changing values of these currencies over time, the rate in any given year tended to be lower than the market rate by as much as 100 *cash*.[109] This manipulation of rates inflated the amount a landowner owed in silver currency and, not incidentally, added much-needed revenue to county coffers. For example, a landowner whose total tax was 500 copper *cash* in 1880 would owe the government 0.434 yuan at the market rate of 1,152 *cash* per yuan, but 0.454 yuan (a 4 percent increase) if the magistrate set the rate 50 *cash* lower, and 0.475 yuan (a 9 percent increase) if he set the rate 100 *cash* lower.

Currency fluctuations.   In the last several decades of the nineteenth century, taxpayers, like rentpayers, were hard hit by the severe depreciation in the value of silver. Since the conversion rates for both the diding and tribute tax were quoted in standard copper *cash*, the devaluation of silver meant that landowners who received foreign silver for the sale of their products had to render ever-larger amounts of that currency to the government as tax. Thus, in absolute terms, the increase in taxes in silver was substantially greater than the increase in taxes in copper during this time. Between the years 1879–81 and 1902–6, for example, the land tax in Chuansha County rose 61 percent in silver but only 27 percent in copper (see Tables 4.4 and 4.5).

In view of the seemingly obvious disadvantage of paying taxes in foreign silver, why would any landowner elect to do so? The decision was not always his to make. As noted above, local governments stood to make a tidy profit by setting the official *cash*–foreign silver exchange rate below the market rate. In some counties, therefore, local officials expressly forbade payment in copper. More important, the type of copper currency that officials were willing to accept, standard *cash* (*zhiqian*), was being eased out of circulation by debased coins 10 to 30 percent lower in value. Landowners who received the substandard coins for the sale of their goods had to convert them into the dearer standard *cash* at a moneychanger's shop at a substantial loss. So paying in copper was not necessarily more advantageous than paying in silver.[110]

The problem of debased copper currency became particularly acute after the turn of the century, with the appearance of massive quantities of newly minted ten-*cash* coins, the real value of which was 8 to 22 percent lower than standard *cash*. Issued by the government in part to deal with the silver deflation and the scarcity of copper currency, the new coins in the end did much more than was bargained for, leading to a severe depreciation in the value of copper currency and a rampant inflation in the copper prices of commodities from about 1903 on. By 1910 Gresham's law had taken effect, and the new debased coinage had all but driven standard *cash* out of circulation. For landowners every percentage difference between the standard copper currency and the new coinage automatically produced a commensurate tax increase, since officials not only continued to express conversion rates in standard *cash* but, for a time at least, would not even accept payment in the debased currency. Conflicts between landowners and local officials over the form of copper payment eventually led the Jiangsu provincial government in 1906 to permit the delivery of 30 percent of the land tax in the new ten-*cash* coins.[111] But this concession was of only marginal benefit to landowners, who still had to convert the ten-*cash* coins into standard currency to cover 70 percent of their tax. As a result, the depreciation of copper currency alone inflated their tax bills by 8 percent in 1906, 6 percent in 1907, and 20 percent in both 1908 and 1909 (see Table B.2).

New surcharges and levies.   Compounding the taxpayer's woes in the first decade of the twentieth century was the collection of additional surcharges (expressed as so many *cash* per tael of diding and so many *cash* per shi of tribute) and land levies (expressed as so many *cash* per mu). For

TABLE 4.4
Rice and Cotton Prices and Land Taxes in Jiangnan, 1879–1909

Category	1879–1881	1882–1886	1887–1891	1892–1896	1897–1901	1902–1906	1907–1909
Prices							
Rice[a]							
Yuan	2.99	3.08	3.17	3.64	4.91	5.72	6.73
Cash	3,422	3,535	3,449	3,843	4,558	5,168	6,316
Cotton[b]							
Taels	9.97	10.94	10.38	11.02	13.92	17.00	18.97
Cash	15,954	17,594	15,792	16,392	18,053	21,393	24,834
Land taxes[c]							
Chuansha							
Yuan	.44	.45	.46	.51	.58	.71	.87
Cash	503	511	496	538	540	639	811
						(650)	(941)
Jiading							
Yuan	—	—	.40	.41	.45	.52	.60
Cash	—	—	436	433	421	470	563
						(478)	(651)
Wu							
Yuan	—	—	—	.46	.67	.82	1.08
Cash	—	—	—	502	624	738	1,007
						(751)	(1,164)

SOURCE: Table B.2; Wang Yeh-chien, *Land Taxation*, pp. 118–19.

NOTE: The figures in parentheses represent the tax when the landowner paid 30 percent in debased 10-*cash* coins and 70 percent in standard *cash*.

[a] Price per shi.

[b] Price per picul.

[c] Tax per mu.

Jiangnan landowners the largest of these supplementary imposts began in 1902, when the Jiangsu and Zhejiang governments added 200 and 300 *cash*, respectively, to the diding to raise their share of the staggering 450,000,000-tael indemnity that the foreign powers had imposed on China in the harsh settlement following the Boxer Uprising of 1900.[112]

Other surcharges and fees were levied to pay for the dynasty's sweeping modernization efforts known collectively as the New Policies (Xin-zheng). In the course of this program, launched by imperial decree in 1902, the civil service system was abolished, and a modern educational system established; military forces and military training were restructured along Western lines; a modern police force came into being; and elective assemblies were set up at the county, provincial, and national levels. With these bold measures, the Qing court hoped to placate popular opposition to its rule, as well as to strengthen and expand the state's control over local society. As elsewhere in China, county governments in the lower Yangzi region financed the reforms primarily through supple-

TABLE 4.5

Index of Rice and Cotton Prices and Land Taxes in Jiangnan, 1879–1909

(1892–96 = 100)

Category	1879–1881	1882–1886	1887–1891	1892–1896	1897–1901	1902–1906	1907–1909
Prices							
Rice							
Yuan	82	85	87	100	135	157	185
Cash	89	92	90	100	119	134	164
Cotton							
Taels	90	99	94	100	126	154	172
Cash	97	107	96	100	110	131	152
Land taxes							
Chuansha							
Yuan	86	88	90	100	114	139	171
Cash	93	95	92	100	100	119	151
						(121)	(175)
Jiading							
Yuan	—	—	98	100	110	127	146
Cash	—	—	101	100	97	109	130
						(110)	(150)
Wu							
Yuan	—	—	—	100	146	178	235
Cash	—	—	—	100	124	147	201
						(150)	(232)

NOTE: The figures in parentheses represent the tax when the landowner paid 30 percent in debased 10-*cash* coins and 70 percent in standard *cash*.

mentary taxes on commerce and land. All other things being equal, the new charges raised a landowner's tax some 4 to 6 percent.[113]

Increases in the absolute tax. The multiplication of surcharges and levies, the depreciation first of silver and then of copper currency, and the upward movement of conversion rates brought about substantial absolute increases in the land tax in the last two decades of the Qing. Tables 4.4 and 4.5 chart the changes in the tax burden per mu for the most common grades of land in the Jiangsu counties of Wu, Chuansha, and Jiading. Several points deserve special mention. First, the data, though limited, suggest that land taxes did not begin to go up substantially until the early 1890's. Second, the rise in the absolute tax from that time on varied according to the type of currency a landowner used as payment. From 1892–96 to 1907–9, the years for which data on all three counties are available, taxes paid in silver and in debased copper coinage experienced roughly the same increase, with taxes paid in standard copper *cash* lagging somewhat behind. Third, while there was an absolute increase in taxes

TABLE 4.6

Percentage Changes in the Real Tax Burden in Jiangnan, 1879–1909

	Chuansha						Jiading						Wu: Rice		
	Rice			Cotton			Rice			Cotton					
	Cash			Cash			Cash			Cash			Cash		
Period	Silver	Std.	Deb'd.	Silver	Std.	Deb'd.	Silver	Std.	Deb'd.	Silver	Std.	Deb'd.	Silver	Std.	Deb'd.
1879–1881															
1882–1886	−1	−1	−1	−7	−9	−9									
1887–1891	−1	−1	−1	+7	+7	+7									
1892–1896	−3	−3	−3	+5	+6	+6	−10	−10	−10	−5	−7	−7			
1897–1901	−16	−16	−16	−9	−9	−9	−19	−19	−19	−14	−12	−12	+8	+5	+5
1902–1906	+5	+5	+7	0	0	0	−1	−1	0	−3	−4	−4	+5	+4	+6
1907–1909	+4	+3	+18	+10	+10	+27	−2	−2	+12	+3	+5	+18	+12	+11	+27
1879–1909	−12	−13	+1	+5	+3	+19	−29	−29	−18	−18	−18	−7			
1887–1909	−11	−11	+3	+5	+6	+23	−21	−21	−9	−14	−12	0			
1892–1909	−8	−9	+6	0	0	+15	−3	−3	+12	0	0	+13	+27	+21	+40
1897–1909	+9	+8	+26	+10	+10	+27							+18	+16	+34

SOURCE: Table 4.4.

NOTE: The tax divided by the price equals the tax burden in real terms, that is, the amount of grain or cotton a landowner would have to sell to obtain the currency to pay his tax. The following formula was used to arrive at the changes:

$$(\text{tax } 2 \div \text{price } 2) - (\text{tax } 1 \div \text{price } 1) \div (\text{tax } 1 \div \text{price } 1) = \text{percentage change}$$

Hence, the change in the real burden from 1879–81 to 1907–9 for Chuansha landowners who grew rice and paid their tax in silver would be calculated as:

$$(.87 \div 6.73) - (.44 \div 2.99) \div (.44 \div 2.99) = (.129 - .147) \div .147 = -12\%$$

in all three counties, the extent of the increase differed considerably: Wu County experienced the greatest rise (2.35 times in silver, 2.01 times in standard *cash*, and 2.32 times in debased *cash*), and Jiading the smallest (1.46, 1.30, and 1.50; Table 4.5).

This discrepancy cannot be explained by dissimilarities in the statutory conversion rates, since the diding rate was uniform from county to county, and the tribute rate, though exhibiting some local variation, was at least as high in Jiading as in Wu. Nor can it be attributed to substantially larger surcharges in Wu than in Chuansha and Jiading. The key difference, as Wang Yeh-chien has pointed out, was that the tribute conversion rate, being more adjustable to price inflation, increased much more than the diding rate; consequently, tax increases would be greater in a county like Wu, which had a particularly heavy tribute quota, than in counties where the diding was of proportionately greater importance.[114]

Increases in the real tax. This same local variation is also evident in changes in taxes relative to the prices of agricultural commodities. Annual fluctuations aside, rice and cotton prices rose steadily in the last three decades of the Qing. Between 1879–81 and 1907–9 rice went up 2.3 times in silver and 1.8 times in copper. Cotton prices grew at a somewhat slower rate, increasing 1.9 times in silver and 1.6 times in copper (Table 4.5). How these long-term price rises affected a taxpayer's burden depended on the county, the type of crop, and the form of payment, whether silver, standard *cash*, or debased *cash*. Table 4.6 shows that until roughly the turn of the century, taxes did not keep pace with prices, and the real burden declined in all categories except cotton land in Chuansha. Then, increases in tax began to outpace the rise in prices, and the real burden became heavier for most landowners, the sole exception being rice growers in Jiading who paid their tax in silver or standard *cash*. But here again, as might be expected from the differences in the absolute tax increases noted above, the impact was greatest in Wu County.

For all this, as Table 4.7 illustrates, these landowners still shouldered a lighter burden than their early-nineteenth-century forebears. From 1798 to 1856 the total tax (diding and tribute) a Changshu landowner owed in standard copper *cash* ranged from 942 to 2,142 a mu. After the Tongzhi reform the figure dropped to 631 *cash*. Thereafter, the rate gradually rose, to reach 1,081 *cash* by 1909, a figure that was in the neighborhood of, but still below, the amounts typical of the 1830's, 1840's, and 1850's.

The contrast between the pre-Taiping and post-Taiping burden in Changshu becomes even sharper when we take into account the simultaneous movements in rice prices. Looking again at Table 4.7, we find that in the first half of the nineteenth century, decreasing rice prices, coupled with the rise in the absolute tax, meant that a Changshu landowner had to sell 0.289 to 1.150 shi of rice per mu to cover his payment. This com-

TABLE 4.7
The Land Tax Burden in Changshu County, 1798–1909
(rates per mu of the most common grade of land)

| Year | Total tax | | Year | Total tax | |
	Cash	Shi		Cash	Shi
1798[a]	1,192	.613	1897	652	.184
1821[b]	942	.289	1898	682	.183
1828	1,218	.610	1899	682	.185
1836	1,590	.698	1900	642	.226
1845	2,142	1.150	1901	692	.235
1846	1,176	.615	1902	777	.176
1853[c]	1,733	.758	1903	777	.184
1853[c]	1,026	.443	1904	747	.227
1856	1,583	.265	1905	727	.244
1867	631	.318	1906	880	.175
1894	677	.230	1907	950	.168
1895	677	.230	1908	1,001	.232
1896	631	.122	1909	1,081	.241

SOURCES: Table 2.3; *Chuanshaxian zhi*, 8: 22b–24b; *Yinxian tongzhi, shihuo*, pp. 210–34; Wang Yeh-chien, *Land Taxation*, p. 65; Zhang Lüluan, pp. 46–52.

NOTE: For the years 1867 on, the total tax in copper *cash* was derived by multiplying the post-Tongzhi reform tribute tax quota (.1006 shi per mu) and the average qianliang quota (.127 tael of silver per mu) by their annual conversion rates. The results were then added to arrive at the total tax in *cash*. For the years 1906 on, a 75-*cash* surcharge, the average for Suzhou Prefecture, was added to both the diding and the tribute conversion rate. For the tax equivalent in rice, the total amount in *cash* was converted into yuan at the prevailing exchange rate. The tax in yuan was then divided by the local average rice price for the months of November and December, the time when landowners sold their grain to get the money to pay taxes.

[a] 1798–99.

[b] 1821–22.

[c] In 1853 the Jiangsu governor, at the urging of Feng Guifen, lowered the tribute conversion rates. The upper figure represents the pre-reform tax and the lower the post-reform tax.

pares with a range of 0.122 to 0.244 in the years 1894–1909. In fact, the rising rice market in the last decades of the Qing mitigated much of the effect of the absolute rise in the tax in copper *cash*.

Popular Resistance to Land Taxes

The landowners of southeastern Jiangsu of course compared years of recent memory, not pre-reform times, and they did not sit idly by when taxes began outstripping prices. The last ten years of the Qing (1902 through the winter of 1911–12) saw a rising tide of protest, with twenty-six collective actions against land taxation (including one incident aimed at both taxes and rents), compared with just three in the preceding thirty years (Table A.2).* At least in this region, then, the Tongzhi reform

---

*Again, if appeals for an investigation of the harvest had tax reductions as a goal, the figures would be twenty-nine for the years 1902–11 and five for the preceding thirty years.

succeeded in curbing popular protest until the last decade of the Qing.

If the volume of agitation against land taxes is a fair measure, the Tongzhi reform was less successful in northern Zhejiang, which experienced five collective actions before the turn of the century.* But in general the Tongzhi tribute tax reduction had not been as thoroughgoing in the Hang-Jia-Hu circuit of northern Zhejiang as in the Su-Song-Tai circuit of southeastern Jiangsu. Despite intense lobbying by Zhejiang officials, the court did not grant the two circuits the same reductions, setting the Hang-Jia-Hu rate at eight-thirtieths (roughly 27 percent as opposed to one-third), on the grounds that the original quota for northern Zhejiang (1,000,419 shi) was substantially smaller than the one for southeastern Jiangsu (1,458,459 shi) and thus in less need of adjustment. As a result the quota for the Su-Song-Tai circuit was slashed by 486,055 shi, against 266,766 shi for Hang-Jia-Hu.[115]

For Zhejiang landowners, the trouble started when the circuit-wide reduction was translated into reductions per mu, the figures that mattered most to them. Provincial officials in both circuits adopted the principle of proportional reduction, granting grades of land different percentage decreases according to the amount of their original quotas. But this principle was followed in a much more elaborate and ultimately much fairer way in the Su-Song-Tai circuit. There the land was divided into nine grades on the basis of the existing quotas, and progressively smaller reductions were then assigned to each grade. For example, all land carrying original tribute quotas of more than 0.2 shi per mu had their quotas lowered to 0.11 shi for a reduction of at least 45 percent. The percentage of reduction then decreased incrementally down through the other categories.[116]

In the Hang-Jia-Hu circuit land was divided into only five grades, with a 30 percent reduction for the highest grade, 25 percent for the next, and so on down the scale to 10 for the lowest grade.[117] Between the circuit-wide reductions and the different methods of translating them, many Zhejiang landowners ended up with higher tribute quotas than their neighbors to the north—for instance, 0.136 shi per mu in Jiashan County, 0.128 in Wucheng, and 0.12 in Xiushui. The highest quota in southeastern Jiangsu did not exceed 0.11 shi.[118]

The conversion rates on these quotas also tended to be much higher than the rates used in Jiangsu, at least until the turn of the century, and altogether less amenable to provincial control. In the 1870's and 1880's, for example, the tribute commutation rates for southeastern Jiangsu, fluctuating from year to year with the rise and fall in rice prices, ranged from 3,152 *cash* to 3,652 *cash* a shi. The rates in northern Zhejiang counties during that time were 1,000 to 3,000 *cash* higher, way out of line with provincial guidelines and way out of line with current rice prices.[119]

---

*Ten if appeals for an investigation of the harvest are included.

The tax burden in northern Zhejiang became only that much more onerous in the final decade of the Qing with the imposition of additional surcharges and levies, the widening gap between conversion rates and rice and currency values, and the depreciation of copper. And in northern Zhejiang as in southeastern Jiangsu, landowners responded by gathering their numbers for protest, mounting twenty-five collective actions (including two aimed at rents as well) from 1902 through the winter of 1911–12.*

Most of these actions, like most of the ones in southeastern Jiangsu, were specifically in protest of the exactions for the New Policy reforms. Fully thirty-eight of the fifty-one incidents recorded in Jiangnan in this period involved the new surcharges and levies. Although the average Jiangnan landowner escaped more lightly than taxpayers in other parts of China, the reforms still inflated his bill by some 4 to 6 percent.[120] The timing of the supplementary imposts contributed in no small measure to their unpopularity. Most were levied from 1906 on, just when Jiangnan landowners also had to contend with reduced yields brought on by a succession of natural disasters and tax conversion rates that no longer adhered much to rice prices and currency values.

As elsewhere in China, popular opposition to the reform institutions and their financing in Jiangnan tended to by-pass local governments and focus almost entirely on the elite.[121] The New Policies relied very much on the initiative of the local elite, who set up numerous new bureaus to carry out the tasks of modernization. The funding for these enterprises came from supplementary taxes on commerce as well as land, taxes the elite managers sometimes took it on themselves to collect. In the case of commercial taxes, as Susan Mann has shown, this task had been routinely farmed out to merchant organizations.[122] Consequently, gentry managers could easily slip into that role, in effect continuing a practice of long standing. But the government, seeking as always to guard its prerogatives in the domain of land taxation, expressly forbade elite managers from levying and gathering the New Policy taxes directly from landowners.[123] That was to be left to the county governments, which were to collect the money along with the regular land taxes and then disburse the funds to the appropriate reform institutions. The effort to prevent elite encroachment into land taxation was only partially successful, however. In some locales the managers of newly founded schools gathered an educational levy directly from landowners, and more commonly, self-government bureaus, in the course of taking the census in preparation for elections, collected a population levy directly from rural households.[124]

*The number of incidents would be thirty-three if appeals for harvest investigation are included.

As gentrymen came to be more closely identified with land taxation, either as collectors themselves or as the designated recipients of funds gathered through regular channels, peasant protests against taxes, which had heretofore been aimed exclusively at the state, expanded to include the elite as a target of attack. Groups of landowners, numbering anywhere from several hundred to as many as ten thousand, attacked schools, police stations, self-government bureaus, and the residences and sometimes the persons of gentry managers. The implementing of the New Policies and the resulting expansion of the elite's role in the public sphere thus introduced a distinct anti-elite element into peasant resistance to taxation in the last decade of the Qing.

LEGACIES OF THE RECONSTRUCTION ERA

The era of reconstruction left the lower Yangzi region with several enduring legacies. It bequeathed to the region the lowest land tax quotas in at least half a millennium. Although the rate of taxation did rise in the last years of the Qing, the burden was still not as heavy as it had been before the Tongzhi reform. The reduced quotas remained in force after the fall of the Qing and helped to keep the tax burden on Jiangnan landowners comparatively light throughout much of the Republican period.

Several developments during the reconstruction era also exerted a downward pressure on fixed rents in kind. In the Suzhou counties of Wu, Yuanhe, and Changzhou, the Tongzhi rent reduction decreased actual rents (shizu) by 2 to 15 percent. More generally, because possession of the topsoil usually brought the tenant a lower actual rent, the widespread expansion of co-ownership of land in the post-rebellion years resulted in a similarly widespread reduction of in-kind rents. As we shall see in the next chapter, growing state involvement in the landlord-tenant relationship in the Republican period brought conversion rates more in line with prevailing rice prices, thus also lightening the burden of those peasants who paid commuted rents. Together, the lowering of fixed rents paid in kind during the reconstruction period and the lowering of fixed rents converted to currency during the Republican era significantly decreased the level of tenant rents in Jiangnan.

Finally, there emerged during the postbellum period a new pattern of interaction among the state, landlords, and tenants, a pattern that first arose in the Suzhou suburban counties in the several decades following the rebellion and then came to dominate rural society in much of the rest of Jiangnan in the Republican period. The growing interdependence between landlords and officials in their efforts to stabilize rent relations represented the intersection of the two much broader developments of the time—the expansion of elite influence and greater state intrusiveness in local society. Through the mobilization of their collective resources, landlords became better able to get local officials to pour more money and manpower into the collection of rents. And local officials became much more interventionist in the regulation of the burden of rent. Growing state involvement placed rent relations on an entirely new footing, one that ultimately worked to the great disadvantage of landlords.

CHAPTER 5

Landlords, Tenants, and the State in the Republican Period, 1912 – 1937

After the fall of the Qing in early 1912, China entered a period of disunity in which political power became decentralized into the hands of various provincial military governors and regional warlords. Unlike much of the rest of the country, however, Jiangnan did not suffer horribly from the ravages of warlordism. The series of militarists in control of the region, content merely to tap into the existing systems of revenue extraction, interfered little with local rural society. Nor was the Jiangnan countryside subjected to much warfare. Only in 1924 did contending warlord factions do battle in the region, and then only in the environs of Shanghai.

In early 1927 the Northern Expeditionary Army of the KMT (Guomindang, or Nationalist Party) and the CCP (Chinese Communist Party) drove the militarists out of the region. Shortly thereafter, in April, as is well known, the KMT general Chiang Kai-shek turned against the CCP in a bloody crackdown in Shanghai, thus ending the brief period of unity that the parties had shared as allies in a united front against imperialism and warlordism. In the following year, 1928, the KMT set up a national government in Nanjing that exercised firm control over parts of the country, Jiangnan included, and only nominal control over most of the rest. In keeping with its reformist and modernizing ideology, the KMT in Jiangsu and Zhejiang was much more interventionist than its militarist predecessors, attempting, on the one hand, to institute and/or expand various programs of modernization and, on the other, to raise the level of revenue extraction in order to finance these efforts.

Within this political context, much of the rest of the lower Yangzi region followed the earlier path of the three suburban Suzhou counties

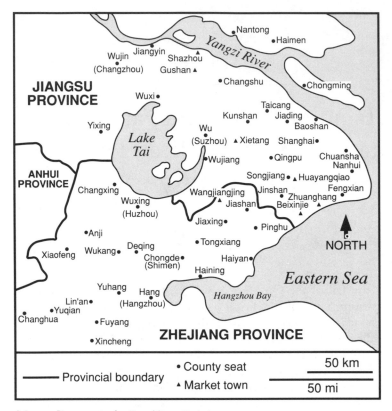

Map 5. Jiangnan in the Republican Period

toward landlord mobilization and official intervention in rent relations. And as there, the common interest of landlords and local officials in maintaining a stable rural order and ensuring efficient rent collection resulted in a great deal of cooperation. But there was also much room for disagreement on how exactly these goals were to be met. Conflict on this score became particularly acute under KMT rule (1927–37), when the government's effort to implement agrarian reform pushed landlord tolerance for state intervention to the breaking point.

The potential for conflict was exacerbated by the fact that the concerns of landlords and local officials, while overlapping, were by no means identical. For landlords, successful rent collection was an end in itself, but for the state, it was merely a means to another end—successful tax collection. The state thus had separate interests of its own that very much dictated the nature of its involvement in rent relations and that, moreover, frequently placed it in direct opposition to landlords. Equating the state with the landlord ruling class, as some mainland Chinese historians do, oversimplifies a complex two-sided relationship.

LANDLORD MOBILIZATION

As in the late Qing, landlord mobilization in the Republican period was partly a response to the increasing urbanization and diversification of elite interests. The shift away from resident proprietorship of land continued unchecked, and by the 1920's and 1930's at least half of the landlords in many counties and as many as 90 percent in some were absentee owners.[1] For these urban-dwelling landlords landownership was seldom the sole means of support. A survey of 161 large landholders (1,000 or more mu) in southern Jiangsu in 1930 shows that none invested his time, labor, or capital exclusively in land. Most (117) were involved in commerce, finance, and/or industry. The other 44 held military or government posts.[2]

In this context landlord mobilization represented a collective effort to put rent relations on a more stable and efficient footing. Bursaries continued to spread in the three Suzhou suburban counties (amalgamated into the single county of Wu after the 1911 Revolution) and also developed in Wujiang, Kunshan, Changshu, and Wuxi in Jiangsu and Pinghu and Jiaxing in Zhejiang.[3] In Wujiang, according to the field investigation of Fei Hsiao-t'ung in the 1930's, the rent collection agencies, called "bureaus" (*ju*, not to be confused with state rent-dunning bureaus), operated in the following fashion:

> Rent is collected in various ways. The simplest system is the direct one; the landlord comes in person to the village. . . . But this direct system is limited to a small group of petty landlords. The majority collect their rent through agents. Landlords of big estates establish their own rent-collecting bureaus and petty landlords pool their claims with them. . . . The tenants do not know and do not care who is their landlord, and know only to which bureau they belong. Names of the tenants and the amount of land held by each are kept in the bureau records. At the end of October, the bureau will inform each tenant of the amount of rent that should be paid that year.[4]

These Wujiang bureaus had first been organized in 1911 to cope with the widespread rent resistance accompanying the fall of the Qing dynasty.[5]

The agencies in Kunshan, Jiaxing, and Pinghu not only bore the same name as the Suzhou institutions (*zuzhan*, a term meaning merely "rent granary" and thus referring to the granaries of both individual landlords and managers) but also, from contemporary descriptions at least, typically performed the same functions. An investigator wrote of the Pinghu agencies that they "do not merely collect the rent for their own land [i.e. land of the granary owner], but also collect rent on behalf of other landowners. This is because it is not convenient for small- and medium-scale Pinghu landlords, those in possession of only several tens of *mu* or one hundred *mu* of land, to set up their own rent rice granaries."[6] In Wuxi and Changshu the equivalent was called *cangfang* or *cangting,* "granary," and the available material suggests that they too took care of the property of other landholders.[7]

Why bursaries came into being in some counties and not others was a function of three factors: the incidence of tenancy, the extent of absentee landlordism, and the presence of large-scale landlords. The first two factors help to explain the source of bursary clients, since one would expect to find these agencies principally in areas where tenants, rather than cultivator-owners, constituted the majority of the farming population and where a large number of landlords would find personal rent collection inconvenient because of the physical distance separating them from their land. The third factor accounts for the source of bursary owners, since it was generally larger-scale, politically influential landlords who expanded their granary operations to include the management of the property of others. Wu, Wujiang, Changshu, Kunshan, Wuxi, Pinghu, and Jiaxing were all characterized by high tenancy rates, a considerable amount of absentee landownership, and the presence of large-scale landlords.[8]

It was in Wu County where these institutions most lived up to their promise—a hardly surprising fact, given their relative longevity, their numbers (300 to 400 in the 1930's[9]), and the status and wealth of their owners. The Wu County bursaries formed a powerful group that dominated the local landowner association, set rent ceilings for the entire county, and lobbied vigorously for official participation in the prompting of rents. Though the Wujiang, Jiaxing, Pinghu, and Wuxi bursaries had a degree of success as the dominant landlord voices in their counties during the Republican period, they did not have the same clout with the local government as the Wu establishments. The bursaries of Changshu and Kunshan, the weakest of the lot, rarely acted together to pursue their common interests.

The three Suzhou suburban counties also provided the model for the other institution through which landlords mobilized to act collectively during the Republican period: the landowner association (*tianye hui, tianye gonghui,* or *tianye lianhehui*). Inaugurated in the fall of 1910 with a membership of over 200 landlords, the most prominent of whom were also bursary owners, the Suzhou association put forward as its goals the improvement of agricultural production and the adoption of fair and uniform rental commutation rates (zhejia). All members were obligated to uphold the approved rate on pain of expulsion. But the group's activities encompassed more than these publicly stated aims. Of equal importance was securing official aid in rent dunning and securing reductions in land taxes.[10] Over the next two decades landlords in Wujiang, Wuxi, Jiangyin, Changshu, Kunshan, Jiaxing, and Hang counties organized their own groups.*

STATE INVOLVEMENT IN RENT COLLECTION

As these institutions grew in number and influence, so did the Jiangnan landlords' power to command state assistance in the collection of rents. During the Republican period official involvement in this aspect of the landlord–tenant relationship developed along two lines. In the first place, the state brought a vastly expanded pool of personnel to this enterprise, thanks to the organization of modern police forces (*jingchadui*) in the first decade of the twentieth century and the subsequent formation of public security bureaus (*gonganju*) during KMT rule. Growing professionalization on this front also saw a greater specialization of function, including the introduction in some areas of "rent prompting police" (*zhuizujing* or *cuizu jingli*) charged with the specific duty of pressuring tenants for the payment of rent.[11] The establishment of county military units—peace preservation corps (*baoandui*) and the larger defense corps (*baoweituan*)—in the 1910's and 1920's provided magistrates with additional manpower to aid landlords in rent collection and to suppress tenant protest.

Whereas this sort of official participation is best seen as an intensification of the assistance that local governments had extended landlords since the late Ming, a more striking development in the twentieth century

---

Shenbao, 12/17/25, 10/14/26; Zhang Yaozong, "Zhou Shuiping," p. 185; Qiao Qiming, "Jiangsu Kunshan Nantong Anhui Suxian nongdian zhidu," p. 109; Kojima Yoshio, "Shinmatsu Minkoku shoki," pp. 192–93; Zhang Zuyin, "Zhenze zhi nongmin," p. 225. Landlord efforts to establish landowner associations did not always succeed. In the fall of 1912 several landlords in Huating County (soon to be combined with Lou County to form Songjiang County) set up an association to gain a larger voice in the setting of county rent rates, a process till then dominated by the benevolent societies (*shantang*). In response one Yang Liaogong, identified only as a "populist" (*pingminzhuyi*), promptly announced his intention to form a tenant association (*dianhuhui*) and passed out handbills in the countryside to recruit members. In the end the Jiangsu military governor ordered the landowner association dissolved on the grounds that it, and by extension, the proposed tenant association, would disrupt public order. Thereupon Yang Liaogong decided there was no need for an organized opposition and abandoned his plans for the tenant association. No doubt partly as a result of this aborted effort, Songjiang County remained without a landowner association (*Shenbao*, 12/3, 12/7/12).

was the widespread institutionalization of state resources into specialized dunning agencies. Here too local governments took their lead from Suzhou city and its suburban counties, which had established dunning bureaus in the last decades of the Qing. By the 1930's state prompting agencies (variously called *cuizuju, cuizuchu, zhuizuju,* and *zhuizuchu*) and tenant debtor prisons (*yadian gongsuo,* literally "tenant detention office" and *dianzu chufensuo,* "office for handling tenant rents") had been set up throughout much of the region—Wu, Songjiang, Jiaxing, Pinghu, Wuxi, Changshu, Taicang, Qingpu, Haining, Wujiang, Jinshan, and Kunshan.[12]

As this lineup of counties indicates, dunning bureaus were most common in the rice-growing areas, where the widespread co-ownership of land ruled out most other methods of dealing with rent delinquency.[13] Since landlord–subsoil owners did not receive security deposits from their topsoil-owning tenants, they had no cushion against default. But they could not evict the defaulter until the amount of his arrears equaled the original purchase price of the topsoil. And even then in trying to rid themselves of the troublesome tenant, they risked an expensive lawsuit. Landlord–subsoil owners thus had little recourse other than incessant dunning. In the cotton areas, where dual ownership was comparatively rare, landlords had both security deposits and a much more real threat of eviction as defenses against default and, as a result, relied much less on just dunning alone.

Like the Suzhou dunning bureaus of the late Qing, the Republican agencies were staffed by both permanent government employees and temporary deputized personnel. Typically the main bureau was headed by a county magistrate or a specially appointed rent-prompting official (*cuizu weiyuan*) and was located within the county administrative compound; clerks in the county complex, often those whose responsibilities encompassed land taxation, saw to the secretarial and bookkeeping chores; and policemen or public rent dunners (called *zuchai, cuizu gongyi, cuizhengli,* or *cuizuli*) had the task of pressing peasants for back rent. In years when tenants proved especially intransigent, local military forces might accompany the dunners on their house-to-house dunning missions. Counties often also established branch bureaus in major market towns. Wu County, for instance, had branches in twenty-eight towns. Local police chiefs or deputized rent-prompting officials were in charge of these operations, and as with the central bureaus in the county seats, policemen, specially hired rent dunners, and local military units carried out the actual dunning.[14]

Financial support for these agencies came from three sources: the county government, landlords, and the tenants themselves. Since magistrates, county clerks, and police chiefs generally received no extra compensation for this kind of work, the major expenditures were supplies and services (stationery, printing, telephone, stamps, and the like) and the wages and travel expenses of the public dunners. Landlords bore a portion of the cost through the purchase of dunning request forms. In Songjiang in the mid-1920's such a form, which could be filled in with the names of as many as thirty tenants, cost 0.4 yuan; the Haining and Jiaxing bureaus in the mid-1930's required one form for each peasant at a price of 0.1 yuan apiece.[15] When dunners went to the villages, their expenses were billed to either the landlord or the tenant, the amount being set by the distance traveled and the amount of rent to be collected.[16] In some counties the bureaus and/or dunners earned a certain portion of any rent successfully acquired from peasants. In Changshu the landlord received 80 percent and the dunner(s) 20 percent; in Taicang the bureau deducted 0.22 yuan from each yuan of rent paid.[17] All the rest of the operating expenses were picked up by the local government and, on occasion, landowner associations.[18]

By all accounts the bureaus did a brisk business. Aggregate figures on the number of default cases routed through these agencies are not available, but scattered data give some sense of the scale of their operations. In the winter and spring of 1924, the bureau in the market town of Wangjiangjing (Jiaxing County) accepted the names of 1,046 households in arrears. Of that number, a little more than half paid their back rent under direct bureau pressure by the end of the summer, and nearly a quarter more eventually delivered what they owed on their own initiative.[19] In 1934, during the depths of the depression, the Changshu rent-dunning bureau reportedly received more than 14,000 written requests from landlords, each listing six peasants, for a total of more than 84,000 names.[20] And from December 1935 to June 1936, the Pinghu County bureau handled 2,726 cases of tenant default.[21]

Jiangnan landlords made use of the government dunning network not only to collect rents but also to collect debts. It was common practice in the lower Yangzi region for farmers to borrow against a future harvest to tide over those periods of food shortages during the late spring and late summer when "the green and the yellow do not meet" (*qinghuang bu jie*)—that is, those times during the agricultural cycle when the past crop had been consumed but the present one was not ready for harvest. As the names applied to some of these loans indicate ("one grain eight," *yili ba*, or "one grain nine," *yili jiu*, meaning that the debtor must return 1.8 or 1.9 shi for every shi of borrowed grain), the interest rates were exceedingly high. When the creditor was the peasant's landlord, as was often the case, failure to repay the debt after the next harvest could land the cultivator in the same difficulties as failure to deliver rent—relentless dunning and perhaps a stint in a tenant lockup.[22]

Landlords were able to secure the detention of a tenant simply by fill-ing in a blank arrest warrant supplied by the local government.[23] Most, however, were reluctant to interrupt a peasant family's work and reserved this form of coercion for peasants whose rent debt had become particularly large. The records for the Gongshou bursary of the Fei family of Suzhou show that though fully 175 of the 250 peasants who farmed 551 mu fell behind in their payments at some point in the four years from 1906 to 1909, just seven spent any time in jail.[24] Incarcerated tenants thus represented only a small minority of defaulting peasants, but even so their numbers in any given year in a single county jail typically ranged from several hundred to more than a thousand.[25] These figures do not include tenants detained elsewhere, in market town bureaus and prisons.

In some counties the dunning bureaus doubled as prisons. In others separate jails for the detention of tenants were established. The bureaus also had access to the regular prison system. But whatever the facilities, overcrowding, poor sanitation, and insufficient food were staples of prison life. In 1918 a rural investigator described the conditions in the Zhenze (Wujiang County) tenant detention office:

> After the establishment of the Republic, . . . landlords feared that they would lack the means to intimidate peasants. They therefore organized a group called the landowner association, which opened up a humble shack, surrounded it with bars, and named it "the tenant detention office." There landlords detain peasants who have done something to incur their displeasure. Since the room is small and the number of inmates large, they at times must stand pressed together, unable to bend in any direction. Excrement and rubbish lie scattered about, and lice proliferate. Often one hears of death among the prisoners. They are given only two meals a day, each consisting of a single bowlful of food no bigger than a fist.[26]

Some women may have been among these unfortunates, for according to descriptions of tenant prisons in other locales, they represented a substantial proportion of the detainees. In the mid-1930's, for instance, women reportedly accounted for 15 percent of the 1,000 peasants imprisoned annually in the tenant jail in Suzhou city.[27] These women had been taken into custody in place of their male relatives, the legal tenants, who had fled to escape the same fate and protect the family's productive capacity.

As deplorable as jail conditions were, at least imprisoned tenants in the Republican period, unlike their late Qing predecessors, did not routinely endure flogging as the legal penalty for default. In 1910 the Qing court adopted a revised law code that forbade, among other practices, the extortion of confessions through torture and all forms of corporal punishment except the death penalty. Republican jurisprudence continued this prohibition.[28] As one observer commented in 1928, the ban proved to be very effective, much to the consternation of Jiangnan landlords. "Such cases [the flogging of tenants] were common under the monarchical regime, but are very rare now, as such punishment is considered illegal, and the district magistrates would not inflict it upon the request of the landlord. The latter now often complains that the magistrates are too lenient in handling such cases, and the tenants are more and more out of control."[29] The flogging of tenants by government personnel did not entirely disappear in the twentieth century, but no longer condoned by law, it was the exception rather than the norm.[30]

Whether the physical abuse of tenants by private individuals—landlords and their dunners—similarly declined, stayed the same, or increased in the Republican period is difficult to determine. According to stories collected during land reform in the early 1950's, bursaries and large landholders in Wu County had maintained chambers of horror, where they supposedly chained and beat peasants. Other, more imaginative forms of torture reputedly included "suffering the bamboo chopstick" (*chi maozhu kuai*), in which a sharpened chopstick was driven underneath the victim's fingernails; "sitting on cold bricks" (*zuo leng fangzhuan*), in which a peasant was stripped of his clothing and forced to sit on frozen bricks; "tossing the willow basket" (*pao badou*), in which the tenant was tied up inside a large basket and then rolled around on the ground until he lost consciousness; "the lantern for drawing off water" (*fangshui deng*), in which the landlord and his minions would push a peasant into the frigid water of a stream or canal, fish him out, and then burn his buttocks; and "irrigating the belly and lungs" (*guan dufei*), in which they would force water down the victim's throat and then apply fire to his chest and abdomen.[31] Since contemporary sources reported similar practices in Suzhou Prefecture in the late Qing, it is not inconceivable that some bursaries and landlords in Republican Wu County did indeed commit the crimes of which they stand accused.[32] But the corporal punishment of tenants was surely not so widespread as the reports would have us believe. Rural reformers of the 1920's and 1930's were just as determined as the Communists to expose landlord abuses, yet their accounts make only occasional mention of the chaining and beating of tenants and none whatsoever of the more gruesome types of torture.

This is not to minimize the extent to which dunning operated on blatant mental and physical intimidation. Physical abuse happened often enough for peasants to see bodily injury as a very real threat. Add to that the mental anguish a visit from a dunner or the prospect of imprisonment could evoke, and it is not surprising that suicide seems to have claimed as many tenant lives in the years 1912–37 as death at the hands of dunners and death from illness in prison.[33] Such suicides were so common in Wuxi that peasants there put them in a special category: "a wildcat ate a person" (*yemao chi ren*), the "wildcat" referring to the landlord and his dunners.[34]

Tenants of the twentieth century also suffered much legal injustice, for the dunning bureaus and debtor prisons, like their late Qing predecessors, separated rent delinquent peasants from the regular judicial process. But until the last Qing years, detaining and beating peasants in default had been permissible, so the only illegal aspect of government dunning practices had been the failure to try the accused in a magistrate's court. In the Republican period not only were tenants denied due process of law, but the very act of holding them in custody violated the new legal codes, which transformed rent default from a criminal to a civil offense.

The decriminalization of rent default took place in 1910, when the Qing court, in its revised legal statutes, drew a distinction between criminal and civil affairs, a distinction that had not existed previously in Chinese law and that placed rent default wholly within the realm of civil offenses.[35] Subsequent civil laws in the Republican period then specified how rent default was to be handled. In the 1910's the Supreme Court (Daliyuan) decreed in a series of decisions on lease contracts that a contract could be terminated if the tenant failed to pay his rent in full, and that the landlord could then pursue his claim for the unpaid portion through the litigation procedures creditors normally employed against debtors.[36] The KMT civil code, which went into effect in piecemeal fashion beginning in 1929, dealt with the question of rent default in more detail in the three sections concerning lease, superficies (*dishangquan*, defined as "the right to use the land of another person with the object of owning thereon structures or other works or bamboo or trees"), and permanent tenure (*yongdian*). In the event of default under a lease, the landlord could "fix a reasonable period" and order the tenant to pay up. If he did not do so by the prescribed deadline, the landlord could terminate the lease. For default in the other two categories, the landlord could revoke the superficies or the permanent tenure when the amount in arrears added up to the equivalent of two years' worth of rent.[37]

The decriminalization of rent default had mixed effects on the treatment of tenants. As noted earlier, the ban on corporal punishment seems to have resulted in a marked decrease in the number of peasants beaten for default. But the redefinition of default as a civil offense had, at best, only intermittent success in curbing the incarceration of delinquent tenants. Under militarist rule (1912–27), aside from a few attempts to route cases of default through the courts, the governors of Zhejiang and Jiangsu generally sanctioned the dunning bureaus and debtor prisons, even to the extent of formulating some sketchy regulations regarding their operation.[38]

In late 1927 and early 1928 provincial approval of the illegal practices gave way to censure under the influence of the KMT. The KMT central government prohibited the bureaus and prisons on the legal grounds that they violated the laws of the Republic and on the political grounds that they were "tools of warlord oppression."[39] Henceforth, the KMT instructed, all disputes over rents should be referred to the local arbitration committees that were to be set up in conjunction with its announced rent reduction campaign.

The KMT alternative to the network of dunning bureaus and debtor prisons failed to take hold at all in Jiangsu; most counties did not even go to the trouble of setting up the arbitration committees. In Zhejiang, where greater efforts were made to carry out the KMT rent reduction program, the committees were duly formed, but the cases that came under their scrutiny were few in number and generally concerned matters other than simple default. Of the forty-nine unresolved disputes referred by lower-level committees to the Zhejiang Reconstruction Office (Jiansheting) in 1928 and 1929, for instance, 70 percent involved a landlord's retrieval of fields from a tenant either to cultivate himself or to lease to another party, and 22 percent involved disagreements over the amount of rent in light of the reduction campaign.[40] Figures for the 124 cases brought before the Jiaxing County committee in 1930 show a larger proportion of conflicts over alleged default (35 percent), but here too the majority of cases turned on the retrieval of land and the proper amount of rents (31 and 27 percent, respectively.)[41] For Zhejiang landlords committee resolution of default cases was too slow, and the results too uncertain, to be an attractive alternative to conventional government dunning.

The KMT prohibition of public dunning agencies thus had little chance of success. Jiangnan landlords, carrying on their forebears' tradition of pleading insolvency because of tenant rent delinquency, played on the KMT's concern for adequate tax revenue, and after a brief suspension, two to three years at most, the network of prompting bureaus and debtor prisons was fully restored.

In some locales a more intimate connection between tax and rent collection encouraged continued official participation in tenant dunning. We earlier saw how holders of topsoil rights in Jiaxing County came to bear permanent responsibility for land taxes amid the expansion of dual ownership after the Taiping Rebellion.[42] And in Pinghu County a unique custom, called "the short head" (*duantou*), had developed, permitting a landlord to shift the tax liability temporarily to a tenant who had defaulted on rent.[43] In these counties government dunning of tenants served the dual purpose of securing both rent and tax payments.

Apart from tax revenues, another powerful consideration prompted the county administrations in Jiangnan to acquiesce in the resurrection of the dunning apparatus in violation of the legal code and KMT prohibitions. Government participation in rent collection was a resource that local officials could either offer or withhold in their efforts to assert the interests of the state against those of landlords. Compliance with county-approved rent ceilings usually constituted a prerequisite for receiving official assistance in dunning.[44] Additionally, in a few places such aid was denied landlords who had not yet paid their taxes; landlords had to show their tax receipts to bureau personnel before dunners would be sent to pressure tenants.[45] Finally, some county governments, in a move reminiscent of Taiping practices, made official help conditional on the registration of land, an attempt to uncover fraud of ownership and enter previously concealed property on the tax rolls.[46]

STATE INVOLVEMENT IN SETTING RENTS

In the domain of rent collection, the state simply stepped up and expanded its activities; support for rent collection was nothing new. But in involving itself in determining acceptable levels of rent, it radically departed from earlier practices. Before the Taiping Rebellion, as we have seen, the Qing government had regarded the level of rent as essentially a private affair between a landlord and his tenant. After the policy of tying compulsory rent reduction to tax remissions was revoked, this non-interventionism had extended even into years of crop failure, when local officials were constrained by imperial decree to use moral suasion alone to induce landlords to lower rents.

Government intervention in this aspect of rent relations became routine in many Jiangnan counties in the twentieth century—Wu, Changshu, Songjiang, Qingpu, Wujiang, Wuxi, Taicang, Jinshan, Jiading, Kunshan, Pinghu, Jiaxing, and Shanghai. In Wu local official participation in the setting of rent ceilings predated the 1911 Revolution; in the other counties it was more clearly a product of the Republican period. As in all else, the procedure varied from county to county. On the whole, however, two distinct patterns emerged. In counties where large-scale landowners were comparatively numerous and exhibited a strong sense of solidarity, landowner associations or groups of bursary owners represented general landlord interests in negotiations with the local magistrate over rent ceilings. In counties where landownership was more dispersed and landlord solidarity weaker, managerial gentry played a more prominent role in the process than individual private proprietors.

Wu, Wuxi, Changshu, Kunshan, Wujiang, Pinghu, and Jiaxing exemplified the first pattern.[47] To take Wu County as a concrete illustration, every year, sometime in the first half of November, the landowner association convened a meeting of its members either at the Yuanmiao Temple in the heart of Suzhou city or at the offices of the Fan charitable estate. Anywhere from seventy to more than two hundred landowners might participate in a given conference. Also in attendance was a delegate or two from the magistrate's office, who expressed the county administration's views and whose presence lent an air of legal authority to the proceedings. After the association had determined ceilings that met with county approval, the Wu magistrate would issue a formal directive ordering all landlords to abide by the decision.[48]

The second pattern prevailed in Songjiang, Shanghai, Jinshan, Taicang, Jiading, and Qingpu, where landlords were not as economically or politically influential as their counterparts to the west.[49] Here gentry managers, particularly but not exclusively the managers of charitable institutions (shantang), conducted negotiations with county officials. For the landholders of Songjiang (formerly Huating and Lou counties), this did not change things much. They had already been following the rental rates set by the area's two largest charitable foundations—and with roughly 3,500 mu each in the 1880's, two of its largest landowners—the home for destitute women (*quanjietang*) and the home for orphans (*yuyingtang*).[50] After the 1911 Revolution the managers of these charities continued to exert a great influence in the setting of rents, but they were no longer the sole voice as the government expanded the deliberations to include gentry managers of other organizations. By the mid-1920's the standard procedure in Songjiang was for those government offices in charge of administering county-owned property—the education bureau (*jiaoyuju*) and the office for the management of public funds and property (*gong kuanchan jinglichu*)—to hold a meeting every autumn to set the year's rates. All interested parties were invited to attend: the managers of the charitable institutions, the managers of the educational promotion office (*quanxuesuo*), the heads of the merchant association and the agricultural association, and the managers of market towns (*zhendong*), as well as a few local men of wealth and prominence (*difang shenshi* or *shenfu*), among whom were undoubtedly some landlords.[51] The gentry managers in this list may well have owned substantial amounts of land, but at the conferences they formally represented not their own interests (although those probably were on their minds), but the public interests of their respective institutions, associations, and jurisdictions.

At the conferences on rent, whether in Songjiang, Wu, or some other place, deliberations followed a three-step formula: the evaluation of crop yields, the determination of the rent rate, and the setting of the conversion rate for fixed rents commuted into currency. Assessment of crop yields, called the harvest *chengse*, was expressed as a percent of an average harvest. Hence, a chengse of 80 percent meant that fields had suffered a 20 percent decline in normal yields.

The officials, landlord representatives, and others in attendance at the conference then used the harvest chengse to settle the rental chengse—the highest percentage of rent tenants would be required to pay. In their calculations the decision-makers took into account the distinction between nominal and actual rents, a distinction that had become more common after the Taiping Rebellion with the extension of co-ownership and its accompanying lowered rents. Consequently, the rental chengse did not exceed the customary actual rent for the county. Even in years of superlative countywide yields, the rental chengse was no more than 80 to 90 percent of the nominal rent, or whatever the highest actual rents for the county might be. With a rental chengse of this percentage, tenants would receive no reductions beyond the slight discounts that individual landlords or bursaries normally made for prompt payment. In 1930, for instance, when Songjiang County enjoyed its best rice harvest of the Republican era, with yields of more than three shi per mu, the rental chengse was set at only 85 percent. This figure represented not a 15 percent reduction but full payment of actual rents. For substandard yields the chengse was reduced accordingly. To take Songjiang again as an example, in 1917 a harvest chengse set at 70 to 80 percent because of an infestation of rice-stalk borers translated into a rental chengse of 70 percent; and in 1936 an average harvest (2 to 2.5 shi) resulted in a rental chengse of 77 percent. For a Songjiang peasant who carried a nominal rent (xuzu) of 1.2 shi per mu, therefore, the actual rent (shizu) in kind would have been 0.84 shi in 1917, 1.02 in 1930, and 0.924 in 1936.[52]

After deciding the rental chengse, the group then turned its attention to the zhejia, the conversion rate for fixed rice (or cotton) rents into currency. Commuted rent had become increasingly widespread in Jiangnan after the Taiping Rebellion, and by the Republican era it was an important form of payment in many Jiangnan counties.[53] As we have seen, commuted rents were particularly susceptible to manipulation by landlords, who commonly set the rates at least 10 to 20 percent higher than the prevailing market price for the crop, effectively raising rent by the same percentage. To correct this abuse the committees, at their autumn meetings, studied lists of prices that wholesalers had been paying peasants for their products, averaged those prices for the past ten to thirty days, and then designated that average as the highest permissible commutation rate.[54] On the whole the government conversion rates stayed abreast with rice prices, even during the depression of the 1930's, when the deliberative committees would have been tempted to elevate the zhejia to spare landlords the consequences of declining grain prices (see Table B.3).

As complicated as this procedure for setting rent ceilings seems, it became even more complex in years of less-than-average crop yields, when landowners realistically could hope for a tax remission from the provincial government. At those times a magistrate would ask the provincial financial department (*caizhengting*) to dispatch a deputy to assess the quality of the harvest. His findings then formed the basis for deliberations among local officials and landlord representatives over the appropriate discounts in tax and rent. When the process went smoothly, the assembly would accept the deputy's crop evaluation without demur and then ask the provincial financial department for a commensurate tax cut. The authorities would agree to their request, whereupon county officials and landlord representatives, taking into account both the harvest and the tax chengse, would decide on reductions in rent that met with full tenant approval.

The process seldom went this smoothly, however, for the number of competing claims on the fixed harvest ruled out easy compromise. Contention first arose over the question of the harvest chengse. Understandably, the provincial government would want a higher harvest chengse to ensure a higher rate of tax collection, and tenants a lower one to ensure a lower rate of rent collection. Landlords, for their part, had to walk a fine line between a higher and a lower harvest assessment. They would want an estimate lower than the provincial one to decrease the amount of tax, but not so low as to jeopardize their collection of rent. Conversely, they would want an estimate higher than the tenants demanded to get a better rental return, but not so high as to harm their chances of securing a remission in taxes from the provincial government.[55]

At the center of this swirl of rival claims stood the local magistrate, whose concerns sometimes coincided with and sometimes conflicted with those of the other parties. As an agent of the state, he was vitally interested in collecting as much in land taxes as possible, not only to gain the monies to run his own county administration, but also to better his administrative record and hence his career prospects. At the same time he was by no means unsympathetic to peasant demands for rent reduction, if only out of a desire to contain social conflict and maintain domestic peace. Yet a magistrate who urged a remission in rent most likely would have to join forces with landlords to lobby the provincial government for a reduction in tax, since landlords typically attempted to make their acceptance of a rent reduction contingent on a tax remission.[56] A county magistrate thus faced three unpalatable options. He could accept the higher provincial harvest chengse and make that the basis for his proposed rent and tax reductions, thereby satisfying the provincial financial department and his own county coffers but incurring the displeasure of both landlords and tenants. Or he could attempt to uphold a lower harvest assessment, thereby pleasing tenants but displeasing landlords and the provincial government and possibly harming his own tax collection. Or, finally, he could support the harvest chengse proposed by landlords at the risk of displeasing both tenants and the provincial finance department.

Once a compromise, however much disputed, was reached on the harvest chengse, contention then invariably arose over the rent and tax chengse. The harvest assessment furnished only a rough guideline for the determination of tax and rent reductions. A harvest chengse of, say, 60 percent did not automatically translate into 40-percent reductions in tax and rent. The negotiations over these cuts provided officials, landlords, and tenants with an opportunity to rectify any perceived injustices in the harvest evaluation. In general officials supported higher rent cuts and lower tax cuts, landlords of course the reverse, and tenants even more substantial rent cuts.[57]

Negotiations over rent and tax in Wu County in late 1917 and early 1918 demonstrate just how convoluted and prolonged the process could be. In 1917 rice-stem borers infested the crop immediately before harvest. In response to peasant requests, the magistrate in early November toured the countryside to examine the damage and estimated it at a 20-percent decline in yield. On the basis of his informal assessment, the landowner association decided to lower rents by a uniform 10 percent. The magistrate then reported the situation to the provincial government, requesting an investigation of the harvest and a remission in land taxes. The finance department refused to do either on the grounds that the county's land taxes had already been figured into the budget and thus could not be changed.

Wu tenants, meanwhile, felt that the 10-percent rent reduction was not only too small but unjust, failing to take into account the geographical variation in the degree of the insect devastation. In the middle of November they demanded a rent cut of 40 to 50 percent and backed up the demand by refusing to accept the payment notices issued by jingzao and private rent dunners (*cuijia*) on behalf of the Suzhou bursaries and by attacking the dunners' residences.

Soon after the eruption of this protest, which quickly spread to eleven rural townships (*xiang*) in the former counties of Changzhou and Yuanhe, the landowner association met at the offices of the Fan charitable estate to discuss larger rent reductions. The meeting ended in a stalemate, with some landlords insisting on more discounts and others refusing to consider the possibility. A few days later the group reconvened, this time with the magistrate, who urged them to decrease rents further. After much heated debate the landowner association agreed to lower rents in old Changzhou an additional 15 percent and those in old Yuanhe an additional 20 percent, but only on the condition that the magistrate join them to lobby for a tax remission from the provincial government.

Eventually, in late December, the provincial finance department granted Wu County a 12-percent reduction in the tax chengse, bringing it down to 88 percent. Now it was the Wu landlords' turn to cry injustice, since neighboring Changshu County had received a remission of 17 percent even though the devastation to the rice harvest there had not been as severe. Since the magistrate declined to dispute the provincial figure, several prominent Wu landlords traveled to the capital to petition personally for a remission of 17 percent. This trip resulted in a substantial concession to the landlords, a remission of 15.2 percent, but the Wu landlords continued to hold out for 17 percent. Finally, in mid-January 1918, a full month after the normal beginning of the tax collection period, the Wu landlords and the provincial financial department compromised on a tax remission of 16.5 percent.[58]

As this case demonstrates, with tax decisions made at the provincial level and rent decisions at the county level, a magistrate's mediation of claims and counterclaims, already difficult because of the competing interests involved, was further complicated by institutional inefficiency. Despite the widespread violent resistance to rents, Wu landlords initially were reluctant to grant further reductions because of the provincial authorities' unresponsiveness to the county's request for a harvest investigation and a tax remission. Only after the magistrate had promised to work with them to gain a remission did they agree to further concessions in rent. And even then nearly two months passed before a final decision on the tax rate was reached. Had the Wu magistrate himself had the authority to lower taxes, the dispute over rents might have been settled much more quickly and much more peacefully.

That inefficiency made itself felt in other ways, too. At times the provincial finance department was slow to respond to county requests for harvest investigations. Until such an investigation was carried out, farmers could not proceed with the harvest because the provincial deputies had to examine standing crops. Should the delay extend beyond the best time for reaping, the fields could suffer further declines in yield. This problem was especially acute during an insect infestation, since the longer the crops remained unharvested, the greater the threat that the pests would spread to undamaged stalks.[59] Moreover, without the provincial deputy's evaluation as an indication of what tax remission, if any, might be granted, the deliberative committees were reluctant to announce the rental chengse. This delay in turn made the tenants uneasy; in the absence of proof to the contrary, they often assumed that landlords were not going to reduce rents. The longer the delay, the more likely they were to resort to collective action to press for harvest investigations and remissions in rent.[60] Bureaucratic inefficiency, then, was frequently a factor promoting tenant protests.

THE BURDEN OF RENT IN
REPUBLICAN JIANGNAN

The rent-reduction procedures that evolved in Republican Jiangnan differed from the Qing methods in several crucial respects. First, the state had appropriated from landlords the right to decide whether and to what extent rents should be reduced in years of below-average yields. Unlike the Qing statutes, Republican law expressly made rent reductions a right of tenants. A Supreme Court decision of 1917 held that "the tenant's claim against the landlord for a reduction or remission of rent on account of a diminution of receipt from the land through *force majeure* being a right lawfully belonging to the tenant, there is no ground on which the landlord can refuse."[61] The KMT civil code also guaranteed a tenant's right to a reduction in such circumstances.[62]

Second, in the Republican period, the link between tax remission and rent reduction was transformed. After mandatory rent reductions were abolished in the second quarter of the eighteenth century, the Qing had merely recommended rent reduction in the event of tax remission and had further suggested a seventy-thirty split as the appropriate division. Under this formula the landlord always fared better than the tenant. A one-third reduction in tax for a mu of land that carried, say, a tax of 0.1 shi and an actual rent of 1.0 shi would cut 0.033 shi from the landowner's tax bill and a mere 0.01 shi (.033 × 30%) from the tenant's rent bill. The landlord thus ended up with a 33-percent remission in tax but the tenant got only a 1-percent reduction in rent. Furthermore, the Qing method of calculation guaranteed that any landlord who chose to transmit some of the benefits of a tax remission to his tenants would not suffer for his generosity. In the example just cited, the landlord, after paying the reduced tax of 0.067 shi, would retain 0.923 shi of the reduced rent of 0.990 shi— in fact 0.023 shi more than the 0.9 shi he would have earned without a remission. In short, the Qing formula ensured that remissions in tax more than covered reductions in rent.

In contrast, the Republican government sometimes ordered rent reductions while maintaining or even increasing the level of taxation, but never granted landlords a tax remission without also granting tenants a rent reduction.[63] In these circumstances the oft-quoted phrase "taxes come from rents" acquired a new significance. Once used by landlords solely to secure official assistance in rent dunning, it now figured prominently in their appeals for tax cuts. Since taxes came from rents, they argued, taxes should be reduced when rents were reduced. This rationale for tax cuts was a striking inversion of the tenants' old argument that rents should be reduced when taxes were reduced. Tellingly, that tenant rationale, after a final appearance in several collective actions around the time of the 1911

Revolution, vanished completely in Jiangnan as a justification for rent reduction.

When officials did see fit to lower taxes as well as rents, the one usually did not offset the other. The most landlords could hope for, but something they rarely received, was a tax chengse of the same percentage as the rent chengse. Even with such a generous tax cut, however, they would still suffer an overall decrease in net income from their land.[64]

State intervention in the determination of rents not only compelled landlords to lower their demands on tenants in years of dearth, but also acted as a check on what they could charge in years of plenty. As a result, there is little evidence, either anecdotal or statistical, to suggest a substantial increase in real rents over the period 1912–36. Rural investigators of the 1920's and 1930's routinely deplored the onerous burden of rent on Jiangnan tenants but seldom stated that the burden was growing heavier; and as will be discussed in the next chapter, none of the 126 tenant collective actions of the Republican era were in protest of rising rents. Moreover, the few scattered reports of rent hikes generally concerned cotton areas like Baoshan County in the eastern part of the region, where the new procedure for setting rents either was not well developed or had not taken hold at all.[65]

In the rest of Jiangnan, especially in those areas where official intervention had become the norm, one would be hard put to document significant increases in rent in any form—nominal rents, actual rents, or conversion rates for commuted rents. The customary dictate against raising the fixed amount in kind, especially on land jointly owned by a landlord and a tenant, was just as strong in the Republican period as it had been in the Qing. And actual rents did not exceed the 80 to 90 percent common during the Qing; in some places, such as northern Zhejiang, they may well have decreased.[66] In addition, the introduction of county-approved commutation rates curbed the landlord practice of setting them some 10 to 20 percent higher than the price of rice. Evidence from the Suzhou bursaries indicates that although the county rates did not command complete landlord compliance, their very existence acted as a check on what tenants were charged. Consequently, with the sole exception of the year 1929, even when the bursary rate exceeded the county rate, it was still in line with current rice prices (see Table 5.1). Similarly, though the average commutation rates charged by Pinghu landlords from 1929 to 1935 were consistently 0.3 yuan per shi higher than the county rates, they still fell below the going market price of rice.[67]

In the Republican period, then, commutation rates became much more closely pegged to the price of rice. This development had a twofold effect on the levels of rent in the twentieth century. First, it restrained the real increases that could occur in commuted rents. Table 5.2 shows that the

TABLE 5.1

Real Rents in Suzhou, 1878–1936

(actual rent figured at 1.0 shi per mu)

Year	Zhejia (*cash* per shi)	Exchange rate (*cash* per yuan)	Zhejia (yuan per shi)	Rice price (yuan per shi)	Rent (shi)
1878	2,400–2,800	1,102	2.18–2.54	1.5–2.0	1.09–1.69
1879	2,200	1,131	1.95	1.3–1.4	1.39–1.50
1880	2,000	1,152	1.74	1.3	1.34
1881	2,000	1,105[a]	1.81	1.5–1.8	1.01–1.21
1883	2,200–2,300	1,075[a]	2.05–2.14	1.7–1.8	1.14–1.26
1899	2,900–4,000	944	3.07–4.24	4.3–4.4	0.70–0.99
1900	2,524	933	2.71	2.0	1.36
1903	3,355	855	3.92	3.7–4.0	0.98–1.06
1904	3,062	865	3.54	2.0–2.4	1.48–1.77
1905	2,831	889	3.18	2.84	1.12
1914			4.51	4.45	1.01
1923			7.73	7.65–8.50[b]	0.91–1.01
1926					
B			6.92	11.50	0.60
G			10.30	11.50	0.90
1927					
B			8.94	7.5–9.0[b]	0.97–1.16
G			7.80	7.5–9.0[b]	0.87–1.04
1928					
B			8.42	8.4–9.1[b]	0.93–1.00
G			8.60	8.4–9.1[b]	0.95–1.02
1929					
B			13.03	11.0–11.9[b]	1.09–1.18
G			11.00	11.0–11.9[b]	0.92–1.00
1930					
B			6.07	9.5	0.64
G			9.00	9.5	0.95
1933			6.50	5.5–6.0	1.08–1.18
1935			8.00	8.0	1.00
1936			7.10	8.5–8.6	0.83–0.84

SOURCES: Table B.3; *Shenbao*, 10/22, 11/16/Guangxu 4 (1878), 10/26/Guangxu 5 (1879), 9/28/Guangxu 6 (1880), 10/27, 12/1/Guangxu 7 (1881), 12/28/Guangxu 9 (1883), 11/11/23, 11/14/27, 11/12/28, 11/7/29, 11/16/30, 11/7/36; *Huibao*, 10/23, 10/30/Guangxu 25 (1899); *Tongwen hubao*, 1/9/Guangxu 27 (1901), 9/12/Guangxu 29 (1903), 10/11, 11/25/Guangxu 30 (1904); Qiao Qiming, pp. 86–87; He Menglei, pp. 33153–54; Hong Ruijian, "Suzhou," pp. 1552–53.

NOTE: B = bursary, G = government. The zhejia and the rice prices are all for unpolished nonglutinous rice (*caogeng*), the principal strain grown in Suzhou.

[a] Autumn exchange rate in Suzhou city; the other figures are the annual average rates in Ningbo.

[b] November retail price in Suzhou city; the other figures are the local prices paid to peasants after harvest.

TABLE 5.2
Rice Prices and Bursary Commutation Rates in Suzhou, 1912–1936
(period averages)

	Rice price		Bursary commutation rate	
Period	Yuan per shi	Index	Yuan per shi	Index
1912–1916	7.22	100	4.42	100
1917–1921	7.88	109	4.44	100
1922–1926	11.89	165	7.10	161
1927–1931	13.75	190	9.12	206

SOURCE: Table B.3.

Suzhou bursary commutation rate increased 2.06 times from 1912 to 1931, against only 1.90 times for the price of rice. Real rents (in silver) thus went up at most only 8 percent during these twenty years, a very modest increase compared with the 48-percent rise in commuted bursary rents paid in copper and the 54-percent rise in commuted rents paid in silver in the final fifteen years of the Qing.*

Second, the narrowing of the gap between conversion rates and rice prices meant that, in the absence of significant increases in the fixed rent in kind, tenants of the Republican period gave a smaller proportion of their harvest to landlords than their predecessors of the late Qing. Table 5.1 shows how much husked rice a bursary tenant who owed one shi per mu had to sell to pay the commuted rent. (The commutation rate, or zhejia, divided by the local November rice price equals the amount of rice in shi the peasant would have to market.) In the late Qing commuted rents cost the tenant 0.70 to 1.77 shi of rice. During the Republican period, because of conversion rates more in line with the price of rice, the range was much lower—0.60 to 1.18 shi. In the case of commuted rents, therefore, official involvement in the setting of conversion rates significantly lightened the tenantry's burden.

Overall the Republican record suggests that the landlords' observance of the county ceilings, though by no means complete, was at least extensive enough to restrain potential increases and, in the case of commuted rents, even to ease the tenantry's actual burden. Part of the reason for this compliance, of course, was that many large landlords had a say in the deliberations on rents and were thus likely to uphold the collective decision. But on occasion magistrates did go against their wishes and decree a larger reduction than they were willing to undertake. In those instances local officials employed other means to compel compliance. Since county pronouncements on rent carried the force of law, errant landlords were

*Copper *cash* was little used in the lower Yangzi valley in the Republican period. The rents referred to here are in foreign silver.

sometimes arrested, fined, and/or ordered to refund the overpayment to their tenants.[68] More important, county officials withheld state dunning resources from landowners who did not abide by the rent ceilings; the dunning bureaus would press tenants only for amounts that fell within the legal limits.[69] This form of coercion was particularly effective against large landholders who had come to rely heavily on state assistance in rent collection.

Landlords who violated the county regulations also had to answer to their tenants. Considering how frequently peasants in the past had used government-decreed tax remissions to shore up their opposition to rents, one can imagine how much capital they made out of government-decreed rent ceilings in the Republican period. It was as much the tenants' refusal to pay more than the permissible amount as the threat of direct government action that persuaded reluctant landlords that their interests were better served by observing the legal limit.

THE KMT RENT REDUCTION CAMPAIGN: THE LIMITS OF INTERVENTION

Landlord tolerance for government intervention in rent relations was not inexhaustible. This the KMT discovered when it attempted to implement a permanent reduction in tenant rents in Jiangsu and Zhejiang provinces in the late 1920's. The literature on Republican China generally has dismissed the KMT agrarian reforms as being little more than elaborate schemes on paper.[70] That indeed was the case for most places under KMT control, but not for Zhejiang, where the party made a concerted effort to carry out the program. In the end the opposition of landlords and local officials, the provincial government's concern with land taxation, and the profound difficulties of changing a complex agrarian system with a few sweeping measures forced the KMT to end its campaign even there. But it left its mark on rent relations in Zhejiang for all that.

To review the campaign's history elsewhere briefly, it began in October 1926, when the KMT adopted a 25-percent reduction in rent as the central plank of its agrarian platform at the Second National Congress. Subsequently, in 1927, the five provinces of Guangdong, Hunan, Hubei, Jiangsu, and Zhejiang issued reduction decrees at the behest of the KMT. In Guangdong, Hunan, and Hubei, the proposed reforms quickly fell victim to the bloody break between the CCP and the KMT and were formally revoked by the end of 1927.[71]

In Jiangsu the campaign enjoyed a longer life as official policy but was stillborn in actual application. In December 1927 the KMT pressured a very reluctant provincial government to formulate guidelines for rent reduction. In doing so, the Jiangsu Department of Agriculture and Industry (Nonggongting) explicitly eschewed the flat 25-percent decrease proposed by the KMT, arguing that it failed to take local conditions into account. In its place, the department drafted and secured KMT approval for a provisional plan that set one-third of the autumn harvest as the rent standard. Current amounts at or below that level were to remain in force; those above it were to be lowered.[72] Revisions of the regulations over the next several years gradually raised the ceiling to 37.5 percent and also prohibited tenants whose rents did not exceed that standard from demanding any reduction.[73]

The considerable time and labor expended in devising and revising the new rent laws for Jiangsu all went for naught, because little, if any, attempt was made to put the reform into effect.[74] From the outset government officials, knowing the battles that would have to be fought with powerful landlord lobbies, showed little enthusiasm for the campaign. It was all the more distasteful, no doubt, because they were just then in the course of trying to suppress Communist-led peasant uprisings that had as one goal a 25-percent reduction in rent. Even the KMT's commitment to the reforms in Jiangsu paled quickly, and party activists chose to concentrate their efforts in Zhejiang instead.

Initially, Zhejiang seemed to offer the best prospects for effecting the 25-percent reduction. Regarded by the KMT as a model province, Zhejiang had a progressive government led by men sympathetic to KMT reforms and willing to institute various modernization projects. However, the KMT agrarian reformers, in their first rush of enthusiasm, seriously overestimated the support they would receive from those men and just as seriously underestimated the opposition they would face from landlords.

The agrarian reforms began in Zhejiang in November 1927, with the issuance of a set of regulations detailing the methods of rent reduction. For Zhejiang, as for Jiangsu, the phrase "twenty-five percent rent reduction" (*erwu jianzu*) is a misnomer, implying as it does a simple, across-the-board reduction of 25 percent in all land rents. Such a measure, the Zhejiang reformers argued, was unfair to both tenants and landlords, serving only to reinforce existing disparities in amounts. Tenants who already enjoyed low rents would receive the same reduction as those who suffered excessively high ones, and landlords who already charged low amounts would be penalized to the same extent as their rack-renting peers.[75] The reformers thus sought to equalize as well as to reduce rents. They first set the maximum rent at 50 percent of the average yield of the primary crop, thereby abolishing charges for auxiliary crops, and then reduced that amount 25 percent, for a final ceiling of 37.5 percent of the average yield. Thus a landlord who charged a tenant more than half the main crop first had to lower the rent to that level and then apply the reduction of 25 percent, and one who demanded less than half the main crop merely had to observe the 37.5 percent ceiling. The reduction in rent would amount to more than 25 percent in the first case and to less than 25 percent in the second. As the framers of the 1927 regulations were soon to discover, this circuitous method of calculation was too easily abused by landlords, who applied the 25-percent reduction to the current rent without first lowering it to 50 percent of the standard yield. As a result the Zhejiang land law was revised in 1929 to state simply that the maximum annual rent was to be 37.5 percent of the main crop.[76]

The task of directing the rent reduction campaign in the Zhejiang counties fell to KMT party branches, which in turn drew on the assistance of local government officials and peasant associations. In addition, anticipating that the reforms would bring about a temporary escalation in rural conflict, the KMT set up special arbitration committees at all administrative levels to handle disputes between landlords and tenants. Called first "committees for the arbitration of disputes between landlords and tenants" (*yedian jiufen zhongcai weiyuanhui*) and then "tenant-landlord administration bureaus" (*dianye lishi ju*), these bodies were composed of representatives from the party, the government, the public security organs, and the peasant associations.[77]

The extent to which the KMT program was followed in Zhejiang varied widely from county to county, depending on the relative strength of the interested parties. No county could claim a thorough implementation (some did not even try), but there were pockets here and there throughout northern Zhejiang where rents were indeed reduced.[78] One such area was the second and third wards (*qu*) of Jiaxing, the site of a detailed field investigation conducted under the auspices of the county government and National Zhejiang University. The researchers discovered that as a result of the campaign, the highest rents charged in these two wards had dropped in the late 1920's from 1.2 shi per mu to no more than 0.7 shi, a level still in force in 1935, the year of the survey. They attributed the success of the reform here not to landlord magnanimity but to the widespread existence of co-ownership of land. Both the rent laws and the KMT civil code provided that tenants with permanent tenure, including surface rights, could not be evicted so long as they paid their rents. In the context of the KMT campaign, this meant that a landlord had no legal grounds for eviction as long as the topsoil holder dutifully paid the new and lower rent. Those landlords who attempted to use the mediation committees or the courts to compel tenants to quit the land or to pay more in rent invariably met with failure.[79]

Like these Jiaxing tenants, peasants elsewhere in northern Zhejiang did not wait patiently for their landlords' permission to deliver the reduced amounts. They took matters into their own hands, unilaterally deciding to pay only what the reforms called for or withholding rents entirely in an effort to force landlords to consent to the permanent decrease. The result, many contemporaries noted, was a deterioration of relations between landlords and tenants. One observer wrote that even though the 25-percent reduction had not been widely implemented, "its influence was nevertheless extremely great. Tenants deliberately seized the pretext of rent reduction to take revenge against landlords for their oppressive treatment in the past. The bond of reciprocity (*ganqing*) between landlords and tenants was thus severed, and conflicts broke out in seemingly limitless numbers."[80]

The rent-reduction campaign and the peasant resistance it inspired seriously threatened the landlords' income from their holdings. And landlords felt the threat all the more keenly because of concurrent hikes in land taxes. As will be discussed in more detail in the following chapter, land taxes in Jiangnan increased precipitously after the imposition of KMT rule in 1927. Between 1926–27 and the mid-1930's, for instance, the tax for paddy land nearly doubled in Wuxing County and rose 60–70 percent in Jiaxing and Pinghu.[81] The combination of decreased rent and increased tax dealt landlords a mighty financial blow, cutting their net gain by as much as a half between 1927 and 1929.[82]

Predictably, the declining profitability of landownership drove land prices down, adding a fall in property values to the list of landlord grievances against the KMT reform. Land prices in northern Zhejiang dropped 20 percent between 1925–26 and 1929–30.* By contrast, in southern Jiangsu, where little effort was made to carry out the reform, land prices climbed throughout the late 1920's, reached a peak in 1930, and only declined thereafter because of the depression.[83]

Zhejiang landlords adopted a number of strategies to undermine the rent reduction campaign. They fired off petitions, some bearing several hundred signatures, to the central Nationalist government in Nanjing. In these documents, carefully worded to conceal their opposition to the idea of a permanent reduction, landlords accused tenants of violating the new laws by refusing to pay the reduced rents in full and charged the arbitration committees with unjustly favoring peasants in their handling

---

*Qian Chengze, *Jiaxingxian zhi zudian zhidu*, p. 30273; Zhang Zongbi, "Zhejiang Pinghu nongye," pp. 594–95. Both subsoil rights in the dual ownership system and land without any division of rights declined in value. Interestingly, the price of tenant topsoil rights increased greatly in those areas where a more determined effort was made to carry out the rent reform. In Jiaxing County the price for topsoil rights rose from the 3–5 yuan per mu typical of the years before 1927 to 10–15 yuan after the start of the reduction campaign (Feng Zigang, *Jiaxingxian nongcun diaocha*, pp. 36–37). This threefold increase greatly outpaced the rise in rice prices for the same period (see Table B.3), suggesting that reduced rents increased the profitability and hence the value of topsoil rights.

of disputes. According to Lucien Bianco, who has studied the surviving documents housed in the Second Historical Archives in Nanjing, the petitioners often ended their appeals with expressions of regret that because of their straitened financial circumstances, they might not be able to pay their taxes.[84]

Closer to home, landlords sought to undercut peasant support for the reform by evicting tenants who insisted too forcefully on their right to a reduction. The new land laws attempted to prevent such retribution by specifying the circumstances in which a landlord could legally require a peasant to vacate a tenancy. The revised regulations of 1928 stipulated that a landlord could evict a tenant only if he wished to farm the land himself or if the tenant had defaulted. In a case of default, however, eviction was still not permissible if the tenant had paid a security deposit that the landlord could draw on for the arrears or if he owned the topsoil of the property.[85] These regulations were honored more in the breach than in the observance, and cases of unlawful eviction accounted for most of the litigation handled by the arbitration committees.[86]

In some areas landlords attempted to sabotage the reforms by using them as an excuse to raise rather than reduce rents. In Pinghu County, for example, landlords had been charging tenants actual rents ranging from 50 to 90 percent of the nominal amounts. For land with a nominal rent of, say, 1.2 shi per mu, actual rents varied from 0.6 to 1.08 shi, or about 25 to 45 percent of a rice harvest of 2.4 shi, the standard yield used in the calculations for reduction in Pinghu. Tenants with actual rents of 50 to 70 percent (0.6 to 0.84 shi) were thus already paying less than 37.5 percent (0.9 shi) of a harvest. Although the regulations explicitly stated that amounts lower than the 37.5-percent ceiling were to remain unchanged, many landlords in Pinghu imposed increases that pushed rents up to that level.[87] To tenants, they justified their actions by insisting, in the words of one rural investigator, that "the government has already decreed that rents should be 37.5 percent [of a standard harvest]. If we continue to collect the amounts we have been collecting, then we would be breaking the law."[88] Thanks to the misconceptions they fostered among the Pinghu peasantry, many tenants there opposed the reform.[89]

Of all the landlord strategies, the one that sealed the fate of the 25-percent reduction in Zhejiang was a refusal to pay land taxes in full. Over the period 1928–31 the province's losses in tribute and diding revenue were enormous, off 27 to 36 percent a year from the amount collected in 1927.[90] (By contrast, Jiangsu's revenue from these items decreased only slightly in the first post-reform years, down 3 percent in 1928 and 7 percent in 1929; moreover, it then increased substantially, to stand 45 percent over the 1927 level in 1930 and 33 percent in 1931.[91]) In northern Zhejiang, where a firm KMT hold of the local governmental apparatus resulted in the strongest reform effort, the decline in land tax revenue was especially pronounced, with some counties collecting in 1928 and 1929 only 40 to 50 percent of the amounts collected in 1927.[92]

The drastic drop in tax revenue could not have been more untimely, for the Zhejiang provincial government was embarked on an ambitious modernization program that added extra expenditures to an already burdened budget. The governor also feared that hard-pressed landlords would be unwilling or unable to purchase the bonds that were to finance such projects as railway and road construction. In April 1929 he announced the termination of the rent campaign on the grounds that it had done little more than create new conflict in the countryside. The provincial KMT branch, reacting swiftly to what it called a betrayal of the ideology of Sun Yat-sen, appealed for assistance to the central government, which sent a representative to Hangzhou to mediate the dispute. With his help the party branch and the provincial government hammered out a compromise that kept the rent laws on the books but granted Zhejiang officials full and exclusive responsibility for their enforcement. Now free of any party supervision in the matter, the provincial government in 1930 simply ceased all efforts to carry out the reforms, and the 25-percent reduction campaign in Zhejiang came to an end.[93]

Landlord opposition to the KMT reform thus ultimately proved to be its undoing. In this, Zhejiang landlords reacted quite differently from the way their counterparts in Jiangsu had reacted some sixty years earlier to a similar government effort to legislate a permanent decrease in rents. The Tongzhi rent reduction in Suzhou had been relatively successful. Rent relations immediately after the Taiping Rebellion were in shambles, and Suzhou landlords, not having received much from tenants for a number of years anyway, perceived the need for a permanent reduction to regain control over their land and its product. In northern Zhejiang in the 1920's, by contrast, rent relations, though continually threatened by tenant resistance, enjoyed a large measure of stability, in no small part because of state intercession. Landlords thus saw no immediate benefit to be gained from a permanent reduction in rents.

Of at least equal importance was the fact that the Tongzhi reform had required no economic sacrifice from Suzhou landlords. On the contrary, the permanent decrease in land taxes had more than compensated for the decreases in rents, leaving them ahead financially. The KMT, however, sought to enforce a permanent reduction in rent even while imposing a significant increase in tax. Each alone would have been difficult for landlords to accept, but the two together were much more than they were able to bear. At the same time, by taking the issue of rent reduction completely out of the landlords' hands, the KMT demanded that they surrender a bargaining chip that had been of great use in the past in keeping land taxes in check. No longer would they be able to make their willingness to undertake a reduction in rent contingent on a remission in tax. The loss of this leverage, as well as the financial hardship caused by falling rents and rising taxes, brought landlords into overwhelming opposition to this instance of state intervention.

Nevertheless, the KMT campaign, while falling far short of its architects' intent, left its mark on the northern Zhejiang countryside. Rents in certain locales were reduced and remained at their reform levels even after the provincial government abandoned its efforts to enforce the new law. More generally, the campaign created a climate that made it all the more difficult for landlords to raise rents. To that degree, it strengthened the state's hand in the matter of setting rents and helped to restrain increases in the tenantry's burden in the Republican period.

CHAPTER 6

Popular Resistance in the Republican Period, 1912 - 1937

Increasing state participation in rent relations, along with growing landlord mobilization, transformed the context within which Jiang-nan tenants acted collectively. And by all evidence, the new context encouraged them to do so. From the fall of 1912 through the fall of 1936, at least 126 tenant collective actions, each involving anywhere from fifty to several thousand people, took place in the region, a figure far exceeding the twenty-eight incidents of the turbulent 1840's and 1850's and the thirty-eight incidents of the final four decades of the Qing (see Table 6.1).[1] This escalation in frequency was accompanied by a rise in scale; the incidents of the Republican era tended to be of wider geographical scope and to have more participants than earlier ones.

Moreover, rent resistance displaced organized protest against land taxation as the principal form of peasant collective action. In fact, Republican Jiangnan experienced only sixteen tax protests, a marked decline from the twenty-nine cases of the 1840's and 1850's and the fifty-nine cases of 1873–1911 (Table 6.1).

This development calls for a reconsideration of the dynamics of state penetration of local society and the types of rural protest that that process provoked. Generally, China scholars, following the arguments of Charles Tilly and James Scott, have seen tax resistance as the typical community response to state-building efforts.[2] As the state levied more and more taxes to support its modernization programs, they say, villagers mobilized to resist the new claims on their harvest. That was clearly the case in North China, with its overwhelmingly cultivator-owner population. But it was not the case in Jiangnan, with its very different farming population. There, a more intrusive state presence in local society prompted

TABLE 6.1
Collective Actions in Jiangnan, 1840–1936

Target	1840–1859		1873–1911		1912–1936	
	Number	Percent	Number	Percent	Number	Percent
Rents	28	49%	35	31%	116	81%
Taxes/levies	29	51	56	50	6	4
Rents and taxes	—	—	3	3	10	7
Unknown[a]	—	—	18	16	12	8
TOTAL	57	100%	112	100%	144	100%

SOURCE: Appendix A.

[a] Actions connected with the reporting of poor harvests (baohuang) that may have been aimed at either rents or taxes or both.

not an escalation in tax resistance, but an escalation in rent resistance and a reorientation of tenant protest toward the state.

POPULAR RESISTANCE TO RENTS

The escalation in tenant collective action during the Republican period can be linked to a number of factors: a succession of natural disasters, adverse economic conditions in the 1930's, the new context of greater landlord mobilization and state involvement in rent relations, and better peasant organization. What it cannot be attributed to, let me reiterate, is rising rents.[3] As we saw in the preceding chapter, except perhaps for a few counties in the cotton belt in Jiangsu, real rents did not significantly increase in the Republican period; in fact, in places where local officials routinely participated in the setting of ceilings, they may even have been lower than in the late Qing. Moreover, the crux of the disputes was not rent hikes but rather the landlords' failure to decrease the regular amounts during years of low yields. In 101 of the 120 collective actions in which the tenant demands are clearly spelled out in the sources, a reduction in the usual rent was the primary claim.*

The overwhelming majority of the incidents, then, took place during years of poor harvest due to inclement weather or insect infestation. Natural calamities—some local, some relatively widespread—in 1917, 1918, 1919, 1920, 1921, 1925, 1926, 1928, 1929, 1931, 1934, and 1935 were the precipitating factor in 84 percent of the tenant collective actions of

---

*The other 19 incidents were peasant association- or CCP-led protests against landlord oppression (12) or acts of revenge against police and other public or private dunners for severe punishment of rent defaulters (6) or, in one case, retaliation on a tenant who, in defiance of the decision of his fellow villagers, had paid his rent on the sly. The motives in six cases are simply unknown.

the Republican era. Only twenty protests, all in 1927–28 and most led by peasant associations and CCP activists, were not linked to poor yields.

In the 1930's the effects of these natural disasters were greatly exacerbated by the depression. The price of wheat declined 37 percent between 1930 and 1934, and though it recovered enough to make good most of this loss by 1936, the average wheat price was still 20 percent lower in 1931–36 than in the years 1929–30.[4] Rice fell off even more drastically, primarily because of extraordinarily high prices in 1930. From that year to 1933 the price dropped 53 percent and then remained 60 to 70 percent below the 1930 level (Table B.3). The average price in 1931–36 was 25 percent lower than the 1926–30 average. Raw cotton also declined but less drastically than either rice or wheat. The price peaked in 1930, fell 35 percent by 1933, and then began to rise. The fall-off between the 1926–30 and 1931–36 averages was 18 percent.[5]

The depression reserved its worst blow for peasants engaged in sericulture. The contraction of the world market for silk textiles drove the price of silkworm cocoons down 53 to 73 percent between the years 1930 and 1934.[6] Sericulture became a losing proposition, and peasants cut their losses by converting their mulberry fields to paddy. In Wuxi, for example, 30 percent of the total cultivated acreage had been planted in mulberry in 1927; by 1932 the figure had been slashed to 6.6 percent.[7]

The depression of the 1930's, coupled with a string of poor harvests, meant that even if landlords did not demand any more from tenants, the burden of rent became heavier because of the decline in total household income. The result was an intensification of rent resistance in the 1930's, and more tenant actions (54) in the five years 1932–36 than in any other five consecutive years in the whole of the restive Republican period (Table A.3).

THE NEW CONTEXT FOR
TENANT COLLECTIVE ACTION

To explain what prompted rent resistance during the Republican era is not to explain why peasants chose to act collectively rather than individually, or how they were able to do so once the decision was made, or what form those actions took. For that, one must look beyond simple economics to the larger political context. Growing landlord mobilization and increasing state involvement in setting and collecting rents changed power relations in rural society, and this in turn influenced the Jiangnan tenantry's incentive, opportunity, and capacity to act collectively.

Indirect confirmation of the importance of the new political context can be found in the protests' shift of geographical focus. Generally, though not invariably, those counties where state participation in rent relations and the mobilization of landlords were most advanced show the greatest increase in tenant collective action. The most telling example is the suburban area of Suzhou city (Changzhou, Yuanhe, and Wu counties of the Qing; Wu County of the Republican period), which stood at the forefront of the changing relationship among landlords, tenants, and the state. During the period 1840–59 no tenant collective actions were reported for this area. But in succeeding years it experienced more tenant protests than any other part of Jiangnan, fifteen collective actions in 1873–1911, for 39 percent of the regional total, and fifty-six in 1912–36, for 44 percent. Other counties where power relations changed more slowly and more moderately exhibited similar but less dramatic increases—for example, Songjiang County (Huating and Lou counties of the Qing), from five cases in 1840–59 to fifteen in 1912–36, and Kunshan County (Kunshan and Xinyang of the Qing) from no incidents in 1840–59 to six in 1912–36. (See Appendix A.)

In what ways, then, did the new context promote a rise in the incidence of tenant collective action?[8] Landlord mobilization and greater state intrusion, I argue, presented tenants with both increased threats and expanded opportunities, and it was the combination of the two that accounts in large measure for the escalation in collective resistance to rents. The new coercive capabilities of landlords and the state increased the tenants' incentive for collective resistance by making rent collection more efficient and thus more of a threat to their subsistence. At the same time, we shall see, the larger role of the state in setting rents increased the likelihood that tenants would and could act collectively against this threat by providing an opportunity for legitimate protest (*baohuang*), by facilitating mobilization, and by ensuring that the action would have some chance of success.

The first point is less clear-cut than the second. For the enlarged capacity for coercing the recalcitrant in fact had contrary effects on the tenantry's ability to mobilize. On the one hand, it no doubt discouraged such activity by raising the costs of collective action. Although the evidence is inconclusive, violent confrontations between tenants and their foes in the Republican period appear to have claimed more peasant lives and to have resulted in more peasant arrests than conflicts of similar scale in the Qing. More obviously, peaceful rent strikes, which officials might have ignored in the past because of inadequate resources, were now more likely to invite government suppression, thus resulting in a greater loss of life and liberty for the tenant participants.

On the other hand, the heightened repressive-coercive capabilities of the state and landlords encouraged tenant collective resistance by raising the costs of nonaction. As dunning grew more systematic and extensive, peasants became less able to escape the consequences of individual rent delinquency. If they did *not* engage in a concerted effort to defend their default, they risked certain economic hardship and possible incarceration. More efficient dunning thus increased their incentive to take collective action.

The license to do so certainly played a role in not a few cases. In their newfound role as the regulators of acceptable levels of rent, local officials permitted groups of peasants to appeal to them for reduction through the procedure of baohuang, the reporting of a poor harvest, a new addition to the tenantry's repertoire of resistance strategies. In the past baohuang had been used almost exclusively by groups of landowners in the hope that a magistrate would examine the condition of their crops and then work to get them a remission in taxes. Tenants had rarely, if ever, used the procedure to secure reductions in their rents, appealing instead directly to their landlords. In the twentieth century, as the state assumed the role of arbiter of rents, local officials displaced landlords as the tenantry's first court of appeal, and instances of baohuang accounted for one-third of the tenant collective actions of the Republican era.

Moreover, as officials took on greater responsibility for the dunning and setting of rents, tenants of different landlords found a common ground for action. Cultivators who in the past might have organized merely against their own landlord now joined with the tenants of other landlords to march on a county office or to drive away government collectors. This enlarged potential recruitment pool eased the difficulties of mobilization, with the result that actions against official personnel involved more people from a wider area than those aimed exclusively against landlords and their private dunners. The number of tenant participants in actions directed at officials averaged about 850, versus only 410 for private dunners. And whereas actions against dunners seldom involved protesters from more than a handful of contiguous communities, those directed at officials, particularly baohuang at county yamens, drew together people from numerous villages and sometimes even from several rural townships (*xiang*).

Finally, what also helped to tip the balance toward collective action was the fact that it so often worked. Peasant protesters scored clear-cut victories (meaning that officials and/or landlords acceded wholly or partially to their demands) in a full third of the Republican-period conflicts in which rent reduction was the primary claim. To a certain extent this rate of success was the cumulative effect of the volume of collective action; the more that tenants demonstrated their intent to realize their interests through means both peaceful and violent, the more willing their adversaries were to grant them concessions in order to prevent further conflict and ensure that at least a portion of the rent would be paid. But an equally important reason for their success was a growing landlord and government vulnerability to tenant claims. The understanding that underlay the collaboration of prominent landholders and local officials— the need to regulate the burden of rent—made them more apt to concede the legitimacy of tenant demands.

TENANT ORGANIZATION AND MOBILIZATION

The changing interaction between landlords and officials thus created conditions conducive to collective rent resistance. But it is unlikely that the relationship between landlords and the state would have changed in the direction it did had it not been for peasant resistance in the first place. Tenant collective action was not simply a by-product of the new context but was instrumental in shaping and sustaining it. Moreover, peasants would not have been able to deal with either the increased coercion or the expanded opportunities of the period had they not already possessed considerable ability to act.

As noted earlier, tenants in the Qing relied primarily on existing vil- lage communal structures (family and lineage ties, temple societies, and the connections formed through cooperative labor in water conservancy) to rally their numbers for collective resistance to rents. This in turn in- jected an element of parochialism into their collective actions, which, several notable exceptions aside, tended to be confined to peasants from a few neighboring villages.

Twentieth-century tenants still drew predominantly on these sorts of ties in their mobilization for resistance, with the result that actions as limited in scale as the nineteenth-century ones remained quite common. But they also began to forge links with peasants outside their normal communal structures under the umbrella of rent resistance associations. These groups sprang up in many locales, as the situation demanded, with such names as the One Dime Society (Yijiaohui) of Zhaowen (1900), the Thousand People Society (Qianrenhui) of the Wuxi-Jiangyin-Changshu border area (1911), the Tenant Society (Dianhuhui) of Huating (1912), and the Peasant Organization (Nongtuan) of Pinghu (1918).[9]

Detailed information on the formation, structure, procedures, and membership of most of these associations is lacking, but a look at the United Hearts Associations (Qixinshe) of Jinshan County, organized in 1917, can provide some sense of how they operated. The force behind the Jinshan associations was Jiang Jiyun, who had already earned local notoriety for his organization of a tenant struggle five years earlier. Jiang had worked as an accountant for a landlord family, a position from which he was fired for some unspecified reason. In 1912, perhaps partly out of pique, he rallied peasants from more than a score of villages in the northern township of the county for a rent strike. His efforts soon landed him in jail. Several hundred to several thousand of his followers then converged on the magistrate's office and threatened to attack the prison if Jiang was not set free. The magistrate released their leader, and the peasants returned home.[10]

These ties stood Jiang in good stead when he set out to mobilize the tenants in 1917. That year, an infestation of rice-stalk borers reduced the countywide harvest by as much as 40 percent. After consulting with landlord representatives, the Jinshan magistrate set the rental chengse at 65 percent, an amount that disgruntled tenants because it failed to take account of cultivators who had suffered a far more serious decline in yield. Assured of substantial peasant backing, Jiang Jiyun again decided to take up the banner of protest and founded in the northern township of Jinshan a tenant society (*dianhuhui*) with himself as its head. He then sent people to other areas of the county to agitate for the establishment of similar groups, the United Hearts Associations.

These efforts paid off, and United Hearts Associations were quickly formed in various locales in the southeastern and western as well as the northern township. As their first order of business, the new groups decided to present roasted pig heads as bribes to resident dibao and precinct managers. (The peasants considered this delicacy a very effective way of ensuring silence because they believed anyone who ate it would be physically unable to open his mouth.) Next the societies instructed tenants to pay rent regardless of the quality of their harvest, but only at the exceedingly low commutation rate of 1.3 yuan per shi. Any peasant who delivered more would be fined ten times the amount he had paid in rent, and if he failed to pay the fine, his house would be destroyed. The penalty payments would be distributed to those cultivators who, despite a complete crop failure, had managed to deliver rent in compliance with the associations' rate.

The extent to which the United Hearts Associations of Jinshan carried out this risk-sharing program is difficult to determine. There is some evidence to suggest that they did enforce the prohibition against paying more than the stipulated 1.3 yuan, but none to indicate that they then redistributed the fines to more unfortunate peasants. It is clear, however, that Jiang's resistance had considerable impact. As of mid-January 1918, when accounts of the movement vanished from newspapers, landlords had received no more than 20 to 30 percent of the reduced (65-percent chengse) rent.[11]

Their success notwithstanding, the United Heart Associations of Jinshan did not endure. Like the other tenant organizations of the twentieth century, they rose in response to a specific need and then disappeared once the crisis had passed. But however ephemeral, they served their purpose, enabling tenant leaders to mobilize peasants from a much larger area (almost the entire county in the case of Jinshan) than they could have done if they had depended solely on communal structures.

Clearly, mobilization on this scale was aided by the development noted earlier, the fact that tenants of different landlords now shared a common adversary—the county government. But it was also aided in no small part by the connections that peasants from different villages made at the marketplace as they became increasingly drawn into the commercial economy. Jiangnan rural society, already highly commercialized before the Taiping Rebellion, became even more so afterwards, with a growing foreign market for silk textiles and a growing domestic market for cotton goods. Additionally, the widespread commutation of rent and tax payment compelled even peasants who grew only food crops to become involved in the market. Commercial development in turn brought the formation of new towns. Between the Daoguang reign (1821–50) and the end of the Qing, the number of towns doubled from 100 to 206 in Suzhou Prefecture and rose from 105 to 185 in Changzhou Prefecture. Other Jiangnan prefectures as well experienced significant new town formation in the late Qing.[12] This increasing density of the marketing network shortened the physical and social distance between peasants of different communities and helped to overcome village parochialism in matters of common concern.

The Peasant Movement in the Lower Yangzi Region

One of the striking features of tenant collective action in the lower Yangzi region was its spontaneity. Only sixteen percent (20) of the 126 protests were organized by peasant associations and/or KMT or CCP activists. In this respect Jiangnan differed sharply from Guangdong and Hunan, where peasant associations formed during the First United Front between the KMT and the CCP in the mid-1920's were instrumental in galvanizing the tenantry for resistance to landlord demands.[13]

Given the lower Yangzi valley's rich tradition of popular protest, its high degree of land concentration, and its escalating tensions between landlords and tenants, one would have expected the region to be especially fertile ground for party activists. That it was not was due to geopolitical factors, the presence of a particularly hostile and repressive elite and government, and, more generally, the inability of both the KMT and the CCP to rally peasant support for their policies and programs.

Geopolitical factors made Jiangnan, initially at any rate, less a focus of party mobilization than Hunan and Guangdong. Until the Northern Expedition of 1926–27, the central leadership of the KMT and the CCP was located in Guangzhou (Canton). This restricted the geographical range of the parties' activities, and accepting that reality, they did not spend precious resources on relatively distant Jiangnan. The low priority initially accorded the region can be seen in the recruitment figures for the Canton Peasant Movement Training Institute, a United Front school established in 1924 to train rural organizers. The first five classes, in session from July 1924 to December 1925, drew no students from Zhejiang or Jiangsu. Only with the sixth form (May to September 1926) do we find any recruits from these two provinces, but they numbered only fifteen in a total class membership of 318.[14]

Data on the peasant associations (*nongmin xiehui*) formed during the First United Front also reflect the comparatively low level of party mobilization in Jiangnan. By the start of the Northern Expedition in the summer of 1926, Guangdong claimed a peasant association membership of 665,441, Hunan a membership of 60,000, and Hubei a membership of 72,000. During the course of the march north, mass movements expanded greatly, and by the late spring and early summer of 1927, peasant association membership had reportedly risen to 700,000 in Guangdong, 4,517,140 in Hunan, and 2,842,239 in Hubei.[15] The fact that there are no aggregate figures for Jiangsu and Zhejiang suggests that the membership there was too insignificant to warrant even a statistical survey.

Qualitative evidence confirms this impression. Before the arrival of the Northern Expeditionary Army in the lower Yangzi region in March 1927, CCP and KMT activists had made some attempt to establish peasant associations, but the repressive power of the hostile warlord government and the elite ensured that they had little chance of success. Associations were set up in several townships in Songjiang, Jinshan, and Qingpu in 1926, for instance, but they were forced in short order either to disband for fear of arrest and execution or to go underground, where their effectiveness as a vehicle for peasant mobilization was severely limited.[16]

The difficulties of organizing the peasantry in such an inhospitable environment can be seen most clearly in the fate that befell Zhou Shuiping, Jiangnan's closest approximation of Guangdong's famous peasant leader Peng Pai.[17] Zhou was born into an educated but impoverished family in a small market town in Gushan township, Jiangyin County. His father, a graduate of a teachers training institute, was unable to find regular employment during the boy's early years, and the family had to rely on the mother's earnings from cotton weaving. In 1905 the eleven-year-old Zhou Shuiping learned tailoring from his maternal uncle, a trade that he engaged in for the next several years. Finally, in 1912, he had the opportunity to receive a formal education when his father accepted a position at a school in nearby Shazhou. In that year, at age eighteen, the youth entered an upper primary school; he then enrolled in a normal school, from which he graduated in 1917, at the age of twenty-three.

After a brief stint as a teacher, Zhou went to Japan for two years of study. In 1919 he participated in the May Fourth demonstrations in Tokyo, for which he was arrested and detained in jail for several days. The following year the newly politicized youth returned to Gushan, where he taught Chinese language and literature in the public school system, established a night school for commoners as well as a progressive organization for young people, and assisted the poor in their lawsuits against the rich. He soon ran afoul of the authorities in Jiangyin because of his exposure of the corruption of some educational officials, and was dismissed from his post. Over the next several years the peripatetic Zhou taught physical education and Chinese in schools in Zhejiang, northern Jiangsu, Chuansha, and Shanghai, all the while continuing his political activities. Sometime during this period he joined the KMT, and after he returned to his home in the summer of 1925, he helped to organize a party branch in Jiangyin. He also founded a study group devoted to the improvement of education for commoners, published a vernacular newspaper dedicated to exposing the social ills of the county, and, in early October 1925, organized a peasant association called the Tenant Cooperative Self-help Society (Dianhu Hezuo Zijiu Hui).

To advertise his society and to recruit peasants to its cause, Zhou delivered lectures and passed out tens of thousands of handbills in villages in the Jiangyin-Wuxi-Changshu border area. In his speeches and writings he repeatedly emphasized the paramount importance of organization and solidarity. As one of his handbills explained:

> If rent collectors want to collect too much rent, then everyone, united in spirit, will hold a meeting and select representatives to negotiate for a reduction. The representatives should be courteous in their conduct and absolutely should not speak in a coarse and rude manner. If the collectors do not agree to our request, then everyone, united in spirit and action, will agree not to deliver any rent. If one of us is taken to jail, then all of us will go together. Should anyone pay rent on the sly, then we will decide publicly on a suitable punishment.

Only when all tenants cooperated in this fashion, the leaflet concluded, would landlords be forced to reform their rack-renting ways.

Zhou's mobilization of tenants quickly caught the attention of several members of the elite, who drew on their connections with some provincial assemblymen to engineer his arrest in the middle of November 1925. For the next several months Zhou's fate hung in the balance. The Jiangsu governor instructed the local authorities to set him free on bail and to go easy on him when he came to trial, but the Jiangyin magistrate, under pressure from the gentrymen who had secured Zhou's arrest, kept him in jail and lobbied for a severe punishment. Finally, in January 1926, the impasse was broken when Sun Chuanfang, the warlord in control of

Jiangsu at the time, demanded that landowners pay a portion of their next year's tax immediately. The gentrymen seized on this as an opportunity to bring the Zhou case to the warlord's notice. In an inflammatory petition carefully worded to appeal to Sun's avarice and anticommunism, they lamented that they would be unable to prepay their taxes because of the rent resistance movement of Zhou Shuiping and his Tenant Cooperative Self-help Society. Zhou Shuiping, they informed him,

> advocated communal property, propagated communism, mobilized peasants for rent resistance, and plotted conspiracies. Peasants throughout the countryside are refusing to deliver any rent and are ready to make even more trouble. The situation has become extremely dangerous. The landlords [literally *shenfu*, "the gentry and the wealthy"] of the county have not received one grain of rent and thus cannot prepay next year's land tax.

Sun Chuanfang responded by ordering the activist's immediate execution, and Zhou Shuiping was beheaded on January 17, 1926.[18]

Zhou Shuiping's fate suggests that the warlord government of Jiangsu was less tolerant of peasant organizers than the militarists in control of Guangdong and Hunan. Peng Pai's much more radical Haifeng peasant movement survived for two years (1922–24) in no small measure because of the support he received from Guangdong's comparatively progressive governor Chen Jiongming. And in Hunan the upsurge in open peasant organization in 1926–27 was made possible by the politically expedient alliance forged between the KMT and the militarist governor Tang Shengzhi. Though both Chen and Tang eventually turned on the mass movements, their initial acceptance of them, however grudgingly given, created an atmosphere in which the peasant movement could flourish. No such atmosphere existed in Jiangnan under Sun Chuanfang.

Not until the revolutionary forces had driven Sun and his cohorts from the lower Yangzi area in March 1927 did the KMT and CCP have the opportunity to organize there openly. The KMT peasant department sent out activists, many of whom were Communists, to establish village, township, and county peasant associations and to rally the rural masses for struggles against "local bullies and evil gentry" (*tuhao lieshen*). Yet even in the more hospitable climate of early spring 1927, the Jiangnan associations did not serve as vehicles for tenant mobilization to the extent that their counterparts in Hunan had in the previous autumn. According to the available evidence, they provided leadership for only six collective protests (four attacks on landlord residences, one attack on a bursary, and one demonstration against landlord oppression), an insignificant number compared with the Hunan actions, even allowing for the hyperbole in Mao Zedong's famous 1927 report on the subject.[19]

The extremely limited mobilization in Jiangnan was due in part to the fact that the associations, set up mostly at the county and subcounty levels, tended to be supravillage groups without a firm basis among the peasantry,[20] but also in part to a sheer accident of timing. The associations had but a few short months to make an impact before the political climate in Jiangnan shifted decisively to the right following Chiang Kai-shek's coup against the CCP in Shanghai on April 12. But since these months of late winter and early spring were neither rent nor tax collection time, the activists could not appeal directly to immediate peasant interests.

After Chiang's coup the KMT government in Zhejiang and Jiangsu shut down mass associations that evinced too great a passion for serving the people or else purged them of their more radical elements.[21] During the late spring and summer of 1927, CCP activists, now working underground, formed clandestine peasant organizations in several counties. The new groups' first opportunity for overt action came in the fall of 1927 in response to the CCP's call for Autumn Harvest Uprisings, in which the peasant masses were to be mobilized to storm the cities, unite with the proletariat, and overthrow the KMT government.

In the lower Yangzi region the Autumn Harvest Uprisings turned out to be quite limited in scope. All together, despite some evidence of preliminary preparations elsewhere, uprisings occurred in only Yixing, Jiangyin, Wuxi, and Qingpu, counties where the underground Communist network was particularly active.[22] And only in Yixing did the revolt follow the course plotted by the CCP: a peasant march on the cities. There the local CCP branch, capitalizing on the landowners' opposition to a tribute tax surcharge recently imposed by the KMT and promising rent reductions to tenants, mobilized several thousand peasants to attack Yixing city on November 1, 1927. The ill-equipped peasant army held the city for two days before being routed by KMT military forces. During that time they killed nine officials, tried and executed five "evil gentry and local bullies," destroyed the houses of more than thirty others, and looted three hundred shops.[23]

In the other counties the Autumn Harvest Uprisings were less coordinated, less focused on the capture of cities and towns, and more anti-landlord than anti-government in intent and action. In November and December CCP members in Wuxi and Jiangyin led groups of peasants, ranging in number from a hundred to a thousand, in attacks on the residences of landlords and rent dunners living in villages and market towns. In their raids the peasant forces destroyed land registers and contracts, set fire to houses, and killed landlords or members of their families. The demands they set forth were wholly contradictory, coupling as they did rent reduction with the confiscation and redistribution of landlord land. The only explicitly anti-government demand was a call for a reduction

TABLE 6.2

*Number of Participants in Tenant Collective Actions
in Jiangnan, 1912–1936*

Participants	Actions	Participants	Actions
50–99	4	800–899	1
100–199	9	900–999	0
200–299	15	1,000–1,999	14
300–399	13	2,000–2,999	8
400–499	7	3,000–3,999	2
500–599	4	4,000–4,999	0
600–699	1	5,000+	1
700–799	4		

SOURCES: See Table A.3.

NOTE: No estimates are available on 43 of the 126 rent protests in the Republican period.

in land taxes, and with only one exception, KMT officials escaped attack altogether.[24]

Anti-landlord sentiment was even stronger in the Autumn Harvest Uprising in Qingpu. The CCP organizers there, working through peasant associations, advertised their planned uprising as a rent resistance movement, and their goals and methods reflected this orientation to a considerable extent. The peasant association of the eastern part of Qingpu, for example, drew up a detailed list of essentially moderate demands that included a 25-percent rent reduction, the return of all peasant rental deposits, the right to decide whether fixed rents were to be paid in kind or in cash, and the abolition of all rental debts, dunners' fees, and overlarge rent measures. The association urged tenants to withhold their autumn rents until landlords had accepted these demands.[25]

As long as the Qingpu activists adhered to the goals and methods of rent resistance, they were able to draw a fair number of peasants to their cause. But when they attempted to transform the movement into an armed uprising against the KMT government, peasant support dissipated. Like the Autumn Harvest Uprisings in Yixing, Wuxi, and Jiangyin, the armed rebellion in Qingpu involved no more than several hundred to several thousand people, a figure that did not exceed the typical number of participants in Jiangnan tenant collective actions (see Table 6.2).[26]

However ill-orchestrated and bereft of popular support the Autumn Harvest Uprisings of 1927 turned out to be, they marked the high point of the Communists' mobilization of the Jiangnan peasantry. Thereafter, as the KMT white terror took its toll on Party members and others suspected of leftist leanings and as the CCP's base of operation shifted from regional lowland cores to mountainous hinterlands, Communist-led peasant struggles grew increasingly infrequent. Party activists led a hundred to a thousand peasants in attacks on rich households in Jiading County in April 1928, in Zhuanghang market town in Fengxian County in January 1929, and in Beixinjie market town in Songjiang County in February 1929.[27] After this last incident no peasant resistance to rents or taxes in Jiangnan had any Communist connection.

In general, then, CCP peasant organizers made little headway in the lower Yangzi valley. The hostile political climate and immense repressive power of the state and elite made participation in anything more radical than rent and tax resistance a risky and potentially life-threatening venture, and ensured that attempts at insurrection would be put down swiftly and surely. But these factors did not wholly account for the lack of success. Another equally important reason was that CCP programs had little appeal to Jiangnan tenants, who over the years had worked out their own strategies for coping with landlord demands. They were not an amorphous mass woefully in need of CCP guidance. Moreover, as the Qingpu case in particular suggests, Communist organizers were most successful in mobilizing tenants when they limited their goals to rent resistance, and least successful when they added to that objective a host of others, including, in the Autumn Harvest Uprisings, overthrowing the KMT government. That was taking the peasants farther than they were willing to go. Tenant protest in the lower Yangzi valley remained remedialist in nature, aimed not at overthrowing the system, but at rectifying its abuses.

Not just the goals, but the methods of the Communists as well, differed radically from those of typical peasant protest. In their attacks on class enemies from 1927 to 1929, the CCP activists and their supporters sought out and killed at least sixty-one landlords, merchants, officials, and private and public dunners. This sort of calculated bloodshed had never been part of Jiangnan tenant collective action. Rent protesters directed their premeditated violence against property (looting and burning houses and granaries and the like), and unlike the Communists and their peasant bands, who typically stole up on their quarry at night, they usually approached their targets noisily in broad daylight, making sure to give their foes ample opportunity to vacate the premises. When tenants did kill, it was to protect themselves from death, injury, or arrest; virtually all their victims were private and public dunners, yamen runners, soldiers, and policemen.* In short, the role of violence was quite different in the two types of collective action. On their own, peasants

---

*Over the entire 1840–1937 period (excluding the Taiping Rebellion), so far as I know, only one landlord was killed by tenants in collective actions not organized by party activists. That death occurred in Wujiang in early 1912 (*Shibao* 2/22, 3/27/1912).

usually resorted to violence against people only in self-defense, whereas the Communists and their followers, as befitted a class war, used it to eradicate their enemies.

Targets of Tenant Collective Action

As Table 6.3 shows, the tendency to make local government officials and private and public dunners the targets set twentieth-century tenant protest apart not only from the CCP actions of 1927–29 but also from earlier collective resistance to rents. (The actions led by Party activists have been excluded from the table, so as not to obscure the changes that occurred in the typical tenant protests.) In 1840–59 and even in 1873–1911, landlords were the objects of either peaceful appeal or violent attack in the majority of cases—in the first period, overwhelmingly so, involving 87 percent of the incidents. This compares with a mere 8 percent in 1912–36. By contrast actions aimed at private rent dunners rose from 9 percent in 1840–59 to 25 percent in 1912–36. More significantly, those aimed at official personnel climbed from 35 percent to 83 percent, with county magistrates and the heads of subcounty administrative units (xiangzhang, quzhang, and zhenzhang) heavily on the receiving end. In the following pages, we will take up each of these categories, beginning with private rent dunners.

When tenants felt aggrieved, it was far easier to attack the private dun-

TABLE 6.3

Targets of Tenant Collective Actions in Jiangnan, 1840–1936

Target	1840–1859		1873–1911		1912–1936	
	Number of cases	Percent	Number of cases	Percent	Number of cases	Percent
Landlords	20	87%	15	52%	7	8%
Private dunners	2	9	6	21	22	25
Official personnel	8	35	13	45	74	83
Officials[a]	3	13	4	14	49	55
Functionaries[b]	—	—	3	10	9	10
Public dunners[c]	5	22	6	21	16	18

SOURCES: See Appendix A.

NOTE: Targets could be determined in only 23 of the 1840–59 actions, 29 of the 1873–1911 actions, and 89 of the 1912–36 actions. The column totals exceed these figures because protests were often directed at multiple targets.

[a] County and subcounty magistrates in the Qing; county magistrates and subcounty officials (xiangzhang, "township head"; quzhang, "ward head"; and zhenzhang, "market town head") in the Republican period.

[b] Dibao, jingzao, baozheng, tudong, qudong, and baojiazhang (the heads of baojia groups).

[c] Yamen runners in the Qing; state dunning bureau personnel, policemen, and soldiers in the Republican period.

ners living in their own or a neighboring village than to attempt to enter the heavily guarded market towns and cities where the bursaries were located and the landlords resided. In Wu County, where the network of private dunners, known there as *cuijia*, was especially well developed, assaults on these landlord proxies became a regular feature of peasant protest. In some of the confrontations, the damage sustained by the dunners was far from negligible. Tenants set fire to the houses of twenty-six dunners in the fall of 1917, and sixty more were burned in October 1934.[28]

The animosity Wu tenants so vividly expressed against private dunners stemmed in no small part from their egregious abuse of power, abuse that the following passage suggests often went on without the landlord's knowledge, and often also to his disadvantage:

> Because private dunners habitually make the rounds of the villages year after year, they are extremely familiar with the peasants and the land. Landlords thus employ them to dun and collect rents in their stead. . . . Originally the dunners just issued rent notices. . . . But now the Suzhou landlords, frequently with a keen eye for petty advantages, hand over even the collection of rent to them. Peasants who live far from the city and thus dislike having to travel a considerable distance to deliver rent also feel that this arrangement works to their benefit. After the dunners collect the rent, they remit it to the landlord, and herein lies the problem of their reliability. The trustworthy among them deliver to the landlord all of the rent, but the untrustworthy either embezzle it all or keep a portion of it for themselves. . . . At times of poor harvest, the dunners have the great authority to decide on reductions in rent and, because landlords do not know the location of their land or the actual names of their tenants, they are able to distort the facts to suit their own ends, deceiving the landlords on the one hand and cheating the peasants on the other. . . . The landlords care only that their lives are comfortable and that rent collection is convenient; they are not interested in anything else. Since they normally only hear the dunners' side of things, they have no way of finding out about the real situation among peasants. They are completely ignorant of even the great hostility existing between dunners and tenants. This, it may be said, is a major cause of tenant rent resistance.[29]

In 1936 the Wu authorities, taking note of the role all this played in precipitating violent protest against rent, ordered landlords and bursaries to discontinue employing private rent dunners. The order went completely unheeded. Despite the grievances landlords may have had against the dunners, the network of intermediaries had become too entrenched and served the interests of absentee landowners and bursaries too well to be so easily eradicated.[30]

Unlike private dunners, who became more frequent targets in both absolute and relative terms, public dunners show a slight percentage decrease (22 percent of the cases in 1840–59 to 18 percent in 1912–36) but an overall absolute increase. Most of this increase came at the expense of soldiers (six cases) or policemen (five); state dunning bureau personnel were the targets in only five cases. Soldiers and police were, of course, involved in many of the Republican-era incidents as suppressors of tenant actions targeted against others, but in the cases noted here they functioned as rent dunners and became objects of attack for that reason.

Similarly, subcounty functionaries (dibao, jingzao, baozheng, tudong, and the like) could find themselves under attack when they served as dunners. But just as often, functionaries, particularly precinct and ward managers, aroused tenant ire by underreporting the extent of crop damage in their jurisdictions, an action that could cost peasants the reductions they felt they deserved.

The most significant change, statistically as well as politically, was the new focus on local officials (county magistrates and heads of subcounty administrative units). Where they had once borne the brunt of only 13–14 percent of the tenants' protests, they now became their favorite targets, with a 55-percent share. Moreover, once peasants could take the path of baohuang, the reporting of poor harvests, to secure rent reductions, the potential for violence increased. Officials, well aware that the harvest chengse and the consequent reductions they assigned tenants would influence the amount of tax landlords would be willing to pay, sometimes dismissed requests for crop investigations, underestimated (at least from the cultivators' perspective) the extent of the damage, or did not reduce rents as much as the tenants wanted. These responses often provoked tenants to resort to more drastic measures to press their suit, and baohuang, an essentially peaceful appeal, was transformed into its violent counterpart, *naohuang* ("agitation over poor harvests"). Fully thirteen of the forty-nine tenant actions aimed at government officials from 1912 through 1936 entailed violence against the persons, offices, and/or residences of county magistrates and district, ward, and market town heads.

By involving itself in rent relations, the government had thus placed itself squarely in the line of tenant fire. To be sure, official personnel had not remained aloof from contention over rents in the past, but their role in the Qing had been largely confined to supporting the landlords' dunning efforts and suppressing violent protest, and what enmity they incurred was merely consequential. In the twentieth century the local government and its personnel came to share center stage with private rent dunners as the primary targets of tenant collective action, with landlords for the most part being relegated to the wings.

This position was not an unenviable one, for it helped to shelter landlords from the violence of peasant resistance. In the 106 Republican tenant collective actions not led by peasant associations or the CCP, only six landlords met with any harm to their persons or possessions, compared with seventy-five in the twenty-eight incidents of the 1840's and 1850's and at least twenty-three in the thirty-eight incidents from 1873 to 1911. The assaults that might otherwise have been the fate of the Republican-period landlords were deflected by the tenants' perception of dunners and local officials as the people who truly counted in the matter of rents.

A series of tenant struggles in Wu County vividly illustrates this point. In 1935 the rice crop in certain areas of the county had sustained much insect damage. In late 1935 and early 1936 tenants in a number of the affected rural townships, dissatisfied with the rental chengse of 60 to 70 percent and the rental conversion rate, converged on township, ward, and market town offices to appeal for further concessions. Their peaceful requests denied, crowds of peasants then launched attacks on government offices, public security bureaus, and the houses of private rent dunners. In response the magistrate dispatched the peace preservation corps (*baoandui*) to suppress the protesters and, adding a carrot to the stick, instructed bursaries to decrease the chengse by an additional 10 percent. Such generosity failed to move the tenants, however, who continued over the next several months to resist payment so tenaciously that the magistrate began sending armed peace preservation soldiers out with police and dunners as they made their house-to-house searches for defaulting peasants. In retaliation tenants gathered for demonstrations, made more assaults on government offices and the residences of private dunners, and fought pitched battles with police and soldiers. At the end of April 1936 the magistrate granted the peasants in the most heavily devastated townships an additional reduction of 20 percent and also lowered the conversion rate for commuted rents, but these concessions came too late to appease the resisters, and violent confrontations continued until the end of June. All told, from December 1935 through June 1936, thirty-three separate episodes of collective action against rents occurred in Wu County. In none of these incidents was a landlord the direct target of protest.[31]

The shift in the focus of rent resistance in the lower Yangzi region defies conventional notions about the alignment of forces in rural collective action. As an expression of conflict in the fundamental class relation in' rural society, rent resistance should pit tenants and landlords against each other. Conversely, when peasants engaged in collective action against the government, land taxes, not rents, should be the issue of dispute. But developments in Jiangnan blurred this customary distinction between tax and rent resistance. As the role of the state in the landlord-tenant relationship grew, tenant protest similarly expanded to include the government as a target of protest.

To the extent that tenants and cultivator-owners came to share the state as a target, they found a common ground for action that had eluded them in the past. Until the twentieth century tax and rent resistance had remained distinct phenomena with different sets of antagonists. None of the peasant collective actions of the 1840's and 1850's, for example, took as its goal the reduction of both land taxes and rents. Beginning in the last decade of the Qing, however, tenants and cultivator-owners on occasion joined forces to march to a government office to request a harvest investigation and remissions in both taxes and rents. (Of course, for peasants who were both tenants and cultivator-owners, this single action served two purposes.) Of the 144 cases of peasant collective action in the years 1912–36, ten were clearly combined resistance to taxes and rents, and another twelve may have been, although the sources only mention that groups of peasants appealed to officials for harvest investigation and do not specify whether the ultimate aim was a lowering of rents or a lowering of taxes, or both (see Table 6.1). The blending of rent and tax resistance in this fashion would not have been possible had the state not become a target of rent protest.

The appearance of this element in tenant collective action and the concurrent decline in direct attacks on landlords, however, should not be interpreted as signifying a drastic reorientation in peasant consciousness. Lucien Bianco, for example, commenting in part on the 1935–36 protests in Wu County, writes that "the anger aroused in the tenants by the collusion between the exploiters and the authorities turned almost exclusively against the latter. Thus the anti-rent disturbances, which are deemed social rebellion *par excellence*, were aimed less at the rich than at the authorities."[32] He concludes that this tendency revealed a weak class consciousness among the peasantry. "Of the representatives of the elite, it was the official, not the landlord, who was the most common target. The spontaneous orientation of peasant anger suggests that the peasants of Republican China were more conscious of state oppression than of class exploitation."[33]

Bianco's characterization of peasant consciousness as being more anti-state than anti-landlord fails to take fully into account the complex interaction among landlords, officials, and tenants during the Republican period. Neglecting the state's role in determining rents, he concentrates solely on its role in collecting them. And even in this regard, his portrayal of peasant sentiment is somewhat misleading. To be sure, the collusion between officials and landlords in rent collection made the state a much more oppressive presence in tenant lives. And tenants reacted with attacks on officials and government dunning personnel. But the Jiangnan peasantry's new sense of state oppression did not mean, as Bianco seems to imply, that their resentment toward rack-renting landlords waned as a consequence, for, as we have seen, assaults on private landlord dunners had also became more commonplace in the Republican period. At least with respect to rent dunning, tenants exhibited both anti-state and anti-landlord feelings.

With respect to the setting of rents, however, the relationship between tenants and the state was of a different order. Officials served as mediators of the rival claims of landlords and tenants and did not necessarily side with landlords in a dispute. The large number of cases of peaceful appeals to officials, in fact, suggests that tenants perceived the local government as much more receptive to their demands than landlords. In these instances the peasants' targeting of officials instead of landlords was not an expression of their anger against state oppression, but rather a strategic decision about which party would give their case the more favorable hearing. In short, official intervention in rent relations was dual-faceted, and so too was the tenants' perception of the state. Peasants reacted strongly against the state's participation in dunning, but welcomed, and indeed by their very actions encouraged, its participation in determining rents.

POPULAR RESISTANCE TO LAND TAXES

One of the most striking aspects of peasant collective action in the lower Yangzi region in this period was the absolute decrease in the number of cultivator protests against land taxation. Collective resistance to taxes, which had averaged roughly 1.5 incidents a year in 1840–59 and 1873–1911, dropped to a mere 0.6 cases a year in 1912–36. This decline runs counter to the trend evident in other parts of Republican China, where an increasingly onerous tax burden provoked an escalation in this type of rural collective action.[34] To see why Jiangnan took a different path, we must examine the changes that took place in two domains: the land tax burden and the process by which landowners, peasants and landlords alike, asserted their claims against the government.[35]

Tables 6.4–6.6 chart the tax burden in yuan per mu for the most common grade of land in the six counties of Chuansha, Wu, Wuxi, Wujin, Changshu, and Wuxing. As we see, land taxes in all those places rose substantially from the early 1910's to the late 1920's and early 1930's, with the bulk of the increase occurring from 1927, the year the KMT assumed rule of the region. In Chuansha, for instance, land taxes more than doubled over the period 1912–32; three-fourths of the total increase (0.57 of 0.76 yuan) came in the final six years. In Wuxing the entire increase occurred after 1926 (since by then the higher rates of the middle of the period had been reduced, and taxes had been slightly below the 1912 figure for several years).

The absolute increase in taxes in Jiangnan during these two decades cannot be ascribed to any changes to speak of in the per-mu tax quotas.

TABLE 6.4
Rice and Cotton Prices in Jiangnan, 1912–1933

Year	Rice (yuan per shi)	Cotton (yuan per dan)	Year	Rice (yuan per shi)	Cotton (yuan per dan)
1912	7.94	5.00	1923	11.20	7.55
1913	7.21	5.00	1924	10.29	7.29
1914	6.42	5.00	1925	10.95	7.85
1915	7.40	5.00	1926	15.77	11.18
1916	7.12	5.00	1927	14.77	9.92
1917	6.52	5.00	1928	11.17	8.45
1918	6.62	5.00	1929	13.51	10.38
1919	6.94	5.00	1930	17.02	11.13
1920	9.61	6.90	1931	12.29	9.54
1921	9.68	7.20	1932	11.35	8.75
1922	11.26	7.94	1933	8.06	7.25

SOURCES: Zou Dafan et al., p. 236; *Fengxianxian zhi*, p. 659.

The militarist governments of Jiangsu and Zhejiang and then the KMT for the most part retained the essentials of the Qing land tax system. As during the imperial period, a landowner's payment was calculated by multiplying a fixed quota (taels [*liang*] per mu for the diding and shi per mu for the tribute tax) by conversion rates expressed as so many yuan per tael for the diding and so many yuan per shi for the tribute tax. The provincial governments of Zhejiang and Jiangsu also retained the statutory quotas that had been in force since the Tongzhi reduction, the only modifications being slight decreases in the amounts per mu.[36]

Nor can the tax hikes be linked to conversion rates. Unlike the Qing rates, those of the Republican period were quoted in foreign silver, the dominant medium of exchange in the region. Currency fluctuations therefore no longer exerted an inflationary effect on the landowner's tax bill. Moreover, the Republican rates, again unlike the Qing ones, were remarkably stable. In Jiangsu the provincewide statutory conversion rate for the tribute tax was set at 5.0 yuan per shi in 1912 and stayed at that level through the rest of the period. The Jiangsu diding conversion rate was set at 1.8 yuan per liang in 1912, raised to 2.1 yuan in 1914, and then lowered to its final figure, 2.05 yuan, in 1917.[37] In Zhejiang the diding rate was 1.8 yuan throughout the period; the tribute rate, set at 3.0 yuan in 1912, rose to 4.0 yuan in 1915, and then declined annually after 1920 (despite climbing rice prices) to stand at 3.3 yuan from 1926 on.[38]

In fact, it was the imposition of new land levies (*mujuan*, expressed as so many yuan per mu) and of surcharges (*fujiashui*, expressed as so many yuan per liang of diding or per shi of tribute) that caused taxes to jump so dramatically.[39] With few exceptions the revenue from these levies and surcharges was earmarked exclusively for county use. These county

TABLE 6.5

Land Taxes in Jiangnan, 1912–1933

(yuan per mu of the most common grade of land)

| Year | Chuansha | Wu | Wuxi[a] | | Wujin | Changshu | Wuxing |
			Buck	Chen			
1912	.60	.70			.75		.79
1913	.60	.70			.75		.79
1914	.65	.76	.58		.75		.79
1915	.69	.78	.56	.63	.75	.75	.91
1916	.69	.80	.57	.63	.75	.75	.91
1917	.66	.65	.56	.62	.75	.75	.91
1918	.67	.70	.55	.63	.75	.75	.91
1919	.71		.57	.63	.85	.73	.92
1920	.72		.56	.63	.95	.74	.92
1921	.72		.56	.63	.75	.74	.76
1922	.72	.64	.57	.63	.78	.75	.76
1923	.74	.74	.58	.63	.78	.74	.74
1924	.76		.59	.73	.85	.86	.73
1925	.77		.70	.65	.85	.72	.72
1926	.79		.79	.99	.85	.73	.71
1927	1.15	1.32	.90	.94	.99	1.01	1.13
1928	1.14	1.33	.87	.96	1.10	1.24	1.20
1929	1.14		.69	.95	.85	1.03	1.23
1930	1.26		.81	1.12	1.09		1.30
1931	1.26		1.09	1.04	1.03		1.23
1932	1.36		1.19	.92	1.09		1.33
1933	1.17			1.18	.85		1.27

SOURCES: *Chuanshaxian zhi*, 8: 22b–24b, 26a–30a, 37a, 68a–70b; Muramatsu, *Kindai Kōnan no sosan*, pp. 717–19; Buck, *Land Utilization*, pp. 161–66; Chen Hansheng, p. 216; *Zhejiang Wuxing Lanxi tianfu diaocha baogao*, pp. 59–69.

[a] Buck's data, used here for Wujin and Changshu as well as Wuxi (and converted from hectares to mu), have come under some suspicion of incompleteness. But the similarity between the two sets of Wuxi statistics suggests that he is not too far off the mark in this case. In addition, Buck's data for Wujin parallel quite closely the yuan-per-mu figures that can be compiled from the detailed information on regular taxes, surcharges, and levies in Wan Guoding et al., pp. 53–54, 58–59. According to those calculations, an owner of the most common type of land in Wujin had to pay 0.89 yuan in 1927, 1.02 in 1928, 0.79 in 1929, 1.02 in 1930, 1.02 in 1931, and 1.10 in 1932.

imposts were piled on thick and fast after the KMT assumed power in the region in 1927 and embarked on its ambitious program of modernization. In 1926, for instance, Chuansha landowners had paid a public welfare surcharge, a police levy, a household registration levy, a water conservancy surcharge, and an educational tuition levy, which together came to 0.14 yuan per mu, or some 18 percent of their total tax of 0.79 yuan. By 1933 they had to pay five new levies (for public security, road construction, agricultural reform, self-government, and land surveying) and larger amounts for the old ones, for a total of 0.55 yuan, or 47 percent of the total tax of 1.17 yuan per mu.[40] Similarly, Wuxi's levies and

TABLE 6.6

Index of Rice and Cotton Prices and Land Taxes in Jiangnan, 1912–1933

(1915–18 = 100)

Category	1912–1914	1915–1918	1919–1922	1923–1926	1927–1930	1931–1933
Rice price						
Yuan per shi	7.19	6.92	9.37	12.05	14.12	10.57
Index	104	100	135	174	204	153
Cotton price						
Yuan per dan	5.00	5.00	6.76	8.47	9.97	8.51
Index	100	100	135	169	199	170
Land tax						
Chuansha						
Yuan per mu	.62	.68	.72	.77	1.17	1.26
Index	91	100	106	113	172	185
Wu						
Yuan per mu	.72	.73	.64	.74	1.33	—
Index	99	100	88	101	182	—
Wuxi (Buck)						
Yuan per mu	.58	.56	.57	.67	.82	1.14
Index	104	100	102	120	146	204
Wuxi (Chen)						
Yuan per mu	—	.63	.63	.75	.99	1.05
Index	—	100	100	119	157	167
Wujin						
Yuan per mu	.75	.75	.83	.83	1.01	.99
Index	100	100	111	111	135	132
Changshu						
Yuan per mu	—	.75	.74	.76	1.09	—
Index	—	100	99	101	145	—
Wuxing						
Yuan per mu	.79	.91	.84	.73	1.22	1.28
Index	87	100	92	80	134	141

SOURCE: Tables 6.4–6.5.

surcharges jumped from two in 1926 to eight in 1931, and Wuxing's from two in 1926 to eleven in 1933.[41] Wuxing, Wuxi, and Chuansha all had a fairly modest number of supplementary charges. The dubious honor of having the most went to Changshu, which in 1934 boasted twenty-six different varieties.[42]

This multiplication of surcharges and levies resulted in a phenomenon noted by scholars for other regions of China. Many landowners ended up paying at least as much in surcharges and levies as they did in statutory tax, and conversely, more government income from land taxation derived from levies and surcharges than from the statutory quotas.[43] In the lower Yangzi valley in the early 1930's, the ratio of revenue from surcharges and levies to that from statutory taxes ranged between 0.96 and 2.48, with most counties falling under 2.00. (A ratio of, say, 1.5 meant that revenue from levies and surcharges was 50 percent higher than revenue from the statutory tax.)[44]

What is intriguing about Jiangnan is not that the absolute tax burden nearly doubled over the course of several decades, or that surcharges and levies came to surpass statutory taxes by the margins noted above, but that these represented such modest changes compared with other regions, including even northern parts of Jiangsu Province itself. In Nantong County, just across the Yangzi River, for instance, the total tax burden for the most common grade of land rose nearly six and a half times between 1912 and 1931.[45] In Suining County, located in the northwest, the diding tax and its attendant surcharges went up three and a half times between 1915 and 1930, and in Feng County, also in the northwest, the diding and its surcharges rose eighteen and a half times, and the tribute tax and its surcharges nearly six times between 1912 and 1929.[46] Other northern Jiangsu counties also experienced greater tax increases than the counties in the southeast.[47]

Since the tribute and diding conversion rates were uniform throughout the province, the greater increases in the north resulted from proportionally larger levies and surcharges. In the early 1930's the ratio of irregular to regular tax ranged from 2.72 to an astonishing 26.20 (Haimen County), for an average of 8.79. In the southeast the average ratio was only 1.67.[48]

What accounts for this disparity? Why did the counties in the southeast escape the kind of increases imposed in the ones to the north? The answer lies in their respective tax bases. Where the whole of the diding and tribute tax once had to be forwarded to the upper reaches of the government, a set portion of both now remained with the county. In Jiangsu after 1917, this amounted to 15 percent of the diding and 20 percent of the tribute tax.[49] Since the tax base inherited from the Qing was set by land fertility, the more productive southeastern counties commanded larger amounts of income from these regular taxes than the northern counties and thus had less need to impose heavy surcharges and levies to satisfy their new budgetary demands.

Table 6.7 illustrates this point. In general, county budgets, while showing much variation, did not differ categorically between the north and the southeast. County governments in the poorer, northern section had similar budgetary needs and commanded the same amounts of revenue as many of the wealthier places to the south. The proportion of total land tax (both regular statutory taxes, or *zhengshui*, and irregular taxes, or *fushui*) in their budgets also did not differ much; land taxes were as crucial a source of income for the southeastern counties as for the northern ones. In the southeastern counties, however, regular taxes supplied an average of 13 percent of total budgeted revenue (vs. 60 percent for irregular taxes).

TABLE 6.7
*Land Tax Revenue as Proportion of County Budgets in
Southeastern and Northern Jiangsu, 1933–1934*
(Thousands of yuan)

County	Budget	Land tax		Statutory taxes		Irregular taxes	
		Total	Budget share	Land tax share	Budget share	Land tax share	Budget share
Southeast							
Shanghai	282	125	44.3%	23.2%	10.3%	76.8%	34.0%
Wu	1,607	845	52.6	22.2	11.7	77.8	40.9
Jinshan	285	172	60.4	25.0	15.1	75.0	45.3
Wujin	1,022	689	67.4	20.9	14.1	79.1	53.3
Wuxi	1,124	775	69.0	15.4	10.6	84.6	58.4
Chuansha	159	109	68.6	11.0	7.6	89.0	61.0
Fengxian	283	199	70.3	24.1	17.0	75.9	53.3
Baoshan	417	308	73.9	7.8	5.8	92.2	68.1
Songjiang	690	529	76.7	21.4	16.4	78.6	60.3
Nanhui	558	427	76.5	14.5	11.1	85.5	65.4
Kunshan	635	500	78.7	22.2	17.5	77.8	61.2
Qingpu	468	380	81.2	24.2	19.7	75.8	61.5
Taicang	433	349	80.6	22.3	18.0	77.7	62.6
Wujiang	873	708	81.1	19.9	16.2	80.1	64.9
Changshu	1,200	1,027	85.6	14.5	12.4	85.5	73.2
Jiading	459	398	86.7	11.1	9.6	88.9	77.1
Yixing	756	639	84.5	16.1	13.6	83.9	70.9
North							
Nantong	1,098	685	62.4%	2.9%	1.8%	97.1%	60.6%
Suqian	276	180	65.2	5.0	3.3	95.0	61.9
Siyang	266	186	69.9	4.3	3.0	95.7	66.9
Haimen	709	526	74.2	1.0	0.7	99.0	73.5
Huaiyin	339	253	74.6	2.4	1.8	97.6	72.8
Tai	762	589	77.3	7.5	5.8	92.5	71.5
Dangshan	171	138	80.7	5.1	4.1	94.9	76.6
Rugao	1,512	1,225	81.0	1.4	1.1	98.6	79.9
Funing	552	454	82.2	2.9	2.4	97.1	79.8
Baoying	451	386	85.6	3.4	2.9	96.6	82.7
Huaian	537	473	88.1	5.3	4.7	94.7	83.4
Suining	192	171	89.1	3.5	3.1	96.5	86.0
Gaoyou	700	625	89.3	2.2	2.0	97.8	87.3

SOURCE: Zhao Ruheng, 2: 743–907.

In the northern counties regular taxes averaged only 3 percent of total budgeted revenue, and irregular taxes fully 76 percent.

What all this meant for the average landowner in the two areas is shown in Table 6.8, which contrasts the land tax burden in two pairs of northern and southeastern counties with similar budgets for the years 1933–34. In the first pair, Wuxi gained about three and a half times more revenue from regular taxation than Nantong (0.0772 yuan per mu as opposed to

TABLE 6.8
Land Taxes and County Revenue in Northern and Southeastern
Jiangsu Counties, 1933–1934

			Nanhui		Funing	
Category	Wuxi	Nantong	1	2	1	2
Individual rates						
Zhengshui (statutory taxes; all per mu)						
Diding (liang)	.0573	.0538	.1129	.1146	.0145	.0560
Tribute (shi)	.0600	.0066	.0867	.0993	.0093	.0234
Total tax per mu (yuan)[a]	.4383	.1505	.6982	.7680	.0800	.2434
Fushui (surcharges; all in yuan)						
Per liang of diding	2.0380	9.8690	—	—	14.3600	14.3600
Per shi of tribute	2.8560	.6000	—	—	1.7500	1.7500
Per mu of land	.1000	—	.4070	.4070	—	—
Total tax per mu[b]	.3882	.5349	.4070	.4070	.2245	.8451
TOTAL TAX						
(yuan per mu)	.8265	.6854	1.1052	1.1750	.3045	1.0885
County totals						
Budget	1,124,000	1,098,000	558,000		552,000	
Zhengshui						
Revenue	119,000	20,000	62,000		13,000	
Budget share	10.6%	1.8%	11.1%		2.4%	
Share per mu[c]	.0772	.0227	.1206	.1337	.0137	.0402
Fushui per mu[d]	.3757	.5005	.3820	.3820	.2245	.8451
TOTAL REVENUE						
(yuan per mu)	.4529	.5232	.5026	.5157	.2382	.8853

SOURCES: Feng Hefa, comp., *Zhongguo nongcun jingji ziliao*, pp. 395–96; Wan Guoding et al., pp. 155, 178; *Nanhuixian xuzhi*, 4: 14b–15a; *Funingxian xinzhi*, 5: 23a; Zhao Ruheng, 2: 753–871 passim.

NOTE: Figures are for the most common grade of land in Wuxi and Nantong and the two most common grades in Nanhui and Funing.

[a] The zhengshui was calculated at the statutory provincial rates of 2.05 yuan per liang for the diding and 5.0 yuan per shi for the tribute tax. Added to that basic tax was a collection fee calculated at the statutory rates of 0.1025 yuan per liang and 0.250 yuan per shi.

[b] To derive the total fushui in yuan, the statutory amounts of the diding and tribute tax were multiplied by their surcharges, and the resulting sums were then added to the amount of land levy. Thus, for Wuxi:

(.0573 liang × 2.0380 yuan) + (.0600 shi × 2.8560 yuan) = .1168 + .1714 + .1000 = .3882 yuan

[c] Counties in Jiangsu retained 0.3 yuan of the diding and 1.0 yuan of the tribute. Thus, to take Wuxi as an example, the amount in yuan of the regular tax retained by the county was computed in the following manner:

(.0573 liang per mu × .3 yuan) + (.0600 shi per mu × 1 yuan) = .0172 + .0600 = .0772 yuan

[d] The counties retained all of the fushui revenue, except for half of the road construction levy, which Wuxi, Nanhui, and Nantong had to hand over to the province.

TABLE 6.9

Percentage Changes in the Real Tax Burden in Jiangnan, 1912–1933

| | Chuansha | | | | | | |
Period	Rice	Cotton	Wu	Wuxi (Buck)	Wuxi (Chen)	Wujin	Wuxing
1912–14 to 1931–33	+38	+19	—	+33	—	−10	+10
1912–14 to 1923–26	−26	−27	−39	−31	—	−34	−45
1923–26 to 1931–33	+86	+63	—	+93	+60	+36	+98

SOURCE: Table 6.6.

NOTE: For the method of computation, see Table 4.6. The Wu, Wuxi, Wujin, and Wuxing changes are figured against rice prices.

0.0227 yuan), the critical difference being the significantly higher statutory tribute quota in Wuxi. In the second pair, Nanhui earned 3.3 and 8.8 times the revenue of Funing for the two most common grades of land, the critical difference here being higher statutory quotas in Nanhui for both the tribute and the diding. Thanks to larger tribute and diding quotas, then, Wuxi and Nanhui counties in the southeast got a larger proportion of their revenue from those sources than Nantong and Funing (roughly 11 percent for Wuxi and Nanhui and 2 percent for Nantong and Funing).

To compensate for a tax base inadequate for their modernizing needs, the governments of Funing and Nantong thus imposed surcharges and levies that were three to four times the amount of the regular tax. In Wuxi and Nanhui, by contrast, the supplementary imposts did not exceed the regular tax. The result was that even though the southeastern landowners bore the heavier total burden per mu, the northern ones, with their rising surcharges and levies, experienced a greater rise in taxes. Somewhat paradoxically, then, it was the agricultural richness of Jiangnan and the high statutory quotas inherited from the Qing that kept tax increases there comparatively modest during the Republican era.

Nevertheless, taxes almost doubled in many Jiangnan counties in the two decades following the 1911 Revolution. This was an absolute increase, however, and must be viewed against the changes in agricultural prices. Table 6.9 shows that in those counties for which a full range of data exists for the years 1912 to 1933, the real burden increased 10 to 38 percent in Chuansha, Wuxi, and Wuxing, but decreased 10 percent in Wujin. The table also demonstrates that taxes relative to rice and cotton prices during these two decades did not move in a unilinear direction, but went through two distinct phases. From 1912–14 to 1923–26 the rise in the price of agricultural products outpaced the rise in taxes, with the result that the real burden in fact declined 26 to 45 percent. Then, with the advent of KMT rule in 1927, real taxes began to climb. During the years 1927–30, tax hikes, particularly the addition of the numerous sur-

TABLE 6.10
Land Tax as Percentage of Rice Harvest,
Wu and Wuxi Counties, 1903–1933

Year	Rice price[a]	Land tax (per mu)		Percent of harvest[b]
		Yuan	Shi	
Wu				
1903	3.85	.87	.226	8–11%
1904	2.20	.85	.386	13–19
1905	2.84	.80	.282	9–14
1914	4.45	.76	.171	6–9
1923	8.08	.74	.092	3–5
1927	8.25	1.32	.160	5–8
1928	8.75	1.33	.152	5–8
Wuxi[c]				
1923	8.33	.58	.070	2–4%
		.63	.076	3–4
1924	7.28	.59	.081	3–4
		.73	.100	3–5
1925	9.00	.70	.078	3–4
		.65	.072	2–4
1926	11.90	.79	.067	2–3
		.99	.083	3–4
1930	10.00	.81	.081	3–4
		1.12	.112	4–6
1932	6.75	1.19	.176	6–9
		.92	.136	5–7
1933	5.45	1.18	.217	7–11

SOURCES: Taxes, Tables 6.5, B.2. Prices, Qiao Qiming, pp. 86–87; *Tongwen hubao*, 9/12/Guangxu 29 (1903), 10/11, 11/25/Guangxu 30 (1904); *Shenbao*, 11/11/23, 11/5/24, 11/14/25, 11/15/26, 11/14/27, 11/12/28, 11/14/30, 11/9/32, 11/16/33.

[a] Autumn Suzhou and Wuxi prices. Where sources give a range of figures, the average has been used.

[b] Percentage of harvests of 2–3 shi of husked rice per mu.

[c] The upper tax figures come from Buck, *Land Utilization*, and the lower ones from Chen Hansheng. Both are for the most common grade of land in the county. The 1933 figure is Chen's.

charges and levies, outstripped the continued rise in prices. During the subsequent years landowners were pinched by both rising taxes and falling prices. As a result, the real burden under KMT rule in the various counties increased 36 to 98 percent from 1923–26 to 1931–33.

Popular protest against land taxes paralleled these developments. From 1912 through 1926, during the decline in real taxes, just three collective actions took place, for an average of 0.2 a year. But from 1927 to 1936, during the rise in real taxes, the average jumped to 1.3, with thirteen protests over the period (Table A.3). Collective resistance to taxes thus

TABLE 6.11

The Land Tax Burden in Southeastern Jiangsu, 1753 and 1933

	1753 tax[a]		1933 tax[a]	
Locality[b]	Shi per mu	Percent of harvest[c]	Shi per mu[d]	Percent of harvest[c]
Suzhou	.2371	8–12%	.2052	7–10%
Songjiang	.2062	7–10	.1843	6–9
Taicang	.0965	3–5	.1252	4–6
Changzhou	.1483	5–7	.1687	6–8
Southeastern Jiangsu	.1778	6–9%	.1757	6–9%

SOURCES: Tables 2.1, 5.1; Wang Yeh-chien, *Land Taxation*, p. 70; Liang Fangzhong, pp. 401–13; Zhao Ruheng, 2: 580–90.

[a] Average tax per mu in husked rice, derived by dividing the area's total tax revenue by the amount of cultivated land.

[b] For ease of reference, the geographical areas are identified by their Qing prefectural names.

[c] Percentage of harvests of 2–3 shi of husked rice per mu.

[d] The original tax data are quoted in yuan. To arrive at the rice equivalents, the tax figures were divided by 5.75 yuan, the average local rice price for late autumn, 1933 (see Table 5.1).

intensified under KMT rule. Yet even so, it did not reach the 1.5 per-year average of 1840–59 and 1873–1911, let alone the averages for the peak decades of agitation in the Qing, 2.3 for the 1850's and 4.2 for 1901–11. Even under the KMT peasant protest against taxation remained comparatively subdued.

This suggests that the KMT's extraction of revenue from the land, although a greater burden on Jiangnan proprietors than under militarist rule, was hardly confiscatory, especially when compared with what the Qing had required in the mid-nineteenth century and in the final decade of its rule. Land taxes in Wu and Wuxi, for instance, now amounted to 3 to 11 percent of an average to superlative rice harvest of two to three shi per mu, twice the mid-1920's burden of 2 to 5 percent, to be sure, but still generally lower than that of the top Qing periods (see Tables 6.10 and 4.7). On the whole, as Table 6.11 indicates, the average tax burden in southeastern Jiangsu under the KMT was comparable to that of the mid-Qing—6 to 9 percent of a rice harvest.

Jiangnan's comparatively light tax burden goes far to explain the decline in peasant collective action against taxes after the 1911 Revolution. But it is not the entire explanation. After all, the burden, however bearable when the harvest was good, could become intolerable when the harvest was poor. And given the high incidence of drought, waterlogging, flood, and insect infestation in these years, Jiangnan landowners did not lack cause for agitating for tax relief. Yet natural disasters did not provoke anywhere near the amount of peasant protest against taxes as they did peasant protest against rents.

The reason for this is not hard to find. The fact is, the initiative in pressing for tax reductions during years of poor harvests had passed from peasants to the elite. More so than their predecessors of the Qing, prominent landholders of the Republican period assumed an active routine role in lobbying for remissions. During the late Qing, aside from the Tong-zhi reform and isolated instances of gentrymen speaking out on behalf of the peasantry, there is little evidence of elite mobilization against land taxes. The Republican record, in contrast, is full of examples of land-owner associations or various ad hoc groups negotiating directly with county magistrates and drawing on their connections with highly placed provincial government and party officials to secure tax breaks for their counties.

Changing interests lay behind this new elite activism. During the Qing the discrepancy between large and small household rates and the business of proxy remittance limited the elite's incentive for agitating for tax reductions. The gentrymen's own very low rates made them less likely to lobby for remission for their own sake, and their desire to maintain the differential rates and hence their returns from proxy remittance made them less likely to lobby for the sake of others. There was thus a divergence of interests between elite and commoner landowners in Jiangnan.

During the Republican era the interests of the two groups converged. Neither the militarist nor the KMT government in Jiangnan continued the Qing practice of granting exemptions on the basis of wealth or status (although no doubt rich and influential landowners were still able to get local functionaries to pare down their bills). Without the underpinning of different tax rates, proxy remittance, once so rampant in the region, also ceased to be a problem worthy of comment. Now charged the same amount as peasant households and no longer anxious about the profitability of proxy remittance, large landholders found it in their interest to push actively for remissions that would benefit themselves and, by extension, all other property owners in their county.

State intervention in rent relations in the Republican period also contributed to the greater concern among large landowners about the level of taxation. As we have seen, it was not uncommon for a magistrate to legislate a rent reduction against the wishes of landlords. In these circumstances, short of blatantly refusing to comply with government orders (and thereby risk official censure and tenant protest), the most that landlords could do was to lobby for a tax remission so as to make the state absorb some of the cost of the rent reduction.

The new activism among large landholders encouraged a certain passivity among the smaller ones. Rather than risk a potentially bloody confrontation with the authorities, peasant cultivator-owners in the Republican period tended to adopt what the newspapers of the time invariably described as a "wait and see" attitude. They sat on the sidelines and waited for the outcome of the tax negotiations between large landowners and government officials.

CHANGING CONFIGURATIONS OF POWER

In the end, one group came out the worse for all the changes. By the late 1920's Jiangnan landlords found themselves caught in a tightening economic vise, pressured from one side by rising state exactions, and by tenant and state demands to maintain and/or lower rents from the other. The effects of these pressures on their profits can be illustrated with several concrete examples. In Wuxi County, throughout the 1920's and early 1930's, the average nominal rent for the autumn rice crop was 0.8 shi of husked rice, and the typical actual rent 90 percent of that, or 0.72 shi.[50] A Wuxi landlord who collected rents in kind had to pay 10–11 percent of that 0.72 shi as tax in 1923 and 9–12 percent in 1926. By 1930, because of hikes in taxes that outstripped the continuing rise in rice prices, tax consumed 11–16 percent of rent. In the early 1930's declining rice prices joined with the rising taxes to push the figure up to 19–30 percent. (See Table 6.10 for the tax figures in shi used in the calculations.)

Landlords who collected commuted rents were similarly hard hit. Table 6.12 shows the proportion of tax to commuted rent in Pinghu for the years 1929 to 1935. Actual rents in this county ranged from 50 to 90 percent of the typical nominal amounts of 1.0 to 1.2 shi per mu of paddy, with larger landlords charging the lower rates and smaller landlords, who were more dependent on income from their land, the higher ones. During the depths of the depression, the combination of increasing taxes and decreasing rental conversion rates cut deeply into landlord profits. In 1933, the year with the highest taxes and the lowest rents, tax payments consumed 52–62 percent of actual rents of 50 percent, 37–45 percent of actual rents of 70 percent, and 29–35 percent of actual rents of 90 percent. According to an investigation of neighboring Jiaxing during the same period, a 42-percent rise in tax and a 36-percent drop in the rental conversion rate eroded landlord returns by as much as two-thirds.[51]

The decline in the profitability of landlord holdings was reflected in falling land prices. The value of land in northern Zhejiang, as we have seen, had already decreased some 20 percent between 1925–26 and 1929–30 in reaction to the provincial attempt to carry out the KMT's 25-percent reduction in rent. Thereafter land prices continued to drop in response to the economic slump and escalating taxes. In Jiaxing County the value of high-grade paddy plunged a further 31 percent between 1930 and 1935.[52]

TABLE 6.12
Land Tax as Proportion of Rent in Pinghu County, 1929–1935
(paddy land)

Item	1929	1930	1931	1932	1933	1934	1935
Land tax[a]	1.069	1.183	1.103	1.130	1.436	1.297	1.290
Nominal rent[b]	1–1.2	1–1.2	1–1.2	1–1.2	1–1.2	1–1.2	1–1.2
Actual rent[b]							
50%	.5–.6	.5–.6	.5–.6	.5–.6	.5–.6	.5–.6	.5–.6
70%	.7–.84	.7–.84	.7–.84	.7–.84	.7–.84	.7–.84	.7–.84
90%	.9–1.08	.9–1.08	.9–1.08	.9–1.08	.9–1.08	.9–1.08	.9–1.08
Average zhejia[c]	5.6	5.9	5.9	5.1	4.6	5.6	5.1
Commuted rent[a]							
50%	2.80–3.36	2.95–3.54	2.95–3.54	2.55–3.06	2.30–2.76	2.80–3.36	2.55–3.06
70%	3.92–4.70	4.13–4.96	4.13–4.96	3.57–4.28	3.22–3.86	3.92–4.70	3.57–4.28
90%	5.04–6.05	5.31–6.37	5.31–6.37	4.59–5.51	4.14–4.97	5.04–6.05	4.59–5.51
Tax as percent of rent							
50%	32–38%	33–40%	31–37%	37–44%	52–62%	39–46%	42–51%
70%	23–27	24–29	22–27	26–32	37–45	28–33	30–36
90%	18–21	19–22	17–21	21–25	29–35	21–26	23–28

SOURCE: Duan Yinshou, pp. 22690–95, 22780–81.
[a] Yuan per mu.
[b] Shi per mu.
[c] Yuan per shi.

In southern Jiangsu the price of top-grade paddy peaked in 1930 and then plummeted 37 to 55 percent by 1933.[53] So unprofitable did landownership become for landlords, in fact, that for the first time in Jiangnan's history the price of subsoil rights in some areas fell below the price of topsoil rights.[54]

POSTSCRIPT: 1945–1951

The economic plight of Jiangnan landlords did not improve when the KMT resumed control of the region after the eight-year Japanese occupation. On the contrary, the KMT again raised its level of land taxation, this time to cope with huge budget deficits, a catastrophic currency crisis that drove prices up an astounding 30,000 times between September 1945 and April 1949, the tremendous task of reconstruction, and the cost of fighting the Communists.[55] In Jiangnan from 1946 through 1948, regular land taxes alone ranged from 0.095 to 0.222 shi of husked rice per mu.[56] The various miscellaneous provincial and county levies and surcharges often equaled or exceeded those figures. The average total tax amounted to 0.211 and 0.221 shi of husked rice in 1947 and 1948 for landowners in Yunlin township (Wuxi County), 0.288 shi in 1948 for landowners in Meigang township (Wujin County), and 0.338 shi in 1948 for landowners in eleven villages near Xietang town (Wu County).[57] The tax burden now amounted to 7 to 17 percent of a rice harvest of two to three shi, substantially higher, at least at the top of the range, than that of the late 1920's and early 1930's—6 to 9 percent.

For many Jiangnan landlords a drastic decline in rental income made the postwar taxes that much more onerous. In Wuxi County, for instance, according to the reports of land reform cadres in the early 1950's, prewar rents averaged a shi per mu. Afterward, landlords resident in the villages could collect at most 0.4 to 0.5 shi, and absentee landholders only 0.2 to 0.3 shi.[58] Similar drops were noted in other counties.[59]

The decrease in landlord income stemmed in part from a government-decreed rent reduction and in part from widespread tenant resistance. In 1945–46 the KMT reaffirmed its ideological commitment to agrarian reform by calling for an immediate 25-percent decrease in rent and an eventual redistribution of land to the tiller.[60] This time Jiangnan's landlords and county officials proved to be much more receptive to a permanent reduction than they had been in the late 1920's, although as in the earlier case its implementation was by no means complete. By the autumn of 1947 landlord representatives and county magistrates in Jiaxing, Changshu, Fengxian, and Wu were using the 25-percent formula to fix ceilings at 37.5 percent of the main crop at their annual conferences on rent.[61]

In the following year, 1948, as the Communists scored a string of victories in North China and ventured into northern Jiangsu to engage KMT troops at the decisive battle for Xuzhou, the idea of agrarian reform became even more compelling. As the governor of Zhejiang, a strong advocate of rural reform, explained, rent reduction was essential "to counteract the land reform campaign of the Communist Party and to save common unenlightened [*hutu*, literally, "confused"] landlords from suffering Communist struggles of retribution."[62] The fear of an imminent Communist attack prompted other Jiangnan county governments (Kunshan, Nanhui, and Jiading) to reduce rents that fall. The amount of the reduction was also increased that year, to 31 percent, lowering the ceiling from 37.5 to 34.5 percent of the main crop.[63]

Economic as well as political considerations lay behind this effort. Throughout Jiangnan tenants were defaulting on their payments, partly in response to substandard harvests, particularly during a severe drought in 1947, and partly in response to soaring prices. With the rate of inflation running as high as 100 percent a month, peasants who surrendered some of their harvest to landlords in the autumn would find it even more difficult than usual to purchase grain when their supply ran out in the late spring. They therefore sought to hold onto as much of their crop as possible as a hedge against inflation, even if that meant repudiating their rental obligations. In these circumstances the agrarian reforms of the 1940's, much like the reduction campaign in Suzhou Prefecture after the Taiping Rebellion, were a calculated attempt to get tenants to deliver more in rent.

But this concession to tenants did not stem the tide of resistance. Peasants not only continued to default widely even after the reforms, but frequently engaged in collective action to protect their harvests from landlords and public and private dunners. In Changshu County alone, there were at least eight such incidents between 1945 and 1949, and Wu County experienced seven protests in 1947 and 1948.[64]

The inability of many landlords to collect enough rent to cover their taxes and the shortfall in revenue that the government suffered on that account led a number of county administrations to institute the practice of collecting taxes directly from tenants.[65] And by doing so, local officials, like the Taipings nearly a century earlier, placed themselves in more direct competition with landlords over the cultivator's harvest. In Wu County in 1947, for example, county officials offered rent reductions as a reward to tenants for their prompt payment of taxes. Tenants who paid tax in full during the first month of collection would receive a discount of 40 percent over and above the 25–percent rent reduction, and those who paid in the second and third months would receive additional discounts of 30 and 20 percent. Moreover, the officials exempted all impoverished tenants from rents, requiring them only to pay tax.[66] With this fiscal arrangement, the Wu county government thus protected its collection of taxes at the expense of the landlords' collection of rents.

Predictably, Wu tenants seized on their payment of taxes as a pretext to default on rents. In 1947 roughly half the 371 tenant households in several villages in Huangkang township refused to pay anything at all. In the following year, the situation was even worse; 90 percent of the households withheld rents.[67] In the postwar period, as in the past, rent resistance was both a cause and a consequence of the policy of going directly to tenants for taxes.

These developments took a heavy financial toll on landlords. Even when they were able to collect in full the reduced rents allowed by the government, their net income after taxes was lower than it had been during the worst years of the depression in the 1930's.[68] The margin of profit, of course, was even smaller for landlords who did not receive the entire reduced amounts because of tenant resistance. The narrowing of the gap between taxes and rents made the ownership of property even more unprofitable in the late 1940's than it had been in the 1930's. The price of subsoil rights fell way below the price of topsoil rights in every corner of the region; subsoil in some locales was worth only one-fifth to one-sixth the value of topsoil.[69]

In the case of the elite landowners, the difficulties were merely part of a more general economic crisis. For these large landholders, as we have seen, landownership formed just one link in a chain of activities that included commerce, industry, and military and civil officeholding. With the economy in shambles, their income from these other sources also plummeted. The rapid rate of inflation greatly reduced consumer purchasing power and increased the costs of production, thus forcing hundreds of factories in Jiangnan cities into bankruptcy and closure and producing in turn a severe contraction in commerce. The hyperinflation also reduced the real incomes of salaried military officers and government employees to only a fraction of their prewar levels. By the end of 1948 the collapsing economy and the threat of an imminent Communist advance into Jiangnan persuaded many members of the elite to flee to the sanctuaries of Hong Kong and Taiwan.[70]

When the Communists gained control of the lower Yangzi valley in May 1949, they thus confronted a much weakened elite, and this helped to shape the form that land reform took there. Land reform in Jiangnan in 1950–51 differed sharply from the process that had taken place in North China during the civil war in the sense that it was carried out through orders from above, not through class struggle from below. "Peaceful land reform" (*heping tudi gaige*) did not have the approval of the Party central, which continued to emphasize the political mobilization of the peasants and their active participation in the confiscation and redistribution of land.[71] But Party leaders also wanted to see the land law of June 1950 implemented as soon as possible, and to that end they ordered local cadres in Jiangnan to complete redistribution by the spring of 1951.[72] In setting this deadline, they deprived their people in the field of the time needed to educate the peasants fully about class struggle and to involve them integrally in the process of land reform.

Faced with these contradictory orders, the Jiangnan activists launched an essentially orderly campaign, though they took care to wrap it in the trappings of class struggle. In the villages local cadres classified the inhabitants into the appropriate categories of landlord, rich, middle, and poor peasant, and hired laborer, and then simply equalized ownership by taking land away from some and giving it to others.[73] What class struggle there was took place one step removed from the villages, at the ward and township levels, where various landlords were subjected to peasant "speak bitterness" sessions. Interestingly, the high point of the struggle movement in southern Jiangsu came in January and February of 1951, which is to say, after nearly half the area had already completed the reallocation of land.[74] Class struggle here was carried out not so much to mobilize mass support for land reform as to satisfy the directives of the Central Committee. As a result, it was not as integral a part of land reform as it had been in North China. In his most recent work, Philip Huang, recounting the process of land reform in a cluster of villages near Songjiang city, observes:

> For the Huayangqiao villagers, the overturn in class relations that came with the Revolution was not a blood-and-guts affair involving mass struggles against specific, hated landlords with names and faces. Rather, it occurred almost unnoticed and at some remove from their daily lives. It was done chiefly by administrative fiat, the revolutionary authorities outlawing by a stroke of the pen the collection of rents.[75]

In Huayangqiao, as elsewhere in Jiangnan, the redistribution of land was completed by March 1951. Had landlords remained a formidable enemy in the lower Yangzi region, land reform there could not have been as peaceful and orderly as it turned out to be.

CONCLUSION

Landlordism in the lower Yangzi region was destroyed not by revolutionary action, but by the cumulative weight of centuries of structural change. The transformation in the relationship among the state, the elite, and the peasantry had its roots in the late Ming and early Qing periods, when advancing commercialization brought about a wholesale restructuring of the interaction between landlords and tenants. Large landholders moved to the cities and towns to take advantage of the commercial opportunities and social and cultural amenities offered there. Large-scale landownership became increasingly absentee and fragmented, a process that in turn limited landlords' participation in the cultivation of their property, in the welfare of their tenants, and in village affairs in general.

The removal of large landholders from the countryside had a number of important consequences for the relationship among landlords, the state, and the tenantry. The attenuation of the personalistic ties between landlord and tenant, elite and peasant, created a leadership vacuum in rural communities that necessitated greater state intervention in matters such as water conservancy and famine relief. At the same time, it resulted in a recasting of the nature of elite involvement in local affairs and a shift in the basis of elite power. Where once members of the elite had performed vital community tasks themselves in their capacity as large resident landlords, gentry managers and the local government now took over. Elite domination of rural society thus came to be based less on private control of land and close ties with the peasantry than on semibureaucratic public activity and personal connections with local officials.

Rent relations in Jiangnan directly reflected the depersonalization of elite-peasant ties. For the tenant, absentee landlordism brought greater freedom to participate more fully in the market economy, as well as new terms of tenure, such as fixed rents and topsoil rights, that strengthened his control of the land and his rights to any increases in its yield. For the landlord, it made close supervision of tenants all but impossible, and in the case of topsoil owners, eviction extremely difficult. The changing relationship between the two brought about an intensification of conflict as each sought to secure his claims to the harvest within the context of a commercializing economy. Landlords resorted variously to security deposits, larger-than-standard rent measures, surcharges, and, when possible, higher rents; and tenants to the adulteration of rent rice, foot-dragging on payments, and an outright individual or collective refusal to pay what they owed.

For the state, the escalation of tensions between landlord and tenant posed a direct threat to its own main source of revenue. In regions with high tenancy rates such as Jiangnan, the state's ability to extract land taxes depended on the landlords' ability to extract rents. To secure its tax base in the face of widespread tenant default, officials began to lend active assistance to landlords in the collection of rents. The imperial court declared rent default a crime in the early eighteenth century, thereby permitting landlords to use the judicial system to pressure delinquent tenants for payment. More locally, Jiangnan officials deployed yamen runners and rural functionaries to dun peasants for rent in arrears.

The turmoils of the mid-nineteenth century, I argue, constituted the critical turning point in the interaction of landlords, tenants, and the state. Collective action against rent increased in frequency from the early 1840's on, to reach a peak in widespread tenant uprisings against landlords in 1853, the year of the Taipings' arrival in Nanjing and Zhenjiang and of the Small Sword Society's uprising in Songjiang and Taicang, and another in 1860, when the Taipings launched their successful campaign to capture the lower Yangzi delta. Taiping rule of the region from 1860 to 1864 further weakened the elite's already tenuous hold over rural society. The gentry found itself shut out of a significant proportion of local offices, including many of the highest ones.

Taiping rule also made its presence felt in rent and tax relations. The rebels reached the lower Yangzi region with their revolutionary agenda much compromised by the exigencies of war and their desperate need for revenue. At this point they not only had no plans for implementing land redistribution; they had shifted ground completely, forced by circumstances merely to tap into the existing mechanisms of revenue extraction. Nevertheless, their radical message, however muted, struck responsive chords among Jiangnan peasants, who through their opposition to the payment of rents and taxes, helped to shape the direction of rebel policies. Taiping rulers in Jiangnan adopted a number of novel measures that undermined landlord control of the land and its product, the most important being tenant payment of taxes, mandatory rent reduction, and bureau rent collection. Compounding the difficulties of the elite landlords was the fact that, even as their rental income declined, they were charged the full panoply of land taxes and then some, for the Taiping government at once terminated their exemptions and saddled them with special levies and contributions.

Though defeated, the Taipings had raised the specter of class war and left a legacy that compelled greater state involvement in rent relations. First in the Suzhou suburban counties of Wu, Changzhou, and Yuanhe in the several decades following the rebellion and then throughout much of the rest of Jiangnan in the Republican period, local officials began to intervene in setting ceilings on rent. Yet ever mindful that taxes came from rents, they also undertook to help landlords much more fully in the collection of rents and, to that end, established government dunning bureaus and tenant debtor prisons. The state thus played a dual role in rent relations. It sought at one and the same time to appease tenant interests by limiting rents and to appease landlord interests by enforcing the payment of rents, thereby ensuring its own fiscal base.

Linked to this greater state intervention in rent relations was a growing landlord mobilization that expressed itself in the form of bursaries, charitable estates, and landowner associations. Landlord mobilization constituted just one aspect of a more general extension of elite influence in the post-rebellion period. Yet even as the elite took on expanded functions and organization, its position vis-à-vis rural society became still more tenuous. The expansion of elite influence was, in the main, an urban phenomenon that drew the gentry's attention and energy even further away from the villages and even more toward the cities and towns. In the context of the continuing urbanization and diversification of elite interests, landlord mobilization represented a collective effort to reassert a control over rural society that no individual landlord had the ability or the inclination to attempt. It was, moreover, an effort heavily dependent on government assistance.

For its part, growing official intervention in rent relations can be seen both as a continuation of the earlier trend toward greater government involvement in matters like rural relief, water conservancy, and rent dunning and as a facet of a modernizing state's aggressive attempt to strengthen its hold over local society. In the end state intrusion worked to the disadvantage of the landlords. By assuming the right to regulate rent, the state undermined their authority over tenants, inadvertently promoted an escalation in tenant resistance, and made it much more difficult for landlords to raise rents to cope with escalating taxes.

RENTS AND POPULAR RESISTANCE

The particular features of Jiangnan land tenure had not made the landlords' lot an easy one, in any case. The spread of security deposits and topsoil rights in the early and mid-Qing brought tenants actual rents at least 10 to 20 percent lower than the former nominal amounts. Once fixed rents were reduced in this fashion, landlords found it virtually impossible to raise them, especially in the rice-growing areas, where dual ownership became widespread because of the heavy investment of capital and labor needed in polder maintenance.

To cope with the inflexibility of fixed rents, landlords, particularly after the Taiping Rebellion, resorted increasingly to requiring tenants to pay them in currency. Commuted rents afforded landlords a way to up the income from their property without altering the fixed rents in kind. In the final years of the Qing, this commercialization of rental payments enabled landlords, themselves hard pressed by tax hikes, to impose substantial increases on tenants, with the result that in some areas, the real burden of commuted rents rose as much as half again.

During the Republican era state intervention made it difficult for landlords to manipulate the conversion rates for commuted rents to the same degree. Though county zhejia ceilings did not command complete landlord compliance, they nevertheless did hold potential increases in check. Moreover, since the county ceilings were now more closely pegged to rice prices than the late Qing landlords' private commutation rates, peasants had to market significantly less of their harvest to meet their rents. As a result, tenants of the Republican period actually bore a lighter burden than their predecessors of the late Qing.

Paradoxically, this decline, far from discouraging popular resistance to rents, was accompanied by a rising tide of tenant collective actions. Contrary to the orthodox Chinese Marxist approach, which would impute such an escalation of conflict to rising rents and increasing peasant pauperization, this study has argued that it was due primarily to landlord mobilization and state intervention and secondarily to new openings for peasant organization and mobilization.

From the tenants' perspective, state intervention and landlord mobilization presented both increased threats to their livelihood and expanded opportunities for collective resistance. With the professionalization of police forces, the increase in county military units, and the establishment of bursaries, state dunning bureaus, and debtor prisons, rent collection became much more coercive, giving peasants new incentive to act collectively to safeguard their subsistence. At the same time, with growing official involvement in the setting of rents, tenants acquired an avenue of legitimate, state-sanctioned protest (baohuang), a common target that facilitated mobilization, and an audience that proved to be more receptive than landlords to appeals for rent relief.

The altered political context, however, cannot account entirely for the escalation in tenant resistance in the Republican era, for peasants would not have been able to act collectively to deal with the new threats and/ or to seize the new opportunities had they not enjoyed a fair degree of village solidarity and an already considerable capacity for organization and mobilization. The frequency and scale of tenant collective actions during the twentieth century suggest that, contrary to the predictions of the moral economy approach, state penetration and commercialization did not erode the community ties so necessary for effective resistance. Indeed, they had the opposite effect. Greater state intrusion in rent relations promoted both intra- and intervillage solidarity by providing a common target against whom tenants of different landlords and from different communities could rally. And the increasing density of the market network helped to forge personal connections among peasants from various villages that could be drawn on for collective resistance. Both processes enabled tenants to overcome some of the parochialism that had plagued their attempts to mobilize widely in the past.

Besides the increase in frequency, tenant collective action of the Republican period was characterized by a striking shift in the focus of protest. Because of the local officials' expanded role in the setting and dunning of rents, they displaced landlords as the most frequent target of tenant attack and tenant appeal. An anti-official element thus came to be part of peasant collective action against rents. But, as we have seen, this did not mean that an anti-state consciousness had replaced an anti-landlord consciousness among the tenantry, for the tenants' perception of the state, reflecting the two aspects of government intervention in rent relations, was equally dual-faceted. In its role as rent dunner, the state was seen as an oppressor, but in its role as the monitor of rents, it was seen as a potential ally.

The complex relationship between tenants and the state accounts in large measure for the difficulties that CCP activists encountered when they sought to organize the masses in the lower Yangzi valley in the 1920's. Its rich tradition of collective resistance notwithstanding, the Jiangnan peasantry was not particularly receptive to Communist overtures. The immense repressive power that the elite and the government brought to bear against radical political groups no doubt discouraged many would-be recruits. But, more important, CCP methods and goals did not appeal to a tenantry that had acted not because it was bent on overthrowing an oppressive state or eradicating a strong landlord class, but rather because it faced a sympathetic state and diminishing landlord power.

LAND TAXES AND POPULAR RESISTANCE

In one sense at least, the tenants had the better of the landlords: they did not have to contend with the kind of fluctuations in their rents that landowners endured in taxes. Whereas customary practice, tenant resistance, and state intervention combined to exert a downward pressure on rents, the land tax burden, after a series of sharp climbs and equally sharp drops in the period under study, ended up being as heavy in the 1930's as in the mid-eighteenth century (and even heavier in the late 1940's). It was precisely this failure of rents and taxes to move in tandem that ultimately proved to be the financial undoing of Jiangnan landlords.

In the mid-eighteenth century the average tax in Jiangnan was already high, roughly three and a half times the national average. It became increasingly onerous through the first half of the nineteenth century as the value of silver relative to copper *cash* rose and the price of agricultural commodities fell. By the 1840's and 1850's the tax demanded of commoner "small households" had climbed as high as one-third to one-half of a harvest of rice or cotton, levels much more typical of rent than of taxes. What enabled larger landlords to keep economically afloat in these circumstances was the preferential treatment they received in tax assessment as gentry "large households" and, for those who charged commuted rents, the ability to shift some of the tax burden onto tenants in the form of conversion rates much higher than the going market prices for farm products.

After the Taiping Rebellion the Tongzhi tax reduction significantly eased the burden of Jiangnan landowners, although its effects were not as thoroughgoing in Zhejiang as in Jiangsu. By the turn of the century, however, currency instabilities, as well as increasing exactions associated with the Boxer indemnity and China's state-building efforts, negated much of the benefit of the Tongzhi reforms. Absolute taxes rose throughout Jiangnan in the last fifteen years of the Qing, in many areas at a faster pace than the inflationary trend in prices, resulting in real increases as high as a third. Again, as in the mid-nineteenth century, large landholders escaped the worst of the real tax hike because of preferential assessment and the even more widespread existence of commuted rents.

Though land taxes in the lower Yangzi valley experienced an immediate sharp drop after the fall of the Qing, a reverse trend set in before long, and by the 1930's they had nearly doubled in absolute terms. By far the greater part of this increase took place after 1927, when the KMT, more intent than its militarist predecessors on penetrating and reorganizing local society, imposed new surcharges and levies to support its program of state-strengthening. As a result many Jiangnan landowners ended up paying more in "irregular" taxes than they paid in regular taxes. Yet because of the larger amount of revenue that the agriculturally rich Jiangnan counties derived from regular taxation, both the rise in the absolute burden and the margin between regular and irregular taxes were relatively modest compared with what landowners elsewhere in the country had to endure.

Popular resistance to taxes reflected these rises and falls in the tax burden. In the last century of Qing rule, peasant collective action against state exactions reached two peaks, one in the 1840's and 1850's in response to escalating taxes and declining prices and the other in the final decade of the Qing in response to tax increases that outstripped price inflation. In the Republican period as well, popular protest mirrored the movement of real taxes, climbing particularly during their period of fastest (prewar) growth, 1927–37.

But on the whole the incidence of collective action against land taxes was markedly lower than in the Qing. In part this was because the tax burden, even with its growth under KMT rule, was still considerably lighter than the burden of the 1840's and 1850's and the last decade of the Qing. As important, however, was the emergence of a new elite activism in tax matters. Before, differential rates and the profits to be made from proxy remittance had discouraged elite participation in popular resistance to land taxes. None of the collective actions from the 1840's to the fall of the Qing included gentrymen among their leadership. (And indeed, in the final decade of the Qing, the elite, because of its role in the New Policy reforms, frequently became the target of popular protest against taxation.)

In the Republican period the changing dynamics between the state and the elite encouraged greater elite concern about the level of taxation. Once the state equalized assessments, effectively shutting down proxy remittance, and became heavily involved in rent relations, prominent landlords had an immediate economic incentive to use their political influence to lobby for tax relief, if only to get the government to absorb some of the cost of a rent reduction. This new elite activism, along with the comparatively light burden, accounts for the greater passivity among cultivator-owners in the Republican period. Ironically, then, the transformation in the relationship among the state, landlords, and peasants exerted opposite effects on popular resistance to land taxes and popular resistance to rents. Whereas the altered political context of growing landlord mobilization and enlarged government intervention in rent relations promoted an escalation in tenant collective action, it contributed to a decline in cultivator-owner collective action.

Landlords fared badly in the transformation of the trilateral relationship. Occupying the point of intersection between rent and tax, they were the most vulnerable to changes in both sets of relations. After 1927 in particular, landlords were squeezed by increasing state exactions on the one hand and pressures from the government and the tenantry to keep rents low on the other. Now charged the same conversion rates as peasant cultivator-owners and subject to the same surcharges and levies, they felt the full impact of the rising level of real taxes. At the same time the special characteristics of the tenancy system, as well as state intervention, deprived them of their principal defense against those hikes—the ability to raise rents. By the early 1930's landlords had to deliver anywhere from a fifth to two-thirds of their rental income to the government in taxes. Their difficulties only grew worse in the four final years of KMT rule (1945–49), when taxes shot up to as much as 17 percent of a rice harvest and rents declined further as a result of widespread tenant default and renewed government efforts to implement the 25-percent rent reduction.

The landlords' economic plight was but symptomatic of a realignment in power relations in rural society. In the end what destroyed landlordism in the lower Yangzi region was the interrelated processes of state-strengthening and growing tenant political power. When the People's Liberation Army conquered Jiangnan in 1949, rent relations were already on the verge of collapse. Land reform just dealt the final blow.

APPENDIXES

Collective Actions Against Rents and Taxes in Jiangnan, 1840 – 1936

In the following tables, I have used the guidelines devised by Charles Tilly (*From Mobilization to Revolution*, pp. 250–52) to determine the boundaries for the entries. In Tables A.2 and A.3 the data are grouped on the basis of the agricultural cycle and the rent and tax payment periods, not the calendar year. That is, an action that took place in February 1928, for example, was in protest of the rent or tax for the past (1927) fall harvest, not for the upcoming one. The letter "R" identifies an action aimed exclusively at rent; "T" is for taxes, "R/T" for a joint action, and "BH" for *baohuang*, incidents connected with the reporting of a poor harvest in which the specific aim is not known.

Collective Actions, 1840–1859

Prefecture and county	1840	1841	1842	1845	1846	1847–1849	1852	1853
Changzhou								
Wuxi							1T	1R
Jingui								2R
Wujin/Yanghu								1R,1T
Yanghu								1R
Suzhou								
Wu/Changzhou								
Yuanhe							1T	
Wujiang							1R	
Zhenze								
Changshu								1R
Zhaowen			1R	1T	1R			2R
Taicang								
Zhenyang					1T			2R
Jiading								1R
Songjiang								
Huating							1T	2R,1T
Lou								1R
Huating/Lou			1R					1R
Qingpu							1T	
Shanghai								1T
Jinshan								3R
Nanhui								1T
Fengxian								1T
Nanhui/Fengxian			1T					
Jiaxing								
Xiushui	2R							1R
Jiashan								1R
Pinghu								2R
Tongxiang			1T					1T
Shimen						1T		
Huzhou								
Guian		1T						
Guian/Wucheng								
Changxing								1T
Wukang								
Jiaxing or Huzhou								
Hangzhou								
Xincheng								1T
Lin'an								1T
Yuqian								1T
Yuhang								
TOTALS								
R	2	—	2	—	1	—	1	22
T	—	1	2	1	1	1	4	10
COMBINED TOTAL	2	1	4	1	2	1	5	32

SOURCES: *Xinchengzhen zhi*, 4: 6b, 25: 2b–3a; *Gongzhongdang, Daoguang* 22 (1842) 007079, *Xianfeng* 5 (1855) 006505; Zheng Guangzu, 6: 35b–38a, 7: 43b–50b; "Pingzei jilüe," pp. 222–23; Dou Zheng; "Gouwu guijia lu," p. 80; *Wuyang zhiyu*, 3: 30b–31a, 10: 4a–b; Zhao Liewen, "Luohua chunyu chao riji," p. 38; Ke Wuchi, pp. 9, 15, 18–21; "Guijia riji," p. 382; Zhu Chengcong, pp. 1071–72; *Jinshanxian zhi*, 17: 31a–b; *Danghu waizhi*, in Li Wenzhi, *Zhongguo jindai nongye shi ziliao*, p. 972; Hehu Yiyisheng, pp. 486–527 passim; Yao Ji, "Gouquan jinlu," pp. 1146–48, 1152; *Da Qing Xuan Zongcheng*, 364: 19a–b, 377: 40a–b;

Prefecture and county	1854	1856	1857	1858	1859	Totals R	Totals T	Combined total
Changzhou								
Wuxi						1	1	2
Jingui						2	—	2
Wujin/Yanghu						1	1	2
Yanghu						1	—	1
Suzhou								
Wu/Changzhou						—	—	—
Yuanhe						—	1	1
Wujiang						1	—	1
Zhenze	1T				1T		2	2
Changshu						1	—	1
Zhaowen						4	1	5
Taicang								
Zhenyang						2	1	3
Jiading						1	—	1
Songjiang								
Huatıng	1T					2	3	5
Lou	1T					1	1	2
Huating/Lou						2	—	2
Qingpu						—	1	1
Shanghai						—	1	1
Jinshan						3	—	3
Nanhui						—	1	1
Fengxian						—	1	1
Nanhui/Fengxian						—	1	1
Jiaxing								
Xiushui						3	—	3
Jiashan						1	—	1
Pinghu						2		2
Tongxiang						—	2	2
Shimen						—	1	1
Huzhou								
Guian						—	2[a]	2[a]
Guian/Wucheng			1T			—	1	1
Changxing						—	1	1
Wukang		1T				—	1	1
Jiaxing or Huzhou				1T		—	1	1
Hangzhou								
Xincheng						—	1	1
Lin'an						—	1	1
Yuqian						—	1	1
Yuhang			1T			—	1	1
TOTALS						28	29	57
R	—	—	—	—	—			
T	3	1	2	1	1			
COMBINED								
TOTAL	3	1	2	1	1	57		

379: 23a–b, 391: 22a–b; Zhang Shouchang, p. 217; Wu Wenrong, 26: 1a–15a; Feng Guifen, 5: 33a; Yuan Zuzhi, p. 1019; "Yizhaolou shishi huibian," pp. 379, 391–92; *Da Qing Wen Zongxian*, 104: 15a–16a, 110: 14b–15a, 143: 21a–b, 163: 8b–9a; Fu Yiling, "Taiping Tianguo shidai de quanguo kangliang chao," p. 412; Shen Zi, p. 328.

NOTE: No incidents were found for 1843, 1844, 1850, 1851, or 1855.

[a] Includes an incident dated only as the 1850's.

Collective Actions, 1873–1911

Prefecture and county	1873–1876	1877–1881	1882–1886	1887–1891	1892–1896	1897–1901
Changzhou						
Wuxi						
Jingui						
Jiangyin						
Wuxi-Jiangyin-Changshu border						
Wujin/Yanghu						
Wujin						
Yixing						
Suzhou						
Wu		1R				
Yuanhe				5R		1R
Changzhou		2R				
Wujiang						
Zhenze						
Kunshan			1R			
Xinyang						
Changshu						1R
Zhaowen						1R,1T
Changshu/Zhaowen						
Taicang						
Zhenyang						1R
Chongming						
Songjiang						
Qingpu			1BH			
Shanghai			1T			
Nanhui						
Fengxian			1BH			
Chuansha					1R,1T	
Jiaxing						
Xiushui						
Jiaxing		1T				
Jiashan	1BH					
Tongxiang						
Tongxiang/Haining						
Shimen						
Haiyan						
Huzhou						
Guian			1BH			
Wucheng			1T,1BH			
Guian/Wucheng						
Changxing		1T	1BH			
Wukang						
Deqing		1T	1BH			
Deqing/Guian/Wucheng						

Prefecture and county	1902–1906	1907–1911	Totals				Combined total
			R	T	R/T	BH	
Changzhou							
Wuxi		1R	1	—	—	—	1
Jingui	1T		—	1	—	—	1
Jiangyin		1R	1	—	—	—	1
Wuxi-Jiangyin-Changshu border		1R	1	—	—	—	1
Wujin/Yanghu		2T	—	2	—	—	2
Wujin	2T	3T	—	5	—	—	5
Yixing		1T	—	1	—	—	1
Suzhou							
Wu		2T	1	2	—	—	3
Yuanhe	1R	3R,1R/T,1BH	10	—	1	1	12
Changzhou	1R		3	—	—	—	3
Wujiang		3R,4T	3	4	—	—	7
Zhenze		2T	—	2	—	—	2
Kunshan		2R,2T	3	2	—	—	5
Xinyang	1BH	1R,1T	1	1	—	1	3
Changshu		1R,1T	2	1	—	—	3
Zhaowen			1	1	—	—	2
Changshu/Zhaowen		1BH	—	—	—	1	1
Taicang							
Zhenyang		2T	1	2	—	—	3
Chongming	1T		—	1	—	—	1
Songjiang							
Qingpu		1R	1	—	—	1	2
Shanghai			—	1	—	—	1
Nanhui		1R	1	—	—	—	1
Fengxian			—	—	—	1	1
Chuansha		1T	1	2	—	—	3
Jiaxing							
Xiushui		1BH	—	—	—	1	1
Jiaxing	1T	1T,1BH	—	3	—	1	4
Jiashan		3T,1BH	—	3	—	2	5
Tongxiang		1T	—	1	—	—	1
Tongxiang/Haining		1T	—	1	—	—	1
Shimen		2R,1T,1R/T	2	1	1	—	4
Haiyan		1R	1	—	—	—	1
Huzhou							
Guian		1T,1BH	—	1	—	2	3
Wucheng		1R,1BH	1	1	—	2	4
Guian/Wucheng		2T	—	2	—	—	2
Changxing		2T,1BH	—	3	—	2	5
Wukang		1BH	—	—	—	1	1
Deqing		4T	—	5	—	1	6
Deqing/Guian/Wucheng	1BH		—	—	—	1	1

Continued

TABLE A.2 (cont.)
Collective Actions, 1873–1911

Prefecture and county	1873–1876	1877–1881	1882–1886	1887–1891	1892–1896	1897–1901
Hangzhou						
Renhe						
Renhe/Qiantang		1T				
Yuqian						
Haining						
TOTALS						
R	—	3	1	5	1	4
T	—	4	2	—	1	1
R/T	—	—	—	—	—	—
BH	1	—	6	—	—	—
COMBINED						
TOTAL	1	7	9	5	2	5

SOURCES: *Shenbao; Yiwenlu; Huibao; Tongwen hubao; Shibao; Minlibao; Dongfang zazhi; Chuanshaxian zhi*, 23: 2b; *Jincun xiaozhi*, 1: 8a; *Gongzhongdang Guangxu chao zouzhe*, 15: 601–6; Zhang Zhenhe and Ding Yuanying, parts 1 and 2 passim; Shen Yuwu, "Xinhai Geming qianxi Zhejiang," p. 42; Liao Zhihao

TABLE A.2 (cont.)
Collective Actions, 1873–1911

Prefecture and county	1902–1906	1907–1911	Totals				Combined total
			R	T	R/T	BH	
Hangzhou							
Renhe	2T		—	2	—	—	2
Renhe/Qiantang		1T	—	2	—	—	2
Yuqian		2T	—	2	—	—	2
Haining		1T,1R/T	—	1	1	—	2
TOTALS			35	56	3	18	112
R	2	19					
T	7	41					
R/T	—	3					
BH	2	9					
COMBINED TOTAL	11	72					112

and Li Maogao, p. 91; Yangzhou shifan xueyuan lishixi, comp., pp. 133–34, 183–85, 197–206; *Xinhai Geming zai Shanghai shiliao xuanji*, pp. 696–716; *Baxi zhi*, zaji: 1a–2b; Zhejiangsheng Xinhai Geming shi yanjiuhui and Zhejiangsheng tushuguan, comps., pp. 31–32.

TABLE A.3
Collective Actions, 1912–1936

County	1912–1916	1917–1921	1922–1926	1927–1931	1932–1936	Totals				Combined total
						R	T	R/T	BH	
Wuxi			1R	1R/T	2R,1T	3	1	1	—	5
Jiangyin			1R	3R,1R/T		4	—	1	—	5
Wujin				1R		1	—	—	—	1
Changzhou				1T		—	1	—	—	1
Yixing				1R/T		—	—	1	—	1
Wu		7R	1R	1R,2BH	46R,1R/T,1BH	55	—	1	3	59
Wujiang		1R		1R		2	—	—	—	2
Kunshan		1R	1R,1BH	4R		6	—	—	1	7
Changshu				3R,2T	1R,1R/T	4	2	1	—	7
Taicang					1R	1	—	—	—	1
Jiading				4R,1T	3BH	4	1	—	3	8
Chongming			2R			2	—	—	—	2
Songjiang	1R	6R,1BH	2R,2R/T,1BH	4R		13	—	2	2	17
Qingpu			3R	7R		10	—	—	—	10
Jinshan	1R	5R				6	—	—	—	6
Fengxian				1R/T		—	—	1	—	1
Jiaxing		1R,1R/T,2BH	2R		1R,1R/T,1BH	4	—	2	3	9
Jiashan					1T	—	1	—	—	1
Pinghu		1R				1	—	—	—	1

TOTALS										
R	2	22	13	28	51	116	6	10	12	144
T				4	2					
R/T		1	2	4	3					
BH		3	2	2	5					
COMBINED TOTAL	2	26	17	38	61					144

SOURCES: Accounts in *Shenbao*, *Shibao*, and *Zhonghua xinbao*; Fang Long, pp. 123–30; Zhang Yaozong, pp. 177–233; Run Zhi [Mao Zedong]; Zhang Youyi, 3: 1019–23; Wu Dakun, pp. 83–84; Hong Ruijian, "Suzhou," pp. 1547–62; Gu Fusheng; Yan Xuexi.

APPENDIX B

Tax, Rent, and Price Data

The tables in this appendix draw on the following sources:

B.1 The Land Tax Burden in Jiangnan Under Taiping Rule

Tang Shi, pp. 110, 124–25; Ke Wuchi, pp. 52, 58; Gu Ruyu, pp. 371–73; "Gengshen binan riji," pp. 536–37; Gong Youcun, pp. 438, 463, 468; Liu Zhaoxun, pp. 152, 188, 216; Liaocun Dunke, pp. 26, 38; Shen Zi, pp. 58, 208, 211, 237–38, 288; *Tongxiangxian zhi*, 20: 8b; Li Chun, p. 344; Rong Mengyuan, p. 543; Wang Xingfu and Zhou Qizhong, pp. 195–97; Feng Shi, pp. 708–9.

B.2 Rice and Cotton Prices, Currency Exchange Rates, and Land Taxes in Jiangnan, 1879–1910

Zou Dafan et al., pp. 235–36; *Yinxian tongzhi, shihuo zhi*, pp. 210–34; *Chuanshaxian zhi*, 8: 22b–24b, 26a–29a; *Jiadingxian xuzhi*, 3: 10a–15a; Faure, "Rural Economy of Kiangsu Province," p. 425; Muramatsu Yūji, *Kindai Kōnan no sosan*, pp. 717–19; Wang Yeh-chien, *Land Taxation*, pp. 118–19.

B.3 Currency Exchange Rates, Rice Prices, and Suzhou Rental Commutation Rates, 1872–1936

Yinxian tongzhi, shihuo zhi, pp. 210–34; Zou Dafan et al., pp. 235–36; Ihara Kōsuke, pp. 190–91; Muramatsu Yūji, *Kindai Kōnan no sosan*, pp. 172–73, 642–45, 649, 716–19, 723; Tao Xu, pp. 239–40; *Shenbao*, various issues, 1878–1936; *Shibao*, 10/20/Xuantong 2 (1910), 1/14/12; *Huibao*, 10/30/Guangxu 25 (1899); *Tongwen hubao*, 10/16/Guangxu 28 (1902); He Menglei, pp. 33153–54; Hong Ruijian, "Suzhou," pp. 1552–53.

TABLE B.1
The Land Tax Burden in Jiangnan Under Taiping Rule

(rates per mu)

County and year	Tribute tax (shi of rice)	Diding (cash)	Land levy (cash)	Other (cash)[a]
Northern Changshu and Zhaowen				
1860	.3	200		70, miscellaneous fees
1861	.3–.4	240		50, gunpowder levy
1862	.37	1,000[b]		
Wujiang				
1860	.06			
1861	.154	400[c]		
Wu, 1860	.3			
Changzhou, 1863	.34[d]	—[d]		.12 shi, bureau expenses
Jiaxing, 1862	.48	3,000	360	150, dike levy; 790, firewood levy
Pinghu				
1861	.3			
1862	.7	750	50	
Shimen				
1861	.163			
1862	.163–.183			
1863	.161–.176			
Haiyan				
1861	.1			
1862	.35			
Tongxiang				
1861	.2	700		
1862	.156			800, transport fee
1863	.2		360	400, bureau expenses
Xiushui, 1862	.4	640	540	50, miscellaneous fees

[a] Except Changzhou.
[b] Includes dike levy.
[c] Plus .04 shi of rice.
[d] Diding and tribute taxes.

TABLE B.2

Rice and Cotton Prices, Currency Exchange Rates, and Land Taxes in Jiangnan, 1879–1910

| | Price | | | Land tax (per mu) | | | | | |
| | Rice (yuan per shi) | Cotton (taels per picul) | Exchange rate (cash per yuan) | Chuansha | | Jiading | | Wu | |
Year				Cash	Silver	Cash	Silver	Cash	Silver
1879	3.00	9.90	1,131	513	.45				
1880	3.19	10.00	1,152	500	.43				
1881	2.79	10.00	1,146	496	.43				
1882	2.76	9.70	1,148	501	.44				
1883	2.88	10.90	1,149	513	.45				
1884	2.98	11.50	1,157	504	.44				
1885	2.91	11.60	1,144	521	.46				
1886	3.86	11.00	1,145	518	.45				
1887	3.17	9.80	1,079	493	.46				
1888	3.02	11.30	1,081	493	.47				
1889	3.15	10.00	1,086	493	.45				
1890	3.38	10.00	1,093	501	.46	431	.39		
1891	3.15	10.80	1,094	501	.46	440	.40		
1892	3.30	10.00	1,092	552	.51	443	.41		
1893	3.06	10.70	1,097	520	.47	443	.40	502	.46
1894	3.38	9.90	1,091	554	.51	430	.39		
1895	3.46	12.50	1,089	544	.50	430	.39		
1896	5.02	12.00	956	518	.54	418	.44		
1897	4.72	15.00	908	525	.58	423	.47		
1898	5.85	11.50	932	550	.59	430	.46		
1899	4.80	13.00	944	550	.58	420	.44	641	.68
1900	4.46	13.90	933	516	.55	410	.44	612	.66
1901	4.74	16.20	920	559	.61	422	.46	620	.67
1902	6.66	17.00	932	629	.67	467	.50	732	.79

Year									
1903	6.31	17.50	855	.74	629	.55	467	741	.87
1904	5.48	20.20	865	.71	613	.54	470	733	.85
1905	4.31	15.20	889	.70	618	.52	465	713	.80
1906	5.86	15.10	967	.73	704	.50	482	770	.80
			1,080[a]		763[a]		522[a]	834[a]	
1907	7.51	17.20	976	.78	760	.57	553	1,023	1.05
			1,060[a]		808[a]		588[a]	1,087[a]	
1908	7.06	16.90	908	.89	812	.62	559	975	1.07
			1,170[a]		977[a]		672[a]	1,173[a]	
1909	5.63	22.80	925	.93	862	.62	576	1,024	1.11
			1,190[a]		1,037[a]		693[a]	1,232[a]	
1910	7.13	22.60			862		604	1,170	

[a] Amount in debased *cash*.

TABLE B.3
Currency Exchange Rates, Rice Prices, and Suzhou Rental
Commutation Rates, 1872–1936
(prices and rents per shi)

Year	Exchange rate (*cash* per yuan)	Rice price		Bursary zhejia[a]		Zhejia ceiling	
		Copper	Silver	Copper	Silver	Copper	Silver
1872	1,238	(3,355)	2.71	2,194	(1.77)		
1873	1,252	(3,631)	2.90	2,397	(1.91)		
1874	1,220	(4,270)	3.50	2,229	(1.83)		
1875	1,168	(3,376)	2.89	2,196	(1.88)		
1876	1,192	(3,016)	2.53	2,000–2,400	(1.68–2.01)		
1877	1,172	(4,313)	3.68	2,600	(2.22)		
1878	1,102	(4,055)	3.68	2,400–2,800	(2.18–2.54)		
1879	1,131	(3,393)	3.00	2,200	(1.95)		
1880	1,152	(3,675)	3.19	2,000	(1.74)		
1881	1,146	(3,198)	2.79	2,000	(1.75)		
1882	1,148	(3,168)	2.76				
1883	1,149	(3,309)	2.88	2,200–2,300	(1.91–2.00)		
1884	1,157	(3,448)	2.98			1,900	(1.64)
1885	1,144	(3,329)	2.91				
1886	1,145	(4,420)	3.86				
1887	1,079	(3,420)	3.17				
1888	1,081	(3,265)	3.02				
1889	1,086	(3,421)	3.15				
1890	1,093	(3,694)	3.38				
1891	1,094	(3,446)	3.15				
1892	1,092	(3,604)	3.30				
1893	1,097	(3,357)	3.06	2,151	(1.96)		
1894	1,091	(3,688)	3.38				
1895	1,089	(3,768)	3.46				
1896	956	(4,799)	5.02				
1897	908	(4,286)	4.72				
1898	932	(5,452)	5.85				
1899	944	(4,531)	4.80	2,900–4,000	(3.07–4.24)		
1900	933	(4,161)	4.46	2,524	(2.71)		
1901	920	(4,361)	4.74	3,059	(3.33)		
1902	932	(6,207)	6.66	3,100–3,900	(3.33–4.18)		
1903	855	(5,395)	6.31	3,355	(3.92)		
1904	865	(4,740)	5.48	3,062	(3.54)		
1905	889	(3,832)	4.31	2,831	(3.18)		
1906	967	(5,667)	5.86	3,843	(3.97) 3.75		
1907	976	(7,330)	7.51	4,346	(4.45) 4.40		

Continued

TABLE B.3 (cont.)
Currency Exchange Rates, Rice Prices, and Suzhou Rental
Commutation Rates, 1872–1936

(prices and rents per shi)

Year	Exchange rate (*cash* per yuan)	Rice price		Bursary zhejia[a]		Zhejia ceiling	
		Copper	Silver	Copper	Silver	Copper	Silver
1908	908	(6,410)	7.06	5,579	(6.14) 3.97		
1909	925	(5,208)	5.63	5,711	(6.17) 4.13		
1910			7.13	5,311	4.43	5,600	
1911			7.98				4.0
1912			7.94		4.64		
1913			7.21		3.83		
1914			6.42		4.51		
1915			7.40		4.65		
1916			7.12		4.46		
1917			6.52		4.47		
1918			6.62		4.41		4.2
1919			6.94				4.6
1920			9.61				
1921			9.68				
1922			11.26		6.64		
1923			11.20		7.73		
1924			10.29				
1925			10.95				
1926			15.77		6.92		10.3
1927			14.77		8.94		7.8
1928			11.17		8.42		8.6
1929			13.51		13.03		11.0
1930			17.02		6.07		9.0
1931			12.29				
1932			11.35				6.0
1933			8.06				6.5
1934			10.27				6.0
1935			12.31				8.0
1936			10.43				7.1

NOTE: Parentheses indicate computed figures.

[a] Figures for copper for 1876, 1878, 1880–83, 1899, and 1902 are taken from newspaper accounts. The others come from Ihara (1872–79) and Muramatsu (1893–1936). The Muramatsu figures (i.e. from 1893 on) are means. When data from both Ihara/Muramatsu and newspapers are available, the Ihara/ Muramatsu figures fall within the range of the newspaper figures.

APPENDIX C

The Population of Jiangnan

In the first seven tables, showing the population by prefecture, all the entries are in thousands. Asterisked totals are for adult males only. The Qing figures, especially those for the immediate post-Taiping rebellion years, are not as accurate as Republican ones, but they do give a general sense of changes in the population. The sources used for those tables are as follows:

Liang Fangzhong, pp. 436, 440–41, 448, 450–51; *Chongxiu Chang-Zhao hezhi gao,* 7: 3b–4a; *Kun-Xin liangxian xuxiu hezhi,* 6: 4a–b; *Hangzhoufu zhi,* 57: 1a–28b; *Huzhoufu zhi,* 39: 2b–12b; *Wukangxian zhi,* 6: 3a–b; *Changxingxian zhi,* 7: 12a–13b; *Xiaofengxian zhi,* 4: 3a–4b; *Deqingxian zhi,* 4: 1a–b; *Guianxian zhi,* 8: 4b–11b; *Jiaxing xinzhi,* pp. 223–24, *Zhongguo shiye zhi, quanguo shiye diaocha baogao zhi yi: Jiangsusheng,* 12–16; Wang Yeh-chien, "Impact of the Taiping Rebellion," pp. 124–25, 152; Li Wenzhi, *Zhongguo jindai nongye shi ziliao,* pp. 151–53; Wang Shuhuai, pp. 448–49.

The sources for the estimates of the distribution of the farming population (Table C.8) appear with that table.

TABLE C.1
Population of Suzhou Prefecture, 1820–1932

Counties	1820	1864–65	1870's	1889	1912	1932
Wu	2,110	87			1,027	908
Changzhou	479	265				
Yuanhe	386	261				
Wujiang	572	207	262		489	432
Zhenze	581					
Changshu	652	214*		235*	833	859
Zhaowen	462	186*		202*		
Kunshan	405		107		231	235
Xinyang	261		79			
TOTAL	5,908				2,580	2,434

NOTE: After the 1911 Revolution, the Qing counties of Wu, Yuanhe, and Changzhou became the single county of Wu; the Qing counties of Wujiang and Zhenze became the single county of Wujiang; and so on.

TABLE C.2
Population of Changzhou Prefecture, 1830's–1932

Counties	1830's	1864–65	1876	1880	1912	1932
Wuxi	340*	72*			798	899
Jingui	259*	138*				
Jiangyin	978	102	309		599	717
Wujin						843
Yixing				178	522	496
Jingxi				110		
TOTAL						2,955

NOTE: After the 1911 Revolution, Wuxi and Jingui counties became the single county of Wuxi, and Yixing and Jingxi the single county of Yixing.

TABLE C.3
Population of Taicang Department, 1795–1932

Counties	1795–97	1864	1869	1880–81	1912	1932
Taicang	200		131	164	266	290
Jiading	421	386		398	222	245
Baoshan	376				273	162
Chongming					714	406
TOTAL					1,475	1,103

TABLE C.4
Population of Songjiang Prefecture, 1816–1932

Counties	1816	1864	1881	1912	1932
Songjiang				390	390
Huating	303	269	296		
Lou	261	265	304		
Shanghai	529	544	545	1,170	3,138
Qingpu	210	375	375	279	249
Fengxian	262	264	284	187	200
Jinshan	391	274	278		154
Nanhui	416	515	701	426	482
Chuansha	112	122	125	104	130
TOTAL	2,484	2,628	2,908		4,743

NOTE: After the 1911 Revolution, Huating and Lou counties became Songjiang County.

TABLE C.5
Population of Jiaxing Prefecture, 1799–1933

Counties	1799	1838	1873	1928	1933
Jiaxing	492	620	159	449	422
Xiushui	373	503	134		
Jiashan	354	277	96	221	203
Haiyan	403	523	181	213	210
Pinghu	284	304	109	275	281
Shimen (Chongde)	360	379	158	207	211
Tongxiang	275	327	114	165	167
TOTAL	2,541	2,933	951	1,530	1,494

NOTE: After the 1911 Revolution, Jiaxing and Xiushui counties became the single county of Jiaxing, and Shimen County became Chongde County.

TABLE C.6
Population of Huzhou Prefecture, 1756–1928

Counties	1756	1803–6	1827	1870's	1928
Wuxing					743
Wucheng	174			361	
Guian	81			256	
Changxing	54	360		80	236
Deqing	64	391			179
Wukang	22		108		58
Anji	25			11	81
Xiaofeng	15			21	82
TOTAL	435				1,379

NOTE: After the 1911 Revolution, Wucheng and Guian counties became Wuxing County.

TABLE C.7
Population of Hangzhou Prefecture, 1784–1928

Counties	1784	1820's	1866	1882–83	1911	1928
Hang						817
Qiantang	309			55	378	
Renhe	555			174	303	
Haining	572			43	360	356
Fuyang	137			131	168	206
Yuhang	132			65	105	126
Lin'an	75			38	55	86
Yuqian	86		2	17	41	60
Xincheng	109			25	47	60
Changhua	99	170		37	65	78
TOTAL	2,074			585	1,522	1,789

NOTE: After the 1911 Revolution, Qiantang and Renhe counties became Hang County.

TABLE C.8
Distribution of the Farming Population of Jiangnan in the Republican Period
(Percent)

County	Cultivator-owner	Part-owner, part-tenant	Tenant	Laborer
Wujin				
1912	59.0%	29.0%	13.0%	
1923[a]	55.0	34.0	11.0	
1927[b]	7.0	35.2	45.1	11.3%
1931	49.0	29.0	23.0	
1932	48.0	30.0	22.0	
1933	44.0	30.0	25.0	
1934[c]	42.4	37.2	20.4	
Wuxi				
1912	3.0	15.0	83.0	
1923[b]	10.4	44.4	45.2	
1931	3.0	15.0	83.0	
1932	8.0	20.0	72.0	
1933	10.0	34.0	56.0	
1933[d]	21.0	31.0	48.0	
1934[c]	22.4	41.1	·36.5	
Yixing				
1912	50.0	22.0	27.0	
1931	40.0	29.0	31.0	
1932	44.0	24.0	33.0	
1933	42.0	26.0	33.0	
1934[c]	26.7	39.9	33.4	
Jiangyin				
1912	31.0	57.0	12.0	
1923[a]	38.0	41.5	20.5	
1931	28.0	52.0	21.0	
1932	26.0	52.0	21.0	
1933	24.0	46.0	31.0	
1934[c]	20.6	53.7	25.7	
Wu				
1912	23.0	31.0	46.0	
1923[a]	11.3	16.6	72.1	
1927[e]	16.0		63.0	9.0
1931	18.0	18.0	64.0	
1932	20.0	10.0	70.0	
1933	15.0	10.0	75.0	
1933[d]	6.6	20.0	73.4	
1934[c]	10.0	16.0	74.0	
Changshu				
1912	24.0	33.0	43.0	
1923[a]	10.8	9.2	80.0	
1931	16.0	39.0	45.0	
1932	15.0	35.0	50.0	
1933	14.0	30.0	56.0	
1933[d]	10.0	20.0	70.0	
1934[f]	10.0	20.0	60.0	
1934[c]	8.6	26.6	64.8	

TABLE C.8 (cont.)
Distribution of the Farming Population of Jiangnan in the Republican Period
(Percent)

County	Cultivator–owner	Part-owner, part-tenant	Tenant	Laborer
Kunshan				
1912	11.0%	29.0%	60.0%	
1914[g]	11.7	16.6	71.7	
1923[a]	7.3	12.3	80.3	
1924[g]	8.3	14.1	77.6	
1931	5.0	23.0	73.0	
1932	5.0	20.0	75.0	
1933	5.0	20.0	75.0	
1934[c]	3.0	34.5	62.5	
Wujiang				
1923[a]	13.4	45.9	40.7	
1933	15.0	20.0	65.0	
1934[c]	10.0	72.5	17.5	
Taicang, 1927[h]	40.0	25.0	15.0	10.0
Qingpu, 1934[c]	31.0	23.0	46.0	
Jiading, 1934[c]	71.0	5.0	24.0	
Baoshan, 1933	10.0	90.0		
Shanghai, 1934[c]	54.0	45.0	1.0	
Songjiang				
1933	10.0	10.0	80.0	
1934[c]	3.5	10.0	86.5	
Nanhui, 1934[c]	15.0	27.0	58.0	
Chuansha				
1933	40.0	50.0	10.0	
1934[c]	25.0	70.0	5.0	
Jiaxing				
1912	35.0	30.0	35.0	
1931	20.0	40.0	40.0	
1932	35.0	30.0	35.0	
1933	34.0	33.0	33.0	
1933[i]	21.1	43.3	33.8	1.8
Jiashan				
1912	20.0	50.0	30.0	
1931	5.0	25.0	70.0	
1932	5.0	25.0	70.0	
1933	5.0	25.0	70.0	
1934[c]	10.6	13.7	75.7	
Haiyan				
1912	22.0	34.0	44.0	
1931	15.0	35.0	50.0	
1932	10.0	37.0	53.0	
1933	10.0	37.0	53.0	
1933[i]	20.0	30.0	50.0	
1934[c]	13.6	63.0	23.4	

Continued

TABLE C.8 (cont.)
Distribution of the Farming Population of Jiangnan in the Republican Period
(Percent)

County	Cultivator-owner	Part-owner, part-tenant	Tenant	Laborer
Pinghu				
1912	17.0%	25.0%	58.0%	
1931	9.0	18.0	73.0	
1932	9.0	18.0	73.0	
1933	8.0	18.0	74.0	
1933[i]	5.6	15.2	79.2	
1934[c]	3.5	19.0	77.5	
Chongde, 1933[i]	30.0	50.0	17.0	3.0
Tongxiang, 1933[i]	20.0	50.0	20.0	10.0
Deqing				
1912	39.0	42.0	19.0	
1931	47.0	40.0	14.0	
1932	19.0	65.0	17.0	
1933	33.0	57.0	11.0	
Wuxing				
1912	60.0	10.0	30.0	
1931	65.0	10.0	25.0	
1932	70.0	10.0	20.0	
1933	70.0	10.0	20.0	
1933[i]	9.3	54.9	28.8	7.0
1934[c]	24.0	39.0	37.0	
Changxing				
1912	30.0	35.0	35.0	
1931	15.0	45.0	40.0	
1932	15.0	45.0	40.0	
1933	10.0	50.0	40.0	
1933[i]	25.0	50.0	12.5	12.5
1934[c]	28.3	22.7	49.0	
Hang				
1933[i]	22.0	55.0	20.0	3.0
1934[c]	33.0		67.0	
Haining				
1933[i]	8.0	70.0	20.0	2.0
1934[c]	6.0	54.0	40.0	
Fuyang, 1933[i]	62.0	25.0	12.0	1.0
Yuhang, 1933[i]	10.7	17.8	71.5	

SOURCES: All figures are from *Zhongguo jingji nianjian xubian*, G18, 32–33, and are countywide estimates unless otherwise indicated in the superscript notes.

[a] Dongnan daxue nongke, *Jiangsusheng nongye diaocha lu Su-Chang dao shu* (Shanghai: 1923), data reproduced in Faure, "Rural Economy of Kiangsu Province," pp. 453–55. The figures are the means for the various localities in each county: Wujin (9 localities), Wuxi (12), Jiangyin (10), Wu (10), Changshu (12), Kunshan (6), and Wujiang (7).

[b] Gong Jun, p. 105. Plus estimated landlord population of 1.4 percent.

[c] *Zhongguo jingji nianjian disan bian*, G11, 20–21.

[d] He Menglei, pp. 32977–79.

[e] Yan Dafu, p. 118. Plus estimated landlord population of 12 percent.

[f] Yu Jinru, p. 27. Plus estimated landlord population of 10 percent.

[g] Qiao Qiming, p. 80.

[h] Zhou Tingdong, p. 122. Plus estimated landlord population of 10 percent.

[i] Hong Ruijian, *Zhejiang*, p. 16.

REFERENCE MATTER

NOTES

For complete author names, titles, and publication data for the items cited here in short form, see the References Cited, pp. 287–309. The following abbreviations are used in the Notes.

Gongzhongdang: Palace Memorial Archives in the National Palace Museum, Taibei. Citations are by reign year and memorial number.

Kang-Yong-Qian: *Kang-Yong-Qian shiqi chengxiang renmin fankang douzheng ziliao* (Materials on urban and rural resistance struggles in the Kangxi, Yongzheng, and Qianlong reigns). Comp. Zhongguo renmin daxue Qingshi yanjiusuo and Zhongguo renmin daxue dang'anxi Zhongguo zhengzhi zhidu shi jiaoyanshi. 2 vols. (Beijing: Zhonghua shuju, 1979).

Introduction

1. See, for example, Hu Sheng. This scheme is also the organizing principle for the massive three-volume compilation of primary materials, *Zhongguo jindai nongye shi ziliao* (1957), by Li Wenzhi (vol. 1) and Zhang Youyi (vols. 2 and 3).

2. This approach is articulated most clearly in Scott, *Moral Economy*. For examples of its application to China, see Marks, *Rural Revolution in South China*; and Thaxton, *China Turned Rightside Up*.

3. For arguments about the essentially beneficial effects of China's commercialization and incorporation into the world economy, see Myers, *Chinese Peasant Economy*; Faure, *Rural Economy of Pre-Liberation China*; and Brandt, *Commercialization and Agricultural Development*. On the KMT's inability to establish a viable rule, the importance of the CCP's organizational ability, and the role of the Japanese occupation, see, respectively, Eastman, *Abortive Revolution*; Hofheinz, *Broken Wave*; and Johnson, *Peasant Nationalism and Communist Power*.

4. For the relationship between the nature of peasant production and the frequency and intensity of rural conflict in China, see P. Huang, *Peasant Family*, p. 333.

5. This point is thoroughly explored in Scott, *Weapons of the Weak*.

6. P. Huang, *Peasant Family*, p. 102.

7. A partial exception to this statement is Faure, *Rural Economy of Pre-Liberation China*. His work examines the influence of the world monetary market on rents and taxes in Jiangnan, but it pays little attention to escalating tensions among the state, landlords, and peasants.

8. Kuhn, *Rebellion and Its Enemies*, pp. 189–96; Wakeman, "Rebellion and Revolution," pp. 219–20; Wakeman, "Introduction," pp. 2–4, 21–25.

Chapter 1

1. Some of the archives' memorials relating to land tenure have been reproduced in two collections: *Kang-Yong-Qian*; and *Qingdai dizu boxue xingtai*.

2. Gu Yanwu, chap. 2, part 2, p. 56.

3. *Jiangyinxian zhi*, 3: 2b.

4. Yan Chen, *Mohua yinguan shiwen chao*, quoted in Wang Tianjiang, "Taiping Tianguo geming," p. 129.

5. *Shimenxian zhi* (1821), quoted in *Shimenxian zhi* (1879), 11: 4a.

6. *Wujiangxian xuzhi*, 19: 5a–b; *Wuxian zhi*, 31: 13b, 22b–23a; Shen Shouzhi, p. 22; Liu Zhaoxun, p. 381.

7. *Suzhoufu zhi*, 10: 23b.

8. "Shenyutang zutian bu," hereafter cited as Shenyu register (see n. 25); *Pinghuxian zhi* (1745), 1: 10b–45a; *Pinghuxian zhi* (1789), 1: 13b–72a.

9. "Shilu yiji."

10. P. Huang, *Peasant Family*, pp. 44–46.

11. Ibid., pp. 46–47.

12. Liu Shiji, pp. 142–43. For other data on new town formation in the lower Yangzi region during the late Ming and Qing periods, see P. Huang, *Peasant Family*, pp. 48–49, 343–46; and Elvin, "Market Towns," pp. 441–74.

13. Skinner, "Sichuan's Population," p. 75. The 9.5% figure in the text represents Skinner's own revision of his earlier estimate of 7.4% for the urban population in the lower Yangzi macroregion (Skinner, "Regional Urbanization," p. 229).

14. Liu Shiji, pp. 136–37.

15. Perkins, pp. 13–78 passim.

16. P. Huang, *Peasant Family*, pp. 77–92 passim. Huang also convincingly demonstrates that the expansion in total household output under commercialization was undergirded by declining labor productivity per workday. Hence, the Jiangnan rural economy experienced growth in absolute levels of output, but no transformative development in labor productivity.

17. See the following works for more details on the transformation of landlord-tenant relations in the late Ming and Qing periods: Elvin, *Pattern*, pp. 203–67; Wiens, "Lord and Peasant"; Rawski, *Agricultural Change*; and Perdue, *Exhausting the Earth*.

18. Recent scholarship has demonstrated that kinship organization in China

took many forms. Hence, not all lineages in South China were of the highly stratified rural type described in the text. But since Jiangnan lacked lineage villages of this sort, the general contrast between the two regions still holds. For the latest research on this subject, see the essays in Ebrey and Watson.

19. Dennerline, "Marriage, Adoption, and Charity."

20. *Chongxiu Chang-Zhao hezhi gao*, 15: 1a–21b, 17: 11a–22b. The location of the other six estates is unknown.

21. *Wuxian zhi*, 31: 11a–26a. The location of the other 15 estates is unknown.

22. Pan Guangdan and Quan Weitian, p. 90.

23. Ibid.

24. See, for example, Watson, pp. 37, 68–70, 81. This preference reflects the greater sense of group identification and cohesion among South China lineages. The right to rent lineage land often differentiated members from outsiders.

25. Less productive land did not, of course, bear this rent burden. Information on early and mid-Qing rice yields was drawn from the following sources: *Fenhu xiaozhi*, 6: 10a–15b; Bao Shichen, 26: 4a; Li Wenzhi, *Zhongguo jindai nongye shi ziliao*, p. 100; and Wu Liangkai, p. 64. Data for rice rents were derived from four sets of materials:

A. "Shenyutang zutian bu," a rent register in the Suzhou Museum containing 267 land and housing contracts of the Qu family of Pinghu County, Jiaxing Prefecture, from 1746 to 1755. The documents, all written in the same hand and lacking signatures, appear to be duplicates of original contracts, copied and assembled into a single volume to facilitate bookkeeping. About 100 of the contracts are reprinted in Hong Huanchun, pp. 586–609, 646–52.

B. "Shikai zhichan bu," another land register in the Suzhou Museum. It records the land purchases made by the Shen family of Zhouzhuang market town in Yuanhe County, Suzhou Prefecture, over the years 1659–1823. Occasionally, rent amounts are noted in the margins. "Shikai register" is used to refer to this work. The information on land purchases has been abstracted and reproduced in Hong Huanchun, pp. 90–144.

C. A collection of documents of the Huai family of Jiaxing County, Jiaxing Prefecture, in the Tōyō bunka kenkyūjo, Tokyo University. These documents, dating from 1743 to 1903, include a number of tenancy contracts. I would like to thank Linda Grove of Sophia University for providing me with a copy of this collection, henceforth cited as "Huai papers."

D. *Tōyō bunka kenkyūjo*, 1: 88–90, 2: 21, 141.

26. Bao Shichen, 26: 4a; Li Wenzhi, *Zhongguo jindai nongye shi ziliao*, p. 665; *Baxi zhi*, jingji: 1b; *Tōyō bunka kenkyūjo*, 1: 32–33; Faure, "Rural Economy of Kiangsu Province," p. 393.

27. Liangjiang governor-general, 1739 memorial, reproduced in *Kang-Yong-Qian*, 1: 11.

28. See the Huai papers, and the Shenyu register. The land rental contracts in the Shenyu register of the Qu family permit us to chart the movement of rent when one tenant is replaced by another. Of the 30 cases of replacement from 1746

to 1755, 28 entailed absolutely no change in the amount of fixed rent in kind, and the other two involved a slight decrease in rent. In no instance did the Qus use the occasion of a change in tenants to increase the fixed rent in kind.

29. Landlords defended their use of overlarge rent measures on the grounds that tenants adulterated their rent rice with chaff and substandard kernels. And tenants defended their adulteration of rent rice on the grounds that landlords used overlarge rent measures (*Kang-Yong-Qian*, 1: 10; *Lüxi zhi*, 4: 24b; *Nanxun zhi*, 30: 18a–b).

30. Liu Yongcheng, "Qingdai qianqi de nongye zudian guanxi," p. 87.

31. Tao Xu, *Zuhe* (1884), reproduced in Suzuki, p. 210.

32. *Wu-Qingzhen zhi* (1760), cited in *Wu-Qingzhen zhi*, 7: 7b.

33. Huadong junzheng weiyuanhui tudi gaige weiyuanhui, ed., *Huadong nongcun jingji ziliao*, 1: 7, 14, 77, 205–6.

34. Liu Yongcheng, "Qingdai qianqi de nongye zudian guanxi," pp. 68–69; Jiang Taixin, p. 147.

35. Shenyu register.

36. *Tōyō bunka kenkyūjo*, 1: 88–90.

37. See, for example, *Qingdai dizu boxue xingtai*, 2: 349–51, 360–63, 413–15, 456–57.

38. Shenyu register.

39. Land price data from Shikai register and Nakayama, p. 93.

40. Tao Xu, *Zuhe* (1884), in Suzuki, pp. 229–30. This lowered rent, it should be pointed out, did not mean a smaller return for the landlord–subsoil owner, since subsoil rights cost less than land with no divided rights.

41. The transfer of topsoil rights involved only the seller and the buyer, though their sales contract usually mentioned the amount of rent owed to the subsoil owner. Afterward, the landlord–subsoil owner was to be informed of the change in proprietorship, but he did not draw up a separate rental contract with the new topsoil holder. It was thus the sales contract between the two tenants that set the amount of rent. The fixed nature of rents in the two-tiered ownership system eventually led to the market evaluation of subsoil not in terms of acreage, but in terms of rent in some parts of Jiangnan—for example, as in Pinghu County in the mid-1920's, 40 to 80 yuan of foreign silver per shi of rent. What the purchasers of subsoil were buying was not land as such but the right to receive a certain fixed amount of income from it. (Wu Jing, "Suzhou"; Hayashi, p. 126; Kusano, "Kyū Chūgoku," p. 59; Zhang Zongbi, pp. 594–95.)

42. "Jiangnan zhengzu yuanan" (1788), appendix to Li Chengru, p. 30; Shikai register.

43. There is a great amount of secondary literature on dual ownership in late Ming and Qing China. For recent scholarship on the subject, see Han Hengyu; Fujii; Palmer; and Yang Guozhen. The earliest unequivocal mention of dual ownership in Jiangnan comes from the Jiangyin gazetteer of the Zhengde reign (1506–21; Yang Guozhen, p. 100). Kusano Yasushi argues that dual ownership existed in Jiangnan as early as the Song dynasty. Fujii Hiroshi argues more convincingly for Ming origins (Kusano, "Kyū Chūgoku"; Kusano, "Denmen kankō"; Fujii).

44. Li Chengru, pp. 29–30; *Kang-Yong-Qian*, 1: 10–11.

45. He Menglei, p. 33042; Duan Yinshou, p. 22599; Lieu, pp. 462–63.

46. Li Chengru, pp. 29–30; *Kang-Yong-Qian*, 1: 11, 28; Hong Huanchun, pp. 615–16; Yang Guozhen, pp. 97–110 passim.

47. Huadong junzheng weiyuanhui tudi gaige weiyuanhui, ed., *Huadong nongcun jingji ziliao*, 1: 16, 77, 194–95, 207–8.

48. Liang Fangzhong, pp. 340–41, 402, 405.

49. From the late 1730's to the early 1760's, the price of topsoil rights in Suzhou Prefecture ranged from 1.67 to 2.9 taels a mu, and the price of paddy land with no divided rights from 11 to 19 taels. By the 1790's the price of topsoil rights had reached 12,000 copper *cash*, or approximately 12 taels. The price of paddy land with no topsoil rights increased more slowly, reaching 14,000 to 21,000 *cash*, or 14 to 21 taels, in the 1790's. (Shikai register; *Qingdai dizu boxue xingtai*, 2: 509–11, 515–19, 595–96.)

50. Kusano, "Sōdai no ganden kōso."

51. *Kang-Yong-Qian*, 1: 11.

52. *Gujin tushu jicheng* (1725), 676: 27, quoted in ibid., p. 27.

53. "Kunshanxian fengxian yongjin wandian jibi bei," reproduced in ibid., p. 51; Li Chengru, pp. 9–10.

54. *Kang-Yong-Qian*, 1: 11, 26–27.

55. Ibid., p. 27.

56. Ibid., p. 28.

57. *Jiangyinxian zhi*, 3: 2a–3a; *Wu-Qingzhen zhi*, 7: 4a–b; Wu Zhen, "Yanjin wandian kangzu gaoshi," *Chengjiang zhiji xubian* (n.d.), 2: 35–37, in *Kang-Yong-Qian*, 1: 28–29.

58. Gu Yanwu, *Tianxia junguo libing shu*, quoted in Niida, p. 212.

59. For examples of disputes between Jiangnan tenants over the dingshouyin, see *Qingdai dizu boxue xingtai*, 2: 349–51, 360–63, 456–57.

60. Hamashima, pp. 559–69. It should be noted, though, that the same statute in the Qing code that made rent default a crime also made it illegal for a landlord to beat a tenant or force his wife or daughter to serve as a servant or a concubine (Xue Yunsheng, 4: 912–13).

61. Li Chengru, pp. 30–32; *Kang-Yong-Qian*, 1: 50–51.

62. Pan Zengyi, pp. 2a–b.

63. The poem can be found in *Yuxiang zhi*, 8: 31a.

64. For memorials on Jiangnan rent disputes that led to the death of either a tenant or a landlord, see *Kang-Yong-Qian*, 1: 33–36, 41–43, 54–55; and *Qingdai dizu boxue xingtai*, 1: 135–37, 310–11.

65. For information on collective action by tenants in other regions during the early and mid-Qing periods, see *Kang-Yong-Qian*, 1: 10–164; Mori, "Min-Shin jidai no tochi seido," pp. 229–74; Imahori; Maeda; Shiraishi; and Liu Yongcheng, "Qingdai qianqi diannong kangzu," pp. 54–78.

66. Yu Lin, p. 400. See also P. Huang, *Peasant Family*, pp. 145–48.

67. *Shuanglinzhen zhi* (1870), quoted in Hamashima, pp. 539–40.

68. *Yuanhe yulin qingce*.

69. *Wujiang shuikao zengji*, quoted in Morita, p. 376. The translation here, with

minor alterations, is that of Wiens, "Socioeconomic Change," p. 105.

70. *Qingdai dizu boxue xingtai*, 1: 161.

71. Ibid., pp. 250–51, 2: 349–51, 360–63, 456–57, 515–18, 617–19, 680–81.

72. Huang Zhongjian, "Zhengzu yi," *Xuzhai ji* (1711), 4: 21–23, reproduced in *Kang-Yong-Qian*, 1: 25–26; Chen Hongmou, *Peiyuantang ou cungao wenxi* (1759), 45: 25–26, reproduced in ibid., pp. 40–41.

73. *Tōyō bunka kenkyūjo*, 1: 88; Huai papers.

74. Jing Junjian, pp. 68–71.

75. Xue Yunsheng, 2: 271–72.

76. Jing Junjian, pp. 76–79. See also Sudō.

77. Quoted in Jing Junjian, p. 75.

78. For details on the lijia system in the lower Yangzi valley during the Ming, see Wiens, "Socioeconomic Change," pp. 23–32. Putting the burden of maintaining the polder ditches and embankments solely on a few landowners was not so unfair as it seems, as Hamashima Atsutoshi demonstrates in great detail. Because of the sheer size of Jiangnan polders during the Ming, often several thousand mu larger than during the Qing, the plots in the center were far less easily watered and drained than the well-irrigated and drained land on the periphery, which was accordingly more productive and valuable. This land, as Hamashima also demonstrates, tended to belong to large resident landlords, who had their tenants do the work under their supervision. (Hamashima, pp. 67–90.)

79. Labor service had been allocated not just by the number of male adults in a household, but also according to the amount of property. Thus, cultivator-owners who possessed less than 10 mu of land had also been exempt. (For this reason, it is misleading to refer to the commuted labor service levy as a poll tax, as some scholars tend to do.) According to the early Ming statutes, the only labor service to which a male adult tenant from Jiangnan could be subjected was the equalized labor levy (*jungongfu*) instituted in 1368 for construction work at the new capital of Nanjing, which was calculated at one male adult for each 100 mu of land. Landlords who were unable to provide enough male labor from within their own family could have their tenants perform the service in their stead, but they were also to compensate them with one shi of grain each. This levy ended when the imperial capital was moved from Nanjing to Beijing in 1421. (Wiens, "Socioeconomic Change," pp. 29–32; Tsurumi, pp. 249–59; R. Huang, pp. 35–36.)

80. Hamashima, pp. 54, 167.

81. Ibid., pp. 106–20.

82. Elvin, "Market Towns," pp. 461–67.

83. Mori, "Jūroku-jūhachi seiki." See also Will, pp. 73–75, 79–148 passim.

84. Shigeta Atsushi contends that the merging of the labor service levy and the land tax represented the absolute triumph of landlordism in China and the end of state involvement in landlord-tenant relations in all aspects except official support for rent collection. In his words, the reform "accepted landlordism as the social form of organization through which the state was to maintain its control over the peasantry. [It] put landless tenants beyond the reach of direct state control and meant that landlords were openly entrusted with the task of ruling them." (Shigeta, "Origins and Structure of Gentry Rule," p. 365; see also Shigeta, *Shindai shakai*, pp. 98–122.) Shigeta's argument rests on the assumption that land-

less tenants had been liable for labor service duty or the commuted labor service tax, a liability that would have formed a direct link with the state. In this case the amalgamation of the labor service tax with the land tax in the 18th century would indeed have severed that link. But I have seen no compelling evidence to suggest that landless tenants in Jiangnan were classified as anything other than "odds and ends" households who owed no labor service (see n. 79). Nor have I seen any evidence suggesting that the state became less rather than more involved in local water conservancy and rural relief in the late Ming and early Qing periods.

85. Elvin, "Market Towns," pp. 461–67; Will, pp. 315–16.

Chapter 2

1. Liang Fangzhong, pp. 401–13. One of the principal reasons for Jiangnan's high tax burden was the widespread existence of land specified as "official land" (*guantian*). By the end of the Ming, this property, once farmed by state tenants for a "rent" much higher than the tax on private land, had passed into the hands of individuals, and the rent was transformed into tax. Although the quotas for this category of property were subsequently reduced, they remained higher than the quotas for other land. For a discussion of the origins and high tax quotas of official land in Jiangnan, see Lojewski, "Confucian Reformers," pp. 29–40; and Muramatsu, "Soshō no jūfu."

2. *Wuxian zhi*, 45: 15b–20a. Rice price data from Wang Yeh-chien, *Estimate of Land-Tax Collection*, table 26.

3. Wang Yeh-chien, *Land Taxation*, pp. 49–61; Usui, "Taihei Tengoku," pp. 59–69; Zelin, pp. 46–54.

4. Ch'ü T'ung-tsu, pp. 48–53, 67–68; Feng Guifen, 5: 36a–37b; Sheng Kang, 36: fuyi 3, 5a–b.

5. Usui, "Shindai fuzei kankei sūchi no ichi kentō," pp. 77–79; Xia Nai, pp. 422–24.

6. Lin Man-houng, pp. 256–99. For the copper currency argument, see King; and on the opium argument, Peng Zeyi.

7. Zheng Guangzu, 6: 46a–b, 8: 6a; Bao Shichen, 26: 37b; Usui, "Shindai fuzei kankei sūchi no ichi kentō," pp. 77–79, 93–96. We unfortunately do not have comparable data on the prices of agricultural commodities in taels of silver. This has made it difficult for scholars to spell out precisely the relationship between the silver inflation and the price recession. On this score, one of the most convincing arguments has been advanced by Lin Man-Houng, who notes that if, as some historians contend, the rising value of silver relative to copper was due to a debasement of copper coinage, then the result should have been an increase in the supply of copper *cash* and a depreciation in the value of copper not only to silver but to commodities as well, and hence a rise in the copper prices of farm products. That copper prices fell suggests that the silver-copper crisis of the mid-19th century entailed not only a rise in the value of silver, but also a contraction in the supply of copper *cash* (pp. 191–205).

8. Usui, "Shindai fuzei kankei sūchi no ichi kentō," pp. 78–79.

9. Ibid., pp. 94–95.

10. Ibid., pp. 108–13. Usui's main source for her calculations is the diary *Lou-*

wang yongyu ji by Ke Wuchi of Changshu. Ke's diary records local grain and cotton prices, silver-copper exchange ratios, and tribute rice and qianliang conversion rates for a number of years between 1836 and 1859.

11. Ke Wuchi, p. 5.

12. Feng Guifen, 10: 1a.

13. *Taicangzhou zhi* (1919), noted in Yokoyama, "Chūgoku ni okeru nōmin undō," p. 335.

14. Duan Guanqing, pp. 37–38.

15. Zelin, p. 242. See also Will, p. 106.

16. Ke Wuchi, p. 5.

17. Peng Zeyi, pp. 53, 62.

18. *Chongxiu Huatingxian zhi*, 23: 6a–b.

19. Land price data from the Shikai register; rice price data from Usui, "Shindai fuzei kankei sūchi no ichi kentō," pp. 93–95.

20. Rent information from *Chongxiu Chang-Zhao hezhi gao*, 17: 12a; price data from Zheng Guangzu, 6: 4a–b, 8: 6a; Ke Wuchi, p. 19.

21. See, for example, Lin Man-houng, pp. 72–115 passim; Namiki; Yokoyama, "Chūgoku ni okeru nōmin undō"; Fu Yiling, "Taiping Tianguo shidai de quanguo kangliang chao"; and Chen Zaizheng.

22. Gongzhongdang, Daoguang 25 (1845) 007357, 007840, 008047.

23. *Shenghu zhibu*, 4: 3a–b; Harigaya, "Taihei Tengoku senryō chi-iki no sōsen shūdan."

24. Wakeman, *Strangers at the Gate*, pp. 12–70; Kuhn, *Rebellion and Its Enemies*, pp. 69–76.

25. Qi Sihe et al.; *Yapian zhanzheng*.

26. Qi Sihe et al., 4: 566.

27. Ibid., p. 453.

28. *Danghu waizhi*, 8: 5a.

29. Reproduced in Cheng Ying, pp. 57–58. The song has to do specifically with the 1846 tax uprising.

30. Zheng Guangzu, 6: 35b–38a, 7: 43b–50b. Unless otherwise noted, the account here is based on Zheng's work. For a more detailed analysis of the Zhao-wen rent and tax uprisings, see Kobayashi Kazumi.

31. Zheng Guangzu, 2: 51a; *Chongxiu Chang-Zhao hezhi gao*, 17: 18a, 31: 23b–24a.

32. Min's own reasons for assuming command are not so clear. He may well have been a tenant himself and thus felt the same pressures as the other protesters. Even if he was not a tenant, however, he was still affected indirectly by the burden of rent, since as a guarantor he could be held liable for his clients' default. A guarantor in Min's position, confronted with tenant intentions to oppose payment, might decide to dissociate himself from the conflict for fear of being called to account for the actions of the others. Or, alternatively, he might join the protest in the hope that it would persuade landlords to accept the default and thereby absolve him of any responsibility for his clients' debts. On the role of the guarantor, see Van der Sprenkel, pp. 107–9.

33. Gui Danmeng, 5: 18b–19a; Peng Zeyi, pp. 61–62.

34. Ke Wuchi, p. 6.

35. Gui Danmeng, 5: 18b–21a; Ke Wuchi, p. 6; Li Xingyuan, 12: 34a–40a.
36. Ke Wuchi, pp. 6–7; Gui Danmeng, 5: 23a–b.
37. Li Xingyuan, 12: 47b–48a.   38. Ke Wuchi, p. 8.
39. Li Xingyuan, 12: 55a–56a.   40. Gui Danmeng, 5: 21a.
41. Li Xingyuan, 12: 57b; Ke Wuchi, p. 9.
42. For accounts of the 1853 rent protests in Zhaowen, see Ke Wuchi, pp. 19–21; and "Guijia riji," p. 382.
43. Ke Wuchi, pp. 10–20 passim.
44. Wu Wenrong, 26: 1a–15a.
45. Poem about the 1849 rice riots, reproduced in Dong Caishi, *Taiping Tianguo zai Suzhou*, p. 19.
46. Zheng Guangzu, 8: 6b–8b; Duan Guanqing, pp. 39–40; *Shenghu zhi*, 3: 16a; Yao Ji, "Jiyou beishui jiwen"; Pan Daogen, 12: 16a; Wang Rurun, pp. 184–85.
47. Yao Ji, "Jiyou beishui jiwen," pp. 42–43.
48. Zheng Guangzu, 8: 7a–8b. For other examples, see Yao Ji, "Jiyou beishui jiwen," p. 42; and Duan Guanqing, p. 40.
49. Reproduced in Wu Jing, "1853–1855," p. 58.
50. Unless otherwise noted, the account of the Lili rent struggle is drawn from the description provided in Gongzhongdang, Xianfeng 5 (1855) 006505, a joint memorial by the Liangjiang governor-general Yi Liang and the Jiangsu governor Jierhang'a.
51. Huang Xiling, "Huang Xiling riji," quoted in Wu Jing, "1853–1855," pp. 57–58.
52. Ke Wuchi, p. 15.
53. *Lili xuzhi*, 12: 17a–b.
54. Yin Zhaoyong, "Yin Pujing shilang ziding nianpu," quoted in Wu Jing, "1853–1855," p. 58.
55. "Huang Xiling riji," noted in ibid.
56. Reproduced in Fang Shiming, p. 27. This folksong has the tax resistance leader Zhou Lichun confronting the Qingpu magistrate.
57. Feng Guifen, 5: 33a–b, 9: 23a–b; Suzhou bowuguan et al., *He Guiqing deng shuzha*, p. 216.
58. The Small Sword Rebellion has received a fair amount of attention in the secondary literature. See, for example, Dillon; Fang Shiming; Kujirai; Banno; and Perry, "Tax Revolt."
59. For a detailed description of the establishment of the Small Sword Society, see Lu Yaohua, pp. 208–12.
60. Dillon, pp. 68–69.
61. Ibid., p. 69; Lu Yaohua, pp. 218–19; Perry, "Tax Revolt," pp. 88–89.
62. *Shanghai Xiaodaohui*, pp. 38–39. This argument is advanced by Lu Yaohua, pp. 211–12.
63. *Shanghai Xiaodaohui*, p. 39.
64. *Songjiangfu xuzhi*, 14: 16a. For a discussion of kunbao, see Faure, "Land Tax Collection," pp. 53–61.
65. "Yizhaolou Hong-Yang zougao," p. 1169.
66. Zhu Chengcong, p. 1055; "Huangdu xuzhi," p. 1086. According to another account, the landowners in Zhou's tu had already paid the tax, but the runners

had embezzled the funds ("Qingpuxian zhi," p. 1157).

67. "Huangdu xuzhi," pp. 1085–86.

68. Feng Guifen, 5: 33a; Hehu Yiyisheng, pp. 486, 496, 499; Yuan Zuzhi, p. 1019; *North China Herald*, June 18, 1853; Ke Wuchi, p. 18.

69. Anyone who bought a piece of land or a house was required to pay the government a property deed tax (*shuiqiyin*), set by law at 3 percent of the purchase price. To avoid paying this tax and the attendant customary fees to yamen personnel, property owners frequently concealed changes in proprietorship. Official investigations of deed slips and tax registers, such as the one mentioned here, were periodically undertaken to uncover such cases of fraud, the statutory penalty for which was a severe beating and the confiscation of the property. For information on the deed tax, see Li Wenzhi, *Zhongguo jindai nongye shi ziliao*, pp. 54–55.

70. Zhu Chengcong, p. 1054.

71. Ibid., pp. 1055–56. According to other accounts, Li Shaoqing himself was one of the smugglers on the opium run ("Qingpuxian zhi," p. 1158; "Huangdu xuzhi," p. 1087).

72. The gang's name derived from the phrase "18 Arhats" (the 18 saints of Buddhism). At the initiation ceremony, the monk Sheng Chuan acted as host at the *tenth* table and his name was listed *eighth* on the written pledge of brotherhood (Wang Rurun, p. 187; Zhu Chengcong, p. 1055; "Yizhaolou Hong-Yang zougao," pp. 1112–13).

73. "Pingyue jiwen," pp. 1115–16. One source has it that Chen Mujin had been a founding member of the Arhat League ("Wu Xu dang'an," p. 1124).

74. *Shanghai Xiaodaohui*, pp. 6–7, 28–29; "Yizhaolou Hong-Yang zougao," pp. 1092–93; "Pingyue jiwen," p. 1116; "Shanghai Xiaodaohui qiyi wenxian," p. 21.

75. Zhu Chengcong, pp. 1055–56; Huang Benquan, p. 973; Huang Baoting, p. 1155. Of the cities attacked by the Small Swords, only Taicang proved capable of repulsing the rebels. There, the acting department head held off the insurgents with a small force of mercenaries until government reinforcements arrived ("Yizhaolou Hong-Yang zougao," pp. 1186–89).

76. Zhu Chengcong, pp. 1053–54; "Pingyue jiwen," pp. 1194–98.

77. Zhu Chengcong, pp. 1057–58; "Huangdu xuzhi," p. 1089; "Yizhaolou Hong-Yang zougao," pp. 1100–1101.

78. "Qingpuxian zhi," p. 1158; "Baoshanxian zhi"; "Nanhuixian zhi," p. 1164; "Chuanshating zhi."

79. The following analysis is based on the sources listed at the end of Table A.1.

80. Dou Zheng; "Pingzei jilüe," pp. 222–23; "Gouwu guijia lu," p. 80.

81. See, for example, the account of a collective action against rent in Taicang in 1853 in "Guijia riji," p. 282.

82. Zheng Guangzu, 6: 36a; *Jinshanxian zhi*, 17: 31a–b; *Danghu waizhi* (1858), reproduced in Li Wenzhi, *Zhongguo jindai nongye shi ziliao*, p. 972; Hehu Yiyisheng, p. 512; Yao Ji, "Gouquan jinlu," pp. 1147–49.

83. Zheng Guangzu, 2: 52a; *Chongxiu Chang-Zhao hezhi gao*, 31: 30a–b, 38b–39a, 41a–b.

84. The last was in fact a failure of duty. Under the practice of *yeshi dianli*,

landlords were obligated either to supply tenants with the funds or material for the construction and repair of polder ditches and embankments or to discount rents as compensation for the resources they had put into such work. When landlords did not honor their obligations, tenants occasionally took what was not willingly given. During the flood of 1849, for instance, peasants in Shuanglin (Guian County) and Shengze (Wujiang County) visited the homes of their landlords to request money, grain, and wooden posts for their water conservancy efforts. When landlords refused the request, the tenants pried the wooden doors and window frames from their houses and stole grain from their granaries. (*Shenghu zhi*, 3: 16a; *Shuanglinzhen zhi*, 1870, quoted in Hamashima, p. 550.)

85. Ke Wuchi, pp. 19–20; "Guijia riji," p. 382.

86. "Pingzei jilüe," pp. 222–23; "Gouwu guijia lu," p. 80; Zhu Chengcong, pp. 1071–73.

87. "Gouwu guijia lu," p. 80.

88. Natsui, p. 12.

89. "Yizhaolou shishi huibian," pp. 379, 391–92; *Wuyang zhiyu* (1888), quoted in Li Wenzhi, *Zhongguo jindai nongye shi ziliao*, p. 949; Shen Zi, p. 328; *Qingshi liezhuan*, noted in Fu Yiling, "Taiping Tianguo shidai de quanguo kangliang chao," p. 412.

90. For examples of gentry leading tax uprisings in other regions in the 19th century, see Hsiao Kung-ch'üan, pp. 447–53; C. K. Yang, pp. 198–201; Yokoyama, "Chūgoku ni okeru nōmin undō," pp. 333–36; Fu Yiling, "Taiping Tianguo shidai de quanguo kangliang chao," pp. 404–13; and Chen Zaicheng, pp. 7–12.

91. Kuhn, *Rebellion and Its Enemies*, pp. 98–99; Wei Yuan, 4: 33b–36a; Wu Wenrong, 11: 5a–11a, 17: 1a–14a, 18: 2a–10a; *Da Qing Xuan Zongcheng*, 402: 26b–27b.

92. Ibid.

93. Perry, *Rebels and Revolutionaries*, pp. 86–87.

94. See, for example, Fu Yiling, "Taiping Tianguo shidai tuanlian kangguan wenti yinlun," pp. 443–52.

95. Kuhn, *Rebellion and Its Enemies*, pp. 171–74; *Shenghu zhibu*, 4: 3a–b; Gunong Tuishi, p. 75; Feng Shi, p. 679.

96. Shen Zi, p. 328; *Nanxun zhi*, 45: 20a–21a.

97. Feng Guifen, 9: 23a–b.

98. For a detailed discussion of the 1853 tax reforms, see Lojewski, "Confucian Reformers," pp. 100–128; and Polachek, pp. 228–30.

99. After the Zhaowen rent uprising in 1846 and a rent protest in Hengjingzhen, Taicang, in 1853, the local landlords were ordered to lower their zhezu rates of collection (Li Xingyuan, 12: 57b; Ke Wuchi, pp. 20–21). Some landlords, of course, reduced rents voluntarily. Sixteen Suzhou gentrymen, for example, lowered the rents on their property in Yuanhe, Changzhou, and Wu counties by some 30 to 40 percent in 1854 ("Yizhaolou shishi huibian," pp. 463–64). Why they made so generous a gesture is nowhere stated, but conceivably the ongoing rent resistance movement against highly placed gentry families in Lilizhen (Wujiang) had driven home the fact that neither their prominence nor their official connections would protect them from similar attacks. Or they may have simply recognized that, given the temper of the times, they would probably not be able to collect full rents anyway.

Chapter 3

1. Ke Wuchi, p. 27; Wang Rurun, p. 190.
2. Ke Wuchi, p. 28.
3. Ibid., p. 47; *Yixing Jingxixian xinzhi,* 5: 7b; Liaocun Dunke, pp. 15–16; Polachek, pp. 228–34.
4. Liaocun Dunke, p. 29.
5. Xie Suizhi, pp. 401–2; Juanpu Yelao, p. 99.
6. There are, however, scattered references to the tu as the unit of militia organization. See, for example, Xie Suizhi, p. 403; and Gong Youcun, p. 348.
7. Hua Yilun, pp. 122–24; "Binan jilüe," pp. 70–71; Xu Peirui et al., "Shuangli bian" (1981), p. 292. Hua Yilun belonged to the Hua lineage analyzed by Dennerline; see "Marriage, Adoption, and Charity," especially p. 183.
8. Letters of the Xu brothers to each other and to local officials are the main content of Xu Peirui et al., "Shuangli bian" (1981). A slightly different version of this work was published in *Jindaishi ziliao,* 34 (1964), along with several collections of satirical poems about the brothers and the Dongyongchang militia bureau. See also Gu Shucun.
9. Shen Shouzhi, p. 22. In 1980 a Chinese research team conducted interviews with elderly residents in the Yongchang area. One informant had heard that the Xus secured the cooperation of their tenants in defense efforts by threatening them with eviction (Yuan Zhen et al., p. 6).
10. *Xiangcheng xiaozhi,* bingfang: 1b.
11. Tao Xu, 1: 3a.
12. Ibid., 1: 3a–5a; "Guanyu Fei Xiuyuan fuzi de ziliao."
13. Tang Shi, pp. 78, 84.
14. Ibid., p. 91.
15. Ke Wuchi, p. 52. This was hardly the end of the Zheng family's tenant troubles. When the family refused to lower rents after a poor cotton harvest in eastern Zhaowen in 1934, some 1,000–2,000 tenants, many of them elderly, appealed to the Zheng household head, offering their bodies in lieu of the rents they could not pay; and when he turned a deaf ear to their pleas, the crowd attacked and damaged the Zheng house, as well as the family's charitable estate offices. (*Shenbao,* 11/10, 11/11/34.)
16. For information on these groups, see Shen Yuwu, "Tianjing leiyu Zhejiang chao"; and the two articles by Zou Shencheng listed in the References. For information on organized peasant opposition to the Taipings in eastern Zhejiang, see Cole's account of the famous peasant resistance leader Bao Lisheng of Shaoxing Prefecture.
17. Ke Wuchi, p. 44.
18. "Pingzei jilüe," p. 259.
19. Tang Shi, p. 77.
20. *Haiyanxian zhi* (1877), final chap.; p. 48, cited in Wang Xingfu, p. 34.
21. Xie Suizhi, p. 392.
22. Registers for various Taiping units in Jiangnan record the names, ages, native places, and tasks of a number of local people who, to use the Taiping phrase, "entered the camp" (*ruying*). Locals served the rebels as cooks, porters,

guards, water carriers, grooms, tailors, etc. See *Taiping Tianguo wenshu huibian*, pp. 343–406.

23. Canglang Diaotu, p. 158. For a contrast of the conduct of the two armies, see Wang Xingfu, pp. 60–65.

24. Curwen, pp. 86, 103.

25. For a more extensive discussion of the confused command structure, see Li Chun, pp. 274–77.

26. Gu Ruyu, p. 359.

27. "Gengshen binan riji," p. 483.

28. Ibid.; Liaocun Dunke, p. 25; Feng Shi, pp. 675, 679.

29. Tang Shi, pp. 87–90. The price of the door placards for Wangshi, one yuan of foreign silver (about 1,000 *cash*), was average. Generally, the fee ranged from 200 to 4,000 *cash*, although there are a few cases in which even more was demanded. In some areas the Taipings charged rich households some two to three times as much as poorer families. (Li Chun, pp. 385–86; Shen Zi, p. 59; "Gengshen binan riji," p. 528; "Binan jilüe," p. 60; Zhao Liewen, "Nengjing jushi riji," p. 157; Cao Guozhi, p. 639.)

30. "Gengshen binan riji," p. 486; Liaocun Dunke, pp. 22, 25.

31. Hua Yilun, pp. 123–24; Tao Xu, 1: 6a–b.

32. While the formula outlined here is the one mentioned most often in "The Land System of the Heavenly Dynasty," the document does present at one point an alternate method of organizing the population units. In place of the 5–25–100–500–2,500–12,500 ordering, it offers a 5–26–105–526–2,631–13,156 scale, in which the leaders of the groups and presumably their families as well are counted from the second (liangsima) tier up as additions to their respective units. For example, the 25-member liangsima group of the more common scheme becomes here a 26-member group (five five-member units plus the group leader, the liangsima); the 100-member zuzhang division is transformed into a 105-member group (four 26-member liangsima units plus the zuzhang), and so forth. Most primary sources follow the first formula in their discussions of the rebel social organization. See Li Chun, pp. 286–88.

33. Gu Ruyu, p. 370; *Yixing Jingxixian xinzhi*, 5: 11b; Juanpu Yelao, p. 99; *Taiping Tianguo wenshu huibian*, p. 128.

34. Tang Shi, p. 110; Zhang Naixiu, p. 609.

35. Li Chun, pp. 328–37.

36. Shen Zi, p. 73.

37. Li Chun, pp. 309–15.

38. Tang Shi, pp. 109–10.

39. "Binan jilüe," pp. 60–61.

40. Tang Shi, p. 110.

41. Ibid.; Liaocun Dunke, p. 41.

42. For the peasant-power theory, see, for example, Shen Yuwu, "Taiping Tianguo"; and Dong Caishi, "Taiping Tianguo de xiangguan." For the feudal-power theory, see Wang Tiangjiang, "Taiping Tianguo xiangguan"; Sun Zuomin; and Lin Qingyuan.

43. Kuhn, *Rebellion and Its Enemies*, pp. 189–96; Wakeman, "Rebellion and Revolution," p. 220.

44. For an English translation of "The Land System of the Heavenly Dynasty," see Michael, 2: 309–20.

45. Luo Ergang, "Zai lun 'Tianchao tianmu zhidu,'" pp. 104–7.

46. The only historical accounts from Jiangnan that mention the land program are retrospective ones. See, for example, Xie Suizhi, p. 406.

47. Shen Zi, p. 73; *Taiping Tianguo wenshu huibian*, pp. 145–46, 209–10; Gong Youcun, pp. 390, 415.

48. Tang Shi, pp. 97–98; Yang Yinchuan, p. 176.

49. *Taiping Tianguo wenshu huibian*, pp. 145–46.

50. "Pingzei jilüe," pp. 267, 278; "Binan jilüe," p. 67; Gu Ruyu, pp. 370–71; Xu Rixiang, p. 436; Cai Shaoqing, p. 176.

51. See, for example, Rong Mengyuan, pp. 537–38. The classic statement of this position is Luo Ergang, *Taiping Tianguo shishi kao*, pp. 207–10. Luo has since concluded, on the basis of new evidence, that tenant payment of taxes, while ultimately beneficial to tenants and harmful to landlords, did not constitute the transfer of landownership rights to tenants. For his new view, see his 1984 article "Zai lun 'Tianchao tianmu zhidu.' "

52. Folk tales and songs about the Taiping Rebellion mention land redistribution and rebel prohibitions against rent collection as a matter of course. The historical source for these legends may well have been the *zhuodian qizheng* policy. For a collection of such stories and songs, see *Taiping Tianguo geyao chuanshuo ji*.

53. "Pingzei jilüe," p. 279. 54. Tang Shi, p. 110.
55. Gu Ruyu, p. 371. 56. Ibid., pp. 370–71.
57. "Pingzei jilüe," p. 279. 58. Feng Shi, p. 671.

59. Tang Shi, p. 110; Ke Wuchi, p. 50.

60. "Binan jilüe," p. 73; Shen Zi, p. 193; "Gengshen binan riji," p. 496.

61. "Jingzhai riji," 39a; "Pingzei jilüe," pp. 276, 278; Gong Youcun, p. 415; *Taiping Tianguo wenshu huibian*, pp. 134–35; Ke Wuchi, p. 53.

62. Tang Shi, p. 124; Gong Youcun, pp. 416, 420, 468; *Taiping Tianguo wenshu huibian*, p. 146; Liu Zhaoxun, pp. 152, 156, 163; Juanpu Yelao, pp. 101, 106.

63. Tang Shi, p. 125; "Pingzei jilüe," pp. 278–79, 281; "Gengshen binan riji," p. 515.

64. Liu Zhaoxun, pp. 152, 163; *Lili xuzhi*, 12: 18a–b.

65. *Taiping Tianguo wenshu huibian*, pp. 145–46; Gu Mou, p. 166; "Pingzei jilue," pp. 278–79; Shen Zi, p. 202; Gong Youcun, pp. 396–97, 406–7, 416–17; Heqiao Jushi, p. 198.

66. Gong Youcun, p. 468.

67. Ibid., pp. 396, 462–63; Liu Zhaoxun, pp. 222–23; "Lihu yuefu," p. 172.

68. Tang Shi, p. 124.

69. "Binan jilüe," p. 73.

70. Gong Youcun, p. 460; Zhou Jian, pp. 83–84.

71. Liu Zhaoxun, p. 156.

72. Ke Wuchi, p. 53; "Gengshen binan riji," p. 514.

73. Juanpu Yelao, p. 104.

74. "Pingzei jilüe," pp. 278–79; Juanpu Yelao, p. 106; "Binan jilüe," p. 73.

75. Tang Shi, p. 125; "Pingzei jilüe," p. 281. See also Gong Youcun, pp. 396–97.

76. *Taiping Tianguo wenshu huibian*, pp. 51–52. The Suzhou tax receipts bear official stamps that read in part "taxes have been reduced 10 percent as ordered" (Liao Zhihao).

77. Curwen, p. 120; Canglang Diaotu, p. 149.
78. See, for example, Shen Zi, p. 237.
79. See, for example, Li Chun, pp. 338–59 passim.
80. Tang Shi, pp. 121–22; Ke Wuchi, p. 73; Zhou Jian, p. 83.
81. Shen Zi, pp. 76, 96, 153, 160, 187.
82. Ibid., p. 193.
83. Ibid., pp. 138, 238; Juanpu Yelao, pp. 100, 102, 106.
84. Tang Shi, pp. 116–17, 123, 125; Gu Ruyu, pp. 371–73; Gong Youcun, pp. 401, 434, 442; "Gengshen binan riji," pp. 514–15, 525.
85. Tang Shi, pp. 119, 122; "Gengshen binan riji," pp. 528, 540; Gong Youcun, pp. 451, 456; Feng Shi, p. 710.
86. Ke Wuchi, pp. 58, 68–69.
87. Qi Longwei.
88. Yuan Zhen et al., pp. 26–27; *Meili zhi*, 7: 34a; *Shenbao*, 2/6/Tongzhi 12 (1873).

Chapter 4

1. Wright, p. 63.
2. The role the Taiping Rebellion and gentry militarization played in the expansion of elite influence in the late Qing was first analyzed by Philip A. Kuhn in his seminal work *Rebellion and Its Enemies*. Frederic Wakeman then elaborated on some of Kuhn's themes in "Rebellion and Revolution," pp. 219–20, and "Introduction: The Evolution of Local Control," pp. 2–4, 21–25.
3. Wang Yeh-chien contends that the Tongzhi tax reduction should be seen as "a product of an old tax cut movement, with the Taiping Rebellion merely facilitating its realization" ("Impact of the Taiping Rebellion," p. 134). For an example of the opposite view, which holds that the tax reduction was primarily a reaction to the political disturbances of the mid-19th century, see Takahashi, pp. 269–81.
4. *Xiaofengxian zhi*, 4: 1b; *Shenbao*, 4/16/Guangxu 6 (1880); Ma Xinyi, 3: 50b–51a.
5. Zhu Xuechin, ed., *Jiaoping Yuefei fanglüe*, 371: 26, quoted in Wang Yeh-chien, "Impact of the Taiping Rebellion," p. 128.
6. Wang Yeh-chien, "Impact of the Taiping Rebellion," pp. 127–28, 150; Li Zongxi, 4: 3a.
7. Wang Yeh-chien, "Impact of the Taiping Rebellion," pp. 128–29; Ding Richang, 4: 11a.
8. "Binan jilüe," p. 72; Hua Yilun, p. 130; "Pingzei jilüe," p. 325; Juanpu Yelao, p. 111; Lu Yun, p. 111.
9. Ke Wuchi, p. 93.
10. Ibid., p. 93; "Gengshen binan riji," p. 558; *Tongxiangxian zhi*, 7: 15b.
11. Ke Wuchi, p. 93; "Pingzei jilüe," p. 294.
12. Heqiao Jushi.
13. This contention is based on a careful reading of two late Qing Shengze gazetteers, *Shenghu zhi* (1874) and *Shenghu zhibu* (1900).
14. For examples of the deliberate exclusion of former xiangguan from involvement in gentry affairs, see "Pingzei jilüe," p. 324; and Shen Zi, pp. 306–7.

15. Xu Peirui et al., "Shuangli bian" (1981), pp. 251–308; Yuan Zhen et al., pp. 3, 6–7.

16. McCord.

17. For examples of militia formation in the post-Taiping period, see *Shenbao*, 9/7/Guangxu 2 (1876), 2/12/Guangxu 3 (1877), 11/4/Guangxu 3 (1877); *Yiwenlu*, 11/5/Guangxu 17 (1891); *Huibao*, 8/26/Guangxu 26 (1900); and *Baoshanxian xuzhi*, 9: 12a–16a.

18. Rankin, *Elite Activism and Political Transformation*. For elite activities in Zhejiang in the late Qing and early Republican period, see also Schoppa, *Chinese Elites and Political Change*.

19. *Shenbao*, 10/26/Tongzhi 11 (1872), 4/24/Tongzhi 12 (1873), 11/14/Guangxu 3 (1877), 12/4/Guangxu 5 (1879), 1/20/Guangxu 6 (1880); *Baoshanxian xuzhi*, 3: 22b–23b.

20. *Wuyang zhiyu*, 6: 21b; Liaocun Dunke, p. 14; Feng Shi, p. 687; *Yixing Jingxixian xinzhi*, 1: 9b.

21. Kojima, "Shinmatsu no gōson tōchi ni tsuite," pp. 22–26; Ocko, pp. 137–39.

22. *Wuxi Fu'anxiang zhigao*, 1: 1b, 11: 6a.

23. *Shenbao*, 2/9/Guangxu 5 (1879); *Tongwen hubao*, 9/12/Guangxu 28 (1902).

24. Wang Shuhuai, p. 57.

25. *Wuxian zhi*, 30: 7a–21b. The gazetteer lists a total of 75 charities, but gives the date of founding and/or rebuilding for only 70. The remaining five are thus not included in the tabulation in the text.

26. Rankin, p. 16.

27. The term "public sphere" must be used with caution. The original conception comes from Jürgen Habermas, who employs it in his study of the roots of European democracy in *The Structural Transformation of the Public Sphere*. He juxtaposes the notion of a public sphere against that of a private sphere and adds to that mix yet another dichotomy—the state and civil society. Although he is never quite clear on the content of these different realms and the way they interrelated, he does suggest that the public sphere historically in Europe embraced both a civil realm and a state realm. If we are to apply the concept of public sphere to late Qing China, then, we must consider not only the expansion of the civil realm of the public sphere, but also the expansion of its state realm. I am grateful to Philip Huang for pointing out this distinction to me. For a review of the use of Habermas's work by historians of China, see Rowe, "Public Sphere in Modern China." For a more recent study employing the notion of public sphere, see Brook, "Family Continuity and Cultural Hegemony," especially pp. 43–50.

28. The central government received 70–80 percent of the quotas for Suzhou and Songjiang prefectures in the 1830's, 50–60 percent in the 1840's, and only 40 percent in the 1850's. Similarly, the tax revenue from the three northern Zhejiang prefectures declined from 70–80 percent in the 1840's to 50–60 percent in the 1850's (Liu Kexiang, p. 310).

29. Ibid., p. 311.

30. Ding's memorial is reproduced in Sheng Kang, 37: 9a–11a.

31. Feng Guifen, 9: 5a; Liu Kexiang, p. 311.

32. Lojewski, "Confucian Reformers," pp. 153–203 passim; Wang yeh-chien, *Land Taxation*, pp. 35–36; Xia Nai, pp. 453–68; Liu Kexiang, pp. 308–21.

33. Li Hongzhang, 9: 8a–9b; Shen Zi, pp. 309–10; Juanpu Yelao, p. 114; Lu Yun, pp. 141–42; Ke Wuchi, pp. 96–97.

34. Li Hongzhang, 9: 8b.

35. Lu Yun, pp. 141–42; Li Hongzhang, 9: 9b; Fang Zhiguang, pp. 10–11.

36. Shen Zi, pp. 309–10; Tao Xu, *Zuhe*, in Suzuki, p. 231; Juanpu Yelao, p. 114; Wang Bingxie, 6: 2a; Jiang Yinsheng, pp. 437–38. Evidence that tenant payment of the levy occurred in Jiaxing County comes from several 1864 "tenant receipts" (*diandan*) in the Huai papers. The receipts were apparently issued to tenants on completion of a field survey. In addition to noting the names of the tenant and landowner and the amount and location of the field in question, the documents state that the tenant is to pay the tax until such time as the landlord registers his property with the county government. If the amount of land he reported matched the figure on the tenant's receipt, he was to be issued a copy of the document and would be permitted to collect rent after discounting the amount the tenant had already paid in levies.

37. Lu Yun, p. 142.

38. Juanpu Yelao, pp. 114, 116.

39. Li Hongzhang, 9: 8b–9a; Juanpu Yelao, p. 118; Ke Wuchi, p. 101; "Gengshen binan riji," p. 591; Liu Zhaoxun, pp. 333–34, 351; Lu Yun, pp. 145–46.

40. Ke Wuchi, p. 101; Lu Yun, pp. 145–46; "Gengshen binan riji," p. 591.

41. Juanpu Yelao, p. 118.

42. Ibid., p. 117; Lu Yun, pp. 145–46.

43. Ma Xinyi, 7: 53b; Liu Yao, pp. 38–39; Li Wenzhi, "Lun Qingdai," pp. 84–85.

44. Liu Yao, pp. 38–39.

45. Ma Xinyi, 7: 50b; Wang Desen, 4: 6a–b; *Jiaxingxian zhi*, 11: 49a; *Meili beizhi*, 2: 27a; *Xiaofengxian zhi*, 4: 3b–4b; *Yiwenlu*, 7/28/Guangxu 10 (1884).

46. *Jiaxingxian zhi*, 11: 49a–51a.

47. See, for example, *Xinchengzhen zhi*, 4: 7a; *Wu-Qingzhen zhi*, 40: 11a–12b; *Shenbao*, 9/12/Guangxu 4 (1878); *Huibao*, 3/10/Guangxu 25 (1899); and *Tongwen hubao*, 6/25/Guangxu 29 (1903).

48. *Yixing Jingxixian xinzhi* (1882), 5: 1b, translated in Wang Yeh-chien, "Impact of the Taiping Rebellion," p. 131.

49. Ma Xinyi, 7: 50b.

50. Ibid., 7: 52b–53a.

51. *Shenbao*, 4/2, 4/16/Guangxu 6 (1880), 4/19/Guangxu 7 (1881).

52. Ma Xinyi, 3: 53b–55b, 7: 51a–53a.

53. Li Wenzhi, "Lun Qingdai," pp. 81–96; Li Wenzhi, "Taiping Tianguo geming," pp. 82–94.

54. Mao Jiaqi, pp. 111–25.

55. Wang Tianjiang, "Taiping Tianguo geming," pp. 126–42.

56. Tao Xu, *Zuhe*, in Suzuki, p. 209; *Jinshanxian zhi*, p. 739.

57. Ding Richang, 4: 11a.

58. Wang Desen, 4: 6a–b; Wang Tianjiang, "Taiping Tianguo geming," p. 130.

59. Li Wenzhi, "Lun Qingdai," pp. 83–84.

60. Ibid., p. 84; Wang Tianjiang, "Taiping Tianguo geming," pp. 129–30, 138.

61. Liu Kunyi, 2: 569–70; Li Wenzhi, "Lun Qingdai," p. 85.

62. Li Wenzhi, "Lun Qingdai," pp. 89, 92–94.

63. Ibid., pp. 87–88; Wang Tianjiang, "Taiping Tianguo geming," pp. 139–40; *Jiaxingxian zhi*, 11: 49a; *Shenbao*, 9/12, 12/3/Guangxu 4 (1878), 4/16/Guangxu 6 (1880), 4/19/Guangxu 7 (1881).

64. *Yixing Jingxixian xinzhi*, 3: 6a–b; *Shenbao*, 12/28/Guangxu 8 (1882); Li Wenzhi, "Lun Qingdai," pp. 84–85.

65. Shen Baozhen, an 1877 memorial, reproduced in Sheng Kang, 39: 23b; *Jiashanxian zhi*, 10: 5a–b.

66. *Jiashanxian zhi*, 10: 5a–b.

67. *Shenbao*, 12/22/Guangxu 5 (1879).

68. Huai papers; Shilu register.

69. Li Wenzhi, *Zhongguo jindai nongye shi ziliao*, p. 252; *Min shangshi xiguan diaocha baogao lu*, 1: 317, 462; Liu Yao, pp. 43–47.

70. The shift in the tax liability from landlord to tenant is shown in the post-rebellion land purchase contracts in the Huai papers. At the end of each contract the person or persons who had been responsible for the tax payment prior to the transaction are named. Many are clearly identified as tenants (*dianhu*).

71. Kojima, "Dennō no zeiryō futan," pp. 66–67; *Min shangshi xiguan diaocha baogao lu*, 1: 462.

72. For a discussion of how an abundance of land affected peasant resistance strategies, see Adas.

73. Li Wenzhi, "Lun Qingdai," p. 82; Wang Tianjiang, "Taiping Tianguo geming," pp. 128–29; Mao Jiaqi, p. 112.

74. Natsui, p. 25; Lojewski, "Soochow Bursaries," p. 53.

75. Feng Guifen, 4: 12b.

76. *Wuxian zhi*, 1: 36a–b. According to Feng Guifen, 4: 12b, however, the reduction was to be 3 percent, not 2 percent, for rents of one shi and below, bringing a rent of 1.3 shi down to 1.12 shi (0.97 + 0.15).

77. *Wujiangxian xuzhi*, 8: 12b; *Kun-Xin liangxian xuxiu hezhi*, 6: 79a. The regulations for Wujiang and Kunshan-Xinyang, though purportedly copied from the Suzhou city regulations, allowed for marginally higher maximum rents, 1.21 and 1.22 shi, respectively, as opposed to the 1.2 ceiling in the suburban Suzhou measure.

78. Tao Xu, *Zuhe*, in Suzuki, p. 210.

79. On Suzhou bursaries, see Muramatsu, *Kindai Kōnan no sosan*, pp. 233–34, 324–26, 470–75, 504–6, 570; Lojewski, "Soochow Bursaries," pp. 48, 54–55; and Natsui, pp. 30–33. For examples of the phrase "reduced actual rent," see two rental contracts, dated 1875 and 1876, for land of the Suzhou Pan family in the Land Documents Collection, Tōyō bunka kenkyūjo, Tokyo University.

80. Natsui, pp. 30–33; Lojewski, "Soochow Bursaries," p. 55.

81. Natsui, p. 25.

82. Ibid., pp. 1–39.

83. The 88 estates were established in Changzhou, Wu, Yuanhe, Changshu, Zhaowen, Kunshan, and Xinyang counties (*Wuxian zhi*, 31: 11a–26a; *Kun-Xin*

liangxian xuxiu hezhi, 10: 37a–38b; *Chongxiu Chang-Zhao hezhi gao*, 17: 11a–22b).

84. Pan Guangdan and Quan Weitian, p. 96; Yamana Hirofumi, pp. 123–26.

85. *Shenbao*, 1/24/Guangxu 4 (1878), 11/17/Guangxu 9 (1883), 12/5/Guangxu 10 (1884).

86. *Shenbao*, 12/10/Guangxu 2 (1876), 12/5/Guangxu 3 (1887).

87. *Jiangsu shengli*, 4: 35a; *Jiangsu shengli xubian*, 5: 1a–b.

88. *Shenbao*, 9/10/Guangxu 10 (1884).

89. Tao Xu, *Zuhe*, in Suzuki, p. 250; *Shenbao*, 9/13/Guangxu 7 (1881), 12/28/Guangxu 9 (1883). See also Table 5.1.

90. In 1876 the newspaper *Shenbao* ran a letter from a reader in response to an article on the harsh treatment of tenants by Suzhou landlords. The author mentioned several humane landlords worthy of emulation, singling out the owner of several thousand mu of land in Wujiang County as especially praiseworthy for setting his rental conversion rate at levels equal to or below the prevailing price of rice (*Shenbao* 12/20/Guangxu 2).

91. *Huibao*, 10/30/Guangxu 25 (1899).

92. The data on which these calculations are based are drawn from Tables 5.1 and B.3; and *Chuanshaxian zhi*, 8: 22b–24b.

93. *Shenbao*, 10/22, 11/16/Guangxu 4 (1878); *Yiwenlu*, 2/4/Guangxu 6 (1880).

94. *Shenbao*, 10/21, 12/28/Guangxu 9 (1883), 9/10/Guangxu 10 (1884).

95. Tao Xu, *Zuhe*, in Suzuki, p. 239; *Shenbao*, 9/10/Guangxu 10 (1884).

96. *Yiwenlu*, 4/24/Guangxu 7 (1881).

97. *Yiwenlu*, 12/12/Guangxu 12 (1886), 11/24/Guangxu 13 (1887); *Tongwen hubao*, 4/14, 11/13/Guangxu 27 (1901), 11/15/Guangxu 28 (1902), 4/5, 11/20/Guangxu 30 (1904), 3/13/Guangxu 31 (1905), 11/13/Guangxu 32 (1906); Zhang Youyi and Liu Kexiang, pp. 172–73.

98. Tao Xu, *Zuhe*, in Suzuki, p. 212.

99. Muramatsu, *Kindai Kōnan no sosan*, pp. 326–27, 353.

100. *Shenbao*, 1/13/12; *Shibao*, 1/12, 1/14, 2/10/12. For more detailed discussions of tenant protests at the time of the 1911 Revolution, see Wong Youngtsu, pp. 333–39; Shen Yuwu, "Xinhai Geming"; Kojima, "Kōso tōsō," pp. 132–42; Kojima, "Shingai Kakumei," pp. 333–53; and Kojima, "Shinmatsu Minkoku."

101. *Minlibao*, 1/13/12, reproduced in *Xinhai Geming zai Shanghai shiliao xuanji*, p. 706.

102. *Shenbao*, 10/3/Guangxu 2 (1876), 11/23/Guangxu 8 (1882); *Huibao*, 5/28/Guangxu 25 (1899).

103. *Shenbao*, 10/3/Guangxu 2 (1876); Kobayashi Yukio, pp. 75–78.

104. Ding Richang, *Fuwu gongdu*, 1: 12–13, reproduced in Li Wenzhi, *Zhongguo jindai nongye shi ziliao*, p. 339; *Shenbao*, 7/25/Guangxu 5 (1879).

105. For a discussion of bursaries and proxy remittance, see Muramatsu, *Kindai Kōnan no sosan*, pp. 681–745.

106. *Yiwenlu*, 1/14/Guangxu 9 (1883).

107. *Chongji Fuyangxian zhi*, 12: 49a–b; Yong An, 7: 9a–b.

108. For a thorough discussion of the increasing use of foreign silver currency for tax payments in Jiangnan, see Kobayashi Yukio, pp. 68–76.

109. Ibid., pp. 70–73; *Jiangsu shengli xubian*, 1: 1a–3a; *Shenbao*, 8/11/Guangxu 3 (1877).

110. Kobayashi Yukio, pp. 74–76.

111. Wang Yeh-chien, *Land Taxation*, pp. 116–19.

112. Ibid., pp. 62–63.

113. *Chuanshaxian zhi*, 8: 22b–24b, 26a–29a; *Jiadingxian xuzhi*, 3: 10a–15a; Wang Yeh-chien, *Land Taxation*, p. 65.

114. Wang Yeh-chien, *Land Taxation*, p. 121.

115. Xia Nai, pp. 457–58, 464–65.

116. Liu Kexiang, p. 319.

117. Dai Pan, p. 271.

118. Kobayashi Yukio, p. 79.

119. *Shenbao*, 12/3/Tongzhi 11 (1872), 4/17/Guangxu 2 (1876), 11/30/Guangxu 4 (1878), 11/25/Guangxu 9 (1883); *Chuanshaxian zhi*, 8: 23a–24b; *Chongji Fuyangxian zhi*, 12: 49a–b; *Chongxiu Yuqianxian zhi*, 19: 39a–b; *Hangzhoufu zhi*, 61: 41a–48a.

120. Wang Yeh-chien, *Land Taxation*, p. 65.

121. On popular reactions to the New Policies in the lower Yangzi region and elsewhere in China, see Yamashita; Lust; Prazniak, "Tax Protest"; Prazniak, "Weavers and Sorceresses"; and Esherick, pp. 117–23.

122. Mann, *Local Merchants*.

123. *Dongfang zazhi*, 7.4 (1910), p. 61.

124. Zhang Zhenhe and Ding Yuanying, part 1, pp. 148–68 passim, part 2, 91–121 passim.

Chapter 5

1. Qiao Qiming, p. 102; *Zhongguo jingji nianjian disanbian*, p. 114; Feng Zigang, pp. 34–35; He Menglei, p. 33237.

2. Chen Hansheng, p. 219.

3. Fei Hsiao-t'ung, pp. 187–88; Qiao Qiming, p. 100; Qian Chengze, pp. 30298–99; Zheng Kangmo, pp. 33938–39; He Menglei, pp. 33125–41 passim; Duan Yinshou, pp. 22688–89; *Shenbao*, 4/15/27.

4. Fei Hsiao-t'ung, pp. 187–88.

5. *Shibao*, 2/22/12.

6. Duan Yinshou, p. 22689.

7. He Menglei, pp. 33125–41.

8. See Table C.8; He Menglei, pp. 32970–75, 33237; Duan Yinshou, pp. 22676–77; Qiao Qiming, p. 102; and Chen Hansheng, p. 207.

9. Hong Ruijian, "Suzhou," p. 1549.

10. *Shibao*, 10/20/Xuantong 2 (1910); Kojima, "Shingai Kakumei zengo," pp. 330–33.

11. *Shenbao*, 5/9/25, 7/23/27.

12. *Shibao*, 1/9/13, 9/12, 10/8/16; *Shenbao*, 12/8, 12/9/17, 5/9/25, 3/5/26, 7/23/27, 1/5, 1/11/28, 12/15/30, 1/21/35, 3/11/37; Zhao Xiong, p. 82; "Jiaxing chengli cuizuchu"; He Menglei, pp. 33186–210; Tan Yuqing, pp. 12–14; Zhang Zuyin, pp. 225–26; Qiao Qiming, 108–10.

13. According to one estimate of the 1930's, dual ownership rights figured in 90 percent of the rental arrangements in Wu County, 80 percent in Changshu, and 50 percent in Wuxi (He Menglei, p. 33042). According to another, 70–80

percent of the land in Wujiang County was divided into topsoil and subsoil rights (Chen Guofu, *dizheng*: 30). Finally, in Pinghu County, also in the 1930's, about 67 percent of the peasant population worked land for which they owned the surface rights (Duan Yinshou, pp. 22677–78).

14. *Shibao*, 1/9/13, 12/30/17; *Shenbao*, 2/28/21, 12/27/27; "Jiaxing chengli cuizuchu"; He Menglei, p. 33199; Tan Yuqing, pp. 12–14; Xingzhengyuan nongcun fuxing weiyuanhui, *Jiangsusheng nongcun diaocha*, p. 60.

15. *Shenbao*, 5/9/25; Tan Yuqing, p. 13; "Jiaxing chengli cuizuchu."

16. "Jiaxing chengli cuizuchu"; *Shenbao*, 1/15/28.

17. Zhao Xiong, p. 82; *Shenbao*, 3/11/37.

18. He Menglei, pp. 33196–98; Tan Yuqing, pp. 12–14; *Shenbao*, 10/23/36; *Shibao*, 9/12, 10/8/16; Zhang Youyi, 2: 130; Fang Long, pp. 125–26; Amano Motonosuke, p. 132.

19. *Shibao*, 8/12/24.

20. *Dawanbao* (Shanghai), 10/10/34, reprinted in Feng Hefa, *Zhongguo nongcun jingji ziliao xubian*, p. 32.

21. Duan Yinshou, p. 22702.

22. Zhao Xiong, p. 82; Zhang Zuyin, pp. 226–28; Kuhn, "Local Self-Government," p. 291.

23. Muramatsu, *Kindai Kōnan no sosan*, pp. 326–27, 353; Zheng Kangmo, p. 33940; *Shenbao*, 1/9/28.

24. Muramatsu, "Documentary Study of Chinese Landlordism," pp. 572, 588, 591.

25. He Menglei, pp. 33196–99, 33206–11; *Shenbao*, 2/10/13, 2/5/29, 3/3/33.

26. Zhang Zuyin, pp. 225–26.

27. He Menglei, p. 33208; Qiao Qiming, p. 109; Hong Ruijian, "Suzhou," p. 1551.

28. Meijer, pp. 24–25, 66.

29. Lieu, p. 471.

30. Qiao Qiming, p. 108.

31. Huadong junzheng weiyuanhui tudi gaige weiyuanhui, *Dizhu zui'e zhongzhong*, pp. 81–82; *Zui'e de jiu shehui*, 3: 17; Pan Guangdan and Quan Weitian, chap. 1. See also Ash, *Land Tenure*, pp. 43–44.

32. See, for example, Tao Xu, *Zuhe*, in Suzuki, pp. 211–12; *Shenbao*, 1/24/Guangxu 4 (1878), 10/5, 10/7/Guangxu 5 (1879), 12/5/Guangxu 10 (1884); and *Yiwenlu*, 12/22/Guangxu 12 (1886).

33. Huadong junzheng weiyuanhui tudi gaige weiyuan hui, *Dizhu zui'e zhongzhong*, p. 82; *Shenbao*, 3/16, 12/8/24, 9/9/26, 12/26/28, 3/3/, 3/20, 3/21/33, 3/31/37.

34. Ni Yangru, p. 90.

35. Meijer, p. 53.

36. F. T. Cheng, pp. 52–83 passim, 112–19. A 1915 Supreme Court decision provided for the official detention of debtors: "If within the limits of the law an official department detains a debtor in custody on the application of the creditor, it is only exercising lawful powers and no unlawful injury can be spoken of" (p. 25). Presumably the phrase "within the limits of the law" means after a civil suit had established the existence of a debt and a debtor. Thus, this provision

would not sanction any operation that deprived defaulting tenants of the benefits of a civil trial.

37. Hsia Ching-lin et al., pp. 114, 215, 217.

38. *Shibao*, 1/22/12, 9/12, 10/8/16, 12/7, 12/29, 12/30/17; *Shenbao*, 2/10/13, 12/18/17, 2/23/18.

39. Fang Long, pp. 125–26; *Shenbao*, 12/21/27, 1/9, 1/15, 2/28, 6/2/28, 11/10/29.

40. Cai Binxian, pp. 50–54.

41. Qian Chengze, pp. 30306–08.

42. See also Lieu, p. 469; Hong Ruijian, *Zhejiang zhi erwu jianzu*, p. 29; and *Min shangshi xiguan diaocha baogao lu*, 1: 467–69.

43. Lieu, pp. 465, 469; Duan Yinshou, p. 22702; Wu Xiaochen, pp. 119–20.

44. Duan Yinshou, p. 22695; "Jiaxing chengli cuizuchu."

45. *Shenbao*, 1/20/19.

46. Tan Yuqing, pp. 12–14; *Shenbao*, 9/2/25.

47. See, for example, He Menglei, pp. 33153–55, 33166–69; and *Shenbao*, 12/13/18, 1/26/20, 10/14/26, 12/4/29, 11/24/30, 11/15/32, 11/13/34.

48. *Shibao*, 10/2/10; *Shenbao*, 11/13/18, 11/12/23, 10/29/35.

49. *Shenbao*, 11/27, 12/7/17, 11/8, 12/9/27, 12/15/30, 10/18, 11/24/36.

50. Kojima, "1910 nendai," p. 104; Hoang, p. 140; *Shenbao*, 12/7/12.

51. *Shenbao*, 11/23/17, 10/12/23, 11/12/24.

52. *Shenbao*, 11/23/17, 11/5, 11/9/30, 10/28/36.

53. Duan Yinshou, pp. 22692–94; Qian Chengze, p. 30295; Qiao Qiming, p. 91; *Zhongguo jingji nianjian xubian*, p. 51; Xingzhengyuan nongcun fuxing wei-yuanhui, *Jiangsusheng nongcun diaocha*, p. 60.

54. He Menglei, pp. 33153–54; Hong Ruijian, "Suzhou," p. 1553.

55. Fang Long, pp. 123–25; *Shenbao*, 11/11/17, 11/19/31.

56. See, for example, *Shenbao*, 11/27/17, 12/11/25.

57. *Shenbao*, 11/9/33.

58. *Shibao*, 11/19, 12/1–12/3, 12/10/17; *Shenbao*, 11/18, 11/21–11/22/17, 1/7, 1/14, 1/20/18.

59. Hong Ruijian, "Suzhou," p. 1553; *Shenbao*, 11/18/17.

60. *Shenbao*, 11/14/17.

61. F. T. Cheng, p. 117.

62. Hsia Ching-lin et al., pp. 118, 217.

63. See, for instance, *Shenbao*, 10/29, 12/5, 12/21, 12/25/32, 11/22/35, 11/11, 11/19/36.

64. To arrive at this conclusion, I calculated what the actual amounts of rent and tax reduction would have been with different combinations of four sets of variables—nominal rents of 1.0, 1.2, and 1.5 shi per mu; actual rents of 90 percent, 85 percent, and 80 percent of the nominal rents; stipulated taxes equaling 0.1, 0.2, and 0.3 shi per mu; and tax and rental chengse set equally at 85 percent, 80 percent, 75 percent, and so on down to 10 percent. In only five of the 432 possible combinations did the tax reduction completely cover the rent reduction.

65. Zhang Youyi, 3: 256–57.

66. Duan Yinshou, pp. 22690–91; Zhang Zongbi, pp. 593–94; Yu Lin, pp. 414–15; Hu Chuanru, p. 113.

67. Duan Yinshou, p. 22694.

68. *Shenbao*, 7/1/18, 12/13, 12/16/27, 1/10, 1/23/29, 12/25/33.

69. Duan Yinshou, p. 22695; "Jiaxing chengli cuizuchu."

70. Among the exceptions are Miner, "Agrarian Reform"; and Bianco, "Peasant Movements."

71. Lin Chu-ching, pp. 144–45.

72. *Shenbao*, 12/30/27.

73. Geisert, pp. 202–4.

74. Ibid., pp. 206–8.

75. Zheng Kangmo, p. 34008.

76. Miner, pp. 78–79.

77. Qian Chengze, p. 30306; Hong Ruijian, *Zhejiang zhi erwu jianzu*, pp. 37–38, 52–59.

78. Hong Ruijian, *Zhejiang zhi erwu jianzu*, pp. 69–78; Zheng Kangmo, pp. 33985–91; Wu Xiaochen, p. 120.

79. Feng Zigang, pp. 45–46.

80. Qian Chengze, p. 30278.

81. Hong Ruijian, *Zhejiang zhi erwu jianzu*, p. 80; Duan Yinshou, pp. 22780–82; *Zhejiang Wuxing Lanxi tianfu diaochu baogao*, pp. 59–69

82. Hong Ruijian, *Zhejiang zhi erwu jianzu*, p. 80.

83. He Menglei, p. 32984.

84. Bianco, "Peasant Movements," pp. 275–77.

85. Hong Ruijian, *Zhejiang zhi erwu jianzu*, p. 55.

86. Ibid., pp. 58–59; Cai Binxian, pp. 50–54.

87. Zhang Zongbi, pp. 593–94; Duan Yinshou, pp. 22692–93; Wu Xiaochen, pp. 120–21.

88. Wu Xiaochen, p. 120.

89. Ibid., p. 121.

90. Hong Ruijian, *Zhejiang zhi erwu jianzu*, p. 84.

91. Zhao Ruheng, 2: 574.

92. Xingzhengyuan nongcun fuxing weiyuanhui, *Zhejiangsheng nongcun diaocha*, pp. 149–50, 165–73.

93. Miner, pp. 80–82.

Chapter 6

1. This picture may be somewhat skewed, since the advent of newspapers in the 1870's made coverage on the periods 1873–1911 and 1912–36 more complete than for the period 1840–59. (See Appendix A for a list of the sources used.) Nearly all of the cases recorded in the sources for the 1840's and 1850's (memorials, gentry writings and diaries, and local gazetteers) involved violence. There may well have been nonviolent actions that attracted little attention and thus went unrecorded, actions that found their way into newspapers with some regularity. The 1840's and 1850's may thus be underrepresented, and the overall rise in tenant actions from then to the Republican period less dramatic than suggested. On the other hand, the increase from the late Qing (1873–1911) to the Republican era is relatively reliable, since the same sorts of sources, including newspapers, were consulted for both periods.

As pointed out in Appendix A, I have used Charles Tilly's guidelines for enumerating and determining the boundaries of collective actions. In the Republican period the majority of the tenant actions fall within his category of "distinct, but linked" events, defined as those that "occur in the same or consecutive months and meet any of these conditions: (a) concerted action of at least one formation in one event with at least one formation in the other; (b) strong evidence of overlap of personnel; (c) strong evidence of the provision of material assistance by the participants in one event to the participants in the other; (d) overt imitation of the action of one event by a formation in another; (e) overt response as indicated by demands, slogans, or ritual acts" (*From Mobilization to Revolution*, p. 250).

2. On this, see, for example, Duara, pp. 250–51; and Bianco, "Peasants and Revolution," p. 315.

3. Nor can the escalation in collective rent resistance in the Republican era be attributed to any significant increase in the number of tenants in Jiangnan. Tenant actions averaged 1.4 incidents a year in 1840–59, 0.97 a year in 1873–1911, and 5.04 a year in 1912–36. For changes in population to have been the key to such a dramatic rise in frequency, the number of tenants would have to be 3.6 times greater in the Republican period than in 1840–59 and 5.2 times greater than in 1873–1911. But in fact Jiangnan's total population was not larger in the Republican era than in the 1840's and 1850's (see Tables C.1–C.7), and the proportion of tenants had not increased significantly. Indeed, some counties may have had proportionately fewer tenants as a long-term result of the devastation of the Taiping Rebellion.

4. Faure, *Rural Economy of Pre-Liberation China*, p. 133.

5. *Fengxianxian zhi*, p. 659.

6. Xu Daofu, pp. 273, 278–79; He Menglei, p. 33014; Feng Zigang, pp. 76–77.

7. Bell, p. 118.

8. The discussion here, particularly the questions asked of the historical materials, owes much to Tilly, *From Mobilization to Revolution*. The analysis of the Republican-era tenant collective actions is based on the sources listed at the end of Table A.3.

9. *Huibao*, 11/26/Guangxu 26 (1900); Yangzhou shifan xueyuan lishixi, pp. 183–85, 197–206; *Shenbao*, 12/3, 12/7/12, 1/25/18; *Shibao*, 1/14/12; Kojima, "Kōso tōsō," pp. 137–40.

10. *Shenbao*, 12/22, 12/26, 12/27/12.

11. Information on the 1917 rent resistance in Jinshan comes from *Shenbao*, 11/27, 11/30, 12/3, 12/7, 12/14, 12/19, 12/27/17, 1/4, 1/14/18.

12. Liu Shiji, pp. 73–119, 142–56.

13. On the peasant movement in Guangdong and Hunan, see Marks; McDonald; Hofheinz; and Yokoyama, "Peasant Movement in Hunan."

14. Hofheinz, p. 79; Berkley, p. 167.

15. Hofheinz, p. 104; Zhang Youyi, 2: 685.

16. Gu Fusheng, p. 9.

17. The biographical information on Zhou Shuiping is drawn from Zhang Yaozong, pp. 183–231 passim.

18. Ibid., pp. 190–92, 232.

19. *Shenbao*, 4/9, 4/14, 4/15/27; Gu Fusheng, pp. 9–11.

20. *Shenbao*, 4/7, 4/9, 4/10, 4/15, 4/25/27.

21. *Shenbao*, 4/23/27, 2/3/28; Geisert, pp. 109–12.

22. Jiangsusheng dang'anguan, pp. 31–122.

23. Yan Xuexi; Shenbao, 11/3, 11/5, 11/11/27.

24. Shenbao, 11/11–11/13, 11/15, 11/18, 11/20, 12/21/27. See also Chen Zhenbai, pp. 51–58; and Hang Guoren, pp. 63–70.

25. Gu Fusheng, pp. 12–18.

26. Ibid., pp. 9–30 passim.

27. Shenbao, 4/14, 4/17, 4/18/28, 1/24, 1/27, 1/30, 2/13/29.

28. Shibao, 12/3/17; Fang Long, p. 127.

29. Hong Ruijian, "Suzhou," pp. 1548–49.

30. Ibid., pp. 1560–61.

31. In determining the initial rental chengse of 60 to 70 percent, the magistrate and landowner association used as their basic units not individual fields, but whole precincts (tu), thus granting all tenants in any given precinct the same discount regardless of the quality of their harvest. Predictably, the peasants disputed this procedure, pointing out that it gave discounts to cultivators who had suffered no crop damage, yet required a relatively large rent from those who had suffered complete crop failure. Adding to the peasants' woes, a precipitous decline in the price of rice in the brief period between the setting of the zhezu conversion rate and the opening of landlord granaries for collection translated automatically into a 6-percent increase for those tenants who paid commuted rents. The chengse and the conversion rate constituted the main issues of contention in these collective actions. Of secondary concern, especially for peasants who paid their rent in kind, was a recent 6-percent enlargement of the Suzhou shi measure as part of the KMT standardization of weights and measures. Peasants feared that this would mean a corresponding rise in their rents—a fear that was not unfounded, given the landlords' habit of manipulating the measures. (Hong Ruijian, "Suzhou," pp. 1547–62; Zhang Youyi, 3: 1021–23; Shenbao, 12/29/35, 1/6, 1/14, 2/28, 4/20, 4/23, 4/24, 4/26, 4/29, 5/8, 5/16, 5/29, 6/9, 6/10, 6/14, 6/28, 6/29/36.

32. Bianco, "Peasant Movements," p. 275.

33. Ibid., p. 301.

34. See, for example, P. Huang, Peasant Economy, pp. 278–91 passim; Perry, Rebels and Revolutionaries, pp. 40, 163, 177–82; Thaxton, pp. 44–47; Duara, pp. 65–79, 250–51; and Bianco, "Peasant Movements," pp. 280, 288.

35. Just as the rise in the incidence of peasant resistance to rent cannot be linked to any significant increase in the number of tenants, so the decline in the incidence of resistance to taxes cannot be attributed to any significant decrease in the number of cultivator-owners. (For population changes to have been the principal cause of the decline, the number of cultivator-owners would have had to be 2.5 times smaller in the Republican period than in 1840–59 and 1873–1911.) The data in Table C.8 show that in many places either cultivator-owners or part-owner part-tenants constituted the largest single group among the peasantry, and, moreover, that those two categories combined represented the majority of the farming population in a number of counties. Despite tenancy rates that were among the highest in the country, Republican Jiangnan did not lack for cultivator-owners who could mobilize their considerable numbers for collective action.

36. This was particularly the case in northern Zhejiang, where tribute quotas were reduced in 1921 to rectify some of the inequalities that had remained after the

Tongzhi tax reduction (*Zhejiang Wuxing Lanxi tianfu diaocha baogao*, pp. 59a–60b).

37. *Chuanshaxian zhi*, 8: 22b.

38. *Zhejiang Wuxing Lanxi tianfu diaocha baogao*, p. 61b. Attached to the diding and tribute tax were collection fees (*zhengshoufei*), Republican equivalents of the Qing meltage and wastage fees, calculated at 0.1025 yuan per tael of the diding and 0.25 yuan per shi of the tribute in Jiangsu, and at 0.162 yuan per tael and 0.122 yuan per shi in Zhejiang (ibid., p. 64b; *Shanghaixian zhi*, 1: 7b).

39. Xingzhengyuan nongcun fuxing weiyuanhui, *Zhejiangsheng nongcun diaocha*, p. 12. Land-tax surcharges and levies in Jiangnan were generally expressed in this form and exacted from individual landowners. Unlike their counterparts in the North China plain, landowners of the lower Yangzi region did not suffer in the Republican period from the special exactions called *tankuan* ("shared-out fund"), which were imposed on whole villages and became one of the principal forms of irregular taxation. For an analysis of tankuan, see P. Huang, *Peasant Economy*, pp. 278–89.

40. *Chuanshaxian zhi*, 8: 65a–70b.

41. Yu Lin, pp. 406–7; *Zhejiang Wuxing Lanxi tianfu diaocha baogao*, pp. 64b–70b.

42. Zhao Ruheng, 2: 757–60.

43. See, for example, P. Huang, *Peasant Economy*, pp. 278–86; Gunde, pp. 26–28; and Duara, pp. 77–78.

44. Zhao Ruheng, 2: 586–91; Xingzhengyuan nongcun fuxing weiyuanhui, *Zhejiangsheng nongcun diaocha*, pp. 147–48, 159, 161–62.

45. Wan Guoding et al., pp. 117, 155, 160–61; Zhongyang daxue jingji ziliaoshi, pp. 155–59.

46. Zhongyang daxue jingji ziliaoshi, pp. 226–38.

47. Ibid., pp. 18–38, 162–224 passim.

48. Zhao Ruheng, 2: 586–91.

49. For Jiangsu, this means that counties kept 0.30 yuan of the diding commutation rate of 2.05 yuan per tael and 1.0 yuan of the tribute rate of 5.0 yuan per shi. Zhejiang counties began retaining 1.0 yuan of the tribute rate in 1915 (*Chuanshaxian zhi*, 8: 22b; *Zhejiang Wuxing Lanxi tianfu diaocha baogao*, pp. 61b–62b).

50. He Menglei, p. 33150; Yu Lin, pp. 395, 414.

51. Hong Ruijian, *Zhejiang*, pp. 79–80.

52. Qian Chengze, p. 30273.

53. He Menglei, p. 32984.

54. Huadong junzheng weiyuanhui tudi gaige weiyuanhui, *Huadong nongcun jingji ziliao*, 1: 196; Yu Jinru, p. 30; Amano, p. 127; Zhang Zongbi, pp. 594–95.

55. Eastman, *Seeds of Destruction*, pp. 71–88, 172–202; Pepper, pp. 160–63.

56. *Shenbao*, 10/24, 11/1/46, 9/21, 10/26/47, 12/9/48; Huadong junzheng weiyuanhui tudi gaige weiyuanhui, *Huadong nongcun jingji ziliao*, 1: 109–10, 137–39, 178–81. The collection of the land tax had largely reverted to kind because of the highly unstable currency situation and the need to provision troops. The tax amounts, originally expressed by the government in *shishi* (a new volume measure), have been converted here at the rate of 1.0 shishi equals 1.05 shi to facilitate comparison with the KMT taxes in the late 1920's and 1930's. For the conversion of unhusked to husked rice, I have used the government rate of 1.0 shishi of unhusked rice equals 0.525 shishi of husked rice. Where the sources give the amount

of tax in *shijin* (a new weight measure), I have used the government rate of 108 shijin equals 1.0 shishi. (*Shenbao*, 1/24/49; Faure, *Rural Economy of Pre-Liberation China*, pp. 212–15.)

57. Huadong junzheng weiyuanhui tudi gaige weiyuanhui, *Huadong nongcun jingji ziliao*, 1: 109–10, 137–39, 178–81.

58. Ibid., p. 108.

59. Ibid., pp. 180, 250; *Shenbao*, 11/28, 12/19/45, 5/2/47, 12/28/48.

60. Eastman, *Seeds of Destruction*, pp. 82–84; Pepper, p. 230.

61. *Shenbao*, 11/28/45, 10/5, 10/25/46, 9/16, 9/21, 10/25/47.

62. *Shenbao*, 10/6/48.

63. *Shenbao*, 10/22, 11/30, 12/23/48.

64. *Shenbao*, 12/22/45, 1/27, 2/1, 12/12/46, 2/23, 2/27, 2/28, 3/23, 3/25, 9/24/47, 5/17, 5/18, 6/15/48, 1/28/49.

65. Jiaxing, Wu, Changshu, and Kunshan counties, among others (*Shenbao*, 5/2, 9/16, 9/21/47, 12/17, 12/28/48.

66. *Shenbao*, 9/16/47.

67. Huadong junzheng weiyuanhui tudi gaige wciyuanhui, *Huadong nongcun jingji ziliao*, 1: 202.

68. *Shenbao*, 10/21/46, 9/16, 9/21, 10/25, 10/26/47, 11/30/48; Huadong junzheng weiyuanhui tudi gaige weiyuanhui, *Huadong nongcun jingji ziliao*, 1: 108–110, 137–39, 178–81.

69. Huadong junzheng weiyuanhui tudi gaige weiyuanhui, *Huadong nongcun jingji zialio*, 1: 56, 60, 73, 123, 145, 196, 2: 221–22.

70. Eastman, *Seeds of Destruction*, pp. 172–202 passim; Pepper, pp. 108–31.

71. Shue, pp. 82–85.

72. Ash, "Economic Aspects of Land Reform," part 1, pp. 284–85.

73. For a detailed description of the process of peaceful land reform in a Jiangnan village, see P. Huang, *Peasant Family*, pp. 165–71.

74. Ash, "Economic Aspects of Land Reform," part 1, p. 291.

75. P. Huang, *Peasant Family*, pp. 168–69.

REFERENCES CITED

The contemporary periodicals I have consulted (the journal *Dongfang zazhi* and the newspapers *Huibao, Minlibao, North China Herald, Shenbao, Shibao, Tongwen hubao, Yiwenlu, Zhonghua xinbao*) are cited in full in the Notes. The following abbreviations are used in this list:

Jianji: *Taiping Tianguo shiliao congbian jianji* (Selected historical materials on the Taiping Rebellion). Comp. Taiping Tianguo lishi bowuguan. 6 vols. Beijing: Zhonghua shuju, 1961–63.

Shanghai Xiaodaohui: *Shanghai Xiaodaohui qiyi shiliao huibian* (Compendium of historical materials on the Shanghai Small Sword uprising). Comp. Shanghai shehui kexueyuan lishi yanjiusuo. Shanghai: Shanghai renmin chubanshe, 1980.

Taiping Tianguo: *Zhongguo jindaishi ziliao congkan, II: Taiping Tianguo* (Collection of material on modern Chinese history, part 2: The Taiping Rebellion). Comp. Xiang Da et al. 8 vols. Shanghai: Shenzhou guoguangshe, 1952.

TTSLX: *Taiping Tianguo shi lunwen xuan* (Selected articles on the history of the Taiping Rebellion). Ed. Beijing Taiping Tianguo lishi yanjiuhui. 2 vols. Beijing: Sanlian shudian, 1981.

Xiao Zheng, ed.: *Minguo ershi niandai Zhongguo dalu tudi wenti ziliao* (Materials on the land problem in mainland China during the 1930's). 200 vols. Taibei: Taibei chengwen chuban youxian gongsi, 1977.

Zhuanji: *Taiping Tianguo ziliao zhuanji* (A special compilation of historical materials on the Taiping Rebellion). Comp. Suzhou bowuguan, Nanjing daxue, and Jiangsu shifan xueyuan. Shanghai: Shanghai guji chubanshe, 1979.

Adas, Michael. "From Avoidance to Confrontation: Peasant Protest in Precolonial and Colonial Southeast Asia," *Comparative Studies in Society and History*, 1981, no. 23, 217–47.

Amano Motonosuke. *Shina nōson zakki* (Random notes on Chinese villages). Tokyo: Seikatsusha, 1942.

Ash, Robert. "Economic Aspects of Land Reform in Kiangsu, 1949–52," *China Quarterly* (2 parts), 66, 67 (June, Sept. 1976), 261–92, 519–45.

————. *Land Tenure in Pre-Revolutionary China: Kiangsu Province in the 1920s and 1930s.* London: Contemporary China Institute, School of Oriental and African Studies, 1976.

Banno Ryōkichi. "Shanghai Shōtōkai no hanran" (The rebellion of the Shanghai Small Sword Society), *Rekishigaku kenkyū,* 353 (1969), 1–13.

Bao Shichen. *An Wu sizhong* (Four treatises on the governance of Wu; 1888). Reprint. Taibei: Wenhai chubanshe, 1968.

Baoshanxian xuzhi (Continuation of the gazetteer of Baoshan County). 1921.

"Baoshanxian zhi (zhailu)" (Excerpts from the gazetteer of Baoshan County), in *Shanghai Xiaodaohui,* p. 1160.

Baxi zhi (Gazetteer of Baxi). 1935.

Bell, Lynda Schaefer. "Merchants, Peasants, and the State: The Organization and Politics of Chinese Silk Production, Wuxi County, 1870–1937." Ph.D. dissertation, University of California, Los Angeles, 1985.

Berkley, Gerald W. "The Canton Peasant Movement Training Institute," *Modern China,* 1.2 (April 1975), 161–79.

Bernhardt, Kathryn. "Rural Society and the Taiping Rebellion: The Jiangnan from 1820 to 1911." Ph.D. dissertation, Stanford University, 1984.

Bianco, Lucien. "Peasant Movements," in *The Cambridge History of China,* vol. 13: *Republican China 1912–1949, Part 2.* Ed. John K. Fairbank and Albert Feuerwerker. Cambridge: Cambridge University Press, 1986, pp. 270–328.

————. "Peasants and Revolution," *Journal of Peasant Studies,* 3.2 (1975), 313–36.

"Binan jilüe" (A refugee's brief account), in *Zhuanji,* pp. 55–75.

Brandt, Loren. *Commercialization and Agricultural Development: Central and Eastern China, 1870–1937.* Cambridge: Cambridge University Press, 1989.

Brook, Timothy. "Family Continuity and Cultural Hegemony: The Gentry of Ningbo, 1368–1911," in *Chinese Local Elites and Patterns of Dominance.* Ed. Joseph W. Esherick and Mary Backus Rankin. Berkeley: University of California Press, pp. 27–50.

Buck, John Lossing. *Chinese Farm Economy: A Study of 2866 Farms in Seventeen Localities and Seven Provinces in China* (1930). Reprint. New York: Garland Publishing, 1982.

————. *Land Utilization in China, Statistics.* Chicago: University of Chicago Press, 1937.

Cai Binxian. "Zhejiang dianye jiufen anjian tongji zhi shibian" (Examination of the statistics on disputes between Zhejiang tenants and landlords), *Zhejiangsheng jianshe yuekan,* 4.4 (Oct. 1930), 46–58.

Cai Shaoqing. "Li Xiucheng yu Taiping Tianguo zai Jiang-Zhe diqu de tudi zhengce—guanyu Taiping Tianguo houqi tudi zhengce de jige wenti de kaocha" (Li Xiucheng and the Taiping land policy in the Jiangsu-Zhejiang region: An investigation of several questions concerning the land policy in the late Taiping period), in *Taiping Tianguo shi luncong* (Collection of articles on the history of the Taiping Rebellion). Ed. Nanjing daxue xuebao bianjibu and Nanjing daxue Taiping Tianguo shi yanjiushi. 2 vols. Nanjing: 1979, vol. 1, pp. 170–205.

Canglang Diaotu [pseud.]. "Jieyu hui lu" (Record of the aftermath of the Taiping disaster), in *Jianji,* vol. 2, pp. 135–71.

Cao Guozhi. "Taiping Tianguo zashui kao" (An investigation of the miscellaneous taxes of the Taipings), in *TTSLX*, vol. 1, pp. 631–47.

Changxingxian zhi (Gazetteer of Changxing County). 1892.

Chen Guofu. *Jiangsu shengzheng shuyao* (A summary account of the provincial administration of Jiangsu; 1933). Reprint. Taibei: Wenhai chubanshe, n.d.

Chen Hansheng. "Xiandai Zhongguo de tudi wenti" (The land problem in contemporary China), in *Zhongguo tudi wenti he shangye gaolidai* (The land problem and commercial usury in China: 1937), in *Zhongguo jindai guomin jingji shi cankao ziliao, I: Lunwen ji* (Reference material on the modern history of the Chinese national economy, part 1: Collection of articles). Ed. Zhonghua renmin daxue guomin jingji shi jiaoyanshi. Beijing: 1964, pp. 205–29.

Chen Zaizheng. "Shijiu shiji sishi niandai guonei jieji maodun de jihua yu Taiping Tianguo geming" (The intensification of domestic class contradictions in the 1840's and the Taiping Rebellion), *Xiamen daxue xuebao zhexue shehui kexue ban*, 1980, no. 1, 1–19.

Chen Zhenbai. "Ershi niandai zai Wuxi de geming huodong jingli he jianwen" (My experiences in the revolutionary activities in Wuxi in the 1920's), *Jiangsu wenshi ziliao xuanji*, 1980, no. 5, 28–58.

Cheng, F. T., tr. *The Chinese Supreme Court Decisions Relating to General Principles of Civil Law, Obligations, and Commercial Law* (1923). Reprint. Arlington, Va.: University Publications of America, 1976.

Cheng Ying, comp. *Zhongguo jindai fandi fanfengjian lishi geyao xuan* (Selection of modern Chinese historical anti-imperialist and anti-feudal folksongs and tales). Beijing: Zhonghua shuju, 1962.

Chongji Fuyangxian zhi (Newly compiled gazetteer of Fuyang County). 1902.

Chongxiu Chang-Zhao hezhi gao (A draft of the revised edition of the combined gazetteer of Changshu and Zhaowen counties). 1904.

Chongxiu Huatingxian zhi (The revised gazetteer of Huating County). 1878.

Chongxiu Yuqianxian zhi (The revised gazetteer of Yuqian County). 1900.

Ch'ü T'ung-tsu. *Local Government in China Under the Ch'ing*. Stanford, Calif.: Stanford University Press, 1962.

"Chuanshating zhi (zhailu)" (Excerpts from the gazetteer of Chuanshating), in *Shanghai Xiaodaohui*, p. 1165.

Chuanshaxian zhi (Gazetteer of Chuansha County). 1936.

Cole, James H. *The People Versus the Taipings: Bao Lisheng's "Righteous Army of Dong-an."* Berkeley: Institute of East Asian Studies, University of California, 1981.

Curwen, C. A. *Taiping Rebel: The Deposition of Li Hsiu-ch'eng*. Cambridge: Cambridge University Press, 1977.

Da Qing Wen Zongxian (Xianfeng) huangdi shilu (Veritable records of the Xianfeng Emperor, Wen Zongxian, of the Qing dynasty). Reprint. Taibei: Huawen shuju, 1964.

Da Qing Xuan Zongcheng (Daoguang) huangdi shilu (Veritable records of the Daoguang Emperor, Xuan Zongcheng, of the Qing dynasty). Reprint. Taibei: Huawen shuju, 1964.

Dai Pan. *Dai Pan sizhong jilüe* (Four chronicles of Dai Pan). Reprint. Taibei: Huawen shuju, 1968.

Danghu waizhi (Unofficial gazetteer of Danghu). 1858

Dennerline, Jerry. "Marriage, Adoption, and Charity in the Development of Lineages in Wu-hsi from Sung to Ch'ing," in *Kinship Organization in Late Imperial China, 1000–1940*. Ed. Patricia Buckley Ebrey and James L. Watson. Berkeley: University of California Press, 1986, pp. 170–209.

Deqingxian zhi (Gazetteer of Deqing County). 1923.

Dillon, Maureen F. "The Triads in Shanghai: The Small Sword Society Uprising, 1853–55," *Harvard Papers on China*, 23 (July 1970), 67–86.

Ding Richang. *Ding Zhongcheng (Richang) zhengshu* (The political papers of Ding Richang). Reprint. Taibei: Wenhai chubanshe, 1980.

Dong Caishi. "Taiping Tianguo de xiangguan duo shi dizhu fenzi ma?" (Were most of the Taiping *xiangguan* landlords?), in *TTSLX*, vol. 1, pp. 706–22.

———. *Taiping Tianguo zai Suzhou* (The Taipings in Suzhou). Nanjing: Jiangsu renmin chubanshe, 1981.

Dou Zheng. *Zishu* (A personal account). Nanjing University microfilm collection of Taiping materials, reel 212.

Duan Guanqing. *Jinghu zizhuan nianpu* (The chronological autobiography from Mirror Lake). Beijing: Zhonghua shuju, 1960.

Duan Yinshou. *Pinghu nongcun jingji zhi yanjiu* (Study of the rural economy of Pinghu). Vol. 45 of Xiao Zheng, ed.

Duara, Prasenjit. *Culture, Power, and the State: Rural North China, 1900–1942*. Stanford, Calif.: Stanford University Press, 1988.

Eastman, Lloyd E. *The Abortive Revolution: China Under Nationalist Rule, 1927–1937*. Cambridge, Mass.: Harvard University Press, 1974.

———. *Seeds of Destruction: Nationalist China in War and Revolution, 1937–1949*. Stanford, Calif.: Stanford University Press, 1984.

Ebrey, Patricia Buckley, and James L. Watson, eds. *Kinship Organization in Late Imperial China, 1000–1940*. Berkeley: University of California Press, 1986.

Elvin, Mark. "Market Towns and Waterways: The County of Shanghai from 1480 to 1910," in *The City in Late Imperial China*. Ed. G. William Skinner. Stanford, Calif.: Stanford University Press, 1977, pp. 441–74.

———. *The Pattern of the Chinese Past*. Stanford, Calif.: Stanford University Press, 1973.

Esherick, Joseph. *Reform and Revolution in China: The 1911 Revolution in Hunan and Hubei*. Berkeley: University of California Press, 1976.

Fang Long. "Suzhou nongmin baodong de jingguo yu qianzhan" (The course and causes of the Suzhou peasant riots), *Laodong jibao*, 1935, no. 4 (Feb.), 123–30.

Fang Shiming. *Shanghai Xiaodaohui qiyi* (The uprising of the Shanghai Small Sword Society). Shanghai: Shanghai renmin chubanshe, 1965.

Fang Zhiguang. "Shilun Taiping Tianguo 'zhuodian shouliang' zhidu" (A preliminary discussion of the Taiping system of "the collection of land taxes from tenants"), in *Taiping Tianguo shi luncong* (Collection of articles on the history of the Taiping Rebellion). Ed. Nanjing daxue xuebao bianjibu, Nanjing daxue Taiping Tianguo yanjiushi, and Jiangsusheng shehui kexueyuan lishi yanjiushi. 2 vols. Nanjing: 1980, vol. 2, pp. 1–13.

Faure, David. "Land Taxation in Kiangsu Province in the Late Ch'ing," *Ch'ing-shih wen-t'i*, 3.6 (Dec. 1976), 49–75.

———. "The Plight of the Farmers: A Study of the Rural Economy of Jiangnan and the Pearl River Delta, 1870–1937," *Modern China*, 11.1 (Jan. 1985), 3–37.

———. "The Rural Economy of Kiangsu Province, 1870–1911," *Journal of the Institute of Chinese Studies of the Chinese University of Hong Kong*, 9.2 (1978), 365–469.

———. *The Rural Economy of Pre-Liberation China: Trade Increase and Peasant Livelihood in Jiangsu and Guangdong, 1870 to 1937*. Hong Kong: Oxford University Press, 1989.

Fei Hsiao-t'ung. *Peasant Life in China: A Field Study of Country Life in the Yangtze Valley*. New York: Dutton, 1939.

Feng Guifen. *Xianzhitang ji* (Collected essays from Xianzhi Hall). Suzhou: n.p., 1876.

Feng Hefa, comp. *Zhongguo nongcun jingji ziliao* (Materials on the Chinese rural economy). Shanghai: Liming shuju, 1933.

———. *Zhongguo nongcun jingji ziliao xubian* (Materials on the Chinese rural economy, supplement). Shanghai: Liming shuju, 1935.

Feng Shi. "Huaxi riji" (Diary of the flowery stream), in *Taiping Tianguo*, vol. 6, pp. 665–728.

Feng Zigang, ed. *Jiaxingxian nongcun diaocha* (Investigation of villages in Jiaxing County). N.p.: Guoli Zhejiang daxue and Jiaxingxian zhengfu, 1936.

Fengxianxian zhi (Gazetteer of Fengxian County). Comp. Shanghaishi Fengxianxian zhi xiubian weiyuanhui. Shanghai: Shanghai renmin chubanshe, 1987.

Fenhu xiaozhi (A short gazetteer of Fenhu). 1847.

Fu Yiling. "Taiping Tianguo shidai de quanguo kangliang chao" (The countrywide tide of tax resistance during the Taiping period) and "Taiping Tianguo shidai tuanlian kangguan wenti yinlun" (Introductory discussion of the problem of resistance to officials by militia during the Taiping period), in his *Ming Qing shehui jingji shi lunwen ji* (Collection of articles on the social and economic history of the Ming and Qing). Beijing: Beijing renmin chubanshe, 1982, pp. 397–417, 443–52.

Fujii Hiroshi. "Ichiden ryōshu-sei no kihon kōzō" (The basic structure of the system of dual ownership), *Kindai Chūgoku* (4 parts) 5 (April 1979), 83–150, 6 (Sept. 1979), 70–119, 7 (Feb. 1980), 34–87, 8 (Oct. 1980) 53–118.

Funingxian xinzhi (New gazetteer of Funing County). 1934.

Geisert, Bradley Kent. "Power and Society: The Kuomintang and Local Elites in Kiangsu Province, 1924–1937." Ph.D. dissertation, University of Virginia, 1979.

"Gengshen binan riji" (Diary of seeking refuge in 1860), in *Jianji*, vol. 4, pp. 473–600.

Gong Jun. "Wujin (Jiangsusheng)" (Wujin, Jiangsu Province), in "Gedi nongmin zhuangkuang diaocha" (Investigation of the peasantry's condition in various localities), *Dongfang zazhi*, 24.16 (Aug. 25, 1927), 105–9.

Gong Youcun. "Ziyi riji" (Diary of Ziyi), in *Jianji*, vol. 4, pp. 337–472.

Gongzhongdang Guangxu chao zouzhe (Memorials from the Guangxu reign in the Palace Memorial Archives [Taibei]). Taibei: Guoli gugong bowuyuan, 1982.

"Gouwu guijia lu" (A historical record of Wuxi, 1853–54), in *Zhuanji*, pp. 76–84.

Gu Fusheng, "Qing-Song nongmin qiushou qiyi" (The Autumn Harvest Uprising among peasants in Qingpu and Songjiang), *Jiangsu wenshi ziliao xuanji*, 1980, no. 4, 9–30.

Gu Mou. "Lihu yixiang xu" (Preface to *Strange Sounds from Lake Li*), *Jindaishi ziliao*, 34 (1964), 164–66.

Gu Ruyu. "Haiyu zeiluan zhi" (Record of the Taiping calamity in Changshu), in *Taiping Tianguo*, vol. 5, pp. 345–96.

Gu Shucun. "Dajin Taiping Tianguo neibu de dizhu 'Yongchang Xu Shi'" ("Mr. Xu of Yongchang": A landlord who infiltrated the Taiping Rebellion), in *TTSLX*, vol. 1, pp. 365–78.

Gu Yanwu. *Rizhi lu* (Record of daily knowledge; 1695). 6 vols. Reprint. Taibei: Taiwan shangwu yinshuguan, 1956.

"Guanyu Fei Xiuyuan fuzi de ziliao" (Materials concerning Fei Xiuyuan and his son), in *Zhuanji*, pp. 85–89.

Gui Danmeng. *Huanyou jilüe* (Brief account of life as an official; n.d.). Reprint. Taibei: Guangwen shuju, 1972.

Guianxian zhi (The gazetteer of Guian County). 1882.

"Guijia riji" (Diary of 1853–54), in *Jianji*, vol. 2, pp. 379–83.

Gunde, Richard. "Land Tax and Social Change in Sichuan, 1925–1935," *Modern China*, 2.1 (Jan. 1976), 23–48.

Gunong Tuishi [pseud.]. *Kounan suoji* (Jottings about the bandit calamity; 1861). Reprint. Taibei: Taiwan xuesheng shuju, 1969.

Habermas, Jürgen. *The Structural Transformation of the Public Sphere*. Tr. Thomas Burger with the assistance of Frederick Lawrence. Cambridge, Mass.: Massachusetts Institute of Technology Press, 1989.

Hamashima Atsutoshi. *Mindai Kōnan nōson shakai no kenkyū* (A study of Jiangnan rural society during the Ming period). Tokyo: Tokyo University Press, 1982.

Han Hengyu. "Shilun Qingdai qianqi diannong yongdianquan de youlai ji qi xingzhi" (A preliminary discussion of the origins and nature of tenant permanent rights in the early Qing period), *Qingshi luncong*, 1 (1979), 37–53.

Hang Guoren. "Da geming qianhou Wuxi gongnong yundong de huiyi pianduan" (Fragmentary reminiscences of the worker and peasant movement in Wuxi at the time of the Great Revolution), *Jiangsu wenshi ziliao xuanji*, 1980, no. 5, 59–70.

Hangzhoufu zhi (The gazetteer of Hangzhou Prefecture). 1922.

Harigaya Miwako. "Taihei Tengoku kōki no gōson tōchi: 1860 nen igo no Sekkō ni okeru" (Village governance in the latter part of the Taiping Rebellion: Zhejiang after 1860), *Hitotsubashi ronsō*, 83.1 (1980), 124–43.

———. "Taihei Tengoku senryō chi-iki no sōsen shūdan: Taiko shūhen chi-iki o chūshin ni shite" (Gunboat gangs in Taiping-occupied territory: The area around Lake Tai), *Rekishigaku kenkyū*, 522 (Nov. 1983), 17–35.

Hayashi Megumi. *Chūshi Kōnan nōson shakai seido kenkyū* (Study of the social system of rural Jiangnan in Central China). Tokyo: Yūhikaku, 1953.

He Menglei. *Suzhou Wuxi Changshu sanxian zudian zhidu diaocha* (Survey of the tenancy system in the three counties of Suzhou, Wuxi, and Changshu). Vol. 63 of Xiao Zheng, ed.

Hehu Yiyisheng [pseud.]. "Guichou jiwen lu" (Record of 1853), in *Zhuanji*, pp. 476–535.

Heqiao Jushi [pseud.]. "Shengchuan baisheng" (Unofficial historical record of Shengchuan), in *Jianji*, vol. 2, pp. 179–206.

Hoang, Peter. "A Practical Treatise on Legal Ownership" (condensed translation from the French), in George Jamieson, ed., "Tenure of Land in China and the Condition of the Rural Population," *Journal of the China Branch of the Royal Asiatic Society*, n.s. 23 (1889), 118–43.

Hofheinz, Roy, Jr. *The Broken Wave: The Chinese Communist Peasant Movement, 1922–1928.* Cambridge, Mass.: Harvard University Press, 1977.

Hong Huanchun, comp. *Ming Qing Suzhou nongcun jingji ziliao* (Materials on the rural economy of Suzhou during the Ming and Qing). Nanjing: Jiangsu guji chubanshe, 1988.

Hong Ruijian. "Suzhou kangzu fengchao zhi qianyin houguo" (Causes and consequences of the rent resistance riots in Suzhou), *Dizheng yuekan* 4.10 (Oct. 1936), 1547–62.

——. *Zhejiang zhi erwu jianzu* (The 25-percent rent reduction in Zhejiang). Nanjing: Graduate School of Land Economics, Central Political Institute, 1935.

Hsia Ching-lin, James L. E. Chow, and Chang Yukon, trs. *The Civil Code of the Republic of China* (1930). Reprint. Arlington, Va.: University Publications of America, 1976.

Hsiao Kung-ch'üan. *Rural China: Imperial Control in the Nineteenth Century.* Seattle: University of Washington Press, 1960.

Hu Chuanru. "Jiangyin (Jiangsusheng)" (Jiangyin, Jiangsu Province), in "Gedi nongmin zhuangkuang diaocha" (Investigation of the peasantry's condition in various localities), *Dongfang zazhi*, 24.16 (Aug. 25, 1927), 113–16.

Hu Sheng. *Imperialism and Chinese Politics.* Beijing: Foreign Languages Press, 1955.

Hua Yilun. "Xi-Jin tuanlian shimo ji" (Complete account of militia in Wuxi and Jingui), in *Taiping Tianguo ziliao* (Materials on the Taiping Rebellion). Comp. Zhongguo kexueyuan jindaishi ziliao bianjizu. Beijing: Kexue chubanshe, 1959, pp. 121–31.

Huadong junzheng weiyuanhui tudi gaige weiyuanhui, ed. *Dizhu zui'e zhongzhong* (Various evils of landlords). N.p., n.d.

——. *Huadong nongcun jingji ziliao* (Materials on the rural economy in eastern China), vol. 1: *Jiangsusheng nongcun diaocha* (Survey of rural villages in Jiangsu Province); vol. 2: *Zhejiangsheng nongcun diaocha* (Survey of rural villages in Zhejiang Province). N.p.: 1952.

Huai papers. Land documents of the Huai family of Jiaxing County. Originals in the Tōyō bunka kenkyūjo, Tokyo University.

Huang Baoting. "Nansha zashi (xuanlu)" (Selections from miscellaneous information concerning Nansha), in *Shanghai Xiaodaohui*, pp. 1154–56.

Huang Benquan. "Xiaolin xiaoshi" (Short history of a wicked force), in *Shanghai Xiaodaohui*, pp. 971–81.

Huang, Philip C. C. *The Peasant Economy and Social Change in North China.* Stanford, Calif.: Stanford University Press, 1985.

————. *The Peasant Family and Rural Development in the Yangzi Delta, 1350–1988.* Stanford, Calif.: Stanford University Press, 1990.

Huang, Ray. *Taxation and Governmental Finance in Sixteenth-Century Ming China.* Cambridge: Cambridge University Press, 1974.

"Huangdu xuzhi (zhailu)" (Excerpts from the continuation of the gazetteer of Huangdu), in *Shanghai Xiaodaohui,* pp. 1086–89.

Huzhoufu zhi (The gazetteer of Huzhou Prefecture). 1874.

Ihara Kōsuke. "Hanshi giden ni okeru Shinmatsu no kosaku seido" (The tenancy system in the late Qing as seen in the Fan charitable estate), *Hiroshima daigaku bungakubu kiyō,* 26 (1966), 180–207.

Imahori Seiji. "Shindai kōso ni tsuite" (Rent resistance in the Qing period), *Shigaku zasshi,* 76.9 (Sept. 1967), 37–61.

Jiadingxian xuzhi (A continuation of the gazetteer of Jiading County). 1930.

Jiang Taixin. "Qingdai qianqi yazuzhi de fazhan" (The development of the system of rent deposits in the early Qing), *Lishi yanjiu,* 1980, no. 3, 133–49.

Jiang Yinsheng. "Yinsheng rilu" (Daily records of Yinsheng), in *Zhuanji,* pp. 421–47.

Jiangsu shengli (Jiangsu provincial regulations). Nanjing: Jiangsu shuju, 1869.

Jiangsu shengli xubian (Supplement to Jiangsu provincial regulations). Nanjing: Jiangsu shuju, 1875.

Jiangsusheng dang'anguan, comp. *Jiangsu nongmin yundong dangan shiliao xuanbian* (Compendium of selections of archival material on the Jiangsu peasant movement). Beijing: Dang'an chubanshe, 1983.

Jiangsusheng nongcun yinhang, comp. *Wuxixian nongcun jingji diaocha, diyi ji* (Investigation of the rural economy in Wuxi County, part 1; 1931), in *Zhongguo nongcun jingji ziliao* (Materials on the Chinese rural economy). Comp. Feng Hefa. Shanghai: Liming shuju, 1933, pp. 389–99.

Jiangyinxian zhi (Gazetteer of Jiangyin County). 1840.

Jiashanxian zhi (Gazetteer of Jiashan County). 1892.

"Jiaxing chengli cuizuchu" (Jiaxing establishes a rent-dunning office), *Laodong jibao,* 1934, no. 2 (July), 132.

Jiaxing xinzhi (New gazetteer of Jiaxing). 1929.

Jiaxingxian zhi (Gazetteer of Jiaxing County). 1891.

Jincun xiaozhi (Short gazetteer of Jincun). 1924.

Jing Junjian. "Lun Qingdai juanmian zhengce zhong jianzu guiding de bianhua: Qingdai mintian zhudian guanxi zhengce de tantao zhi er" (On the changes in the regulations concerning rent reduction in the Qing policy of tax remission: An examination of the Qing policy concerning landlord-tenant relations on commoner land, Part 2), *Zhongguo jingji shi yanjiu,* 1986, no. 1 (March), 67–79.

"Jingzhai riji" (Diary of Tranquility Hall). Undated manuscript in the History Department Library of Nanjing University.

Jinshanxian zhi (Gazetteer of Jinshan County). 1878.

Johnson, Chalmers A. *Peasant Nationalism and Communist Power: The Emergence of Revolutionary China, 1937–1945.* Stanford, Calif.: Stanford University Press, 1962.

Juanpu Yelao [pseud.]. "Genggui jilüe" (Brief account of 1860 to 1863), in *Taiping Tianguo ziliao* (Materials on the Taiping Rebellion). Comp. Zhongguo kexueyuan lishi yanjiusuo disansuo jindaishi ziliao bianjizu. Beijing: Kexue chubanshe, 1959, pp. 92–119.

Kang-Yong-Qian shiqi chengxiang renmin fankang douzheng ziliao (Materials on urban and rural resistance struggles in the Kangxi, Yongzheng, and Qianlong reigns). Comp. Zhongguo renmin daxue Qingshi yanjiusuo and Zhongguo renmin daxue dang'anxi Zhongguo zhengzhi zhidu shi jiaoyanshi. 2 vols. Beijing: Zhonghua shuju, 1979.

Ke Wuchi. *Louwang yongyu ji* (Collected essays of the fish who escaped the net). Beijing: Zhonghua shuju, 1959.

King, F. H. *Money and Monetary Policy in China, 1845–1895.* Cambridge, Mass.: Harvard University Press, 1965.

Kobayashi Kazumi. "Taihei Tengoku zenya no nōmin tōsō: Yōsukō karyū deruta chitai ni okeru" (Peasant struggles on the eve of the Taiping Rebellion: The Lower Yangzi delta region), in *Kindai Chūgoku nōson shakai shi kenkyū* (Studies on the history of modern Chinese rural society). Ed. Tōkyō kyōiku daigaku Ajia shi kenkyū-kai. Tokyo: Tōkyō kyōiku daigaku, 1967, pp. 1–61.

Kobayashi Yukio. "Shinmatsu no Sekkō ni okeru fuzei kaikaku to sessen nōzei ni tsuite" (Land tax reform and the commutation of tax payment in Zhejiang in the late Qing), *Tōyō gakuhō*, 58.1–2 (Dec. 1976), 49–85.

Kojima Yoshio. "Dennō no zeiryō futan ni kansuru ichi kōsatsu" (An examination of the tax burden on tenants), *Shichō*, 112 (1973), 64–75.

———. "1910 nendai ni okeru Kōnan no nōson shakai" (Jiangnan rural society in the 1910's), *Tōyōshi kenkyū*, 32.4 (March 1974), 87–105.

———. "Kōso tōsō: Kōnan deruta chitai o chūshin ni shite" (Rent resistance struggles: The Jiangnan delta region), in *Kōza Chūgoku kin-gendai shi* (Lectures on modern and contemporary Chinese history). Ed. Nozawa Yukata and Tanaka Masatoshi. Tokyo: Tokyo University Press, 1978, vol. 2, pp. 127–45.

———. "Shingai Kakumei zengo ni okeru Soshūfu no nōson shakai to nōmin tōsō" (Rural society and peasant struggles in Suzhou Prefecture before and after the 1911 Revolution), in *Kindai Chūgoku nōson shakai shi kenkyū* (Studies on the history of modern Chinese rural society). Ed. Tōkyō kyōiku daigaku Ajia shi kenkyū-kai. Tokyo: Tōkyō kyōiku daigaku, 1967, pp. 297–363.

———. "Shinmatsu Minkoku shoki ni okeru Sekkōshō Kakōfu shūhen no nōson shakai" (Rural society in Jiaxing Prefecture, Zhejiang Province, in the late Qing and early Republican periods), in *Yamazaki sensei taikan kinen Tōyō shigaku ronshū* (Symposium on East Asian history in honor of the retirement of Professor Yamazaki). Tokyo: n.p., 1967, pp. 185–96.

———. "Shinmatsu no gōson tōchi ni tsuite: Soshūfu no ku to tō o chūshin ni" (Village governance in the late Qing: *Qu* and *tu* managers in Suzhou Prefecture), *Shichō*, 88 (1964), 16–30.

Kuhn, Philip A. "Local Self-Government Under the Republic: Problems of Control, Autonomy, and Mobilization," in *Conflict and Control in Late Imperial China.* Ed. Frederic Wakeman, Jr., and Carolyn Grant. Berkeley: University of California Press, 1975, pp. 257–98.

———. *Rebellion and Its Enemies in Late Imperial China: Militarization and Social Structure, 1796–1864.* Reprint of 1970 ed. with a new preface. Cambridge, Mass.: Harvard University Press, 1980.

———. *Soulstealers: The Chinese Sorcery Scare of 1768.* Cambridge, Mass.: Harvard University Press, 1990.

Kujirai Nobuko. "1853 nen Chōkō karyū-iki no nōmin ikki" (Peasant uprisings in the lower Yangzi region in 1853), *Ochanomizu shigaku*, 1960, no. 3 (Nov.), 20–34.

Kun-Xin liangxian xuxiu hezhi (Revised supplementary gazetteer of Kunshan and Xinyang counties). 1880.

Kusano Yasushi. "Denmen kankō no seiritsu" (The origins of the practice of topsoil rights), *Hōbun ronsō*, 39: 61–88.

———. "Kyū Chūgoku no denmen kankō" (The practice of topsoil rights in traditional China), *Tōyōshi kenkyū*, 34.2 (1975), 50–76.

———. "Sōdai no ganden kōsō to denko no hō-mibun" (The rent resistance of obstinate tenants and the legal status of tenants during the Song), *Shigaku zasshi*, 78.11 (Nov. 1969), 1–35.

Li Chengru, ed. "Jiangsu Shanyang shouzu quanan" (Complete record on rent collection in Shanyang, Jiangsu)," *Qingshi ziliao*, 1981, no. 2, 1–32.

Li Chun. *Taiping Tianguo zhidu chutan* (Preliminary study of Taiping institutions). Rev. ed. Beijing: Zhonghua shuju, 1963.

Li Hongzhang. *Li Wenzhong gong (Hongzhang) quanji* (Complete works of Li Hongzhang; 1905). Reprint. Taibei: Wenhai chubanshe, 1965.

Li Wenzhi. "Lun Qingdai houqi Jiang-Zhe-Wan sansheng yuan Taiping Tianguo zhanlingqu tudi guanxi de bianhua" (Transformation of land relations in the late Qing in the former Taiping-occupied territory in the three provinces of Jiangsu, Zhejiang, and Anhui), *Lishi yanjiu*, 1981, no. 6, 81–96.

———. "Taiping Tianguo geming dui biange fengjian shengchan guanxi de zuoyong" (The effect of the Taiping Rebellion on the transformation of feudal relations of production), in *TTSLX*, vol. 1, pp. 82–94.

———, comp. *Zhongguo jindai nongye shi ziliao* (Materials on the modern history of Chinese agriculture), vol. 1. Beijing: Sanlian shudian, 1957.

Li Xingyuan. *Li Wengong gong zouyi* (Memorials of Li Wengong; 1865). Reprint. Taibei: Wenhai chubanshe, 1974.

Li Zongxi. *Kaixian Li Shangshu (Zongxi) zhengshu* (The political papers of Li Zongxi of Kai County; 1885). Reprint. Taibei: Chengwen chubanshe, 1969.

Liang Fangzhong. *Zhongguo lidai hukou, tiandi, tianfu tongji* (Statistics on population, cultivated area, and land taxes during China's successive dynasties). Shanghai: Shanghai renmin chubanshe, 1980.

Liao Zhihao. "Suzhou faxian de Taiping Tianguo wenwu kaoshi" (Examination of a Taiping cultural relic discovered in Suzhou), in *Suzhou wenwu ziliao xuanbian* (Selected materials on Suzhou cultural relics). Ed. Suzhou diqu wenhuaju, Suzhou wenwu guanli weiyuanhui, and Suzhou bowuguan. Kunshan: 1980, pp. 193–96.

Liao Zhihao and Li Maogao. "Xinhai geming qijian zichan jieji dui Sunan diqu gongnong douzheng de taidu" (The bourgeoisie's attitude toward worker and peasant struggles in southern Jiangsu during the 1911 Revolution), *Jiangsu shifan xueyuan xuebao*, 1981, no. 3, 90–91.

Liaocun Dunke [pseud.]. "Huku jilüe" (A brief account of the tiger's lair), in *Zhuanji*, pp. 12–54.

Lieu, D. K. "Land Tenure Systems in China," *Chinese Economic Journal*, 2.6 (June 1928), 457–74.

"Lihu yuefu" (Collection of songs and poems about Lake Li), *Jindaishi ziliao*, 34 (1964), 167–76.

Lili xuzhi (Continuation of the gazetteer of Lili). 1889.

Lin Chu-ching. "The Kuomintang Policy of Rent Reduction," in *Agrarian China: Selected Source Materials from Chinese Authors* (1938). Reprint. Arlington, Va.: University Publications of America, 1976, pp. 144–49.

Lin Man-houng. "Currency and Society: The Monetary Crisis and Political-Economic Ideology of Early Nineteenth-Century China." Ph.D. dissertation, Harvard University, 1989.

Lin Qingyuan. "Lun Taiping Tianguo zhengquan de xingzhi ji qi fengjianhua de qushi" (On the nature of Taiping political power and its feudalistic tendencies), in *Taiping Tianguo shi xueshu taolunhui lunwen xuanji* (Selected essays from the academic conference on the history of the Taiping Rebellion). Ed. Zhonghua shuju jindaishi bianjishi. 3 vols. Beijing: Zhonghua shuju, 1981, vol. 1, pp. 111–49.

Liu Kexiang. "Shijiu shiji wushi zhi jiushi niandai Qing zhengfu de jianfu he qingfu yundong" (The Qing government's tax reduction and tax clearance movement from the 1850's to the 1890's), *Zhongguo shehui kexueyuan jingji yanjiusuo jikan*, 7 (Feb. 1984), 295–350.

Liu Kunyi. *Liu Kunyi yiji* (Works of Liu Kunyi, posthumously collected). 3 vols. Beijing: Zhonghua shuju, 1959.

Liu Shiji. *Ming Qing shidai Jiangnan shizhen yanjiu* (Study of market towns in Jiangnan during the Ming and Qing periods). Beijing: Zhongguo shehui kexue chubanshe, 1987.

Liu Yao. "Cong Changjiang zhong-xialiu diqu nongcun jingji de bianhua kan Taiping Tianguo geming de lishi zuoyong" (The historical role of the Taiping Rebellion as seen in the transformation of the rural economy in the middle and lower Yangzi regions), *Lishi yanjiu*, 1979, no. 6, 32–48.

Liu Yongcheng. "Qingdai qianqi de nongye zudian guanxi" (Agrarian rental relationships in the early Qing), *Qingshi luncong*, 2 (1980), 56–88.

——— . "Qingdai qianqi diannong kangzu douzheng de xin fazhan" (New developments in tenant rent resistance struggles in the early Qing), *Qingshi luncong*, 1 (1979), 54–78.

Liu Zhaoxun. "Liu Zhaoxun riji" (Diary of Liu Zhaoxun), in *Zhuanji*, pp. 98–386.

Lojewski, Frank A. "Confucian Reformers and Local Vested Interests: The Su-Sung-T'ai Tax Reduction of 1863 and Its Aftermath." Ph.D. dissertation, University of California, Davis, 1973.

——— . "The Soochow Bursaries: Rent Management During the Late Ch'ing," *Ch'ing-shih wen-t'i*, 4.3 (June 1980), 43–65.

Lu Yaohua. "Shanghai Xiaodaohui de yuanliu" (The origins of the Shanghai Small Sword Society), *Shihuo yuekan*, 3.5 (1973), 207–19.

Lu Yun. "Haijiao xubian" (Supplementary essays from the corner of the sea [Changshu and Zhaowen counties]). Appendix to Ke Wuchi, *Louwang yongyuji*. Beijing: Zhonghua shuju, 1959.

Lu Yunbiao. "Gengshen nian Chenmuzhen jilüe" (Brief account of Chenmu market town in 1860), in *Taiping Tianguo ziliao* (Materials on the Taiping Rebellion). Comp. Zhongguo kexueyuan jindaishi ziliao bianjizu. Beijing: Kexue chubanshe, 1959, pp. 131–35.

Luo Ergang. *Taiping Tianguo shishi kao* (An investigation of historical matters pertaining to the Taiping Rebellion; 1955). Reprint. Beijing: Sanlian shudian, 1979.

——. "Zai lun 'Tianchao tianmu zhidu'" (A reappraisal of "The Land System of the Heavenly Dynasty"), *Lishi yanjiu*, 1984, no. 1, 103–16.

Lust, John. "Secret Societies, Popular Movements, and the 1911 Revolution," in *Popular Movements and Secret Societies in China, 1840–1950*. Ed. Jean Chesneaux. Stanford, Calif.: Stanford University Press, 1972, pp. 165–200.

Lüxi zhi (Gazetteer of Lüxi). 1774.

Ma Xinyi. *Ma Duanmin gong (Xinyi) zouyi* (Memorials of Ma Xinyi; 1894). Reprint. Taibei: Wenhai chubanshe, 1975.

Maeda Katsutarō. "Shindai no Kanton ni okeru nōmin tōsō no kiban" (The basis of peasant struggles in Guangdong during the Qing), *Tōyō gakuhō*, 51.4 (March 1969), 1–38.

Mann, Susan. *Local Merchants and the Chinese Bureaucracy, 1750–1950*. Stanford, Calif.: Stanford University Press, 1987.

Mao Jiaqi. "Taiping Tianguo geming hou Jiangnan nongcun tudi guanxi shitan" (An exploration of land relations in Jiangnan villages after the Taiping Rebellion), in *TTSLX*, vol. 1, pp. 111–25.

Marks, Robert B. *Rural Revolution in South China: Peasants and the Making of History in Haifeng County, 1570–1930*. Madison: University of Wisconsin Press, 1984.

McCord, Edward A. "Militia and Local Militarization in Late Qing and Early Republican China: The Case of Hunan," *Modern China*, 14.2 (April 1988), 156–87.

McDonald, Angus W., Jr. *The Urban Origins of Rural Revolution: Elites and the Masses in Hunan Province, China, 1911–1927*. Berkeley: University of California Press, 1978.

Meijer, Marinus Johan. *The Introduction of Modern Criminal Law in China* (1949). Reprint. Arlington, Va.: University Publications of America, 1976.

Meili beizhi (The complete gazetteer of Meili). 1922.

Meili zhi (Gazetteer of Meili). 1877.

Michael, Franz. *The Taiping Rebellion: History and Documents*. 3 vols. Seattle: University of Washington Press, 1966.

Min shangshi xiguan diaocha baogao lu (Report on the investigation of commercial activities and customs among the people). 2 vols. Nanjing: Sifa xingzhengbu, 1930.

Miner, Noel R. "Agrarian Reform in Nationalist China: The Case of Rent Reduction in Chekiang, 1927–1937," in *China at the Crossroads: Nationalists and Communists, 1927–1949*. Ed. Gilbert F. Chan. Boulder, Colo.: Westview Press, 1980, pp. 69–89.

Mori Masao. "Jūroku-jūhachi seiki ni okeru kōsei to jinushi denko kankei" (Famine relief administration and landlord-tenant relations from the 16th through the 18th century), *Tōyōshi kenkyū*, 27.4 (March 1969), 69–111.

——. "Min Shin jidai no tochi seido" (The land system during the Ming and

Qing periods), in *Iwanami kōza sekai rekishi* (Iwanami lectures on world history). Tokyo: Iwanami shoten, 1971, vol. 12, pp. 229–74.

Morita Akira. *Shindai suirishi kenkyū* (Study of the history of Qing water conservancy). Tokyo: Aki shobō, 1974.

Muramatsu Yūji. "A Documentary Study of Chinese Landlordism in Late Ch'ing and Early Republican Kiangnan," *Bulletin of the School of Oriental and African Studies*, 29.3 (1966), 566–99.

————. *Kindai Kōnan no sosan: Chūgoku jinushi seido no kenkyū* (Bursaries in Jiangnan in the modern period: Studies of the Chinese landlord system). Tokyo: Tōkyō daigaku shuppankai, 1970.

————. "Shindai no iwayuru 'Soshō no jūfu' ni tsuite" (On the so-called "heavy taxation in Suzhou and Songjiang" during the Qing), *Hitotsubashi ronsō*, 45.6 (June 1961), 563–86.

Myers, Ramon. *The Chinese Peasant Economy: Agricultural Development in Hopei and Shantung, 1890–1949*. Cambridge, Mass.: Harvard University Press, 1970.

Nakayama Mio. "Shindai zenki Kōnan no bukka dōkō" (The trend in commodity prices in Jiangnan during the early Qing), *Tōyōshi kenkyū*, 37.4 (March 1979), 77–106.

Namiki Yorihisa. "1850 nendai Kanan Rensōkai no kōryō bōdō" (Anti-tax riots by the Lianzhuanghui in Henan during the 1850's), *Chūgoku kindaishi kenkyū*, 2 (July 1982), 1–28.

"Nanhuixian zhi (zhailu)" (Excerpts from the gazetteer of Nanhui County), in *Shanghai Xiaodaohui*, pp. 1163–64.

Nanhuixian xuzhi (Continuation of the gazetteer of Nanhui County). 1929.

Nanxun zhi (Gazetteer of Nanxun). 1923.

Natsui Haruki. "Jūkyū seiki chūyō Soshū no ichi sosan ni okeru shūso jōkyō: Dōchi genso to sore ni itaru katei" (The rent collection of a Suzhou bursary in the mid-19th century: The Tongzhi rent reduction and the process leading up to it), *Shigaku zasshi*, 90.7 (1981), 1–39.

Ni Yangru. "Wuxi Meicunzhen ji qi fujin de nongcun" (Meicun market town, Wuxi, and its neighboring villages), *Dongfang zazhi*, 32.2 (1935), 89–91.

Niida Noboru. "Min-Shin jidai no ichiden ryōshu kanshū to sono seiritsu" (The two-lords-to-a-field custom in the Ming and Qing periods and its establishment), in his *Chūgoku hōsei-shi kenkyū: tochihō torihikihō* (Study of Chinese legal history: Land law, exchange law). Tokyo: Tokyo University Press, 1960, pp. 164–215.

Ocko, Jonathan K. *Bureaucratic Reform in Provincial China: Ting Jih-ch'ang in Restoration Jiangsu, 1867–1870*. Cambridge, Mass.: Harvard University Press, 1983.

Palmer, Michael J. E. "The Surface-Subsoil Form of Divided Ownership in Late Imperial China: Some Examples from the New Territories in Hong Kong," *Modern Asian Studies*, 21.1 (Feb. 1987), 1–119.

Pan Daogen. *Yinqiutang riji jieyao* (The abridged diary from Yinqiu Hall). 1935 preface.

Pan Guangdan and Quan Weitian. *Sunan tudi gaige fangwen ji* (Record of an inquiry into land reform in southern Jiangsu). Beijing: Sanlian shudian, 1952.

Pan Zengyi. "Zuozhi siyi liutiao" (Six personal opinions to assist in governing), in his *Gongfu xiansheng fengyuzhuang benshu* (Mr. Gongfu's [Pan Zengyi] original book on the Fengyu charitable estate). 1834.

Pan Zhongrui. "Sutai milu ji" (My modest account of Suzhou), in *Taiping Tianguo*, vol. 5, pp. 269–305.

Peng Zeyi. "Yapian zhanhou shinianjian yingui qianjian bodongxia de Zhongguo jingji yu jieji guanxi" (The impact of the fluctuating value of silver and copper currency on the Chinese economy and class relations during the decade following the Opium War), *Lishi yanjiu*, 1961, no. 6, 40–68.

Pepper, Suzanne. *Civil War in China: The Political Struggle, 1945–1949*. Berkeley: University of California Press, 1978.

Perdue, Peter C. *Exhausting the Earth: State and Peasant in Hunan, 1500–1850*. Cambridge, Mass.: Council on East Asian Studies, Harvard University, 1987.

Perkins, Dwight H. *Agricultural Development in China, 1368–1968*. Chicago: Aldine, 1969.

Perry, Elizabeth J. *Rebels and Revolutionaries in North China, 1845–1945*. Stanford, Calif.: Stanford University Press, 1980.

———. "Tax Revolt in Late Qing China: The Small Swords of Shanghai and Liu Depei of Shandong," *Late Imperial China*, 6.1 (June 1985), 83–111.

Pinghuxian zhi (The gazetteer of Pinghu County). 1745.

Pinghuxian zhi (The gazetteer of Pinghu County). 1789.

"Pingyue jiwen (xuanlu)" (Selections from "Record of the suppression of the bandits from Guangdong and Guangxi"), in *Shanghai Xiaodaohui*, pp. 1115–23, 1190–98.

"Pingzei jilüe" (Brief account of the suppression of the Taiping rebels), in *Jianji*, vol. 1, pp. 207–336.

Polachek, James. "Gentry Hegemony: Soochow in the T'ung-chih Restoration," in *Conflict and Control in Late Imperial China*. Ed. Frederic Wakeman, Jr., and Carolyn Grant. Berkeley: University of California Press, 1975, pp. 211–56.

Prazniak, Roxann. "Tax Protest at Laiyang, Shandong, 1910: Commoner Organization Versus the County Political Elite," *Modern China*, 6.1 (Jan. 1980), 41–71.

———. "Weavers and Sorceresses: The Social Origins of Political Activism Among Rural Chinese Women," *Modern China*, 12.2 (April 1986), 202–29.

Qi Longwei. "Changshu Taiping Tianguo shoujun de panbian shimo" (Complete account of the mutiny of the Changshu Taiping commander), in *TTSLX*, vol. 1, pp. 347–64.

Qi Sihe et al., comps. *Yapian zhanzheng* (The Opium War). 6 vols. Shanghai: Shenzhou guoguangshe, 1954.

Qian Chengze. *Jiaxingxian zhi zudian zhidu* (The tenancy system of Jiaxing County). Vol. 59 of Xiao Zheng, ed.

Qiao Qiming. "Jiangsu Kunshan Nantong Anhui Suxian nongdian zhidu zhi bijiao yiji gailiang nongdian wenti zhi jianyi" (Comparison of the tenancy systems in Kunshan and Nantong in Jiangsu and Suxian in Anhui and a proposal for the reform of the tenancy problem; 1926), in *Zhongguo nongcun jingji ziliao* (Materials on the Chinese rural economy). Comp. Feng Hefa. Shanghai: Liming shuju, 1933, pp. 80–117.

Qingdai dizu boxue xingtai (The pattern of exploitation through land rents dur-

ing the Qing). Comp. Zhongguo diyi lishi danganguan and Zhongguo shehui kexueyuan lishi yanjiusuo. 2 vols. Beijing: Zhonghua shuju, 1982.
"Qingpuxian zhi (zhailu)" (Excerpts from the gazetteer of Qingpu County), in *Shanghai Xiaodaohui*, pp. 1157–59.
Qiu Zongyi. "Yexiexiang (Jiangsu Songjiang)" (Yexie township, Songjiang, Jiangsu), in "Gedi nongmin zhuangkuang diaocha" (Investigation of the peasantry's condition in various localities), *Dongfang zazhi*, 24.16 (Aug. 25, 1927), 127–28.
Rankin, Mary Backus. *Elite Activism and Political Transformation in China: Zhejiang Province, 1865–1911*. Stanford, Calif.: Stanford University Press, 1986.
Rawski, Evelyn Sakakida. *Agricultural Change and the Peasant Economy of South China*. Cambridge, Mass.: Harvard University Press, 1972.
Rong Mengyuan. "Taiping Tianguo youguan tudi zhidu de gongju" (Official documents pertaining to the Taiping land system), in *TTSLX*, vol. 1, pp. 537–52.
Rowe, William T. "The Public Sphere in Modern China," *Modern China*, 16.3 (July 1990), 309–29.
Run Zhi [Mao Zedong]. "Jiang-Zhe nongmin de tongku ji qi fankang yundong" (The plight of the peasants in Jiangsu and Zhejiang and their resistance movement), *Xiangdao zhoubao*, 179 (Oct. 25, 1926), 1869–71.
Schoppa, R. Keith. *Elites and Political Change: Zhejiang Province in the Early Twentieth Century*. Cambridge, Mass.: Harvard University Press, 1982.
Scott, James C. *The Moral Economy of the Peasant: Rebellion and Subsistence in Southeast Asia*. New Haven, Conn.: Yale University Press, 1976.
———. *Weapons of the Weak: Everyday Forms of Peasant Resistance*. New Haven, Conn.: Yale University Press, 1985.
"Shanghai Xiaodaohui qiyi wenxian" (Documents concerning the Small Sword Society uprising in Shanghai), *Jindaishi ziliao*, 1979, no. 4, 15–21.
Shanghaixian zhi (Gazetteer of Shanghai County). 1935.
Shen Shouzhi. "Jiechao biji" (A diary of life adrift), in *Wuzhong wenxian xiao congshu* (A small collection of literature from Wu). Comp. Jiangsu shengli Suzhou tushuguan. Suzhou: n.p., 1940, vol. 18.
Shen Yuwu. "Taiping Tianguo Zhejiang difang zhengquan xingzhi kaocha" (An investigation of the nature of local political power in Zhejiang during the Taiping Rebellion), *Zhejiang shifan xueyuan xuebao shehui kexue ban*, 1981, no. 1, 87–94.
———. "Tianjing leiyu Zhejiang chao: Taiping Tianguo shiqi Zhejiang gedi renmin qiyi" (The storm in the Heavenly Capital and the tide in Zhejiang: Popular uprisings throughout Zhejiang during the time of the Taiping Rebellion), *Zhejiang shifan xueyuan xuebao shehui kexue ban*, 1979, no. 1, 77–92.
———. "Xinhai Geming qianxi Zhejiang nongmin de fankang douzheng" (Peasant resistance struggles in Zhejiang on the eve of the 1911 Revolution), *Zhejiang shifan xueyuan xuebao shehui kexue ban*, 1981, no. 4, 40–46.
Shen Zi. "Bikou riji" (A diary of evading the bandits), in *Jianji*, vol. 4, pp. 1–335.
Sheng Kang, ed. *Huangchao jingshi wen xubian* (Collected essays on statecraft from the reigning dynasty, continued; 1897). Reprint. Taibei: Wenhai chubanshe, 1972.

Shenghu zhi (Gazetteer of Shenghu). 1874.

Shenghu zhibu (Supplement to the gazetteer of Shenghu). 1900.

"Shenyutang zutian bu" (Rent register of Shenyu Hall), Suzhou Museum.

Shi Jianlie and Liu Jizeng. "Ji (Wuxi) xiancheng shishou kefu benmo" (Complete account of the loss and recovery of Wuxi city), in *Taiping Tianguo*, vol. 5, pp. 239–68.

Shigeta Atsushi. "The Origins and Structure of Gentry Rule" (Translation of "Kyōshin shihai no seiritsu to kōzō"; 1975), in *State and Society in China: Japanese Perspectives on Ming-Qing Social and Economic History*. Ed. Linda Grove and Christian Daniels. Tokyo: Tokyo University Press, 1984, pp. 335–85.

———. *Shindai shakai keizaishi kenkyū* (Studies on Qing socioeconomic history). Tokyo: Iwanami shoten, 1975.

"Shikai zhichan bu" (Shikai register; Register of land purchases of the Shikai Hall), Suzhou Museum.

"Shilu yiji" (Shilu register; Supplementary records of Shilu Hall), Suzhou Museum.

Shimenxian zhi (Gazetteer of Shimen County). 1879.

Shiraishi Hirō. "Shinmatsu Konan no nōson shakai: ōso kankō to kōso keikō" (Rural society in Hunan during the late Qing: The practice of rent deposits and the trend toward rent resistance), in *Chūgoku kindaika no shakai kōzō* (The social structure of Chinese modernization). Ed. Tōkyō kyōiku daigaku Ajia shi kenkyūkai. Tokyo: Tōkyō kyōiku daigaku, 1960, pp. 1–19.

Shue, Vivienne. *Peasant China in Transition: The Dynamics of Development Toward Socialism, 1949–1956*. Berkeley: University of California Press, 1980.

Skinner, G. William. "Regional Urbanization in Nineteenth-Century China," in *The City in Late Imperial China*. Ed. G. William Skinner. Stanford, Calif.: Stanford University Press, 1977, pp. 211–49.

———. "Sichuan's Population in the Nineteenth Century: Lessons from Disaggregated Data," *Late Imperial China*, 8.1 (June 1987), 1–79.

Songjiangfu xuzhi (Continuation of the gazetteer of Songjiang Prefecture). 1884.

Sudō Yoshiyuki. "Shindai zenki ni okeru denko no denso genmen seisaku" (Policy on the reduction and remission of tenant rents during the early Qing period), in his *Shindai Higashi Ajia shi kenkyū* (Studies on the history of East Asia during the Qing period). Tokyo: Nihon gakujutsu shinkō kai, 1973, pp. 415–38.

Sun Zuomin. "Shilun Taiping Tianguo zhengquan de xingzhi: san lun guanyu 'nongmin zhengquan' wenti" (Preliminary discussion of the nature of Taiping political power: Three points on the question of "peasant political power"), in *Taiping Tianguo shi xueshu taolunhui lunwen xuanji* (Selected essays from the academic conference on the history of the Taiping Rebellion). Ed. Zhonghua shuju jindaishi bianjishi. 3 vols. Beijing: Zhonghua shuju, 1981, vol. 1, pp. 78–110.

Suzhou bowuguan, Jiangsu shiyuan lishixi, and Nanjing daxue lishixi, comps. *He Guiqing deng shuzha* (Correspondence of He Guiqing and others). Nanjing: Jiangsu renmin chubanshe, 1981.

Suzhoufu zhi (Gazetteer of Suzhou Prefecture). 1824.

Suzuki Tomō. *Kindai Chūgoku no jinushisei: 'So kaku' no kenkyū yakuchū* (The landlord system in modern China: Research, translation, and annotation of the "Investigation of Rent"). Tokyo: Kyūko shoin, 1977.

Taiping Tianguo geyao chuanshuo ji (A collection of folksongs and legends about the Taiping Rebellion). Comp. Zhongguo kexueyuan Jiangsu fenyuan wenxue yanjiusuo. Nanjing: Jiangsu wenyi chubanshe, 1960.

Taiping Tianguo wenshu huibian (Compendium of official Taiping documents). Comp. Taiping Tianguo lishi bowuguan. Beijing: Zhonghua shuju, 1979.

Takahashi Kōsuke. "Shinmatsu jinushi-sei no saihen to nōmin" (Peasants and the reorganization of the landlord system in the late Qing), in *Kōza Chūgoku kin-gendai shi* (Lectures on modern and contemporary Chinese history). Ed. Nozawa Yutaka and Tanaka Masatoshi. Tokyo: Tokyo University Press, 1978, vol. 1, pp. 265–96.

Tan Yuqing, comp. *Yinianlai zhi Haining xianzheng* (The county government of Haining during the past year). 1937.

Tang Shi. "Qiuwen riji" (The diary of Qiuwen), *Jindaishi ziliao*, 1963, no. 1, 65–127.

Tao Xu. "Zhenfengli gengjia jianwen lu" (Record of things seen and heard in Zhenfengli from 1860 to 1864). Appendix to *Zhouzhuangzhen zhi* (Gazetteer of Zhouzhuangzhen). 1882.

Thaxton, Ralph. *China Turned Rightside Up: Revolutionary Legitimacy in the Peasant World*. New Haven, Conn.: Yale University Press, 1983.

Tilly, Charles. *From Mobilization to Revolution*. Reading, Mass.: Addison-Wesley, 1978.

Tongxiangxian zhi (Gazetteer of Tongxiang County). 1887.

Tōyō bunka kenkyūjo shozō Chūgoku tochi bunsho mokuroku, kaisetsu (Catalogue and explanation of Chinese land documents held by the Research Institute of East Asian Culture). 2 vols. Ed. Tōkyō daigaku Tōyō bunka kenkyūjo fuzoku Tōyō gaku bunken sentā. Tokyo: 1983–86.

Tsurumi Naohiro. "Rural Control in the Ming Dynasty" (translation of "Mindai ni okeru kyōson shihai"; 1971), in *State and Society in China: Japanese Perspectives on Ming-Qing Social and Economic History*. Ed. Linda Grove and Christian Daniels. Tokyo: Tokyo University Press, 1984, pp. 245–77.

Usui Sachiko. "Shindai fuzei kankei sūchi no ichi kentō: Kenryū matsunen yori Dōchi rokunen ni itaru Kōnan ni okeru ginsen hika, senryō sekka, beika, menka-ka, sōbei sekka no hendō to nōzei-ko no fuzei futan no sui-i" (An examination of statistical data pertaining to land taxes during the Qing: Fluctuations in the silver-copper exchange rate, commutation rates for the *qian-liang* tax, prices of rice and cotton, commutation rates for the tribute tax, and changes in the tax burden on taxpayers in Jiangnan from the late Qianlong reign to the 6th year of the Tongzhi reign), *Chūgoku kindaishi kenkyū*, 1981, no. 1 (July), 43–114.

―――. "Taihei Tengoku zen Soshūfu Shōkōfu ni okeru fuzei mondai" (The land tax problem in Suzhou and Songjiang Prefectures before the Taiping Rebellion), *Shakai keizai shigaku*, 47.2 (Aug. 1981), 59–82.

Van der Sprenkel, Sybille. *Legal Institutions in Manchu China*. Rev. ed. London: Athlone Press for the University of London, 1977.

Wakeman, Frederic Jr. "Introduction: The Evolution of Local Control in Late Imperial China," in *Conflict and Control in Late Imperial China*. Ed. Frederic Wakeman, Jr., and Carolyn Grant. Berkeley: University of California Press, 1975, pp. 1–25.

————. "Rebellion and Revolution: The Study of Popular Movements in Chinese History," *Journal of Asian Studies*, 36.2 (Feb. 1977), 201–37.

————. *Strangers at the Gate: Social Disorder in South China, 1839–1861*. Berkeley: University of California Press, 1966.

Wan Guoding, Zhuang Qianghua, and Wu Yongming. *Jiangsu Wujin Nantong tianfu diaocha baogao* (Investigative report on land taxes in Nantong and Wujin, Jiangsu; 1934). Reprint. Taibei: Zhuanji wenxue chubanshe, 1971.

Wang Bingxie. *Wuziqi shi wenji* (Collected essays from Wuziqi Hall; 1885). Reprint. Taibei: Wenhai chubanshe, 1968.

Wang Desen. *Suihan wengao* (A manuscript about the dark cold [Taiping] winter). N.d.

Wang Rurun. "Fufenju riji" (Diary from the Fufen residence), in *Qingdai riji huichao* (Collection of diaries from the Qing period). Comp. Shanghai renmin chubanshe. Shanghai: Shanghai renmin chubanshe, 1982, pp. 169–99.

Wang Shuhuai. *Zhongguo xiandaihua de quyu yanjiu, Jiangsusheng, 1860–1916* (Regional studies on Chinese modernization: Jiangsu Province, 1860–1916). Taibei: Zhongyang yanjiuyuan jindaishi yanjiusuo, 1984.

Wang Tao. "Wengyou yutan (xuanlu)" (Excerpts from the miscellaneous discourses of Wang Tao), in *Shanghai Xiaodaohui*, pp. 1024–25.

Wang Tianjiang. "Guanyu Taiping Tianguo de xiangguan he jiceng zhengquan" (The *xiangguan* and lower level political power during the Taiping period), in *Taiping Tianguo xuekan*. Ed. Beijing Taiping Tianguo lishi yanjiuhui. Beijing: Zhonghua shuju, 1985, vol. 2, pp. 124–45.

————. "Taiping Tianguo geming hou Su-Zhe-Wan sansheng de tudi guanxi" (Land relations in the three provinces of Jiangsu, Zhejiang, and Anhui after the Taiping Rebellion), in *TTSLX*, vol. 1, pp. 126–42.

————. "Taiping Tianguo xiangguan de jieji chengfen" (The class status of the Taiping *xiangguan*), in *TTSLX*, vol. 1, pp. 688–705.

Wang Xingfu. *Taiping jun zai Zhejiang* (The Taiping army in Zhejiang). Hangzhou: Zhejiang renmin chubanshe, 1982.

Wang Xingfu and Zhou Qizhong. "Lun Zhe-Bo cang Shimen Taiping Tianguo wenwu de zhenwei ji qi shiliao jiazhi" (The authenticity of the Taiping documents on Shimen held at the Zhejiang provincial museum and their historical value), in *Taiping Tianguo xuekan*. Ed. Beijing Taiping Tianguo lishi yanjiuhui. Beijing: Zhonghua shuju, 1987, vol. 4, pp. 165–201.

Wang Yeh-chien. *An Estimate of the Land-Tax Collection in China, 1753 and 1908*. Cambridge, Mass.: East Asian Research Center, Harvard University, 1973.

————. "The Impact of the Taiping Rebellion on Population in Southern Kiangsu," *Harvard Papers on China*, 19 (1965), 120–58.

————. *Land Taxation in Imperial China, 1750–1911*. Cambridge, Mass.: Harvard University Press, 1973.

Watson, Rubie S. *Inequality Among Brothers: Class and Kinship in South China*. Cambridge: Cambridge University Press, 1985.

Wei Yuan. *Guweitang neiji waiji* (The first and second collections of the works of Guwei Hall; 1878). Reprint. Taibei: Wenhai chubanshe, 1969.

Wiens, Mi Chu. "Lord and Peasant: The Sixteenth to the Eighteenth Century," *Modern China*, 6.1 (Jan. 1980), 3–39.

————. "Socioeconomic Change During the Ming Dynasty in the Kiangnan Area." Ph.D. dissertation, Harvard University, 1973.

Will, Pierre-Etienne. *Bureaucracy and Famine in Eighteenth-Century China.* Tr. Elborg Forster. Stanford, Calif.: Stanford University Press, 1990.

Wong, Young-tsu. "Popular Unrest and the 1911 Revolution in Jiangsu," *Modern China*, 3.3 (July 1977), 321–44.

Wright, Mary C. *The Last Stand of Chinese Conservatism: The T'ung-chih Restoration, 1862–1874.* New York: Atheneum, 1966.

Wu Dakun. "Zuijin Suzhou de nongmin naohuang fengchao" (The recent tide of peasant agitation over poor harvests in Suzhou), *Dongfang zazhi*, 32.2 (Jan. 16, 1935), 83–84.

Wu Jing. "Suzhou diqu xin faxian de 'Fang Youxing yongyuan bo tianmian wenqi'" (The newly discovered "contract for the irrevocable sale of topsoil rights by Fang Youxing" in the Suzhou area), *Zhongxue lishi jiaoxue*, 1979, no. 2, 59–60.

————. "1853–1855 nian Wujiang Lu Xiaozhong lingdao de kangzu douzheng" (The Wujiang rent resistance struggle led by Lu Xiaozhong, 1853–1855), *Zhongxue lishi*, 1980, no. 4, 57–58.

Wu Liangkai. "Shilun Yapian zhanzheng qian Qingdai nongye ziben zhuyi mengya huanman fazhan de zhuyao yuanyin" (Preliminary discussion of the major reasons for the retarded development of the sprouts of capitalism in Qing agriculture before the Opium War), *Qingshi luncong*, 3 (1982), 63–79.

Wu Wenrong. *Wu Wenjie gong (Wenrong) yiji* (Works of Wu Wenrong, posthumously collected; 1857 preface). Reprint. Taibei: Wenhai chubanshe, 1969.

Wu Xiaochen. "Pinghu de zudian zhidu he erwu jianzu" (The tenancy system in Pinghu and the 25-percent rent reduction), *Dongfang zazhi*, 32.24 (Dec. 16, 1935), 119–21.

"Wu Xu dang'an zhong de Taiping Tianguo shiliao xuanji (xuanlu)" (Excerpts from selected historical materials regarding the Taiping Rebellion in the Wu Xu archives), in *Shanghai Xiaodaohui*, pp. 1124–28.

Wu Yiheng and Chen Shuying. "Shanghai fujin (Jiangsusheng)" (The vicinity of Shanghai, Jiangsu Province), in "Gedi nongmin zhuangkuang diaocha" (Investigation of the peasantry's condition in various localities), *Dongfang zazhi*, 24.16 (Aug. 25, 1927), 125–27.

Wujiangxian xuzhi (Continuation of the gazetteer of Wujiang County). 1879.

Wukangxian zhi (The gazetteer of Wukang County). 1929.

Wu-Qingzhen zhi (Gazetteer of Wu and Qingdun market towns). 1936.

Wuxi Fu'anxiang zhigao (Draft gazetteer of Fu'anxiang, Wuxi County). N.d.

Wuxian zhi (Gazetteer of Wu County). 1933.

Wuyang zhiyu (A remnant of the gazetteer of Wujin and Yanghu). 1888.

Xia Nai. "Taiping Tianguo qianhou Changjiang gesheng zhi tianfu wenti" (The land tax problem in the Yangzi provinces before and after the Taiping Rebellion), *Qinghua xuebao*, 10.2 (April 1935), 409–74.

Xiangcheng xiaozhi (Short gazetteer of Xiangcheng). 1929.

Xiaofengxian zhi (Gazetteer of Xiaofeng County). 1877.

Xie Suizhi. "Linxie congchao" (A miscellany of will-o'-the-wisp and blood accounts), in *Zhuanji*, pp. 387–420.

Xinchengzhen zhi (Gazetteer of Xinchengzhen). 1920.

Xingzhengyuan nongcun fuxing weiyuanhui. *Jiangsusheng nongcun diaocha* (Investigation of rural villages in Jiangsu Province). Shanghai: Shangwu yinshuguan, 1934.

―――. *Zhejiangsheng nongcun diaocha* (Investigation of rural villages in Zhejiang Province). Shanghai: Shangwu yinshuguan, 1935.

Xinhai Geming qian shinian minbian dang'an shiliao (Archival materials on popular revolts during the ten years preceding the 1911 Revolution). Comp. Zhongguo diyi lishi dang'anguan and Beijing shifan daxue lishixi. 2 vols. Beijing: Zhonghua shuju, 1985.

Xinhai Geming zai Shanghai shiliao xuanji (Selected historical materials on the 1911 Revolution in Shanghai). Comp. Shanghai shehui kexueyuan lishi yanjiusuo. Shanghai: Shanghai renmin chubanshe, 1981.

Xu Daofu, comp. *Zhongguo jindai nongye shengchan ji maoyi tongji ziliao* (Statistical materials on agricultural production and trade in modern China). Shanghai: Shanghai renmin chubanshe, 1983.

Xu Peirui et al. "Shuangli bian" (A collection of letters). Appendix to *He Guiqing deng shuzha* (Correspondence of He Guiqing and others). Comp. Suzhou bowuguan, Jiangsu shifan xueyuan lishixi, and Nanjing daxue lishixi. Nanjing: Jiangsu renmin chubanshe, 1981. Originally published in *Jindaishi ziliao*, 34 (1964).

Xu Rixiang. "Gengshen Jiangyin dongnan Changshu xibei xiang riji" (Diary of southeastern Jiangyin and northwestern Changshu in 1860), in *Taiping Tianguo*, vol. 5, pp. 421–39.

Xue Yunsheng. *Duli cunyi* (Concentration on doubtful matters while perusing the substatutes). Ed. Huang Jingjia. 5 vols. Taibei: Chengwen chubanshe, 1970.

Yamana Hirofumi. "Shinmatsu Kōnan no gisō ni tsuite" (Charitable estates in Jiangnan during the late Qing), *Tōyō gakuhō*, 62.1–2 (Dec. 1980), 99–131.

Yamashita Yoneko. "Shingai Kakumei no jiki no minshū undō: Kōsetsu chiku no nōmin undō o chūshin to shite" (Mass movements at the time of the 1911 Revolution: Peasant movements in the Jiangsu-Zhejiang region), *Tōyō bunka kenkyūjo kiyō*, 37 (March 1965), 111–218.

Yan Dafu. "Wuxian (Jiangsusheng)" (Wu County, Jiangsu Province), in "Gedi nongmin zhuangkuang diaocha" (Investigation of the peasantry's condition in various localities), *Dongfang zazhi*, 24.16 (Aug. 25, 1927), 118–19.

Yan Xuexi. "1927 nian Yixing Qiushou qiyi" (The 1927 Autumn Harvest Uprising in Yixing), *Jindaishi ziliao*, 1958, no. 3, 142.

Yang, C. K. "Some Preliminary Statistical Patterns of Mass Actions in Nineteenth-Century China," in *Conflict and Control in Late Imperial China*. Ed. Frederic Wakeman, Jr., and Carolyn Grant. Berkeley: University of California Press, 1975, pp. 174–210.

Yang Guozhen. *Ming Qing tudi qiyue wenshu yanjiu* (Studies on land contracts and documents of the Ming and Qing). Beijing: Renmin chubanshe, 1988.

Yang Yinchuan. "Yeyan lu" (A record of the smoke of battle), in *Jianji*, vol. 2, pp. 173–78.

Yangzhou shifan xueyuan lishixi, comp. *Xinhai Geming Jiangsu diqu shiliao* (Historical materials on the 1911 Revolution in Jiangsu). Nanjing: Jiangsu renmin chubanshe, 1961.

Yao Ji. "Gouquan jinlu" (A recent record of bare survival), in *Shanghai Xiaodaohui*, pp. 1129–53.

———. "Jiyou beishui jiwen" (Account of the flood of 1849), *Jindaishi ziliao*, 1963, no. 1, 40–44.

———. "Xiao cangsang ji" (A short account of the recent vicissitudes), in *Taiping Tianguo*, vol. 6, pp. 441–534.

Yapian zhanzheng moqi Yingjun zai Changjiang xiayou de qinlüe zuixing (The British military's criminal acts of aggression in the lower Yangzi valley during the latter part of the Opium War). Comp. Zhongguo kexueyuan Shanghai lishi yanjiusuo choubei weiyuanhui. Shanghai: Shanghai renmin chubanshe, 1958.

Yinxian tongzhi (General gazetteer of Yin County). 1935.

Yixing Jingxixian xinzhi (New gazetteer of Yixing and Jingxi Counties). 1882.

"Yizhaolou Hong-Yang zougao (xuanlu)" (Selected memorials on the rebellion of Hong Xiuquan and Yang Xiuqing from the Yizhaolou), *Shanghai Xiaodaohui*, pp. 1090–114, 1169–89.

"Yizhaolou shishi huibian" (Collection of information on current events from the Yizhaolou), in *Jianji*, vol. 5, pp. 167–494.

Yokoyama Suguru. "Chūgoku ni okeru nōmin undō no ichi keitai: Taihei Tengoku zen no 'kōryō' undō ni tsuite" (One form of the peasant movement in China: The "tax resistance" movement before the Taiping Rebellion), *Hiroshima daigaku bungakubu kiyō*, 1955, no. 7 (March), 311–49.

———. "The Peasant Movement in Hunan," *Modern China*, 1.2 (April 1975), 204–38.

Yong An. *Yong An shangshu zouyi* (Memorials of Secretary Yong An; 1913). Reprint. Taibei: Wenhai chubanshe, 1970.

Yu Jinru. "Changshu nongcun xianzhuang diaocha" (Investigation of the current condition of the villages in Changshu; 1934), in *Zhongguo nongcun jingji ziliao xubian* (Materials on the Chinese rural economy, supplement). Comp. Feng Hefa. Shanghai: Liming shuju, 1935, pp. 27–33.

Yu Lin. "Jiangnan nongcun shuailuo de yige suoyin" (An index of the decline of Jiangnan villages; 1932), in *Zhongguo nongcun jingji ziliao* (Materials on the Chinese rural economy). Comp. Feng Hefa. Shanghai: Liming shuju, 1933, pp. 400–421.

Yuan Zhen, Li Zhoufang, and Ma Zuming. "Zoufang lu: Taiping jun zai Wuxian" (A record of interviews: The Taiping army in Wu County). Paper presented at the Taiping history conference in Suzhou, 1981.

Yuan Zuzhi. "Suiyuan suoji (xuanlu)" (Selections from the trifling jottings by Yuan Zuzhi), in *Shanghai Xiaodaohui*, pp. 1018–23.

"Yuanhe yulin qingce" (Fishscale register of Yuanhe; 1846), Tōyō bunka kenkyūjo, Tokyo University.

Yuxiang zhi (Gazetteer of Yuxiang). 1840.

Zelin, Madeleine. *The Magistrate's Tael: Rationalizing Fiscal Reform in Eighteenth-Century Ch'ing China*. Berkeley: University of California Press, 1984.

Zhang Lüluan. *Jiangsu Wujin wujia zhi yanjiu* (A study of prices in Wujin, Jiangsu). Nanjing: Jinling daxue nongxueyuan, 1933.

Zhang Naixiu. "Rumeng lu" (A dreamlike record), in *Jianji*, vol. 4, pp. 601–17.

Zhang Shouchang. "Shiliao shiling" (Historical tidbits), *Jindaishi ziliao*, 1980, no. 2, 215–30.

Zhang Yaozong, comp. "Zhou Shuiping lieshi ziliao" (Materials on the martyr Zhou Shuiping), *Jindaishi ziliao*, 54 (April 1983), 177–233.

Zhang Youyi, comp. *Zhongguo jindai nongye shi ziliao* (Materials on the modern history of Chinese agriculture), vols. 2 and 3. Beijing: Sanlian shudian, 1957.

Zhang Youyi and Liu Kexiang. "Taiping Tianguo shibai hou dizu boxue wenti chutan" (A preliminary investigation of the problem of rental exploitation after the defeat of the Taiping Rebellion), *Zhongguo shehui kexueyuan jingji yanjiusuo jikan*, 4 (April 1983), 112–213.

Zhang Zhenhe and Ding Yuanying, comps. "Qingmo minbian nianbiao" (Chronological table of popular revolts during the late Qing) (2 parts), *Jindaishi ziliao*, 49 (1982–83), 108–81; 50 (1983–84), 77–121.

Zhang Zongbi. "Zhejiang Pinghu nongye jingji diaocha baogao" (Report on an investigation [in 1929] of the agricultural economy in Pinghu, Zhejiang), in *Zhongguo nongcun jingji ziliao* (Materials on the Chinese rural economy). Comp. Feng Hefa. Shanghai: Liming shuju, 1933, pp. 593–96.

Zhang Zuyin. "Zhenze zhi nongmin" (The peasantry of Zhenze), *Xin qingnian*, 4.3 (March 15, 1918), 225–28.

Zhao Liewen. "Luohua chunyu chao riji" (Diary from the lair of fallen petals and spring rain), in *Jianji*, vol. 3, pp. 19–70.

———. "Nengjing jushi riji" (Diary of Nengjing jushi), in *Jianji*, vol. 3, pp. 125–430.

Zhao Ruheng, comp. *Jiangsusheng jian* (Yearbook of Jiangsu Province; 1935). 4 vols. Reprint. Taibei: Chengwen chubanshe, 1983.

Zhao Xiong. "Changshu nongmin zhi jingji zhuangkuang" (The economic situation of Changshu peasants), *Xin Zhonghua zazhi*, 2.2 (Jan. 20, 1934), 82–83.

Zhejiang Wuxing Lanxi tianfu diaocha baogao (Report on an investigation of land taxes in Wuxing and Lanxi, Zhejiang). N.p., n.d.

Zhejiangsheng Xinhai Geming shi yanjiuhui and Zhejiangsheng tushuguan, comps. *Xinhai Geming Zhejiang shiliao xuanji* (Selected historical materials on the 1911 Revolution in Zhejiang). Hangzhou: Zhejiang renmin chubanshe, 1981.

Zheng Guangzu. *Yiban lu* (A partial record). N.p., n.d.

Zheng Kangmo. *Zhejiang erwu jianzu zhi yanjiu* (Study of the 25-percent rent reduction in Zhejiang). Vol. 65 of Xiao Zheng, ed.

Zhi Fei [pseud.]. "Wujiang gengxin jishi" (A record of events in Wujiang in 1860–61), *Jindaishi ziliao*, 1955, no. 1, 21–50.

Zhongguo jingji nianjian disan bian (Economic yearbook of China, 3d ed.). Comp. Shiyebu Zhongguo jingji nianjian bianzuan weiyuanhui. Shanghai: Shangwu yinshuguan, 1936.

Zhongguo jingji nianjian xubian (Economic yearbook of China, continuation). Comp. Shiyebu Zhongguo jingji nianjian bianzuan weiyuanhui. Shanghai: Shangwu yinshuguan, 1935.

Zhongguo shiye zhi, quanguo shiye diaocha baogao zhi er: Zhejiangsheng (China industrial handbooks, second series of the reports by the national industrial investigation: Zhejiang Province). Comp. Shiyebu guoji maoyi ju. Shanghai: Shiyebu guoji maoyi ju, 1933.

Zhongguo shiye zhi, quanguo shiye diaocha baogao zhi yi: Jiangsusheng (China industrial handbooks, first series of the reports by the national industrial investigation: Jiangsu Province). Comp. Shiyebu guoji maoyi ju. Shanghai: Shiyebu guoji maoyi ju, 1933.

Zhongyang daxue jingji ziliaoshi, ed. *Tianfu fujiashui diaocha* (Investigation of land tax surcharges). Shanghai: Shangwu yinshuguan, 1935.

Zhou Jian. "Yuechu yu baodi Ziren Xiaocui shu" (Letters of Yuechu to his younger brothers Ziren and Xiaocui), *Jindaishi ziliao*, 1955, no. 3, 83–92.

Zhou Tingdong. "Taicang (Jiangsusheng)" (Taicang, Jiangsu Province), in "Gedi nongmin zhuangkuang diaocha" (Investigation of the peasantry's condition in various localities), *Dongfang zazhi*, 24.16 (Aug. 25, 1927), 122–24.

Zhu Chengcong. "Sangzi wenjian lu" (Record of things seen and heard in my native place), in *Shanghai Xiaodaohui*, pp. 1052–73.

Zou Dafan, Wu Zhiwei, and Xu Wenhui. "Jin bainian lai jiu Zhongguo liangshi jiage de biandong qushi" (Fluctuations in grain prices in the last 100 years of old China; 1965), in *Zhongguo jin sanbainian shehui jingji shi lunji* (Collection of essays on China's social and economic history of the last 300 years). Ed. Cuncui xueshe. Hong Kong: Chongwen shudian, 1979, pp. 235–43.

Zou Shencheng. "Taiping Tianguo shiqi de Zhedong Shibaju qiyi" (The Eighteen Bureaus uprising in eastern Zhejiang during the time of the Taiping Rebellion) and "Zhedong Lianpengdang he Zhitianyi He Wenqing" (The Lotus Cupule Gang and He Wenqing in eastern Zhejiang), in his *Taiping Tianguo shishi shiling* (Historical tidbits on the Taiping Rebellion). Hangzhou: Hangzhou shifan xueyuan xuebao bianjishi, 1981, pp. 53–66, 67–88.

Zui'e de jiu shehui (The evil old society). 3 vols. Shanghai: Shanghai renmin chubanshe, 1978.

CHARACTER LIST

Well-known personal and place names are not included in this list.

Anjixian　安吉縣
Anzhen　安鎮

bachan　霸產
Baihejiang　白鶴江
Bailongdang　白龍黨
baitou　白頭
ban liang zhi fei　辦糧之費
Bao Lisheng　包立生
baoandui　保安隊
baohuang　報荒
baojia　保甲
baojiaju　保甲局
baojiazhang　保甲長
baolan　包攬
Baoshanxian　寶山縣
baoweituan　保衛團
Baoyingxian　寶應縣
baozheng　保正
beiluzhe　被擄者
Beitangzi　北湯字
Beixinjiezhen　北新街鎮
bike yatu　庇客壓土
Bu Xiaoer　卜小二

Cai Lingxiang　蔡嶺香
caizhengting　財政廳
cangfang　倉房
cangting　倉廳
Cao Heqing　曹和卿
caogeng　糙粳
caomi　漕米
Changhuaxian　昌化縣
changjia　長價
changmao　長毛
Changshuxian　常熟縣
Changtian　長田
Changxingxian　長興縣
Changzhoufu　常州府
Changzhouxian　長洲縣
Chen　陳
Chen Jiongming　陳烱明
Chen Mujin　陳木金
Chen Rong　陳溶
Chen Yucheng　陳玉成
chengse　成色
chi dahu　吃大戶
chi maozhu kuai　吃毛竹筷
Chongdexian　崇德縣

Chongmingxian 崇明縣
Chuanshating (xian) 川沙廳（縣）
cuijia 催甲
cuizhengli 催徵吏
cuizu gongyi 催租公役
cuizu jingli 催租警吏
cuizu weiyuan 催租委員
cuizuchu 催租處
cuizuju 催租局
cuizuli 催租吏

da pengche 大輣車
da xianfeng 打先鋒
da xiongzu 打兇租
dahu 大戶
Daliyuan 大理院
dan 擔
Dangkouzhen 蕩口鎮
Dangshanxian 碭山縣
Danyangxian 丹陽縣
Daoguang 道光
Deqingxian 德清縣
di 地
diandan 佃單
diangun 佃棍
dianhu 佃戶
Dianhu hezuo zijiu hui
　佃戶合作自救會
Dianhuhui 佃戶會
diannong 佃農
dianye lishi ju 佃業理事局
dianzu chufensuo 佃租處分所
diaodian 刁佃
dibao 地保
diding 地丁
difang shenshi 地方紳士
digun 地棍
ding 丁
Ding Richang 丁日昌
Ding Shouchang 丁壽昌
dingshouyin 頂首銀
dishangquan 地上權
dizong 地總
Dong 董

Dongtingshan 洞庭山
Dongyongchang 東永昌
Dongzhangshi 東張市
Dongzhoushi 東周市
dou 斗
du 都
duanjia 短價
duantou 短頭
duozhong 奪種
duxiaoju 督銷局

egun 惡棍
erwu jianzu 二五減租

Fan 范
fangshui deng 放水燈
fei 匪
Fei 費
Fei Yucheng 費玉成
Feng Guifen 馮桂芬
Feng Han 馮瀚
Fengxian 豐縣
Fengxianxian 奉賢縣
fujiashui 附加稅
Funingxian 阜甯縣
fushou 浮收
fushui 附稅
Fuyangxian 富陽縣

ganqing 感情
Gaoyouxian 高郵縣
gengzhe you qitian 耕者有其田
gong kuanchan jinglichu
　公款產經理處
gonganju 公安局
gongfei 公費
gongju 公舉
gongsheng 貢生
Gongshouzhan 恭壽棧
gu 股
Gu Yanwu 顧炎武
guan dufei 灌肚肺
guantian 官田
guanye 管業

Gui Danmeng 桂丹盟
Guianxian 歸安縣
Guijiashi 歸家市
Guomindang 國民黨
Gushanxiang 顧山鄉

Haimenxian 海門縣
Hainingzhou (xian) 海寧州（縣）
Haiyanxian 海鹽縣
haiyunju 海運局
Hamashima Atsutoshi 濱島敦俊
Han Chong 翰崇
Hangxian 杭縣
Hangzhoufu 杭州府
haomi 耗米
haoxian 耗羨
Hefei 合肥
hegongju 河工局
Hengjingzhen 橫涇鎮
heping tudi gaige 和平土地改革
Heshi 何市
Hong Ren'gan 洪仁玕
Hong Xiuquan 洪秀全
Houxiang 後巷
Hua Yilun 華翼綸
Huai 懷
Huaianxian 淮安縣
Huaiyinxian 淮陰縣
Huangdaixiang 黃埭鄉
Huangjiaqiao 黃家橋
Huatingxian 華亭縣
Huayangqiao 華陽橋
huifei 灰肥
hushou 斛手
hutu 糊塗
Huzhoufu 湖州府

Ji Cuicui 季萃萃
jia 甲
Jiadingxian 嘉定縣
jian shizumi 減實租米
jiandian 奸佃
jianfuju 減賦局
Jiang Jiyun 蔣積雲

Jiangnan 江南
Jiangyinxian 江陰縣
jianjun 監軍
jiansheng 監生
Jiansheting 建設廳
jiaomi 腳米
jiaoyuju 教育局
Jiaqing 嘉慶
Jiashanxian 嘉善縣
jiashou 甲首
Jiaxingfu (xian) 嘉興府（縣）
Jierhang'a 吉爾杭阿
jilinghu 畸零戶
jin 斤
Jin Deshun 金德順
Jin Shangui 金山桂
Jin Yushan 金玉山
jingchadui 警察隊
Jinguixian 金匱縣
Jingxixian 荊溪縣
jingzao 經造
jinhuatian 金花田
Jinqianhui 金錢會
Jinshanxian 金山縣
jinshi 進士
jizhan 寄棧
juan 捐
jungongfu 均工夫
junshuai 軍帥
juren 舉人
Jurongxian 句容縣

kang 抗
Kangxi 康熙
kangzu 抗租
Ke Wuchi 柯悟遲
kehuang 客荒
kemin 客民
kun 捆
kunbao 捆保
Kunshanxian 崑山縣

Laowushi 老吳市
Laoxushi 老徐市

lezhe 勒折
li 里
Li Hongzhang 李鴻章
Li Shaoqing 李少卿
Li Shixian 李世賢
Li Wenbing 李文炳
Li Wenzhi 李文治
Li Xianyun 李仙雲
Li Xingyuan 李星沅
Li Xiucheng 李秀成
liang 兩
liang cong zu ban 糧從租辦
liangdian 艮佃
Liangjiang 兩江
liangsima 兩司馬
liangzhang 糧長
Lianpengdang 蓮蓬黨
lijia 里甲
Lilizhen 黎里鎮
limi 力米
Lin Zexu 林則徐
Lin'anxian 臨安縣
Liu Kunyi 劉坤一
Liu Lichuan 劉麗川
Liu Shiji 劉石吉
Liu Zhaoxun 劉兆薰
lizhang 里長
Louxian 婁縣
Lü 呂
Lu Xiaoheng 陸孝恆
Lu Xiaozhong 陸孝中
Luohandang 羅漢黨
Lushi 陸市
lüshuai 旅帥

Ma Xinyi 馬新貽
maihuang 賣荒
Mao Jiaqi 茅家琦
Meigangxiang 梅港鄉
Meilizhen 梅里鎮
menpai 門牌
Min Yuanyuan 閔元元
mintuan 民團
Mori Masao 森正夫

mu 畝
mujuan 畝捐
Muramatsu Yūji 村松祐次

Nanhuixian 南滙縣
Nantongxian 南通縣
Nanxiangzhen 南翔鎮
Nanxunzhen 南潯鎮
Natsui Haruki 夏井春喜
naohuang 鬧荒
Niaodang 鳥黨
Ningbodang 寧波黨
Ningbofu 寧波府
Nonggongting 農工廳
nongmin xiehui 農民協會
Nongtuan 農團

Pan Zengwei 潘曾瑋
pao badou 拋笆斗
Peng Pai 彭湃
pengmin 棚民
Pin 鞏
Pinghuxian 平湖縣
pingminzhuyi 平民主義

Qian Guiren 錢桂仁
Qian Rongzhuang 錢蓉莊
Qian Shouren 錢壽仁
qiangchuan 槍船
qiangmi 搶米
qianliang 錢糧
Qianlong 乾隆
Qianrenhui 千人會
Qiantangxian 錢塘縣
Qianxiang 前巷
qiding 旗丁
Qingdunzhen 青墩鎮
qingfu zongju 青賦總局
qinghuang bujie 青黃不接
Qingjinhui 青巾會
Qingpuxian 青浦縣
Qixinshe 齊心社
Qu 屈
qu 區

quanjietang 全節堂
quanxuesuo 勸學所
qudong 區董
quzhang 區長

Renhexian 仁和縣
renken 認墾
rentian 認田
Rugaoxian 如皋縣
ruying 入營

Sandaohui 三刀會
sanri yibi 三日一比
saodimi 掃地米
Sha Ge 沙哥
Shanghaixian 上海縣
shanhouju 善後局
shantang 善堂
Shaoxingfu 紹興府
Shazhou 沙洲
Shen 沈
Shen Gaozhong 沈鎬中
Shen Paishi 沈牌士
Shen Shitang 沈實堂
shendong 紳董
shenfu 紳富
sheng 升
Sheng Chuan 勝傳
shengyuan 生員
Shengzezhen 盛澤鎮
shi 石
Shi Dakai 石達開
Shibaju 十八局
shijin 市斤
Shimenxian 石門縣
shishi 市石
shishuai 師帥
shizu 實租
shou xiongzu 收兇租
shoujiang 守將
shouzuju 收租局
Shuangdaohui 雙刀會
Shuanglinzhen 雙林鎮
shudian 熟佃

shuhuang 熟荒
shuiqi 稅契
shuiqiyin 收契銀
shun 順
shuyuan 書院
Siyangxian 泗陽縣
Songjiangfu (xian) 松江府（縣）
Sufu 蘇福
Suiningxian 睢甯縣
Sun Chuanfang 孫傳芳
Suqianxian 宿遷縣
Suzhoufu 蘇州府

Taicangzhou (xian) 太倉州（縣）
Taiping Tianguo 太平天國
Taixian 泰縣
Taizhoufu 台州府
Tan Shaoguang 潭紹光
Tang 唐
Tang Shengzhi 唐生智
tanggongju 塘工局
tangzhang 塘長
tankuan 攤款
Tao Xu 陶煦
tian gui yuanzhu 田歸原主
tian nai fu zi zhi di, shi wei lei zhi tou
　　　田乃富字之底，實為累字之頭
tiandi 田底
tianduo 田多
tianjia 田甲
tianjuan 田捐
tianmian 田面
tianping 田憑
tiantouzhi 田頭制
tianye gonghui 田業公會
tianye lianhehui 田業聯合會
tianyehui 田業會
Tonglizhen 同里鎮
Tongxiangxian 桐鄉縣
Tongzhi 同治
tu 圖
tuanlian 團練
tuchai 圖差
tudong 圖董

tufei 土匪
tugun 土棍
tuhao lieshen 土豪劣紳
tuntian 屯田
tunzu 吞租

Usui Sachiko 臼井佐知子

wandian 頑佃
wang 王
Wang Shengming 汪勝明
Wang Simazi 王四痲子
Wang Tianjiang 王天獎
Wang Yuanchang 王元昌
Wangjiangjing 王江涇
Wangshi 王市
Wei Changhui 韋昌輝
Weiting 唯亭
Wenzhoufu 溫州府
Wu 吳
Wu Jianzhang 吳健彰
Wu Lin 吳林
Wu Xu 吳煦
Wu Yun 吳雲
Wuchengxian 烏程縣
Wujiangxian 吳江縣
Wujinxian 武進縣
Wukangxian 武康縣
wulai 無賴
wuri yibi 五日一比
Wutazhen 吳塔鎮
Wuxian 吳縣
Wuxingxian 吳興縣
Wuxixian 無錫縣
wuzhang 伍長
Wuzhen 烏鎮

Xianfeng 咸豐
xiang 鄉
xiangdong 鄉董
xiangguan 鄉官
xiangmin 鄉民
xiangyong 鄉勇
xiangzhang 鄉長

Xiaodaohui 小刀會
Xiaofengxian 孝豐縣
xiaohu 小戶
Xiaowushi 小吳市
xiebi 血比
Xietangzhen 斜塘鎮
Xinchengxian 新城縣
Xinguo 新郭
Xinyangxian 新陽縣
Xinzheng 新政
Xiong Wanquan 熊萬荃
xiongzu 兇租
Xiushuixian 秀水縣
Xu Naizhao 許乃釗
Xu Peirui 徐佩瑃
Xu Peiyuan 徐佩瑗
Xu Yao 徐耀
Xuanmiaoguan 玄妙觀
Xue Huan 薛煥
Xue Zheng'an 薛正安
Xuzhou 徐州
xuzu 虛租

yadian gongsuo 押佃公所
yaliju 牙釐局
Yan Chen 嚴辰
Yang Liaogong 楊了公
Yang Xiuqing 楊秀清
Yanghuxian 陽湖縣
yangmi 樣米
yangpin 樣品
yanliju 鹽釐局
yedian jiufen zhongcai weiyuanhui 業佃
    糾紛仲裁委員會
yemao chi ren 野貓吃人
yeshi dianli 業食佃力
Yi Liang 怡良
Yiban lu 一斑錄
Yijiaohui 一角會
yili ba 一粒八
yili jiu 一粒九
Yin Jishan 尹繼善
Yin Zhaoyong 殷兆鏞
yinshi 殷實

Yixingxian　宜興縣
yizhuang　義莊
yong　勇
yongdian　永佃
Yu Cheng　毓成
yuan　元
Yuanhexian　元和縣
yuanzu　原租
Yuhangxian　餘杭縣
yuhuatian　餘花田
yujia　圩甲
Yunlinxiang　雲林鄉
Yuqianxian　於潛縣
yutuan　圩團
yuyingtang　育嬰堂

Zeng Guofan　曾國藩
Zeng Guoquan　曾國荃
Zhang Rongrong　張榮榮
zhangfang xiansheng　賬房先生
Zhao Zhenzuo　趙振祚
zhaoken shengke　召墾升科
zhaotian paiyi　照田派役
Zhaowenxian　昭文縣
Zhapu　乍浦
zhejia　折價
zhendong　鎮董
Zheng Guangzu　鄭光祖
Zhengde　正德
zhengshoufei　徵收費
zhengshui　正稅

zhengzu　正租
Zhenjiang　鎮江
Zhenyangxian　鎮洋縣
Zhenzexian　震澤縣
zhenzhang　鎮長
zhezu　折租
zhiqian　制錢
zhongbao　仲保
Zhou Lichun　周立春
Zhou Murun　周沐潤
Zhou Shuiping　周水平
Zhouli　周禮
Zhouzhuangzhen　周莊鎮
Zhu Chengcong　諸成琮
Zhuanghangzhen　莊行鎮
zhuizuchu　追租處
zhuizujing　追租警
zhuizuju　追租局
zhuodian qizheng　着佃起徵
zhuoji dashu　捉雞大叔
ziye　自業
zongzhi　總制
zu　租
zuchai　租差
zuhu　租斛
zujuan　租捐
Zuo Zongtang　左宗棠
zuo leng fangzhuan　坐冷方磚
zuzhan　租棧
zuzhang　卒長

INDEX

In this index an "f" after a number indicates a separate reference on the next page, and an "ff" indicates separate references on the next two pages. A continuous discussion over two or more pages is indicated by a span of page numbers, e.g., "57–59." *Passim* is used for a cluster of references in close but not consecutive sequence. The entries are alphabetized letter by letter to the first punctuation mark.

Library of Congress Cataloging-in-Publication Data

Bernhardt, Kathryn. .
   Rents, taxes, and peasant resistance : the lower Yangzi region,
1840–1950 / Kathryn Bernhardt.
      p.   cm.
Includes bibliographical references and index.
ISBN 0-8047-1880-6 (cloth : acid-free)
1. China—History—19th century.   2. China—History—Republic,
1912–1949.   3. Peasant uprisings—China—Yangtze River Region—
History.   4. Taxation—China—Yangtze River Region—History.
5. Rent—China—Yangtze River Region—History.   I. Title.
DS755.B47   1992
951'.2—dc20
91-15772
CIP

∞   This book has been typeset by Tseng Information Systems, Inc. in 10/12 Bembo. It is
printed on acid-free paper.